God's Design

God's Design

A Focus on Old Testament Theology

Third Edition

by

Elmer A. Martens

BIBAL Press
N. Richland Hills, Texas

BIBAL Press
An imprint of D. & F. Scott Publishing, Inc.
P.O. Box 821653
N. Richland Hills, TX 76182

God's Design
Third Edition © 1998 by D. & F. Scott Publishing, Inc.
All rights reserved.

First British edition published in 1981 by Inter-Varsity Press, Leicester, as *Plot and Purpose in the Old Testament*

First American edition published in 1981 by Baker Book House Company in the United States of America. First paperback edition issued January 1986.

Second American edition published by Baker Book House Company in the United States and by Apollos (an imprint of Inter-Varsity Press) in the United Kingdom 1994.

Printed in the United States of America

02 01 00 99 98   5 4 3 2 1

Unless otherwise indicated, Scripture quotations are from the New Revised Standard Version, copyrighted 1989 by the Division of Christian Education of the National Council of Churches of Christ in the United States of America.

Library of Congress Cataloging-in-Publication Data
Martens, E. A.
    God's design : a focus on Old Testament theology / by
Elmer A. Martens. -- 3rd ed.
      p. cm.
    Includes bibliographical references and indexes.
    ISBN 0-941037-51-7 (trade paper : alk. paper)
    1. Bible. O.T.--Theology.   I. Title.
BS1192.5.M37 1997   97-43195
230'.0411--dc21   CIP

Graphics provided by Corel Corporation, Ltd.

To Phyllis Jean Hiebert Martens,
a cherished marriage partner
skilled, among much else,
in theological dialogue and literary technique

Contents

Tables

Preface

Writing a theology of the Old Testament is comparable to scaling Mt. Everest—it is a challenge! Different approaches are possible. Whether adventurer or scholar, one aims for the topmost elevation in order to get an overall view and see as much as possible of the landscape in the richness of its contours. However much one sees, one is compelled by the wonder of God's handiwork to tell about it.

A theology of the Old Testament should lay bare, I believe, the essence of the Old Testament message, a message that centers in Yahweh, the God of Israel and the world. This book attempts to sketch the main features in categories taken from the Scriptures themselves, and to show how these relate to each other.

My claim is that the overarching theme of the Old Testament is God's design, a design that incorporates four components: deliverance, community, knowledge of God, and the abundant life. This design is articulated at the exodus, implemented and tested in the monarchy, reaffirmed in the postmonarchy period, and continued into the New Testament.

Confronted with the choice of a synthetic or a diachronic approach, I have incorporated a little of both. The synthetic approach is represented by the fourfold design. The nuances of change and the elaboration of these components is described diachronically in three stages of Israel's history (see the table on page 243). The result is an illustration, possibly, of a multitrack and longitudinal approach, recently advocated in Old Testament scholarship.

It is my conviction that, since the Old Testament is God's Word, a theology of the Old Testament should point beyond the description of the message to an indication of its importance for today's believer. Without being comprehensive, I have set out a sampling of implications in sections subtitled "theological reflections," which are distributed throughout in such a way as to give attention to each component of the fourfold design.

The book is intended for pastors, teachers, and serious students of Scripture, including, I should like to think, those in churches abroad; and for college, university, and seminary students.

My interest in Old Testament theology and my sense of its importance was kindled by professors William H. Brownlee and Rolf Knierim at Claremont Graduate School, Claremont, California, and earlier in seminary by Professor G. W. Peters. While I have moved in directions often quite different from theirs, I want to express my deep gratitude to these able scholarly mentors. Dean John E. Toews, professor of New Testament, is a teaching colleague whose valuable encouragement and help I gratefully acknowledge. The sabbatical period provided by the Seminary Board of Directors enabled me to interact with scholars both in Berkeley, California, and Tyndale House in Cambridge, England.

In a decade of seminary teaching I have repeatedly modified and refined my positions and overall conceptualizations, thanks to the stimulus and probings of my students. I express my gratitude to them, especially to those of recent years who mercilessly critiqued my provisional manuscript. Much help both technically and substantively has come to me from my teaching assistants: Ben Ollenburger, John Fast, John Vooys, and, most recently, Mark Campbell, who also compiled most of the indices.

I acknowledge with gratitude the diligence of Nancy (Mrs. Larry) Ediger, typist, and the help of my daughter Frances, as well as my wife Phyllis, who has been instrumental in giving shape to ideas and who, because of her linguistic expertise, also brought clarity of expression in the final product.

So rich has been my gain from Inter-Varsity Fellowship during earlier student days in Canada that with this volume I wish to repay some of the debt I owe to persons in this fellowship. Inter-Varsity Press has continued the tradition of congenial and competent concern; to the publishers I express my gratitude for kind consideration.

God's design, like the plot of a great drama, provides intriguing reflection, and in this instance soon leads to worship and commitment.

> O the depth of the riches and wisdom and knowledge of God! How unsearchable are his judgments and how inscrutable his ways! . . . For from him and through him and to him are all things. To him be the glory for ever. Amen.
>
> Rom 11:33, 36

Elmer A. Martens
Mennonite Brethren
 Biblical Seminary
Fresno, California
September 1980

Preface to Second Edition

A second edition provides the opportunity to benefit from reviewers' comments on the first edition. To them I am grateful, not only for repeated affirmations, but especially for probings about a theological center and a method that leans so heavily on one text. Clarifications on both points as well as other methodological matters are found in the Appendix.

Two specific weaknesses of the earlier work were noted and are here addressed. One was that with a starting point essentially with the exodus, insufficient attention had been given to creation. Opportunities to teach in seminaries in Asia and East Africa confirmed the need to be more expositional about creation and the way it linked with the more dominant theme of salvation history (see chap. 15). A second issue was also related to salvation history, which, if narrowly construed, settled far too exclusively on Israel as a people, and tended to stay within the bounds of the particular. The way in which the particular relates to the universal is sketched in chapter 16.

Much as both author and publisher wished the revisions in the second edition to utilize gender-inclusive language, and even prepared initial corrections accordingly, considerations of logistics and cost regrettably precluded this improvement. Footnotes and bibliography have been updated. Substantive changes in the content, given the publisher's constraints, are limited to part 5.

My gratitude is tendered, in addition to reviewers and individuals earlier noted, to Professor Allen Guenther, a teaching colleague, and to V. Athithan of India for stimulating dialogue on the content of the new chapters, to the Rev. Woosong Kwak of Seoul, Korea, for intercession to God in my behalf, and to Jim

Weaver, Editor, Academic and Reference Books, Baker Books, for encouragement and good judgment.

Elmer A. Martens
Mennonite Brethren
  Biblical Seminary
Fresno, California
February 1994

Preface to Third Edition

A further edition is improved by the use of gender-inclusive language; in reference to God, however, I remain with the traditional pronouns.

The revisions beyond the second edition are minimal and limited to some restatements and updating of footnotes which now appear as endnotes.

I express sincere gratitude to William R. Scott, President of D. & F. Scott Publishing, Inc., and to the staff at BIBAL Press for a speedy and efficient print process. For major help in placing the entire work on computer disk, I am indebted, as I am also in so many other ways, to Phyllis, my ever-supportive life's companion.

Elmer A. Martens
Mennonite Brethren
Biblical Seminary
October 1997

PART 1

God's Design
Articulated

A Pivotal Text about Yahweh And His Purpose

The task of adequately stating the central message of the Old Testament is a challenging one, and that for several reasons. The diversity of the Old Testament material, quite apart from its size, offers a challenge to anyone who intends to provide a summary statement of its contents. The Old Testament includes stories, poems, laments, judgment speeches, proverbs, songs, and laws. Can one from such diversity of material written over a period of several centuries arrive at a single central theme? Is there even a single theme? Scholars have not been unanimous in their answer.

The challenge of describing the heart of the Old Testament is compounded by the variety of proposals already given by scholars, even in the last sixty years.[1] For some, God's covenant with Israel seems all-important.[2] Others organize their theological statements around the concept of God's sovereignty, or the communion of God with men, or God's promise, or God's presence, or God's election.[3] Asked to summarize the Old Testament message in one sentence, a group of college graduates gave these answers: "God acts in history"; "God is active in reconciling fallen men to himself"; "The central message of the Old Testament is the preparation for the first coming of the Messiah." Some answers get closer to the heart of the Old Testament than others. The answers are not mutually exclusive, of course, though some are more capable of embracing the bulk of the Old Testament material than others. One scholar has aptly said: "When there is one landscape, many different pictures may nevertheless be painted."[4] The challenge remains, however, to paint the best possible picture.

The attempt to describe the core message of the Old Testament is challenging, for clarity about the Christian faith will depend on a grasp of the Old Testament. The Old Testament supplies the fiber for the Christian faith. But unless the message of the Old Testament is clearly articulated, its relevance to the New Testament and to Christians today will remain fuzzy.

The proposal of this book is that God's design is the key to the content of the Old Testament. This proposal assumes that it is legitimate to examine the Old Testament in search of a single central message. The following chapters attempt to offer compelling reasons for such an assumption. The emphasis on a design of God as a unifying and organizing principle of the Old Testament material arises from an exegesis of several comparable biblical texts, the first of which is Exod 5:22 – 6:8.

The approach advocated in this book is distinctive in that the answer to the question about the central message is derived from a specific set of texts. It is in the language of the Bible itself that God's fourfold purpose is described, so that what we have here is a biblical theology rather than a systematic theology. It is with exegesis that we begin in order to get an outline for our picture.[5]

Someone might respond that selections of other texts would yield other outlines of a message. Why choose a certain text in Exodus from which to develop the central Old Testament message? The answer to this question will be clearer once the Exodus text has been understood.

1. A Significant Answer to a Crucial Question: Exod 5:22 – 6:8

Then Moses turned again to the LORD and said, "O LORD, why have you mistreated this people? Why did you ever send me? [23]Since I first came to Pharaoh to speak in your name, he has mistreated this people, and you have done nothing at all to deliver your people."

[1]Then the LORD said to Moses, "Now you shall see what I will do to Pharaoh: Indeed, by a mighty hand he will let them go; by a mighty hand he will drive them out of his land.

[2]God also spoke to Moses and said to him: "I am the LORD. [3]I appeared to Abraham, Isaac, and Jacob as God Almighty, but by my name 'The LORD' I did not make myself known to them. [4]I also established my covenant with them, to give them the land of Canaan, the land in which they resided as aliens. [5]I have also heard the groaning of the Israelites whom the Egyptians are holding as slaves, and I have remembered my covenant.

[6]Say therefore to the Israelites, 'I am the LORD, and I will free you from the burdens of the Egyptians and deliver you from slavery to them. I will redeem you with an outstretched arm and with mighty acts of judgment. [7]I will take you as my people, and I will be your God. You shall know that I am the LORD your God, who has freed you from the burdens of the Egyptians. [8]I will bring you into the land that I swore to give it to Abraham, Isaac, and Jacob; I will give it to you for a possession. I am the LORD.'"

This text presents a dialogue between Moses and God, an observation which the usual chapter division obscures. The conversation occurs after an initial attempt by Moses to seek the Egyptian Pharaoh's permission for the slave people of Israel to leave the country. Moses addresses God, primarily with questions. The larger part of the text is given to God's reply. We may already note a somewhat curious fact, namely that there are two introductions to God's speech. "Then the LORD said to Moses. . ." (v. 1) is followed, though there is no reply by Moses, by "God also spoke to Moses and said to him . . ." (v. 2). The

structure of this text, which consists of a twofold reply to a
speech by Moses, which is also in two parts, is an important clue
to the message of this text unit.[6]

Moses' Crucial Question: Exod 5:22–23

The situation which gives rise to the questions posed by Moses
before God involves a public confrontation with the Pharaoh in
the land of Egypt. Moses' initial appeal to Pharaoh to let the Israelites, for years slaves in Egypt, go to freedom to the land of
promise, has been met with rebuff. Pharaoh has taunted, "Who
is the LORD, that I should heed him and let Israel go?" In defiance Pharaoh has responded: "I do not know the LORD, and I
will not let Israel go" (5:2). Aggressive action has followed asser-
tive word. The production quota imposed by Pharaoh on the Israelites has remained the same, but straw for bricks is no longer
provided by the Egyptians: the Israelites must secure the straw
themselves. The Israelite foremen, not able to meet the new demands satisfactorily, are beaten by their Egyptian task-masters
and complain to Pharaoh. The Pharaoh grants no reprieve.
The foremen turn on Moses, claiming that he is to blame.

Moses takes his frustration before God, from whom he has
received the assignment to lead a people out of bondage. His
speech to God consists of two parts. He asks two questions and
files a complaint.

The questions are already of an accusatory nature. "Why
have you mistreated this people?" Just as the foremen blame
Moses, their superior, so the leader Moses now blames God,
whose call he has reluctantly followed. As often happens in accusations of this kind, Moses overstates the case, for God has
not actively brought evil upon his people. True, the events
which have led to harsh treatment by the Pharaoh have been set
in motion by Yahweh, but only indirectly. The second question
registers impatience, if not accusation: "Why did you ever send
me?" This is hardly a question asking for information. After all,
the directives had been clear when Moses received his commis-
sion at the burning bush: he was to bring a slave population into

freedom. Is there in Moses' question a request for some further clarity, however? Is he calling for a rationale, for purpose, for objective? A hesitation, an uncertainty, underlies his question. In colloquial language one might phrase that question, "God, what are you up to?" The whole enterprise of the anticipated deliverance is called into question. Moses has just entered into his assignment. He thought he knew what was involved, but now that opposition has set in more vehemently, he steps back and in measured cadence asks the elementary but entirely basic question about his mission: "Why did you ever send me?" (5:22).

The questions, posed in a reproachful tone, are followed by a forthright complaint: "Since I first came to Pharaoh to speak in your name, he has mistreated this people, and you have done nothing at all to deliver your people" (5:23). Moses confronts God with a breach of promise. The attempts to gain a favorable response from Pharaoh have met with obstinacy on Pharaoh's part. The glorious promise of God seems at this point to be a hollow promise. With the forthrightness, if not bluntness, characteristic of some of God's servants through the ages, Moses files his complaint. Clearly Moses is in a difficult position. He has been rebuffed by Pharaoh, he has been accused by leaders of the people he is to deliver. Therefore he has turned to God for help.

God's Deliberate Reply

God's reply, like the statement of Moses, is in two parts. The first word from God is reassuring: "Now you shall see what I will do to Pharaoh: Indeed, by a mighty hand he will let them go; by a mighty hand he will drive them out of his land" (6:1). A divine rebuke might be expected in response to the accusations, but Moses receives a promise instead. He is being asked to rely on the naked word of God. This initial reply addresses the last part of Moses' speech, the complaint. The procedure is reminiscent of the lecturer who says, "I will take the last question first." Moses charges, "You have done nothing at all to deliver your people." God's answer is that deliverance is future but sure. The immediate agent for that deliverance will be Pharaoh himself; he will in due time virtually expel the people from his land. Thus the objection of Moses is answered by a straightforward statement, without elaboration.

God's further reply in 6:2–8 is much more extensive. It addresses the weightier part of Moses' speech, for it takes up the question of rationale and objective, a question basic for Moses. The longer reply is clearly structured. The first part revolves around the self-identification of God (6:2b–5); the second part is a series of instructions to Moses. Together the two parts speak to Moses' concern: "God, what are you up to anyway?"

God's self-identification as Yahweh.
God's reply to Moses begins with a simple but highly significant assertion: "I am the LORD" (6:2). In the English translation the force of this statement is not at once apparent. It is essentially the name of the deity that is at issue. In this reply the self-identification formula "I am the LORD" appears three times (vv. 2, 6, 8).

The name for God is given in most English Bibles as "the LORD." The Hebrew consonants are YHWH, and with certain vowels customarily written with these consonants, the pronunciation for the name suggested by earlier scholars was Yehovah (Jehovah). Modern scholars hold that the name of God was pronounced Yahweh. This conclusion is based on an understanding of the way in which in oral reading Jewish people came to substitute a title for the written name of God because of their deep reverence for the name of God. Yahweh, then, is the proper name for God. Some modern translations of the Bible employ the name Yahweh rather than the accustomed "the LORD," and perhaps for good reason. In the English language "Lord" is a title and properly translates *ᵃdōnay*, master. LORD, all in capital letters, as a translation of Yahweh,[7] does not convey the force of a personal name. In this passage it is not a title but a specific name that is revealed. Since great importance was attached to names in ancient Israel, and among Semites generally, it is of considerable importance, especially for a theology of the Old Testament, to gain clarity on the meaning of the name Yahweh.

To answer the question about the meaning of the name Yahweh, we must reach back a little in the narrative. The name had been given to Moses earlier in connection with his call (3:1 – 4:17). There Moses had heard God identify himself as "I AM WHO I AM" (3:14), a phrase that plays on the Hebrew verb "to be." Building on the derivation of the word Yahweh from the verb "to be," some scholars hold that the expressions "I AM WHO I AM" and "Yahweh" refer to the actuality of God's existence. The name, then, marks the certainty of Yahweh's existence. Given a western mindset, such an explanation seems plausible; yet scholars have challenged that interpretation on the basis that such abstractions as "existence" were not characteristic of the Hebrew way of thinking.

Since linguistically the phrase could be translated, "I cause to be that which I cause to be," others have argued that the words refer to the creative activity of God. This view has been contested, however, on the grounds that the specific verb form involved (causative) is not found in the Hebrew for the verb "to be." Still others have suggested that "I will be who I will be" indicated that God was sufficient for every circumstance. Paraphrased, this would mean, "I will be for you the kind of God you have need of." A Jewish scholar holds that the name El Shaddai, which also occurs in the text and is rendered "God Almighty," was a name that was associated with fertility. The patriarchs, this scholar says, knew God as "God Almighty," but did not know God as the one who fulfilled promises; now, at the time of the exodus, the name Yahweh was to be associated with the keeping of promises. That is, Yahweh represents "He who is with his creatures, and He who is constantly the same, that is, he is true to his word and fulfills his promise."[8]

Or, to turn to an approach that sidesteps the attempt to translate the word, some have suggested that the name Yahweh was deliberately enigmatic. To know someone by name is to have a measure of control. One can summon him or her, for instance. Did God give to Israel so strange a name, a name that was no name, so that Israel would not manipulate God?[9] It is a distinct possibility. Human inclination is to use God to one's own advantage. But Yahweh is not a dispensing machine from whom can be secured at will the gifts of bounty, health, wisdom, etc. No, Yahweh remains free to act. Yahweh's acts are carried out in freedom. Yahweh is who he is, and is not determined, except by himself.

Attractive as some of these suggestions may be, it is best, if one wishes to know the meaning of the name Yahweh, to give close attention to the context of Exodus 3. As Eichrodt has noted, the significance of the name lies in part in the promise of his presence. Moses has already been given the assurance of God's presence earlier when God declares, in response to Moses' objection, "I will be with you" (3:12).[10] The context is also one in which God promises deliverance. God says: "I declare that I will bring you up out of the misery of Egypt" (3:17). This promise gives support to the meaning of the name Yahweh as being the saving name. Yahweh is the name by which God represents himself as present, here and now, to act, especially to deliver. It is in this way, essentially in a new way, that Israel will experience Yahweh. Yahweh is a salvation name. This name, the most frequent name for God (YHWH occurs more than 6,800 times in the Old Testament) becomes a frequent reminder that God is the saving God.

The identity of Yahweh, as our text emphasizes, is not to be divorced from the story of the patriarchs. "I appeared to Abraham, Isaac, and Jacob as God Almighty, but by my name 'The LORD' (Yahweh) I did not make myself known to them" (6:3). The same God who now speaks to Moses, though under a new name, Yahweh, had earlier committed himself to the patriarchs through a covenant to them, which, among other things, included the gift of the land of Canaan. With this statement the relationship of God to the patriarchs, described already in Genesis 12, is reviewed, or affirmed, or better yet, made the platform from which the further promises are now launched. The promise of land to Abraham is made in Gen 12:7. The covenant with Abraham is described in greater detail in Genesis 15 and 17 and is related to the initial blessing of a multitude of descendants promised to Abraham (Gen 12:2). Along with the promise of descendants, God promised Abraham territory. "On that day the Lord made a covenant with Abram saying, 'To your descendants I give this land, from the river of Egypt to the great river, the river Euphrates . . .'" (Gen 15:18). The triple promise of descendants, territory, and blessing is embraced in a covenant given to Abraham in his ninety-ninth year (Gen 17:1–8). Reiterated to Isaac (Gen 26:3) and to Jacob (Gen 28:19; 35:9–12), the promise continued to have a threefold gift of descendants, territory, and blessing. God's word to Moses is that he has remembered that covenant, not in the sense of merely recalling it, but in the sense of honoring it. One phase of the promise, that of offspring, is realized in part, for the families of Israel have been exceptionally fruitful (Exod 1:7). Fulfillment of the remaining part of the promise, that of land, will now be brought under way.

The statement of God in Exod 6:3–5 then ties in with the patriarchs historically by reviewing the past, and theologically by providing continuity of the name Yahweh with the name God Almighty. What follows in the Yahweh speech is directed to the future.

Yahweh's purpose.

The name Yahweh, judged by the context in which it is first given (3:14) and the special attention devoted to it in the present passage (5:22 – 6:8), signals a divine presence to save. The name Yahweh, one is led to expect, will introduce a new chapter in God's work in the world. In his reply to Moses, God as Yahweh describes his intention.

Yahweh's initial design for his people is deliverance: "I will free you from the burdens of the Egyptians and deliver you from slavery to them. I will redeem you with an outstretched arm and with mighty acts of judgment' (6:6). These three statements resemble, by reason of parallelism, lines of Hebrew poetry. Three synonyms are used to elucidate Yahweh's action. "I will bring out" (RSV; "free" NRSV) is in the causative form of "go" (*yāṣā²*) and might be rendered: "I will cause you to go out." The causative is also employed in the following verb: deliver (*nṣl*). It is the common verb used to refer to God's actions of rescue. The verbal form (*nṣl*) is repeated with considerable frequency (135 times). The word rendered "redeem" (*gā²al*) has its linguistic home in regulations governing tribal peoples and property. A redeemer (*gō²ēl*) was one whose responsibility it was to buy out the property of a kinsman who had forfeited it, or who was on the verge of forfeiting it, perhaps because of debt. The prophet Jeremiah purchased a piece of land from his cousin Hanamel and so acted as a redeemer (Jer 32:6ff). A more familiar example is Boaz, who as a near relative buys the property of Naomi (Ruth 2:20; 4:4–6, 9). Or the redeemer might buy out a kinsman who had become the slave of a foreigner (Lev 25:47–54), or avenge the blood of a relative who had been murdered. The sense of restoration to a former state or the healing of tribal brokenness is an underlying component of the term. In Exodus the redeemer is Yahweh, and the deliverance is specified to be of large proportion: "from the burdens of the Egyptians" and from their slavery.

Secondly, Yahweh's design is to form a godly community. "I will take you as my people, and I will be your God" (Exod 6:7a). God's purpose is that the people now to be formed are to be distinctly his people. But, characteristically, God's demand is not apart from his promise: he himself will be their God. This second statement makes it clear that deliverance, though it is Yahweh's initial intention, is only preparatory to larger concerns. The redeemed lot are to stand together as a community marked as God's special possession. The vocabulary is covenant vocabulary. The formula, slightly altered, occurs in the major sections of the Old Testament (e.g., Lev 26:12; Deut 26:17ff; Jer 7:23; Ezek 11:20). The implications of this statement will receive attention later.

Thirdly, Yahweh's intention is that there be an ongoing relationship with his people. "You shall know that I am the LORD your God, who has freed you from the burdens of the

Egyptians" (Exod 6:7b). They are to know (that is, experience) him as Yahweh their God. This means, among other things, that he offers himself to be known. God invites his people into the adventure of knowing him. The means by which this knowledge occurs and the nature of the resultant experience can be deduced from the exodus event, but further descriptions of Yahweh's encounter with his people will be in evidence later.

Finally, Yahweh's intention for his people is that they enjoy the good life. The words of the text are: "I will bring you into the land that I swore to give to Abraham, Isaac, and Jacob; I will give it to you for a possession" (Exod 6:8). The land was already earlier the object of promise, where it was the concrete part of God's blessing for his people. Elsewhere the land is described as the land flowing with milk and honey (Exod 3:17), which is to say that it is a land in which life is pleasant and in which living is marked by abundance. The land comes before long to symbolize the life with Yahweh in ideal conditions, a quality of life which might be characterized as the abundant life.

The divine reply to Moses' question, "Why did you ever send me?" embraces a discussion of the name Yahweh, and a disclosure of his purpose. Three times, as we have noted, the self-identification formula surfaces: "I am Yahweh." In the first instance it introduces the historical review in which emphasis is placed on the name itself since it had not been known in earlier times (Exod 6:3). In the second part of the speech, the self-identification formula occurs at the outset of the four statements of divine purpose (6:6). Curiously, and in a sense of finality, the "I am Yahweh" phrase also terminates the speech (6:8). Unless we think of the reply as composed carelessly, we must ask, what is the force of this thrice-repeated assertion? If in the name Yahweh there is disclosed a new feature of Yahweh, and if the covenant with the patriarchs was already made earlier, apart from the name, then we must look for a new feature other than covenant as linked in a particular way with the name Yahweh. Is that new feature not to be found in the statement of the fourfold design? Salvation, a new people, a new relationship, and the gift of the land—these are the components of the purpose. Yahweh is the name that is associated at this crucial juncture with purpose, that which God intends or is about.

One may fully affirm the remark by Brevard Childs in conjunction with this passage: "The content of the message which is bracketed by this self-identification formula is actually an explication of the name itself and contains the essence of God's purpose with Israel."[11] Similarly, the Jewish scholar Cassuto states in commenting on this Exodus text: "In our passage the king of the universe announces His purpose and the amazing plan of action that He proposes to carry out in the near future."[12] We should wish to amend this statement only by noting that the plan is not just for the near future, but embraces a large block of time, in fact the entire history of Israel.

And something more. Both the entire second speech (6:2–8) and specifically the statement of the fourfold design are bracketed by the assertion: "I am Yahweh." Guarantee for the achievement of the purpose rests alone in Yahweh. The entire enterprise about which Moses asks is grounded in a name, which in the Old Testament is shorthand for all that a person is. The perspective is clearly established. Though the plan involves the people of Israel, Egyptians, and the land of Canaan, one must not, either at the beginning or ever, lose sight of God's personal involvement. It is he who will superintend, direct, empower. No human, not Moses himself, will take to himself honor for the achievement of any portion of that plan. Initiative and guarantee are both from Yahweh.

Our exegesis of the Exodus text has established that it speaks to the basic question of what God purposes for his people. Moses has put the question: "God, what is it all about?" Moses has also lodged a complaint. God has replied by reassuring Moses that his action will indeed be a satisfactory answer to that complaint. Furthermore, God has addressed the basic question of purpose which Moses raised, first by establishing his identity in the name Yahweh, and then by explicating a fourfold purpose. The purpose is not something arbitrary or artificial but grows out of the person of Yahweh as signified by his name. Childs put it aptly:

Although there is a history of revelation which includes a past and a future, the theocentric focus on God's initiative in making himself known tends to encompass all the various times into the one great act of disclosure. *To know God's name is to know his purpose for all mankind from the beginning to the end.*[13]

2. A Grid for the Old Testament Message

There is general agreement that the Old Testament has Yahweh for its central subject, but we may ask, what does one say after having said that? We may posit that the text in Exod 5:22 – 6:8 clarifies the way in which the central subject of the Old Testament, Yahweh, is to be elaborated. Yahweh has a plan. This plan is one to bring deliverance, to summon a people who will be peculiarly his own, to offer himself for them to know and to give to them land in fulfillment of his promise. This Scripture passage asks the question posed at the outset, namely, how to understand what the Old Testament is getting at. Formulated by Moses in the context of a frustrating and perplexing experience, the question, "Why did you ever send me?" is helpful in supplying a handle, a definite clue to our investigation about the central message of the Old Testament. As a preliminary check we might test our suggestion that the fourfold purpose of God is a satisfactory grid by casting our eye over one block of the Old Testament, namely the Pentateuch.

The concept of purpose, quite apart from detail, already underlies the book of Genesis. The family stories of Abraham, Isaac and Jacob presage a distinct destiny, especially since they are launched with the statement of design to Abraham: "Go from your country and your kindred and your father's house to the land that I will show you" (Gen 12:1). The Joseph narrative at the conclusion of Genesis also hints at design. Joseph says to his brothers: "Even though you intended to do harm to me, God intended it for good, in order to preserve a numerous people, as he is doing today" (Gen 50:20).

Deliverance, the first phase of Yahweh's intention, is particularly the subject of the first half of the book of Exodus; the covenant community, now given detailed instructions, is the subject of Exodus 19–40. Through the sacrifice and other cultic institutions in Leviticus, God makes himself known and the people experience him as Yahweh. Land, and the regulations pertaining to occupancy, are the frequent subject of Deuteronomy. Thus the fourfold design serves almost as a table of contents to the Pentateuch. Might this outline be pertinent, even adequate, for the remainder of the Old Testament?

It is the thesis of this book that the fourfold design described in Exod 5:22 – 6:8 is an appropriate and also adequate grid according to which to present the whole of the Old Testament material. This is a substantial claim, proof of which must be the pages which follow. Even should it be disputed that the proposed grid is adequate as a set of categories for the presentation of the Old Testament message, the insights gained from this approach promise to be considerable.[14]

Two points could still be raised as requiring clarification. First, it might be asked why this particular passage in Exodus rather than some other in Exodus or elsewhere was chosen. Could some other passage serve equally well? Perhaps, but not too likely. The paragraph of Exod 5:22 – 6:8 commends itself for various reasons. It is the text in which the revelation of the name Yahweh is differentiated from other names of God. Even though a form of it is given to Moses earlier, attention is distinctly called here to Yahweh, the form of the name by which God will be primarily known in the remainder of the Old Testament canon. Secondly, this passage speaks of the beginnings of the people of Israel, with whom much of the Old Testament deals. It could be expected that a programmatic statement would be found here. Moreover, this text is concerned with an interpretation of the exodus event, which according to some scholars is the fulcrum event in the Old Testament.[15] Most important, however, in commending this scripture as the Old Testament message in a nutshell is the consideration that the text addresses the question of God's ultimate purpose. Moses' question is our question too: "God, what are you up to?" More than a clue is given here. The explicit statements supply specific, even if not fully detailed, indications of Yahweh's purpose. Those indications, it may be argued, are the controlling purposes of God within the Old Testament. But someone may still object by saying, "Is not the notion of purpose and design an import from a western civilization which, especially in our time, is fascinated by ideas such as purpose?" The notion of design is basic, for instance, to such western concepts as "management by objective." Since it is our intention to let the Old Testament speak in its own terms, the question is most appropriate. The remainder of the book is an attempt at an answer.

The mention of divine purpose is explicit in several Old Testament texts, a fact which at its minimum establishes that the idea of divine purpose is not foreign to the Old Testament. For a forthright statement on the subject of design, one may begin with Isa 46:9–10, where the exclusiveness of God is emphasized, and with it his purposeful action:

I am God, and there is no other;
I am God, and there is no one like me . . .
Saying, "My purpose shall stand,
and I will fulfill my intention."

In the customary Hebrew parallelism there is a twofold stress on purpose through the use of the two words, purpose (ʿēṣâ) and intention (ḥēpes). The second is more often used in the sense of desire. The meaning of the Hebrew root (ʿēṣâ), plan or purpose, can be discerned from the secular usage which it has in the story of the counselor Ahithophel (2 Sam 15:34). The counsel of the man was a plan he proposed. It was opposed by a plan (ʿēṣâ) offered by Hushai the Archite, whose plan or counsel is regarded in the end as better than that of Ahithophel (2 Sam 17:14).

Using the word ʿēṣâ to mean "plan," we may list a set of texts taken from the wisdom and prophetic material to make the point that God is a God of design. It is not unusual for writers to compare the human plans with the plans of God. Thus God is said to frustrate the plans (ʿēṣâ) of the nations. By contrast, "The plan (*ʿēṣâ*) of Yahweh stands forever, the thoughts of his heart for all generations" (Ps 33:11). Similarly from the book of Proverbs, "Many are the plans in the mind of a man, but it is the purpose (*ʿēṣâ*) of the LORD that will be established" (Prov 19:21). We should expect wisdom literature to have something to say on the subject, since wisdom writers were exercised by the notion of order in the universe.

In the prophetic material, the concept of plan or purpose is even stronger. In a judgment speech against Assyria, the Lord swears: "This is the plan (*ʿēṣâ*) that is planned concerning the whole earth" (Isa 14:26a). Then, to establish the point that this purpose cannot be thwarted, the same speech carries this assurance: "For the LORD of hosts has planned, and who will annul it?" (Isa 14:27). Of interest in our discussion is a Jeremiah text where God's name of Yahweh is particularly identified as "Yahweh of hosts," following which is the accolade: "Great of plan (*ʿēṣâ*) and mighty in performance" (Jer 32:19 NASB). The first statement about Yahweh's name, reminiscent of Exod 6:2–8, is a statement about his plan.

Yahweh is a God with a purpose. In this respect Yahweh is different from other gods represented in ancient Near Eastern literature. Already the Genesis verdict, "God saw that it was good," presupposes a purpose. To this fact of purpose the law gives evidence (Exod 5:22 – 6:8), as do the prophets (Isa 46:10; 14:26; Jer 32:18–19) and so also do the writings (Ps 33:11; Prov 19:21).

With these assertions about purpose generally, and the exegetical treatment of Exod 5:22 – 6:8 specifically, the shape of our task emerges with greater clarity. To comprehend Yahweh's design we shall have to talk about deliverance; about covenant and community; about the knowledge of God; and about land.

Westermann's division of salvation into its two aspects of *deliverance* and *blessing* is helpful in understanding the relationship between these four parts.[16] Deliverance entails God's acts of intervention, particularly in crisis. This work of deliverance aims in turn at the three subsequent purposes: a covenant community, intimacy with God, and the gift of land. All of these can be subsumed under the word *blessing*. Whereas God's work of deliverance is a work of intervention in crisis, his bestowal of blessing is a continuing activity in non-crisis times. The book of Genesis, as we shall see, contains a description of salvation in which both these elements, deliverance and blessing, are evident.

The statement of design in the Exodus text was given in a definite historical situation, and since history is so crucial to the Old Testament material, our discussion of divine design will follow the main historical divisions: the pre-monarchical period; the time of the monarchy; and the exile or post-monarchy period.[17] But first a flashback to the pre-exodus history is necessary in order to determine whether anticipations of God's purpose, clearly given in Exod 5:22 – 6:8, are present in Genesis. After a look at Genesis we shall examine the remainder of the Old Testament in systematic fashion, always with an eye on the fourfold purpose of God. The heart of the Old Testament, we shall seek to demonstrate, revolves around God's design or purpose, as it emerges from a study of Exod 5:22 – 6:8.

Earlier Anticipation of God's Purpose

$\mathbf{G}$od's design is articulated in Exod 5:22 – 6:8. A legitimate question is, are there anticipations of this design prior to the exodus? Does the patriarchal narrative, for example, anticipate such a divine design? Are there early glimpses of this purpose in the primeval history? How does the record in the book of Genesis appear in the light of the pivotal Exodus text? Is the theme of design sufficiently translucent in Genesis, which serves as prologue to the Bible, to make the proposal of the design of God credible as the overarching rubric in an Old Testament theology?

Is there, for example, an indication in Genesis 1–11 that God is a God of purpose? One need look no further than to the first utterance of the Almighty: "Let there be light" (Gen 1:3). This statement of intention is immediately followed by a report of the actualization: "And there was light." The reader/listener senses the force of the purposive word, for it issues at once into fulfillment. Each of God's creative words is expressive of a design, for each successive creative act adds to the fullness and also the harmony of the created order. In certain instances the purpose is most explicit. The heavenly luminaries were spoken into existence "to govern" the day and the night. The creation of man had among its purposes that man should "have dominion" over the fish, the birds, the cattle and creeping things, and over all the earth (Gen 1:26).

Moreover, the Bible's opening chapter repeats the refrain: "And God saw that it was good" (Gen 1:10, 12, 18, 21, 25). Light is good; the distribution of land and water masses is good; so is the vegetation and animal life and so also is the forming of the human creature. "And God saw everything that he had made, and behold, it was very good" (*ṭôb*). Gerhard von Rad, the German scholar, comments on the word *ṭôb*: "The word contains less an aesthetic judgment than the designation of purpose and correspondence."[1]

God spoke a blessing on the sea and air creatures, mandating (purposing) that they fill full the waters of the sea and the earth. God also blessed humankind. The call to multiply is in keeping with design and objective. Of the word *blessing* Kaiser says, "Obviously pride of place must be given to this term as the first to signify the plan of God."[2]

Not only the creation account itself but the remainder of primeval history (Genesis 1–11) points to a God who acts out of purpose. The taking of forbidden fruit proves at least that the prohibition was not an idle prohibition. The subsequent dialogue shows that God is a God with a specified intention, for he promises, "I will put enmity between you and the woman, and between your offspring and hers; he will strike your head, and you will strike his heel" (Gen 3:15). The harmony which existed in Eden before the fall has been shattered. But God announces that the serpent, a chief offender, shall eventually be rendered harmless. The clarification of this purpose and the chronicling of its outworking is prominent in the Old Testament.

In the preparation for the flood God addresses Noah with a declaration of intent: "But I will establish my covenant with you" (Gen 9:9 RSV). In the Babel story the human purpose is deliberately frustrated by the Almighty. In that account, though God's purpose is not specified, it is at least clear that God's purpose and not that of humankind will be the controlling one.

In the patriarchal narratives the initial as well as the concluding statements underscore the fact that God is a God of design. The initial word of God is a call to Abram with a three-fold promise to him (Gen 12:1–3). God intends to bring Abram to a land to give him descendants and through him to bless the nations of the earth. With this programmatic word the Genesis family narrative of Abram, Isaac and Jacob is introduced. More than that: the story of a people and their God is inaugurated. The book's final chapter brings to resolution the story of Joseph and his brothers. In Joseph's word to his brothers there is expressed a central conviction about Yahweh: "Even though you intended to do harm to me, God intended it for good, in order to preserve a numerous people, as he is doing today" (Gen 50:20). To a casual observer, Joseph's life in distant Egypt, a land to which he had come against his will because of family envy, had no connection with God's promise to Abraham to make of him a great nation. And yet the succeeding events—Joseph's rise to power, the storage of grain, the famine, the visit of the Hebrews to Egypt—are such that suddenly the divine hidden purpose is disclosed. God has brought good to Jacob's family in preserving their lives in time of famine. Out of evil, the wicked action of ten men against their brother, God has providentially brought blessing. In the tapestry of Joseph's variegated experiences, design is evident.

In Genesis, therefore, God is so presented that the later disclosure of his purpose at the exodus is congruent with his earlier activity. The specific fourfold goal stated in Exodus, so our argument runs, is not without antecedents in Genesis. We may therefore examine Genesis, this prologue to Hebrew national history, for indications or hints of the specific components of that design—deliverance, community, intimacy, blessing. Our claim is not that in Genesis God's fourfold purpose is explicitly articulated; but that, once God's purpose is plainly stated, as it is in Exod 5:22 – 6:8, a review of the earlier material, both the primeval history (Genesis 1–11) and the patriarchal narratives (Genesis 12–50) will show each of the elements of that design to be present. Reading Genesis from the standpoint of the pivotal text in Exodus has its own fascination.

1. God's Fourfold Purpose Anticipated in Primeval History

The creation narrative (some would say narratives) details the beginnings of the earth and universe, and of plant and animal life upon the earth. The existence of things, whether luminaries in the sky or plants in the ground, comes about through a word of the Almighty God, spoken with intention. The six-day sequence, whatever else its significance, is an indication of an orderly, staged process.[3] Whatever the scientific and anthropological issues the creation narrative raises for modern man, the story, when read in the context of ancient Near Eastern creation stories, sets forth a God who is singularly distinct and independent from his creation and who is therefore presumably acting upon his own purposes. God's primary concern is for people, who are created in God's own image. That image is best understood as consisting in the ability of humankind to relate significantly to others, notably to God; and, like God, to exert dominion over lower forms of life.

The initial scene depicted in the garden is one of harmony. Indeed, God's pronouncement following his act of creation that "it is very good" declares that his expectation has been met and his intention fulfilled. In this initial and ideal depiction of persons, nature and God, the accent is on God's continued activity of blessing. We distinguished in the previous chapter between salvation conceived of as God's intervention in crisis and salvation as God's ongoing work of blessing. In Eden one need not talk of deliverance, for no crisis exists. One speaks rather of a state of bliss, described best by the Hebrew word *šalôm*.[4] *Šalôm* is peace, but it is much more than absence of conflict. The state of *šalôm* is one of inward and outward peace, material and spiritual satiation, harmony of an individual with oneself, with nature, with the world of people, and clearly with God, the Creator. In later eras of human experience, Israelite prophets will describe graphically and with passion the situation of *šalôm* toward which God's acts of deliverance aim. In the eschatological age, the age of God's demonstrated supremacy, the fragmentation of the present will once again be brought into healing and wholeness, or *šālôm*. But in Eden that wholeness exists. Human beings are in tune with God. Adam and Eve are unashamed with each other; they live in harmony with themselves as well as with the animals. Not only their needs but their desires are fully met. Here is the perfect state.

The description of that state of bliss and blessing is most readily given in the categories familiar to us from Exod 5:22 – 6:8. Life in Eden is characterized by covenant. Adam responds enthusiastically to Eve. He acknowledges that she is bone of his bone and flesh of his flesh. He has not been able to find a companion suitable for him among other living creatures, but this one, a person like himself, fashioned by God, is one who satisfies his yearning. The family order is initiated here: "Therefore a man leaves his father and his mother and clings to his wife, and they become one flesh" (Gen 2:24).

Further, there exists a relationship of mutual intimacy between them and God. There is no other God to whom they are tempted to give allegiance. Adam and Eve know God—he is not a stranger to them. God is described as walking in the garden in the cool of the day; Creator and creature converse. God calls to the human family, "Where are you?" (Gen 3:9). (Similarly the comment sandwiched in the genealogies, "Enoch walked with God three hundred years," Gen 5:22, points to personal intimacy with God.) Adam knows God as a solicitous, caring God who earlier responded to Adam's incompleteness by saying, "It is not good that the man should be alone; I will make him a helper as his partner" (Gen 2:18). The pair know God as the one who gives purpose to their lives: dominion over the earth. They know God as the one to whom they are accountable, and who has the prerogative to make demands on them.

Theirs is also a defined territorial space, a gift from their Creator. Adam and Eve are placed in a garden watered by a river divided into four streams. The place for their dwelling is adequate and bounteous.

From these opening chapters, the salvation of God as blessing is easily identifiable. Here are present covenant/community,
knowledge of God, and the gift of land. God's provision in the
spiritual, social, and physical domains of life are adequate and
satisfying.

The disobedience of the first parents is followed in the narrative by increasing disarray, crisis upon crisis. It is this disarray
that throws into singular relief the fourfold design as it is later
articulated.

Now appears the first theme in the fourfold design: intervention, or judgment-deliverance. Very quickly the harmony of
Eden is lost and the human race is corrupted. God contends
with the human race and declares, "My spirit shall not abide in
mortals forever" (Gen 6:3). As a result of the wickedness perpe-
trated by the intermarriage of the sons of God and the daughters of humans, God decreed the punishment of a deluge. It is
the theme of judgment which is dominant, yet Noah is safely
brought through the disaster. Thus the deliverance motif surfaces in the flood story. The world's population is destroyed in
judgment; but deliverance is extended to a remnant. A new beginning is possible because God has intervened to bring deliverance.

From the first, salvation and judgment are two parts of the
same process. The word of judgment was spoken against the
sinful race in Eden and also at the time of the flood. But each
time the judgment was accompanied by a grace word. Claus
Westermann has helpfully pointed out that the primeval history
(Genesis 1–11) embraces human experience in broad compass
and—most important—contains the gospel of God's grace. Sin
vitiated every relationship and brought about judgment; but
the judgment was ameliorated by grace. When Adam and Eve
sinned against *God*, death was threatened as a consequence; yet
with that threat came a word of grace, the promise of an eventual victory over Satan. Cain sinned against his *brother*; a vaga-
bond existence was Cain's punishment, but the mark on his
forehead represented God's grace. The sin of the "sons of God"
against the "daughters of humans" violated the *moral order*.[5]

God threatened total destruction; yet grace prevailed and one family was saved. The sin of pride in the Tower of Babel incident was sin against *civilization and culture*, and God's response was the threat of dispersion. Yet once more the word of grace turned a bleak situation into one of hope—God called out Abraham. The gospel of God's intervention is unmistakable.[6]

A Theological Summary of Genesis 1–11[7]

Incident	Nature of the sin	Divine threat	God's grace word
Adam and Eve (Gen 3)	Against God	Death	A promise of offspring
Cain (Gen 4)	Against man	Fugitive existence	A mark on Cain
Flood (Gen 6–9)	Against natural order	Destruction	Deliverance of one family
Tower (Gen 11)	Against culture	Dispersion	Election of Abraham

The early chapters of Genesis touch not only on deliverance, but on the other three themes of God's fourfold purpose, even if negatively. There is breakdown of community. Even in the first family, solidarity disintegrates when Cain kills his brother Abel. The gregarious nature of people is illustrated by their gathering into communities; yet the community is not whole. The incident at Babel in which the peoples of the world counsel, "Come, let us build ourselves a city, and a tower with its top in the heavens, and let us make a name for ourselves; otherwise we shall be scattered abroad upon the face of the whole earth" (Gen 11:4) illustrates a gregarious impulse, to be sure, but also a selfish, ungodly tendency. The effort at Babel, though it brought people together into community, was not in keeping with God's desire for peoplehood. The community for which he looked was a covenant community whose primary concern would be the honor of God's name and not their own, a people who lived together under God. The Psalmist's statement is sufficient commentary on Babel: "The LORD brings the counsel of the nations to nothing; he frustrates the plans of the peoples.

The counsel of the LORD stands forever, the thoughts of his heart to all generations" (Ps 33:10–11). It is against this background of the failure of community that one is to see God's promise to Abraham that he should become a great nation.

Third in the fourfold design is knowledge of God, defined as experience. The early chapters of Genesis deal with people's experience of God. In fact, the disobedience of Adam and Eve is motivated by the serpent's promise that in the eating of the forbidden tree the two of them shall be as gods knowing good and evil. The phrase "good and evil," as well as indicating the obvious moral aspects of the temptation, is also by its combination of opposites a Hebrew idiom for "everything." The tempter urged mortals to know *something*, in fact everything. God's intent for them was that they should know *Someone*, not something. The craving for an experience of the divine was present. But the reach for that experience was illicit. Here too, one is to see subsequent self-revelations of God against the background of this attempt at an experience of God.

The fourth strand of the design from Exod 5:22 – 6:8 is land. In the primeval story, Eden is hardly an incidental feature. Rather the human pair, the apex of creation, is placed in a garden planted by God for their use (Gen 2:8). The garden is a pleasing place and comes quite naturally to represent loveliness and abundance. Enjoyment of the garden, however, is not without condition. When the two mortals disobey the simple instruction, they forfeit their place in the garden. They are driven out; they no longer have access to Eden; they have lost the gift of territory that God had given. If then the theme of land becomes prominent in the patriarchal story and especially in Israel's story, it should be remembered that its forerunner, theologically, is the garden of Eden. Thus the themes of land, of community, of knowledge of God, and of deliverance are interconnected already in the primeval story.

2. God's Fourfold Design Anticipated in the Patriarchal Narratives

The patriarchal story takes on special significance when it is examined for its literary location and its theological message. On the one hand the story of Abraham, Isaac and Jacob follows the primeval history (Genesis 1–11).[8] On the other, it is the necessary prelude to the story told in Exodus of the deliverance of the people from Egypt. If now our reading of the stories of the patriarchs is informed by the pivotal text in Exodus in which God discloses his purposes, the themes which are specified in the Exodus text readily surface. But it should be noted at once that the accent in these stories is on salvation as blessing. The patriarchal stories open with the promise of blessing (Gen 12:1–3) and must be understood as descriptive of salvation under the rubric of blessing, in contrast to salvation under the rubric of deliverance.

Nevertheless, deliverance is not totally absent. In response to Abraham's intercession, God spares Lot and members of his family from the destruction of Sodom (Genesis 18–19). The deliverance of the peoples of Egypt and the family of Jacob through a remarkable series of events is, as Joseph points out, the work of God.

In protecting his promise of blessing to Abraham, God intervenes on at least two occasions in order to salvage a delicate situation. In each, Abraham perceives his life to be threatened by designs on his beautiful wife by a foreign potentate.[9] In each instance he identifies his wife as his sister. The wife/sister motif stories—three in total (Genesis 12, 20, 26)—are frequently read by moderns in terms of New Testament ethics. The problem, then, to focus for a moment on Abraham and Pharaoh, becomes one of justifying God's punishment on the Pharaoh and explaining the lavish riches God bestows on Abram, who seems to be rewarded for his deception (Gen 12:17ff). The theology of these chapters functions on a different plane, however. The patriarchal narrative is launched with a divine promise (Gen

12:1–3), a promise of blessing, which is, as clarified later, the promise of a son. The question for the Genesis writer is, how does the promise fare? What happens when the recipient of a promise places the promise into jeopardy and a crisis ensues? For by his action Abraham potentially called into question God's promise of a child to Sarah. The theological answer to the question is that even the folly of a believing person will not in the final analysis jeopardize God's promise. The very structure of the stories underscores this conclusion. For prior to each "deception narrative" the promise of descendants is recorded (Gen 12:7; 18:10–15; 26:4), as if to emphasize that the promise is in force. The subsequent "deceptions" will not negate the promise. The theological conclusion toward which these stories about salvation (as deliverance) lead is therefore profound and far-reaching.

The patriarchal stories are particularly rich in describing salvation as a state of blessing experienced as a people—i.e., in community. An earlier echo of the Exodus statement, "I will take you for my people and I will be your God," is found in the patriarchal narrative when God declares to Abraham: "I will establish my covenant between me and you, and your offspring after you throughout their generations, for an everlasting covenant, to be God to you and to your offspring after you" (Gen 17:7). This word to Abraham anticipates the later "covenant formula," "I will be your God; you shall be my people." The initiative for covenant-making comes from God himself. The definition of "covenant" will need to be explicated later; but already here it is clear that a covenant is a special arrangement between two parties, an arrangement that is not to be equated with or confused with contract. It is true that one may speak of "establishing the covenant" (Gen 9:9) or even of "breaking the covenant" (Gen 17:14), expressions that are familiar to us from contract. The essence of a covenant, however, is the bonded relationship between two parties. Circumcision is not itself the covenant but is a "sign" of the covenant. Whether one takes the Genesis 17 statement about covenant or the statement from Exod 6:7 about covenant, it is of interest to note that since the covenant formula is also found in the last book of the Bible, Rev 21:7, the bulk of biblical material is essentially bracketed by this covenant statement.

Another component in God's design according to Exodus 6 is the knowledge of God: "And you shall know that I am God, the LORD your God." The theophanies described in the patriarchal narratives are early evidence of God's intent: "And they shall know that I am God." In a vision Abraham hears God reiterate the earlier promise (Genesis 15). Later when Abraham is ninety-nine years of age, "the LORD appeared to Abram, and said to him, "I am God Almighty; walk before me, and be blameless'" (Gen 17:1; cf. Isaac, Gen 26:23ff, and Jacob, Gen 28:10ff). Once more at the Oaks of Mamre prior to the destruction of Sodom and Gomorrah "the LORD appeared to him" (Gen 18:1). The dialogue and subsequent intercession make the point in a dramatic scene that God responds to the appeal of his servant Abraham. Equally important, the destiny of the community is determined to a considerable extent by the presence in it of righteous persons.

In the life of Jacob two geographical places stand out as marking encounters with God. On his way to Laban at Haran, Jacob stops at a place he later called Bethel (literally, house of God) because there at night in conjunction with the ladder vision he heard God reiterate the earlier promise to Abraham (Gen 28:10ff). As he had met God on his exit from the land, so he is later to be met by the angel of God upon his return to the land twenty years later. At Peniel on the Jabbok, Jacob wrestles with the angel and secures a blessing in the form of a new name, Israel, "he who strives with God" or "God continues to strive" or even "Let God persist" (Gen 32:22–32). In the light of several appearances of God to the three patriarchs, Abraham, Isaac and Jacob, it is strange that Joseph does not record a theophany, though one reads there of significant dreams.

God interacts with the patriarchs with a frequency and intensity that strikes the modern reader as strange. Not only in crisis but in daily events—eating, traveling, child-bearing—they encounter God. These family narratives unmistakably prepare the way for the clarion purpose statement of Exod 6:7, "You shall know that I am the LORD your God."

The final design element, land, is, of all the elements traced, the most easily discernible in the narrative. The Abram story opens with God's call to him to go to a land that he will be shown (Gen 12:1–3). After a stay in Haran, Abram and Sarai with Lot their nephew and all their possessions "set forth to go to the land of Canaan," settling at Shechem (Gen 12:6). Here Abram hears the LORD's word of promise, one that is to be repeated to him many times: "To your offspring I will give this land" (Gen 12:7; cf. 13:14ff; 15:7, 18ff; 17:18ff). The territorial extent is designated as including an area from the river of Egypt to the river Euphrates (Gen 15:18). The river of Egypt is not the Nile but the "Brook of Egypt," which enters the Mediterranean 87 km southwest of Gaza. The north-south boundaries are not spelled out here but are listed elsewhere (e.g., Num 34:3–12).

The land of promise figures also in the lives of Isaac and Jacob. They too receive the divine word that the land is to be theirs (Gen 26:3; 28:4, 13; 35:12). At his death Jacob affirms that though he die in Egypt God will bring his descendants into the land of the fathers (Gen 48:21). The burial place at Mamre which Abraham purchased becomes an important portion, a down payment, so to speak, of the larger land block. Joseph also dies with the hope on his lips, "But God will surely come to you, and bring you up out of this land to the land that he swore to Abraham, to Isaac, and to Jacob" (Gen 50:24). The divine promise of land together with the promise of descendants is a thread which ties the patriarchal stories together and leads quite naturally to the pivotal Exodus text.

Indeed the patriarchal stories are necessary for understanding the LORD's promise to Moses: "I will bring you into the land that I swore to give to Abraham, Isaac, and Jacob; I will give it to you for a possession. I am the LORD" (Exod 6:8). The earlier scene of the drama—the gift of land—has been played. Now the conflict element in the drama has come about through the patriarchs' departure from the land. One awaits the resolution of the difficulty, curious to know how the initial promise of land will fare, for the people of the promise are now held in slavery.

Seen from the perspective of the Exodus text, the book of Genesis is a paradigm in two ways. First, salvation in its two aspects of deliverance and blessing is delineated clearly. Genesis 3–11 describes God's intervention following the crisis brought about by human sin. God's decisive acts bring salvation—deliverance in crisis. In the patriarchal stories (Genesis 12–50) the focus is God's bestowal of blessing. Salvation is a state in which God in providential ways sustains and enriches life. He gives children to barren women such as Sarah, Rebekah, and Rachel (Gen 18:10, 14; 25:21–14; 30:22–24). In providential ways of blessing he uses Joseph to become the provider "to preserve a numerous people" (Gen 50:20). Thus God saves in that he blesses; God also saves in that he rescues from crisis.

There is a second way in which Genesis becomes a paradigm for Old Testament theology. Genesis shows in miniature the larger movement in the Old Testament. That movement consists of a design articulated, then put to the test, and, finally, in post-exilic times, reaffirmed. In Genesis, a similar three-step movement is noticeable. In the first two chapters of Genesis the basic intention of God's purpose, essentially blessing, is stated. The disarray brought on by sin tests that purpose, for it seems that God's intentions are thwarted. But in the patriarchal story each of the themes surfaces anew though still somewhat veiled.[10] In the statement of God to Moses the veil is lifted and momentarily, but with great clarity, the fourfold purpose of God is clearly given. The miniature is helpful, for it anticipates the full-scale model; and to that we now turn.

PART 2

God's Design Implemented

The Pre-Monarchy Era

God's Design: Salvation

God's purpose is first clearly articulated in conjunction with his intervention in the life of an enslaved people in Egypt (Exod 5:22 – 6:8). As we have seen, the elements of the divine purpose are already mirrored in the story of the patriarchs and, for that matter, even in the primeval history.

Given the specific formulation of that purpose in Exodus, the question is, how does God's purpose unfold? The remainder of the Scripture supplies the answer. In following out that question and its answer, we shall divide the Old Testament story into three units: the pre-monarchical era; the age of the monarchy; and the post-monarchy period. By examining each period in turn, we shall not only have manageable blocks of material for consideration, but will be in a position to observe, in the course of history, shifting emphases and nuances of the fourfold purpose. We turn to the first historical block of material, the pre-monarchical era.

If the people of Israel were asked the question, "Who is the Yahweh you claim as God?" their answer, on the bases of his revelation in Exod 5:22 – 6:8 and their experience, would be that he is the God who brings salvation. They would say more than that, but at least the affirmation about God as redeemer and rescuer would be explicit.

Deliverance from calamity is part of what is meant by salvation. The concept of salvation as developed in the pivotal Exodus text and throughout the Bible includes two kinds of divine activity. *Deliverance* is that work of rescue from evil which God brings about through his intervention. *Blessing* is the continuous work of God by means of which he sustains life, empowers persons, and ensures a state of well-being. Salvation may be an act, as for instance the act of deliverance of Israel from Egypt. Salvation as blessing, involving a state of well-being, is illustrated particularly in the stories of the patriarchs, but also in the provisions of sacrifice.[1]

Ancient Israel experienced salvation in two realms: deliverance and blessing. She knew what it meant to be delivered out of an evil situation, for in her history she experienced deliverance often. But Israel also enjoyed the blessings of God. Her state of well-being resulted from her reconciliation with God, as experienced in connection with worship and sacrifice, i.e., the cult. To speak of salvation then we need to discuss deliverance in Israel's history, and also the gift of salvation as blessing in Israel's religious life. We might describe salvation in history as salvation in the external world, and the blessing of forgiveness as salvation in the internal world, but Israel would not have thought in those categories. In the first part of this chapter we investigate deliverance from the vantage point of historical occurrences in the life of Israel. In the next part we give attention to salvation in the form of blessing of forgiveness that relates to guilt. Both sections are limited to the initial centuries of Israel's life and are restricted therefore to the books of Genesis to Judges.

1. Salvation as Deliverance in History

Deliverance from Egyptian servitude was a great experience, though not without moments of panic, especially as the Egyptians in hot pursuit seemed about to recapture the Israelite people pushed up against the Sea of Reeds with mountains on either side. Israel was in trouble. At that crucial moment Moses called to the people, "Do not be afraid . . . see the deliverance that the Lord will accomplish for you today . . . The LORD will fight for you" (Exod 14:13–14). Shortly thereafter, the Egyptians found their chariots mired in the middle of the sea. They exclaimed and explained, "Let us flee from the Israelites, for the LORD is fighting for them against Egypt" (Exod 14:25). The first deliverance was a decisive military victory by Israel's God Yahweh over the Egyptians.

The victory was celebrated in song, a song rich with theology, or God-talk (Exod 15:1–18). Most critics who relegate large parts of the Pentateuch to writers who wrote in David's reign and thereafter, nevertheless regard this hymn by the sea as a very ancient composition.[2] While its language style is early, it is the theological content which interests us, for here one finds theological reflection after the deliverance.

What is to be said about the God Yahweh in view of Israel's deliverance from Egyptian servitude? Much to be sure. The subject of the song, as of the deliverance narrative, is clearly Yahweh. The poem is in three stanzas in which Yahweh's power is successively described in conjunction with the Pharaoh (15:1–7), the sea (15:8–12), and the nations generally (15:13–18). Since the nations—the Edomites and the Moabites mentioned in the song—were not present at the Sea of Reeds, it is possible that the earlier song of Moses was later expanded but in the same vein. Equally likely is the interpretation that Edom and Moab are more distant powers to whom news of God's power will come.

If by resorting to prose descriptive statements we can retain the exhilaration of the song, several assertions about Yahweh, based on Exodus 15, can be identified. These assertions will describe the deliverer. We can then describe the pattern of deliverance.

Yahweh the Warrior

Yahweh is a warrior.[3] "The LORD is a warrior; the LORD is his name" (Exod 15:3). Salvation had been secured in the context of warfare and combat. In wonderful intervention Yahweh had rescued his people when humanly speaking there was no hope.

What theological significance lies in the designation of Yahweh as warrior?

Some older systematic theologians customarily describe God by his attributes. God is said to be omniscient, omnipotent, and omnipresent. While this somewhat philosophical way of putting matters is helpful, it easily tends to be abstract, as though God were a collection of good and great qualities. The Bible itself, while identifying such qualities, presents Yahweh in specific roles. He is king (Zech 14:16). He is shepherd (Ps 23:1). Isaiah exemplifies this way of thinking about Yahweh: "For the LORD (Yahweh) is our judge, the LORD (Yahweh) is our ruler, the LORD (Yahweh) is our king; he will save us" (Isa 33:22).

In the Song by the Sea, Yahweh is presented in the role of warrior. The ancients knew what warriors were and did. The concrete picture was one of struggle, strife, combat. The enemy was Pharaoh, whose status in Egypt was that of god-king. As such he had control over the people of Egypt, Israel included. Yahweh's warrior action here refers to the separating of the waters, but perhaps also to the plagues preceding this event (cf. Josh 24:5). In brief, as warrior Yahweh saves (v. 2), destroys the enemy (v. 6), works wonders (v. 11), leads his redeemed people, guides them to his holy dwelling (v. 13), and reigns for ever (v. 18).

While it may jar modern sensibilities to speak of Yahweh as warrior, one must understand and appreciate the advantage which this kind of language has over the abstract philosophical language of God as infinite, spirit, etc. The personal and relational dimension is highlighted in the designation of Yahweh as judge, king, ruler, warrior. It mattered greatly, for instance, whether a warrior was for or against one's enemy. Relationships, one soon discovers, are crucial in biblical thought.

Yahweh as warrior enters into a relationship with weak, helpless people. The language of Yahweh as warrior is language of God's involvement. He is the salvation-bringer. "The Lord (Yahweh) is my strength and might. And he has become my salvation" (Exod 15:2a). The word "salvation" (*yešû'â*), which will figure so prominently in the Old Testament, is first used in connection with the exodus event. (The use of the word in Jacob's farewell speech, "I wait for your salvation, O Lord," Gen 49:18, is indefinite.) At the Sea of Reeds Moses exhorted the people to faith. "See the salvation of the Lord" (Exod 14:13 RSV). The narrative section concludes, "Thus the Lord saved Israel" (Exod 14:30), to be followed by the confession in song, "He (Yahweh) has become my salvation" (Exod 15:2). As poets and prophets such as David and Isaiah speak of salvation, must we not hear an echo of the exodus?

At base the word "salvation" means "help." It is employed in the story of Moses who came to the rescue of Jethro's daughters when at the well they were being driven off by the shepherds. Moses stood up and *helped* them (Exod 2:19) and the annoyance of the disturbing shepherds ceased. Now at the far end of the Sea of Reeds another help was celebrated. It was Yahweh who had helped by putting an end to the Egyptian aggravation. Israel was now free, thanks unmistakably to Yahweh. Yahweh, Israel knew firsthand, is a God who delivers.

The exodus out of Egypt must be considered together with an entry. Yahweh led his people out of bondage in order to lead them into rest. Thus this hymn mentions his guidance to the "holy abode" (v. 13), which is probably Sinai, their more immediate destiny; the ultimate place of abode is his sanctuary, presumably at Jerusalem, in the land. Or, as we have just noted, the stanza, may be an addition by a people who were in the land and already knew the sanctuary. This connection between exodus and entry found in the Song by the Sea can be found abundantly elsewhere (e.g., Deut 6:21ff; 26:5ff; Josh 24:2ff; Ezek 20:6ff).

But now to pursue the discussion of Yahweh as warrior: he is a god of power. "Your right hand, O LORD, glorious in power—your right hand, O LORD, shattered the enemy" (Exod 15:6). The defeated Egyptians together with their horses and chariots were beaten down beneath the waves. Yahweh is a clever warrior. Had the Egyptians planned strategies such as pursuing and dividing the spoil? Yahweh had but to cause the wind to blow, and the collapsing waters easily frustrated all enemy plans.

Yahweh is incomparable. "Who is like you, O LORD, among the gods?" (Exod 15:11). Those who have made a study of the themes of incomparability hold that although Egyptian and Assyrian peoples entertained similar ideas about their gods (in Canaanite religion the notion of incomparability has not yet been found), Israel did not borrow the notion of incomparability from them. Israel's experiences, from the very beginning of their national history, were to them sufficient evidence that Yahweh was not even in a class with other gods (cf. Exod 9:14).

The conclusion that nothing and no one is even remotely to be compared with Yahweh is important because of the polytheistic setting in which Israel lived. The Egyptians, like other nations, had numerous gods, some of greater power than others. For Israel to claim that no god was even in a position to be compared with Yahweh was to set foot on the firm ground of monotheism, belief in one god. It was also to distinguish the one God from angelic or divine beings, as well as from royalty such as the god-king Pharaoh. The claim, while dogmatic, was not a claim without support. The conquest over Pharaoh and the Reed Sea experience fully justified that claim. It was this uniqueness of Yahweh that accounts for the panic that seized neighboring nations. Thus the Song of the Sea mentions the Edomites, Moabites, and Canaanites as trembling and dismayed in a terror derived from recognizing the greatness of Yahweh's arm (Exod 15:14–16). Yet, to anticipate for a moment the later story of Israel, it is clear that the claim of incomparability came under frequent challenge. The constant danger later on was that of relativizing Yahweh so that he would be reckoned along with other gods.

Yahweh's incomparability is disclosed by his intervention in history in behalf of his people. We need not shrink from describing that intervention as miraculous.

> The intervention of Yahweh in history as the redeeming God, the fighting God, who revealed Himself as the Living, Great, Mighty,

> Holy and Terrible God, the God of Justice, who on the one hand
> renders help to the oppressed, the wronged and the weak, and
> who on the other hand judges the self-sufficient and the haughty,
> the God of the Covenant, the Ruler and the wise Conductor of
> history, was utterly new and unique in the religious world at that
> time.[4]

Further, Yahweh demonstrates covenant loyalty. "In your steadfast love you led the people whom you redeemed" (Exod
15:13). This quality, important as an understanding of Yahweh,
is mentioned later in the Ten Words (Ten Commandments)
where Yahweh is described as one "showing steadfast love to the
thousandth generation" (Exod 20:6). The words "steadfast
love" translate the Hebrew word *hesed*, a word very rich in
meaning. *Hesed*, which is more than "mercy" (so AV), is loving
kindness, but a love in the context of commitment or covenant.
The term *hesed* surfaces here, no doubt, for two reasons. One is
that Yahweh is acknowledged as having honored his covenant
with Abraham. Yahweh identifies with a lowly people who seem
not to count for much, judged by the world of nations. Secondly, as the author makes clear, Yahweh leads the people who
have been redeemed. They are not left, after a great stroke of
deliverance, to fend for themselves. On the contrary, Yahweh
will guide them by his strength to their destiny. Yahweh's link
with his people is deliberate. That which Yahweh has begun, he
can be counted upon to complete. With confidence the singers
address Yahweh concerning their own future: "You brought
them in and planted them on the mountain of your own possession, the place, O LORD, that you made your abode" (Exod
15:17). Of Yahweh's faithfulness to them, Israel can be sure.

Yahweh's rule is for always. "The LORD will reign forever
and ever" (Exod 15:18). Rulership is fitting for a victorious warrior. In this crucial context, Yahweh, monarch and as such a warrior, has prowess over the enemy. The context of the song leads
one to establish that rule as being over Israel. Yahweh has the
right to rule by reason of his deliverance. Those who have been
redeemed give themselves as subjects to the deliverer. The final
line of the song captures the spirit of jubilation that pervades

the song and looks for the utopia of a never-never end to this relationship with Yahweh. To what extent this joyful proclamation continued in Israel's history as reality, and how it relates to the statement of Jesus, "The kingdom of God is here," while legitimate questions, belong to a further study.

The claim of Yahweh's rulership leads to an interesting question, however. Did Israel escape one bondage, to Pharaoh, only to be brought at once by their deliverer into another bondage? Total freedom is perhaps illusory. People merely choose the nature of their overlord. It was a bitter experience to be under Pharaoh's power, asked to produce at his bidding, subject to pressure and oppression. By contrast Israel could conceive at this moment only of the sweetness of being subject to one who was her deliverer, for did she not owe her life to Yahweh?

The Pattern of Deliverance: Yahweh War

Early Israel's experience of deliverance, through the wilderness period, the conquest, and the time of the judges, took the form of war, designated by some scholars as "holy war." The term "holy war" is a translation from the German, for it was German scholars who called attention to an institution of warfare in Israel quite unlike warfare outside Israel.[5] A better designation than "holy war" for the pattern we are about to describe is "Yahweh War."

No single battle record lists in careful chronological order all the elements involved in the ritual of a Yahweh war, but scholars have taken the numerous battle stories in Joshua and Judges and identified the major elements of this unique kind of war.

Of first importance in warfare is a Yahweh directive to engage in battle. Where this is not given outright, as in Yahweh's command to Joshua to take Jericho (Josh 5:13 – 6:5), the people consult God. Thus in the sorry affair of the Benjaminite and his concubine, the people of Israel inquire of Yahweh whether they shall go up to attack their enemies, in this case their own tribe of Benjamin (Judg 20:23–27). In his skirmishes with the Philistines and Amalekites, David observes this requirement most religiously. He inquires of the Lord whether he shall advance (1 Sam 23:25; 30:8). Yahweh's answers are definite. We are not certain of the way in which these answers were conveyed, although a clue may be taken from the life of Saul. "When Saul inquired of the LORD, the LORD did not answer him, not by dreams, or by Urim, or by prophets" (1 Sam 28:6).

After the divine answer the priests offered sacrifice, apparently in the presence of the army. The custom of sacrifice before battle was so firmly established that Saul, impatient to engage in battle, assumed Samuel's priestly role and offered the sacrifice himself (1 Sam 13:5–15).

Following the sacrifice there took place, so it can be assumed, the blowing of the trumpets, a regulation specified in Numbers (Num 10:9). Joshua's conquest of Jericho and Gideon's surprise attack on the Midianites both involved extended use of the trumpets (Josh 6:12–16; Judg 6:34ff). The assurance, akin to a battle cry, given by the leader, pierced the air: "The LORD has given your enemies the Moabites into your hand" (Judg 3:28; 4:14; for the promise by Yahweh, given in similar language, see Josh 6:2; 8:1, 18; 10:19). The assurance, though given in some settings as a promise, was announced at the time of the battle itself as an already accomplished fact.

The men who went into battle were not professional soldiers, though later under David there was a standing army. Men called to fight were eligible to go into battle if they observed regulations of ritual and personal cleanliness (Deut 23:9–11; cf. 1 Sam 21:3–5).

Divine presence as well as leadership was symbolized by the ark, as at the conquest of Jericho (Josh 6:13), and the presence of religious officials. It was the priest who addressed the army. His message is prescribed in Deut 20:3–4: "Do not lose heart, or be afraid, or panic, or be in dread of them; for it is the LORD your God who goes with you, to fight for you against your enemies, to give you victory."

Ammunition was not entirely physical or psychic. Military leaders there were, such as Joshua, Deborah, Barak, Gideon; and fighting men there were also, though as the story of Gideon makes clear, their numbers were not important (Judg 7:2ff). The Israelites obviously had weapons, but little is said about them. More important than military skill or weaponry was faith. Already at the Sea of Reeds, Israel was only to stand by and see the victory of Yahweh (Exod 14:13ff). The battles at the time of conquest too belonged to Yahweh (Josh 10:14, 42). In the battles waged in the conquest, victories were "not by your sword or by your bow. I gave you a land on which you had not labored" (Josh 24:12–13; cf. Acts 13:16–19). Thus as Joshua put it in his farewell speech: "One of you puts to flight a thousand, since it is the LORD your God who fights for you, as he promised you" (Josh 23:10). On the strength of Yahweh's assurance, the leaders were to proceed, and to do so without fear. The battle itself would be turned in Israel's favor by a divinely inspired terror (Josh 10:10). Through natural forces such as thunder (1 Sam 7:10) or by means of internal confusion (Deut 7:23) the enemy became fully vulnerable to Israel's attack.

The spoils gained through battle were set apart as sacred and were under a ban (ḥērem). It appears that booty and spoil were devoted to God and were not for personal use. It was infraction of the rule by Achan that accounted for the army's paralysis at Ai (Josh 6:17ff). Saul is severely reprimanded when he chooses to spare some of the flock acquired from the Amalekites (1 Sam 15:21–23). The spoils were consecrated to Yahweh, one gathers, through the burning of them with fire (Deut 7:24–26).

There remains a question of whether with the establishment of a standing army in David's time and organized conquest of expansion, the pattern of the Yahweh war was observed. Clearly certain details were no longer applicable. God's judgment on David for the census, taken with military considerations in mind (2 Samuel 24), notwithstanding the strange introductory word that God incited David to this act (though compare 1 Chr 21:1), perhaps must be seen against the background of Yahweh war.

But the unique pattern of military warfare remains as the dominant idiom of deliverance for early Israel. Two books, Joshua and Judges, include numerous war accounts to attest to Yahweh's strong deliverance of his people from their enemies.

Following the apostasy described in Judges, Israel cried, as they had done in Egypt, for help from Yahweh. Then, as in Egypt, Yahweh came to their rescue. In the time of the judges, as in the time of the Pharaoh, Yahweh fought for Israel against the enemy, whether Midianite, Moabite, or Philistine. As Moses was an agent in Yahweh's hand, so were Gideon, Samson, Jephthah. In later history Yahweh's role as victorious conqueror is not diminished in the least. The prophet Zechariah will reach for the imagery of Yahweh as warrior to speak about the eschatological deliverer.

The redemption of Israel from Egypt is presented in the category of warfare. By means of this war experience, Israel learned the basic elements of salvation. This deliverance from Egyptian bondage was an external deliverance, a rescue from a visible foe. Since bondage also took other forms, Israel learned about deliverance in other settings.

2. Salvation as Blessing through Cult

Not only in the harsh realities of life in the context of tribal peoples did Israel experience salvation, but in another sphere: the cult. Indeed, it was in the cult that recognition was given to her external deliverance. More significantly, in cult she experienced salvation as the blessing of forgiveness. By cult we mean all forms and acts ritually performed in a worship setting where the people's dealings are with deity. The word "cult" thus embraces public prayer, sacrifice, song, and also ritual structures such as tabernacles and even officiating persons. The word cult is neutral and chiefly descriptive, for cult is found wherever religion is found. Cult, the outward expression of religious life, is to be distinguished from cults, which are aberrant religious groups.

Sacrifice, an early cult form, was connected to an act of deliverance. This deliverance from the angel of death was commemorated in worship rituals: each year Israel was required to observe the Passover. Not all later ritual, however, was associated with deliverance. Other rituals were added which had to do with blessing rather than crisis; festivals were held to celebrate harvest (feast of weeks, feast of tabernacles), forgiveness (day of atonement), new year (feast of trumpets). These rituals commemorated the blessings of the year and maintained Israel's intimate relationship with God.

In Egypt, as a final plague, the angel of death was about to strike, removing the firstborn from every household. The cult provision to escape death was the Passover sacrifice. The Passover was joy to those who observed the divinely given prescription, but disaster to those who disregarded it. Deliverance from the plague in which the eldest was taken came through the sacrifice of a lamb, essentially a blood sacrifice, known as Passover. God spared, delivered the people. The same root word (*nṣl*) is used of the Passover (Exod 12:27) as of the deliverance at the Sea of Reeds mentioned in our pivotal text (Exod 6; 6).

In subsequent history the institution of sacrifice was spelled out in great, almost bewildering detail. What did it all mean? Wherein lay the power of sacrifice? What kind of blessing did it signify? Is there a theology of sacrifice? Or, as some claim, is a coherent theology of sacrifice impossible?

Sacrifice and the Congregation

The intent of sacrifice can be discovered by a closer look at the prescriptions about sacrifice as these apply to the congregation of Israel. Once a year, in the fall, in the seventh month, on the tenth day of the month (corresponding to September-October) a solemn observance involving the priest, people and a sacrifice was called. This ritual observance of the day of atonement was directed to the collective guilt of the people (Lev 16:15ff).[6]

The observance was in two parts, in both of which Aaron the high priest had a decisive role. First, Aaron prepared for the occasion by bathing his body and putting on prescribed garments. Then a bull was slain and presented as a sin offering for himself and his fellow priests (16:11–14). From the main altar Aaron took a censer of burning coal and two handfuls of incense and brought these into the most sacred place, the holy of holies. In the sacred place was the ark, on its lid figures of the cherubim. After incensing the ark, the high priest sprinkled blood once on the lid or mercy seat, and then seven times before it. In this way Aaron made atonement for himself and the priests associated with him.

The second part of the observance dealt with the collective sins of the people. Here two sets of action, each involving a goat, were important. The first goat was slain and through a ritual at the mercy seat, similar to the ritual just described, Aaron made atonement for the holy place. This action was necessary "because of the uncleannesses of the people of Israel, and because of their transgressions" (v. 16).

The transgressions of the people themselves were not yet removed. At this point the second goat was brought in but not killed. Laying his hands on the head of this goat, Aaron confessed over it "all the *iniquities* of the people of Israel, and all their *transgressions*, all their *sins*" (v. 21). The goat was then sent off, or actually taken away into the wilderness to Azazel (vv. 21, 26). Azazel, as best as can be determined, if the word is taken as a name, was probably a desert demon, a leader of the spirits of the wilderness. The goat was to bear all the iniquities upon him to a solitary land (v. 22). Quite probably this action signified that sins were conveyed away from society to a place of death. Through the killing of the first goat and the appropriate sprinkling of blood, the defilement of the officiating priest and the temple furnishing, brought on by the sins of the people, had been cleansed. Through the ritual sending away of the second goat, over whose head Israel's sins had been confessed, the people's *iniquities*, *transgressions*, and *sins* had been carried off (v. 21).

These three words deserve attention in order to reach behind the sacrificial act and so to understand the "calamity" requiring sacrifice. While the three words: *iniquities, transgressions,* and *sins* are synonyms, each carries a distinctive meaning. The word for iniquity (*ʿāwōn*) in its etymology and non-theological usage refers to crookedness. David, in trouble with Saul, arranges a plan with Jonathan and concludes: "But if there is iniquity (*ʿāwōn*) in me, put me to death yourself" (1 Sam 20:8, NASB). Later, David's son Absalom, wanting to see his father who has kept him from the court, speaks similarly: "If there is iniquity (*ʿāwōn*) in me, let him put me to death' (2 Sam 14:32, NASB). Both David and Absalom are making the argument that they are transparent; they are straightforward and not perverse. In each instance they hold that perversity warrants severe reprisal, death. The word *ʿāwōn* is occasionally translated "guilt," and that because in Hebrew holistic thought, an act and its consequences were one entity. This perversity which results in guilt is all of one piece. Used 231 times, the noun is often used religiously in the context of man and God, as when the Psalmist says: "You have set our iniquities before you" (Ps 90:8).

The second term for sin in this list, "transgressions" (*pešaʿ*), refers to overreaching and hence breach. It was earlier regarded as rebellion, but latest research has shown that the term has more subtle shades of meaning.[7] It has sometimes, though incorrectly, been explained from its English translation, "transgression," as going across or against God's commands. The term, taken from the political sphere, deals with insurrection, but not alone with external acts of violence. The term *pešaʿ* indicates a breakdown of trust. In terms of property, the rendering of Exod 22:9 is illustrative: "For every breach of trust (*pešaʿ*), whether it is for ox, for ass, for sheep . . ." (RSV). The evil consists in faulty stewardship in which the steward has violated his trust, possibly through fraud. In terms of relationships between persons, transgression (*pešaʿ*) also involves a breach. The relationship between a subordinate and a superior, regarded as legally binding, has been broken through the overstepping by the subordinate of assigned and understood limits. The relationship is now no longer intact because the subordinate party has overextended himself and damaged, or even in the eyes of the law forfeited, the relationship and therefore become liable. In the fiery indictment by Amos of the nations, the basic evil is a breach of one kind or another which within an understood, judicial context renders them guilty. "For three transgressions of Damascus, and for four, I will not revoke the punishment" (Amos 1:3; cf. 1:6, 9, 11, 13; 2:1, 4, 6). Theologically, whoever sins (*pāšaʿ*) against Yahweh, does not only rebel against him, but breaks off from him, takes from him what was uniquely his. Such breach with Yahweh, rather than obstinacy or pride, is at the core of what the Old Testament calls sin. Sin, while it involves acts, is at its base relational failure. The story of Adam and Eve's disobedience in the garden, if it is to be described theologically by a root word, must be described as transgression (*pešaʿ*) understood as a break of relationship resulting from an over-reaching act. The result was a fractured relationship between God and humankind.

The third word, "sin," in the threefold description of Israel's defilement has its origin in the conversation of the everyday. Sin (*ḥēṭʾ*) is "missing the mark," and the setting for this vocabulary is military target practice. Thus the sharp-hurling warriors in Israel's army in the time of the judges included 700 left-handed stone slingers who were of such a caliber that they could aim at a hair and not "miss" (*ḥāṭāʾ*) (Judg 20:16). From here the term was employed in a moral sense: "one who moves too hurriedly misses the way" (Prov 19:2). Religiously, with the meaning of failure, it comes to be the all-embracing word for sin. In its verbal and nominal form it occurs almost 600 times, and next to the more general word *evil* (*raʿ*) is the most frequent for wrong-doing. Thirty times in the Old Testament one finds, "I have sinned," and twenty-four times, "We have sinned."

It is sometimes erroneously thought that to miss the mark is chiefly a matter of failure to keep the law. While this aspect of failure cannot be excluded, the foremost notion is failure, not of a person over against a code, but of a person-to-person relationship. Eli's statement is programmatic for the meaning: "If one person sins (ḥāṭāʾ) against another, someone can intercede for the sinner with the LORD, but if someone sins (ḥāṭāʾ) against the LORD, who can make intercession?" (1 Sam 2:25; cf. Jer 16:10–12; 1 Kgs 8:46). Or, as Moses makes clear in addressing some tribes of Israel: "But if you do not do this, you have sinned (ḥāṭāʾ) against the LORD; and be sure your sin will find you out" (Num 32:23). Thus the word "sin" (ḥāṭāʾ), like the word "transgression" (pešaʿ), is a relational term.

The three words, "iniquity" (ʿāwōn), "transgression" (pešaʿ), and "sin" (ḥēṭʾ) occur in tandem a total of fourteen times (e.g., apart from Lev 16:21, see Exod 34:7; Num 14:18; Ezek 21:29; Ps 32:1, 5; Isa 59:12). This formal trio of words, each in its own way designating aspects of sin, when found in combination is intended to convey every possible way of wrong-doing. It is this pervasive wrong-doing by Israel that calls for the observance of the day of atonement so that the sin of the people might be sent away. In conjunction with sacrifice Israel experiences the blessing of deliverance from sin.

Sacrifice and the Individual

If we turn from the instructions about sacrifice for the nation, to sacrifice primarily on behalf of the individual, we are confronted with the legislation in the earlier chapters of Leviticus (Leviticus 1–7). Five major types of sacrifice are distinguished: burnt offering, cereal offering, peace offering, sin offering, guilt offering. The last two deal with offenses by individuals, though a sin offering may also be offered for the nation. Since a theology of sacrifice must in large measure be inferred from the practice, a brief sketch of the ritual is appropriate.

As with the prescriptions for the day of atonement, so in this catalogue of regulations, it is the priest who first receives attention. He was to take a young bull, lay his hand on its head, then kill it and bring some of the blood of the bull to the tent of meeting. Some of the blood was to be rubbed on the horns of the altar of incense within the tent of meeting; some was to be poured at the base of the altar of burnt offering (Lev 4:1–7). When the congregation or a ruler sinned, the procedure was essentially the same except that for a ruling person a male blemish-free goat was prescribed (Lev 4:13–26).

The sin offering for the commoner was similar, except that there was a choice: an offering of a female goat or of a female lamb without blemish. The offerer would lay a hand on the animal and kill it. It was the priest, however, who then took the blood, but this time not as before into the tent of meeting. In the case of a community leader or an ordinary layperson, the officiating priest did not enter the holy place but put blood on the horns of the altar and poured the remainder of the blood at the base (Lev 4:27–35). This offering, described as a sin offering, was for someone who "sins unintentionally in doing any one of the things that by the LORD's commandments ought not to be done and incurs guilt" (Lev 4:27). By means of the sin offering such a person was forgiven.

For the individual there was a second offering in many ways similar to the sin offering, known as a guilt offering. In the guilt offering, however, unlike the sin offering, the offerer was to confess his sin. In the guilt offering the individual had additional options. If the offerer could not afford a lamb, a pair of turtle doves or two young pigeons, or at the least, a tenth of an ephah of fine flour could be presented. But more was involved than confession of sin. The guilty one was to make restitution for what had been damaged, plus 20 percent (Lev 5:1 – 6:7).

A number of situations requiring the guilt offering are enumerated. Among them are: utterance of a rash oath; silence when called to testify; deception of a neighbor for whom an item was held in custody; robbing of a neighbor; or defilement through contact with either animal or human uncleanness. It would appear, as Augustine concluded, that a guilt offering was necessary for an overt act, but this cannot be the chief distinction between the sin and the guilt offerings, for transgressions committed unknowingly were also atoned for by a guilt offering (Lev 5:17–19).

The sin offering and the guilt offering are distinguished in Leviticus,[8] though what lies at the base of the distinctions is not easily determined. Following the general outline of the five offerings (Lev 1:1 – 6:7) there is a rehearsal resembling a summary of the instructions which govern each (6:8 – 7:37). In this list the two are treated separately (6:24–30; 7:1–7). Still, since the ritual acts for the priest are virtually identical, one reads, "The guilt offering is like the sin offering, there is the same ritual for them" (Lev 7:7). Josephus, a Jewish historian of the first century AD, explained that the sin offering entailed sins without witnesses, and that by contrast a guilt offering involved sins to which there were witnesses, but this is not borne out by the texts. Others have argued that the sin offering is characterized by "satisfaction," and guilt offerings by reparation. The distinction is most likely that sins requiring the sin offering were sins unknowingly committed, that is, through oversight or negligence. The guilt offering was designed for offenses where damage had been done and a loss incurred. Perhaps, so it has been suggested, the guilt offering would be more accurately called a compensation offering.

More important than distinguishing the two kinds of sacrifices is understanding their intention. Scripture underlines that the worshiper was forgiven the sin (e.g., 4:26; 6; 7). But just what this means involves us in a discussion of some details.

The Significance of Blood Sacrifices

The sacrifices examined so far, whether designed for the collective sins of the people and offered once a year, or whether prescribed primarily for the individual and offered as necessary, were blood sacrifices. Other animal sacrifices such as the burnt offering and the peace offering, because they involved slaughter, also involved blood, but in the sin and guilt offerings the blood had a special role. Unlike the burnt and peace offerings, the blood of a sin/guilt offering was a crucial element. According to the position of the offerer the blood was either taken into the holy place or else applied at the main altar.

The reason for the importance of the blood in these rites is given in Leviticus. Blood is the repository of life. "For the life of the flesh is in the blood; and I have given it to you for making atonement for your lives on the altar; for, as life, it is the blood that makes atonement" (Lev 17:11). The concept that life is concretely associated with blood is found elsewhere (Lev 17:14; Gen 9:4; Deut 12:22–23). It was not the random shedding of blood, but blood applied to the altar that was efficacious for the removal of sin, for the altar, like the mercy seat, was symbolic of deity.

But the question might be asked, what was accomplished by the application of the blood to the altars and veils or the mercy seat? The answer is not far to seek. The offerer was forgiven the offense that had been committed, and on the most solemn fast day of the year the high priest made atonement for the sins of the nation. Absolution was assured by the repeated word of Scripture, "Thus the priest shall make atonement on his behalf for his sin, and he shall be forgiven" (Lev 4:26; cf. 4:31, 35; 5:10, 16, 18; 6:7; 16:34). These scriptures make clear that under the old covenant people were justified from certain sins and accepted by God. They had reason, therefore, to rejoice in the forgiveness of sins. Their God, Yahweh, as Moses had been told by Yahweh himself, was a God "forgiving iniquity and trans-gressions and sin" (Exod 34:7). David states, as might a New Testament Christian: "Happy are those whose transgression is forgiven, whose sin is covered. Happy are those to whom the LORD imputes no iniquity, and in whose spirit there is no deceit" (Ps 32:1–2). While one could argue that in the overall plan of God it was not till Christ that these offerings received their perfect counterpart, yet such argument should not for the moment detract from the reality of God's full acceptance of the worshiper. Forgiveness is one of the great words both in the Isra-elite cult and in Christian proclamation.

One is entitled, however, to inquire more specifically how forgiveness was understood. If atonement (*kippurîm*) was made, what precisely was accomplished? The Hebrew root word—for one can start there—can mean "to cover" if derived from the

Arabic, or "to wipe clean" if its origin is in the Babylonian. But this information is only minimally useful since it affords little help in settling a long-standing controversy. Some hold that making atonement refers essentially to the covering of God's countenance. In this interpretation God's anger against sin is such that he must be appeased or placated. Hence the word "propitiation," which suggests the gracious turning of someone's favor in response to a gift or a bribe, has been employed to explain what transpires in the act of atonement. In this view the directional pointer in a sacrifice is to God, who because of it turns from his anger and looks with favor on the sinner. The transaction is personal.

A second opinion, largely opposite, holds that the offering is a covering, not of God's angry face, but of the sin so that God now sees the worshiper as free from guilt and punishment. An offering makes amends for the past, or repairs the damage; it cancels sin. In this view the directional pointer in a sacrifice is to sin and the sinner. God looks upon the sinner and because of the sacrifice covering the sin, God sees that sinner as righteous. The transaction is judicial.

Although the debate is an old one, it seems pointless to force a decision between the two concepts, because both contain elements of truth. biblical supporting statements can be found for each. Proponents of propitiation point to Gen 8:20; Exod 32:30; Num 25:3–9; Deut 21:1–9; Rom 1:18ff. God's anger against sin is a fact of Scripture (Deut 4:25). It is said that there are more than twenty words to express wrath as it applies to Yahweh. Altogether there are 580 occurrences to be taken into account. Those who advocate expiation adduce Num 35:33; Ezek 16:63; Isa 6:7. But the Old Testament does not pose these as alternatives, and the expression "to atone" (*kipper*) may well encompass both metaphors in the sense that when sin is expiated, God's anger, provoked by sin, is appeased and ceases. As the Hebrew lexicon puts it: "Underlying all these offerings there is the conception that the persons offering are covered by that which is regarded as sufficient and satisfactory by Yahweh."[9]

The two-part refrain is, "Thus the priest shall make atonement on his behalf for his sin, and he shall be forgiven" (Lev 4:26). The second part of this refrain uses the word "forgive" (*sālaḥ*), a word which is used only with God as the subject. Its sense can be understood from words used in parallel with it, such as "atone" (*kipper*), but also in conjunction with other words and phrases such as "lift off," "take away," "Passover," "cleanse," and even "heal" (Isa 57:17–18; Jer 3:22). Taken together, these terms speak in picturesque images of removing sin as "far as the east is from the west" (Ps 103:12), of casting sins behind God's back (Isa 38:17), or of casting sins into the depths of the sea (Mic 7:19). Another common word used to convey forgiveness means to carry or lift up (Exod 34:7). The Hebrew root is *nāśāʾ*, which in space-travel-conscious America calls to mind the acronym NASA (National Aeronautical Space Administration), responsible for the firing of space rockets; "countdown" and "lift-off" are exhilarating vocabulary. In this context a theologically quite appropriate word play can be made: forgiveness (*nāśāʾ*) is a "lift-off" of sin and guilt. The transgressors experience the blessing of deliverance from the burden of guilt.

While the blood is a crucial element, it must not be thought that forgiveness of sins is linked in mechanical fashion to the presentation of blood. In a memorable incident of the golden calf, God extended his forgiveness to a sinful people, not on the basis of blood, but in response to a leader's intercession (Exod 32:30). In another incident, God's forgiveness came as incense was offered (Num 16:46). God was reconciled to his people at the occasion of Israel's adultery with Moabite and Midianite women on the basis of the zeal of Phinehas, who killed the offenders on the spot (Num 25:6ff). Isaiah in the temple, recognizing his sin, exclaimed, "Woe is me! For I am lost; for I am a man of unclean lips." He heard the word of forgiveness: "Your guilt has departed and your sin is blotted out" (Isa 6:7). No sacrifice of blood had been made in his behalf: a divine messenger had touched the lips of Isaiah with a burning coal taken from the altar. As for the levitical legislation, the priestly law provided that a poor person could bring a bloodless offering, namely cereal, as an expiation for sin (Lev 5:11). While these examples are not cited to contradict the generalization, "Without the shedding of blood there is no forgiveness of sins" (Heb 9:22), for as a basic operational principle it remains, yet more thorough examination cautions one not to be overly rigid. The equation between blood and forgiveness must not be too tightly drawn, for it misrepresents both God and the nature of forgiveness.

That the mere act of sacrifice in and of itself was not sufficient to ensure forgiveness can be further substantiated. It is said concerning Eli's sons: "Therefore I swear to the house of Eli that the iniquity of Eli's house shall not be expiated by sacrifice or offering forever" (1 Sam 3:14). While this statement underlines the gravity of Eli's family's transgression, it surely does more: it implies, as prophets later shall make abundantly clear, that no mechanical explanation of sacrifice will do. Is it not already understood that the proper heart's attitude of a worshiper is as integral to sacrifice as the blood of bulls and goats? People like Eli's sons, who hold Yahweh and his prescriptions in contempt, find no remission of sins.

This demand for an interior subordination and compliance is also implicit at the first sacrifice recorded, that of Cain and Abel's offering. It is sometimes claimed that Cain's offering was unacceptable because it was not a blood sacrifice. If one wishes to read Mosaic legislation back into the account, then one must also allow for that Mosaic provision which specified that a cereal offering such as Cain presented was acceptable (Lev 5:11–13). Cain reveals his disposition, as often happens, when he is rebuked. He is angry (Gen 4:5). Here is sufficient evidence that Cain's attitude prior to his sacrifice is perverse (cf. 1 John 3:12). By contrast Abel as a person of faith was accepted (Heb 11:4). The attitude, rather than the materials of sacrifice, was decisive in Yahweh's response to the sacrifice.

It may be that an arrogant, even defiant manner as exhibited by Cain is what is intended by the biblical expression "sins with a high hand." Precisely in the framework of a discussion of a sin offering one reads:

> But whoever acts high-handedly, whether a native or an alien, af-
> fronts the LORD, and shall be cut off from among the people. Be-
> cause of having despised the word of the LORD and broken his
> commandment, such a person shall be utterly cut off and bear
> the guilt (Num 15:30–31).

To understand the "high-handed" sins it should first be stressed
that these are sins different from those committed unwittingly,
that is, because of negligence. Sins with a high hand also differ
from deliberate sins, for some of which there was a provision in
the guilt offering. The sins with a high hand are in a separate
class; they are sins of blatant defiance. They are punishable by
death, as the Numbers text explains, because the person has
"despised the word of the LORD." That is, whenever someone
mocks, despises, or holds in contempt the means by which forgiveness can come, that one is not in that condition eligible for
forgiveness. Those who despise God's provision for sin have exhausted the means of grace, when like Eli's sons they have
treated these means with contempt.

A Theology of Sacrifice

As often lamented by Old Testament scholars, there is no elaborate or even systematic explanation given in the Old Testament
for the ritual of sacrifice. If we want to get at the theology of sacrifice it will be through inference.

Generally, following the history of religions approach,
theologians have seen some similarity between pagan and Israelite sacrifices. The variety of Israel's sacrifices have seemed to
some to correspond with stages in the growth of religions as
shown by the study of primitive religions. Scholars have noted
that sacrifices in these primitive societies were made as food
and nourishment for the gods. It is true that the Scripture
resorts to similar language on occasion, as in Num 28:2: "My
offering, the food for my offerings by fire, my pleasing odor,
you shall take care to offer to me at its appointed time" (cf. Lev
3:11; Ezek 20:41). Such a statement needs to be understood as
anthropomorphic language. For communicative purposes,

statements about God are made as though God is human. Or it may be that Israel adopted the language of Canaan. In addition, one can tell from the reproach given such a physical understanding of sacrifice in Ps 50:12–13 that sacrifice is not to be understood as nourishment for God: "If I were hungry, I would not tell you . . . Do I eat the flesh of bulls or drink the blood of goats?" Certainly the lengthy discussions about sacrifice in the Old Testament do not convey the impression that sacrifices are for the purpose of sustenance of the deity.

The reason for pagan sacrifices is often said to be a gift to the deity, perhaps in thankfulness. These gifts became increasingly costly, and eventually included prostitution of sexual powers and the gift of human sacrifice. But both the offering of sexual powers and the gift of life were disallowed in Israel. Sacrifices as gifts, as in the burnt offering or the peace offering (Lev 7:12–15), a presentation of first fruits, were indeed part of the understanding of sacrifice, but they were restricted to animals and cereals, and there is no indication that they were to serve or could serve, as they did in pagan rites, as bribes. The gift theory of sacrifice, while not irrelevant to Israelite sacrifice, does not exhaust the theology of sacrifice.

Israelite sacrifice is not a matter of serving God or procuring benefits. A more biblical understanding of sacrifice, found also among non-Christians, is that by sacrifice communion with the deity is established. The burnt offering represented thanksgiving and was received by God as sweet savor expressive of thanksgiving. The peace offering, because of the priest as God's representative eating the sacrificial meal, along with the offerer's partaking of the sacrifice, often in the company of his friends, especially signified communion and fellowship with the deity. The worshipers shared in a feast with Yahweh.

But while these were offerings in the context of harmonious relationships with the deity, provisions were also made for contact with the deity when through human failure these relationships were broken. It is these, the sin and the guilt offering, which have been the subject of this chapter. The theology of these sacrifices can be summarized as follows:

(1) These sacrifices were intended to restore the harmonious relationship of the wrong-doer with God. This dimension is clear from three considerations. The burnt offering, cereal and peace offerings which precede in the levitical legislation the sin and guilt offerings are, as has just been said, offerings underscoring the maintenance of communion of the worshiper with God. It is at this point, where through wrong-doing this relationship is fractured, that the sin and guilt offerings become necessary. A second argument underlying the reasons for these sacrifices is that the words for sins, as we have seen, especially "transgression" (*pešaʿ*) and "sin" (*ḥēṭʾ*), are fundamentally words that pivot on the idea of a relationship. Thirdly, to anticipate our discussion, God and Israel were bound together in a covenant relationship. This notion of covenant, which points to intimacy, further underlines the rationale for sacrifice. By means of sacrifice, Yahweh extended forgiveness to the wrong-doer and the broken relationship brought on by the evil was restored. The initiator for this restoration of a ruptured relationship is Yahweh. It is Yahweh who instituted the sacrifice.

(2) These sacrifices, as shown by the stress on blood, revolved around the idea of life. As has been indicated, the blood is brought into contact with the altar, not because the blood is a magical element, but because Yahweh has ordained that the blood, "by reason of the life" it represents, is the tangible element in a sacrifice. Blood is an equivalent, so to speak, or a shorthand way of saying "a life offered." Blood atones, or expiates, since it has life, represents life, or put another way, is the repository of life.

It is commonly believed that the sacrificial animal was regarded as a substitute for the offerer. This may be the theory of atonement presented by the New Testament, but whether the Israelite worshiper explained the ritual in that way to himself and others may be doubted.

No easy equation can be made between the sacrificial animal and the sinner if the biblical details are carefully observed. The victim, the goat or lamb in a sin offering, is regarded as exceptionally holy. The priest is to eat it in a holy place. "

Whatever touches its flesh shall become holy" (Lev 6:27). As applied to the sinner for whom the animal is supposedly a substitute, such language is hardly appropriate. If substitution were the main idea, would one not expect the principal act to be the slaying of the animal since death is the penalty for sin? As it is, the ceremony is taken up with the blood, the disposition of the flesh and the pronouncement of forgiveness. One would also expect the priest to be the one slaying the animal. But it is the sinner who is to slay the lamb.

Moreover, if substitution were the chief point, then one would hardly expect that in instances a cereal offering was acceptable as a guilt offering (Lev 5:11). Such a provision destroys the niceties of a fully fledged substitution theory. The place of the priest in the entire ritual eliminates ideas of self-redemption. The offerer can by laying a hand on the animal designate the animal as an animal for sacrifice, and proceed with the slaughter, but the offerer is passive as the priest presents the blood, carries out other acts, and finally pronounces the worshiper forgiven. In addition one may note the restrained way in which the New Testament treats the matter. Speaking of blood, the author of the book of Hebrews says, "Indeed, under the law *almost everything* is purified with blood, and without the shedding of blood there is no forgiveness of sins" (Heb 9:22; italics added). The claim here made is not that substitutionary language is not employed in the Bible. It is (Deut 21:1–9; Isa 53:4–6). The important text of Lev 17:11 says, "I have given it (the blood) to you for making atonement for your lives on the altar." The claim here made is that substitution, while one language model used to understand the atonement, is only partially representative of the truth. The language model should not be milked for excessive ranges of application. What can be said is that God ordained that, generally speaking, blood, representing life, should be the tangible element in the sacrificial ritual. That this spoke of the high cost involved in forgiveness is self-evident.

That for the Israelites the ceremony of sacrifice called attention to the importance of the priests and the place of blood cannot be doubted. That these ceremonies were understood in early Israel as a form of the doctrine of substitution, however, is not as self-evident. In the literature the idea of substitution is not as much found in the cultic sacrifices as in the intercessions, such as that of Moses, who offered by his death to make atonement. Most impressive of all is the servant mentioned later in Israel's history, who was the mediator and the perfect sacrifice (Isaiah 53). One can argue that the New Testament works with the concept of substitution, but one should be careful not to read back into the early literature a full-blown theory of substitution.[10] More pervasive in the Pentateuch language is the necessity of the mediator, the priest, and his use of the blood in the ritual. The offerers could not in the last analysis look on the slaughtered victims as the source or reason for forgiveness. No, their eyes were properly directed to God because of whose grace they could hear the words, "You are forgiven."

(3) God's forgiveness was extended in consideration of the sacrifice, but not strictly because of it. The mere mechanical ritual was insufficient. The presentation of blood, even understood as representing life, did not in itself guarantee forgiveness. God was not bound at the sight of sacrifice to extend forgiveness. The importance of the repentance of the worshiper is assumed in the levitical legislation as part of the sacrificial experience. By contrast, the prophets were to explain that without a corresponding willingness to obey, sacrifice was unacceptable to Yahweh (Isa 1:12–17). Yet in the mention of sins with a high hand, the point is made even in the levitical legislation that sacrifices are not a magical means whereby Yahweh's favor can be secured. There is no facile equation between sacrifice and forgiveness. Relationship with God as relationship between people is not a balance sheet affair in which a sacrifice automatically raises the credit balance. It is misleading, therefore, to say that because of sacrifice God forgives persons their sin. Rather, one must say, in consideration of sacrifice, which generally by the very act itself indicates willingness to comply with God's provision, God in grace extends his forgiveness to the guilty. Once again there can exist the harmony between

God and people toward which God is forever aiming. But for anyone to establish the precise operational principle involved in sacrifice will not be possible. There remains a mystery, even as God's grace itself is mysterious.

Deliverance can be discussed from the standpoint of cult. In the cultic sense deliverance entails escape from the consequence of sin and the restoration to wholesome relationships. While in Israel's early history deliverance in a historical setting (Egypt) and deliverance via the cult (worship through sacrifice) are separate streams, we shall find later that Isaiah sees these together. Speaking to the situation of the exiles, he sees a time when following forgiveness granted by God (cult) the exiled people will be delivered from their foreign servitude through a new exodus (history). The change of circumstance to come in history is to be grounded in a cultic act involving God's forgiveness. But in early Israel the deliverance models are basically distinct. Salvation as deliverance comes in history. Salvation as blessing is experienced through cult.

3. Theological Reflections

The foregoing pages have described two forms of divine salvation. God fought for Israel and delivered her in a crisis from external bondage; God prescribed a ritual in conjunction with which Israel was blessed with forgiveness and continuing intimacy with her God. The description of these models of salvation is important, but if they are to become more than merely interesting antiquities we must establish their relevance to a modern world. The answer to the quest "What do these models of redemption signify for us today?" is an involved one and would ideally lead to an examination of the New Testament. The application of these models of deliverance for today's believer can, however, be sketched in outline.

Theological Reflections about War
As a Model of Deliverance

Both the exodus pattern of deliverance and the Yahweh war pattern have in recent times been given interpretations that need careful review. The Exodus account has been a convenient point of departure for liberation theologians. Moreover, appeal has been made to the wars in the Old Testament as a justification for war and violence today. Are these valid conclusions to derive from the study of Exodus and the military aspects of the Old Testament?

The twentieth century has witnessed liberation of oppressed peoples. At the same time oppression in its various forms—physical, economic, psychic—has continued. Theologians in Third World countries, along with some in the Christian countries, have stressed the importance of reading the Bible through the eyes, not of an affluent propertied middle class, but of the victimized and oppressed. In part this way of reading the Bible has evolved from current situations of political dictatorships, economic exploitation, self-benefiting manipulations, all of which, because of the media, are no longer remote and secretive. Christian leaders in situations characterized by exploitation have identified their cause with the Israelites in bondage and have advocated bold action. In part, the general Old Testament concern for social justice has inspired participation by Christians in liberation movements.

In addition to the realities of oppression and the biblical call for justice, another stream that has fed the waters of liberation theology is a sympathetic reading of Karl Marx. Since Marx was exercised about throwing off the chains that held the working class captive, he is viewed as a fighter for freedom. While Christian scholars are critical of the capitalist system, others are not; but the theoretical exposition by Marx of the human predicament is placed in a biblical frame, especially in the frame of the exodus story, and the call to liberation in the Scripture is reinforced by the call to freedom in Marx. In a book entitled *Marx and the Bible* the author says, "In the view of the Bible

Yahweh is the God who breaks into history to liberate the oppressed." Elsewhere he applies this conclusion as follows: "Yahweh's intervention in our history has only one purpose. Here it is explicit: to serve the cause of justice." "He who reveals himself by intervening in our history is always Yahweh as savior of the oppressed and punisher of the oppressors."[11]

So large a literature has developed and so extended is the argumentation that more space than is here available is needed for a full exposition and reply.[12] One must agree that the biblical concern for justice, evident throughout, has been a neglected theme. There is need to read the New Testament in the light of such Old Testament emphasis and to ask, what has it to say about political and social aspects of life? World systems such as capitalism need to be examined and not blindly defended. The biblical message about the unacceptability of injustice must be heard. The exodus is related to social justice (Exod 23:9; Lev 25:36–39; Deut 15:12). Action, even political action, may be necessary. But the aggressive stance of liberationists, even of evangelical scholars, needs modification in the light of several considerations. The exodus event was a political event since it involved the escape of a people from Pharaoh, a political power. But the liberation pointed forward to a life with Yahweh, to a covenant community, to a life enriched by Yahweh. This goal of a religious and spiritual nature is crucial. Freedom in the exodus story points to life under the lordship of Yahweh. Elimination of social injustice is important, but the liberation movement, if it is to be theologically underpinned, must ask, freedom for what? If liberationists will appeal to the exodus event for justification of social and political action, then the whole of the exodus must be kept in mind. Yoder put it well: "Exodus is not a paradigm for how all kinds of people with all kinds of values can attain all kinds of salvation."[13]

Yoder also notes that for Israel the exodus meant moving not into security, but into insecurity. While the exodus event is not to be ruled out as model for dealing with oppression, the Bible also presents other models for dealing with oppression. Joseph suffered innocently in prison. The exiles were instructed by Jeremiah to make their living within the circumstances (Jeremiah 29). There is reason to believe that some in that situation favored insurrection. And so, granted that social injustice is not to be accepted without protest, the exodus event is hardly intended to be the model by which all social evil is redressed.

As with the exodus, the war pattern can be used to support a position that upon investigation is vulnerable. To advocate warfare today on the basis of wars commanded by Yahweh in the Old Testament is problematic, in part for cultural reasons. We need to consider the mentality of Middle East peoples in the second millennium BC. It is clear from Egyptian and Assyrian annals that to be able to distinguish oneself in military campaigns was a high, much lauded achievement. In a culture which glorified war and set the military conqueror superior to all others, the revelation of Yahweh was most understandably and forcefully made in a military context. More important is the consideration that the thrust of these Yahweh wars was the faith requirement of the people. The initiative and leadership for the battle lay in Yahweh. For Israel, faith was not some abstract notion, but a life and death matter—a risk of one's safety on the promise that Yahweh would come through as victor. It is this fact—the just shall live by faith—that is basic to Yahweh wars; these wars were not recorded so that warring per se should become a behavior model for Christians today. Furthermore, the enemy is not simply anyone who stands in the way of Israel's advance, but peoples designated *by God* as those whose cup of iniquity is full.

Close attention must be given to the designation "wars of Yahweh." Scripture even refers to a source, "The Book of the Wars of Yahweh" (Num 21:14). As we have seen, these wars were of such nature that only by stretching the word "war" can modern warfare be described by the same word. It would be a misnomer to call World War II a Yahweh War. The elements of directive from Yahweh, the meager attention to equipment, reliance on Yahweh, were surely not characteristic of that event. In the twentieth century, as in secular wars generally, the escalation of military might has been all-important. Yahweh and faith are not in the arsenal in any significant way, nor even in the vocabulary. To the proponents of war, moreover, whether wearing the Christian label or not, one must point to the Old Testament theology of war and its ideals of peace.

The warrior model is strange-sounding to modern Christians. Yet it must not be minimized, for not only is it a datum of Scripture, but it represents a message of hope. The struggle with evil, then as now, is no myth. There is Someone, Yahweh the warrior, who is set as a force against evil. The shape of evil may change, but the combat between God and powers of evil continues, and will climax ultimately, as in Israel's situation, with God as victor. Statements by the prophets about such eschatological matters as the day of Yahweh, if not based on the Yahweh war, were certainly enriched by this imagery.

The event of deliverance with its motif of Yahweh the warrior and the Yahweh war dominate much of the Old Testament and even the New Testament. In Samuel's farewell speech and in other historical resumes, the exodus event is foundational (cf. 1 Sam 12:6; Ezek 20:6–10). Hymns celebrate God's intervention (Pss 78; 136; 77:11–20). Prophets refer to the exodus in the past (Hos 13:4; Jer 2:2–6) but also use it as a paradigm for the future new act of God (Jer 23:7–8; Isa 51:9–11). And the New Testament writings too speak in reference to exodus as a fitting way of speaking of the new act of salvation in Jesus (Col 1:13–14; 1 Pet 1:1, 13–18; 2:9; Rev 15:3).

The war motif makes use of political language. People in societies experience a political dimension in life. Redemption is not to be conceived as only individually oriented. There is a social, even political dimension in redemption. Christ's work includes the defeat of powers, and the church likewise is confronted with and must deal with powers. The way in which God's people understand and live out that phase is variously understood, but at a minimum, the Yahweh war with its divine warrior puts the political aspect of the human experience into the limelight.[14]

To summarize: Yahweh's deliverance can be understood in the context of two patterns: the exodus event and the Yahweh war. While we have separated them in our discussion in order to call attention to the exodus, to which more than any other event Israel returned for its foundation, it is true that the exodus itself is an illustration of Yahweh the warrior at work. There, as in Yahweh war, Yahweh intervenes with power to redeem his people.

Theological Reflection about Sacrifice Models

The two models of salvation—Yahweh war and cultic sacrifices—are of current significance in the life of the church, not least of all in its missionary assignment. One easily conceives of redemption and deliverance in categories that are too limiting. In the western world there is an understanding of guilt. Failure to meet expectations, whether those set by God, society, or oneself, generates feelings of guilt. Psychologists and social scientists have helped us understand that the guilt may be pseudo-guilt, or it may be real guilt. Theologians have understood the word of the gospel to be the good news of forgiveness, the removal of guilt. The sacrifice model used throughout the Bible is a helpful way of visualizing the forgiveness process. Jesus Christ, so evangelists and Bible teachers explain, came to deal with the root cause of the human predicament: sin and its manifestation of guilt. The teaching about sacrifice then becomes an important way of explaining salvation.

Now while it is true that Christ came into the world to deal decisively with the human predicament, and while it is true that the root of the predicament is sin, it does not necessarily follow that the manifestation of that predicament in every culture will be guilt. In certain African cultures, for example, the problem is not so much guilt as fear. In a culture where spirits are perceived as active in the world of everyday experience, there is fear because of the power which these spirits can exert. Evil spirits can be destructive of health or of property or can be responsible for other kinds of calamity. In such cultures, individuals live out of fear. They dread these forces over which they have little if any control, but at whose mercy they are. If in those cultures one proclaims the gospel and defines it as deliverance from guilt, it will be understood, perhaps, but not fully appreciated.

If, however, the gospel is explained as the deliverance made possible by a Savior who is stronger than any opposing force, be it Pharaoh or a demon from the spirit world, and if Yahweh the Savior is understood as the invincible warrior, the listener in the non-western culture will both more fully understand the gospel and be drawn to it.[15] The gospel meets humankind's deepest need, but that need is not defined in exactly the same way all over the world. A biblical theology which represents the act of deliverance, as does the Bible, in alternative models is more likely to communicate than a systematic theology forged in a foreign culture.

In addition to the perceptions about deliverance, one can focus specifically on aspects of forgiveness. If one imagines a worshiper at sacrifice in Old Testament times and asks: "How is this worshiper assured of forgiveness?" the answer cannot turn even primarily on sacrifice. True, God prescribes that when guilt is incurred, a sacrifice is to be offered. But the presentation of a sacrifice in itself is hardly sufficient reason to think that forgiveness has been extended, unless there is a conviction about the consistency and integrity of the one who has promised that he will forgive. Fundamentally then, the worshiper, despite the visual symbols, is pushed back upon the spoken and heard Word. The importance of the spoken word is underscored in that the priest, having processed the sacrificial animal, is to declare forgiveness to the worshiper. The worshiper is clearly cast on the bare word, the statement of forgiveness. The New Testament Christian is in the same position. The Bible makes clear that Christ is the satisfactory and sufficient sacrifice for sin. If we confess our sins God is faithful to forgive and to cleanse (1 John 1:9). That word, along with other similar words, is the word of assurance. Thus the Old Testament worshiper, the New Testament Christian, and even the paralytic of the Gospels, each appropriate the same message essentially: "Son, your sins are forgiven."

God's Design
The Covenant Community

The pivotal text of Exod 5:22 – 6:8 strikes down at once a notion that has surfaced every so often in church history. The erroneous notion is that deliverance, or salvation narrowly conceived, is the climax of God's action: for a people to be "saved" is really all that matters. The aura about the mighty intervention of God in history need not be dimmed, but it must be emphasized that the initial act of deliverance is indeed initial. More is to follow. The salvation experience is a vestibule into the main auditorium of God's design. The vestibule, for all its charm and the reality it offers of being "inside" the temple, and so in God's presence, is nevertheless intended to lead into the larger dimensions of experience with God. Deliverance is the vestibule to a community life, to continuing experience with God, to a rich quality of life. The community at which deliverance aims is a special kind of community, a covenant people under God, as depicted in the statement: "I will take you as my people, and I will be your God" (Exod 6:7a).

The pivotal statement from Exodus consists of a promise: "I will be your God," and a demand, "You shall be my people." We ask, what is entailed in being the people of God? If it includes obligation, then in what light is the promise "I will be your God" to be understood? So strong throughout the Bible is this theme of covenant which underlies peoplehood that some have seen covenant not only as a strand throughout the Bible, but as *the* strand. The Old Testament message, for some, is centered in covenant.[1] Whether covenant is a sufficiently broad concept to encompass all the Old Testament is doubtful, but its importance, reaching as it does into the New Testament, cannot be questioned.

1. The Covenant Formula

In scholarly circles the sentence "I will take you as my people, and I will be your God" has been designated "the covenant formula." Variant forms of it occur about twenty-five times throughout the Bible. The first occurrence is in the pivotal text of Exodus 6, but an earlier partial form is found in conjunction with God's appearance to Abraham. There in the context of covenant discussion and the promise of descendants, a people, God declares: "I will establish my covenant . . . to be God to you and to your offspring after you" (Gen 17:7). Elsewhere, in a chain of blessings that are to follow Israel if they walk in Yahweh's statutes, the final blessing promise is, "And I will walk among you, and will be your God, and you shall be my people" (Lev 26:12). In what resembles a covenant renewal, made in the land of Moab, Moses addresses the leaders of Israel, along with the men of Israel, wives and children, as ready to enter into a sworn covenant which Yahweh their God is now making with them, "that he may establish you today as his people, and that he may be your God" (Deut 29:13). Echoes of this two-part formula are found elsewhere in the Pentateuch (e.g., Deut 26:16–19). Beyond the Pentateuch the full formula is particularly frequent in Jeremiah and Ezekiel (Jer 7:23; 11:4; 24:7; 30:22; 31:1, 33; 32:38; Ezek 11:20; 14:11; 36:28; 37:23). Allusions to it are in Paul's epistle (Rom 9:25–26), Peter's letter (1 Pet 2:9), and John's Revelation (Rev 21:3).

Essentially the formula envisages a people; not an individual, but a community. Even the covenant with Noah is essentially a covenant with the human family: "I am establishing my covenant with you and your descendants after you" (Gen 9:9). So also the covenant with Abraham, where the covenant is made with an individual, has in view at once his descendants. The group, rather than the isolated individual, moves into center stage. There is a sociological understanding of the group, apart from the covenant but basic to it, which differs from western notions of the group. A grasp of the ancient Near East concept of "people" forms a good introduction to the Old Testament distinctive of a covenant people.

A key word to describe Hebrew and ancient Near East understanding of group is "solidarity," a term which conveys the link that exists between members of a group. In western thought individuals and group are quite separate ideas. Several individuals, or several thousand, can be described as a group. But the distinction between one person and the collective units of persons remains clear. It was otherwise for Israel. The unity of a group reached back in time to include the ancestors. In burial, for example, the dead were "gathered to their people," united with their kindred. Or, the group itself could be thought of as an individual. The borderline between individual and group was fluid. It was not a problem to address the group, as does the book of Deuteronomy, using the singular "you" as well as the plural "you." Or, conversely, the individual could think of himself or herself as summing up the group in oneself. The suffering servant of Isaiah 53 can be understood, at one level, as incorporating the group. A term descriptive of this easy back-and-forth movement between individual and group is "corporate personality."[2] It conveys the idea of a corporate society viewed as having personality and therefore to be treated as a unity. It hints also at the idea that a person incorporates the whole, as in the story of the unchaste woman (Ezekiel 16 and 23), or the Son of Man who is at the same time "the people of the saints of the Most High" (Dan 7:13, 27, RSV). Almost certainly the "I" in the Psalms is not in each instance an individual but represents a group, possibly a nation.

Such thinking emphasizes solidarity. The ways in which this concept receives expression are of interest. Genealogies are found in Genesis, Exodus, and Numbers, as well as in books from a later period, such as Chronicles. Genealogies have little or no interest to the casual reader, although it is helpful to be told that genealogy is an ancient accepted way of writing history. If one knew the story of the individual, then it was sufficient in tracing out a history to list the names of individuals. But then history is not all that these genealogies convey. One understands from them that people belong together. The genealogies of Genesis emphasize that all peoples stand in solidarity with each other. Though developed into different tribes and clan groupings, a people share alike in a basic commonality which makes for a kinship of humanity. Genealogies of clan and family establish more directly the bonds of closeness within smaller circles. Individuals are important, but individualism is not. The fundamental unit in Semitic society is the group, and not, as in the West, the individual. Nowadays a person starts with the right of the individual; the Israelite did not.

Group solidarity is illustrated by a look at blessings and curses, for these affect more than the individual. The blessings of Jacob are on his sons, but are given the terms of tribal traits and regional settlements (Genesis 49). The story of Achan makes sense according to Israelite understanding of group: the taking by one person of the forbidden gold and garments, available as spoil at Jericho, incapacitates an entire army (Joshua 7). What has a private action to do with the fortunes of a military campaign? On the basis of group solidarity, a great deal. The individual is not a private person whose actions implicate himself or herself only for good or ill. No, each is part and parcel of a group, and an individual's evildoing affects the entire group. In keeping with the understanding of solidarity, not Achan alone but his family also is stoned.[3]

Blood revenge, the arrangement whereby the kinsman of the murdered pursues the slayer to take vengeance, is also built on the solidarity of the clan or family. For a stranger to take revenge would be out of keeping with the understanding of society.

To speak of peoplehood generally means that such pervasive notions as just outlined are taken into account. But to speak of a people of God, especially as defined by the formulaic statement "I will take you as my people, and I will be your God" is to speak of a particular kind of solidarity, a covenant people. The designation "people of the covenant" requires some grasp of the meaning of covenant. The definition of "covenant" can be determined either by a word study, or through investigation of the contexts in which the word is used, or it can be illumined from the ancient Near Eastern practice. The fullest comprehension of course builds on the insights that come from all these approaches.[4]

The word "covenant" (*bᵉrît*) itself occurs 287 times in the Old Testament. The derivation of the word is not fully clear. Some link it with "to eat," calling attention to the ritual of animal slaughter in making a covenant (Genesis 15), or the partaking of a meal, sometimes a constituent in covenant-making (Exod 24:9–11), or even the term "make" (literally "cut") a covenant, and conclude that covenant originally had a connection with food.

Others see in the Akkadian verb *biritu* the contributing word to the name for covenant (*bᵉrît*) since *biritu* means "fetter," "clasp," or "bond," an idea easily associated with covenant. A recent attempt has been to connect the Hebrew word with a verb found both in the Hebrew and in the Akkadian, used in the sense of appointing to an office and so hinting at both designation and obligation. Clear-cut conclusions are not here advisable, given the competing theories.

Examination of the way covenant is used in the Old Testament is a more helpful approach, although not without difficulties. One study concluded that originally a covenant was made between unequals. The stronger, out of a voluntary action in which he bound himself to the weaker, committed himself to the weaker through a promise. An example supporting this understanding of covenant is furnished by Joshua's arrangement with the Gibeonites. He, the stronger, made a promise to the weaker Gibeonites; the language reflects this unilateral direction in that the covenant is made "for" the Gibeonites. But, so argues this writer, another concept of covenant-making comes closer to a contract, and so "with" is the proper preposition, as in Exod 19:7ff (see especially 24:8).

Other writers, looking to such passages as Joshua's covenant with the Gibeonites, observe that covenant consists in a self-imposed obligation, as for example Joshua's arrangement to let the Gibeonites live (Josh 9:15). Although a covenant did not always mean a reciprocal relationship, it was sometimes used to speak of the obligation God required of people and seems to be equivalent to laws (Isa 24:5). Looking at the way covenant is used in the Old Testament, one is confronted, though not always at one and the same time, with promise, obligation, and reciprocal responsibilities.

The greatest help of all in understanding covenant has come in recent years from research in ancient Near Eastern political treaties.[5] Through archaeological discovery, a variety of treaties can now be examined. Some of these political treaties were between large powers, such as Egypt and the Hittites, and thus treaties between equals. Another type of treaty was that between the imperial ruler and a vassal. Each type followed a particular stereotyped form. This is not surprising since even today business letters, not to mention contracts, follow a convention. What was surprising was the discovery that biblical material in instances followed the same form sequence, especially the form of the suzerainty-vassal treaty in which an overlord made a treaty with an inferior though partially independent city-state.

A look at what may be an offer of treaty between the Hittite emperor and a Ugarit city-state in the fourteenth century BC will illustrate the major features of the treaty.[6] The treaty began with a preamble which identified the persons in the treaty. It was customary to add elaborate epithets to the chief emperor. In the treaty of the Hittite ruler Suppiluliuma, the pompous mood and exaggerated claims are evident from the opening line: "Thus says Suppiluliuma, the great King, King of Hatti, the Sun, to Niqmandu . . ." Modesty seems not to be a virtue of the Hittite rulers!

Following this preamble, a historical prologue reviewed the former relationships between the two parties and so set the up-coming arrangement into a proper framework. In our example, the Hittite king reminds the vassal king Niqmandu that in former times when neighboring kings of city states, such as Ituraddu king of Mukis and Agitessub king of Ni'i, raided Ugarit, Niqmandu in desperation had sent a plea for help: "Kings are raiding me. Save me." In gracious response the imperial Hittite ruler had sent chariots and horsemen and delivered the hapless Niqmandu from his attackers.

A key element in the formal treaty declaration of an ancient time was the basic stipulation. In a nutshell it set out the arrangement that was to govern the two parties. Suppiluliuma the Hittite overlord stipulated the following: "With my friend you shall be a friend and with my enemy you shall be an enemy" (cf. Exod 23:22). This statement in itself sounds like a cliché or stereotype, but it is remarkably concise and clear and unmistakable in intent. Particular conditions or obligations were then itemized. These touched on fugitives, boundaries, throne successions, regulation of itinerant merchant men, etc. In the Suppiluliuma-Niqmandu treaty, a list of places is given, apparently in order to set up boundaries.

The arrangement between the greater lord and the vassal or subject lord was "notarized," to use a western term, by an appeal to the gods. The names of gods, possibly those recognized in both territories, were listed as witnesses. The terminology was the following: "May a thousand gods know it: the god of Hebat, the god of Arinna," etc. Although the Hittite treaty does not contain a list of blessings and curses, this feature was a well-established part of a binding treaty. The blessing section of a treaty between Mursilles and Duppi-Tessub reads: "May these gods of the oaths protect him together with his person, his wife, his son, his grandson, his house and his country."[7] The curses paralleled the blessings: "May these gods of the oath destroy Duppi-Tessub together with his person, his wife, his son, his grandson, his house, his land and together with every thing he owns."[8]

If from this pattern of an ancient treaty scholars are asked to isolate the most striking characteristic, then quite predictably there will not be full agreement. As a minimum, a covenant was an arrangement between two parties drawn up in legal language. Beyond this, there is divergence of opinion. Some see the obligations as basic and hold that essence of the *bᵉrît* (covenant) consists in obligation. The covenant is a relationship under sanctions. Is it the obligation of the subject vassal or that of the overlord that is to be cited as key? Those who stress the obligations of the lesser party convey the impression that the particular conditions of the treaty are crucial and that the covenant will be broken when specific terms are violated. While this is true of a contract, a covenant has more flexibility. It is the superior who makes a covenant; the commitment of the lesser is loyalty to the other. Specifics are there, to be sure, but these are mainly illustrative of what loyalty means. For a working definition of covenant (*bᵉrît*) we may think of an arrangement between two parties in which the greater commits himself to the lesser in the context of mutual loyalty.

2. The Covenant Community and Law

Such an understanding of covenant as just summarized leaves somewhat blurred the role of law and obligation within covenant. But a closer look at the stereotyped formulations and particularly certain Scriptures which are modeled on the international treaty help to clarify how the law section fits into the covenant.[9] Our concern is not the content of the law, but rather a perspective on the law sections as a whole. The initial function of law in Israel's life has been misunderstood. Popular misunderstanding of the place of the law has been damaging for individual Christian experience.

The law as given in Exod 20:1–17 is a good place to begin. Narrowly described, the passage contains the Ten Commandments—a more biblical description of them is the Ten Words. There is some reason to be squeamish about commandment language, partly because the Old Testament designation is not "commandments" but "words" (Exod 20:1; 34:28; Deut 10:4), and partly—this is more crucial—because "commandment" inaccurately describes these statements as legalistic and harsh, so that disobedience brings inevitable punishment. But if Exodus 20 is viewed against the ancient Near Eastern covenant stereotype, the harsh color of "commandment" is quickly softened to "rightful response."

The preamble to the covenant is recognizable in the words: "I am the LORD your God" (Exod 20:2). Here the sovereign identifies himself. There follows the historical prologue, though in a shorter form than in the international Hittite treaties: ". . . who brought you out of the land of Egypt" (Exod 20:2). The prior relationship which now will form the framework for the law is the salvation by Yahweh of his people. The deliverance is the basis for obedience. The Ten Words are given to a people freed from bondage, and must be viewed in the context of redemption.[10] The issue is not to establish a close relationship but rather to perpetuate it. The close relationship of God and people took its beginning from the event at the Sea of Reeds. The giving of instruction and commandments is a sequel to that beginning. It must not be thought that observance of the Ten Words is God's appointed way for humankind to establish acceptance with God. Far more does the covenant context invite us to consider the law as a way of expressing or maintaining the relationship that has already been established. To see the Ten Words in the context of redemption is to see them positively, and not at once and at the first negatively, as condemnatory.

A second Scripture passage to help us understand the place of law is Joshua 24. It too is modeled according to the covenant pattern. The chapter gives credence to the suggestion that Israel observed a covenant renewal festival, but forthright information about such a festival is lacking. As in the Hittite treaty, the preamble is readily recognizable: "Thus says the LORD, the God of Israel." This statement is in third rather than in customary first person. The reason is easily supplied. Joshua is pictured as presenting a farewell speech in which he will call the people to loyalty to their covenant God. That speech, in keeping with the intention of the speech, is modeled after the conventional covenant formulations. The preamble is necessarily in third person, but once God is identified, the historical prologue (Josh 24:2b–13) is in first person: "Then I took your father Abraham from beyond the River and led him through all the land of Canaan" (Josh 24:3).

The historical review is quite detailed, touching on highlights of the exodus, wilderness, and conquest. In hortatory language, but in keeping with the next treaty element, the stipulations, Joshua says: "Now therefore revere the LORD, and serve him in sincerity and in faithfulness." The appeal is not, in the first instance, to observe the individual commandments, though there is an allusion to the second commandment in the admonition, "Put away the gods that your ancestors served beyond the River and in Egypt" (Josh 24:14). But the repetitious "Serve the Lord" (v. 14 twice; 15 twice; 18, 19, 21, 22) calls attention to the basic stipulation, which is that of acknowledging Yahweh and being devoted to him exclusively in service. Of course the details of that basic commitment as represented in the Ten Words are not ignored, but that which holds center stage is the basic stipulation itself. Recognition of this fact is important. Even the covenant at Sinai, like ancient Near Eastern covenants, is an arrangement where the first issue is loyalty and allegiance. Clearly the Sinai command focuses on loyalty to Yahweh.[11]

The law, so we summarize from the Joshua passage, is in its detailed stipulations an explanation of what loyalty to Yahweh means. The individual requirements are not, as individual requirements, important in a detached sort of way. The law, so we must learn, is to be read and followed in the context of personal allegiance to a personal God, Yahweh.

An appreciation of the significance of the loyalty aspect in covenant can come through a contrast of contract and covenant. The contract form differs from the covenant in that its elements are: list of consenting parties, description of transaction,

witness list and date. But beyond this formal aspect there are
other basic differences. The occasion for contract is largely the
benefits that each party expects. Thus for a satisfactory sum one
party agrees to supply a specified quantity of some desired
product for the other party. The contract is characteristically
thing-oriented. The covenant is *person*-oriented and, theologically speaking, arises, not with benefits as the chief barter item,
but out of a desire for a measure of intimacy. In a contract negotiation, arrival at a mutually satisfactory agreement is important. In a covenant, negotiation has no place. The greater in
grace offers his help; the initiative is his. "Gift" is descriptive of
covenant as "negotiation" is descriptive of contract. Both covenant and contract have obligations, but with this difference: the
conditions set out in a contract require fulfillment of terms; the
obligation of covenant is one of loyalty. A covenant, commonly,
is forever; a contract for a specified period. A ticking off of
terms in check-list fashion can reveal a broken contract, and the
point of brokenness can be clearly identified. A covenant, too,
can be broken, but the point at which this transpires is less clear,
because here the focus is not on stipulations, one, two, three,
but on a quality of intimacy. Of all the differences between covenant and contract, the place in covenant of personal loyalty is
the most striking.

The third clearly identifiable passage that is shaped like
the political treaty is the book of Deuteronomy. Here the preamble is lengthier (1:1–6a), and since this is a speech by Moses
with intentions similar to those of Joshua, the pronoun forms
do not entirely conform. The historical prologue stretches from
1:6b to 4:49. The stipulations section is found in chapters 5 to
26. The list of witnesses is found in 31:19–22; 31:28 – 32:45. A
separate and very impressive section is devoted to the blessings
and curses (27:15 – 28:68). This schema of covenant presents a
helpful way of approaching the book of Deuteronomy, for it
offers a unity and cohesiveness that is not so easily discerned if
the book is viewed as a collection of exhortations.[12]

Deuteronomy is helpful in understanding the place of the
law within covenant at two points. First, the law is for Israel's

benefit. The law is intended to ensure Israel's well-being, for observance of it would ensure long life. Israel, by means of it, could enjoy life to the full, for the law was given "that it may go well with you" (Deut 5:33; cf. 6:18; 12:28). The way in which Israel was to view the law is best articulated in the statement: "The LORD commanded us to observe all these statutes, to fear the LORD our God, for our lasting good, so as to keep us alive, as is now the case" (Deut 6:24; cf. 4:5). Israel held, and holds today, that the law put her in a privileged position. Moses asks, "And what other great nation has statutes and ordinances as just as this entire law that I am setting before you today?" (Deut 4:8). It will not do, therefore, to assess the law as a set of arbitrary restrictions intended to inhibit people and make them miserable and guilty. No, the law, though regulatory, has a rich life as its object.

A Comparison of Contract and Covenant

Category	Contract	Covenant
Form	1 List of parties 2 Description of transaction 3 List of witnesses 4 Date	1. Preamble 2. Historical prologue 3. Stipulations 4. Provisions for deposit and/or public reading 5 Witnesses 6 Blessings and curses
Occasion	Expected benefits	Desire for relationship
Initiative	Mutual Agreement	The stronger (frequently)
Orientation	Negotiaion Thing-oriented	Gift Person-oriented
Obligation	Performance	Loyalty
Termination	Specified	Indeterminate
Covenant breaking	Yes	Yes

Although the statements from Deuteronomy are sufficiently clear, a piece of rabbinic exegesis about the law emphasizes that stress on the law as beneficial is no recent idea. In rabbinic exegesis the words of the law are likened to a medicine of life.

> . . . like a king who inflicted a big wound upon his son and he put a plaster upon his wound. He said, "My son, so long as this plaster is on your wound, eat and drink what you like and wash in cold or warm water and you will suffer no harm. But if you remove it, you will get a bad boil." So God says to the Israelites: "I created you with an evil *yēṣer* (inclination) but I created the law as a drug. As long as you occupy yourself with the law the *yēṣer* (inclination) will not rule over you. But if you do not occupy yourself with the Torah, then you will be delivered into the power of the *yēṣer* and all its activity will be against you."[13]

Deuteronomy, as the most complete example of the political treaty pattern, has an extended section on blessing and curses (Deut 27:15 – 28:68), and herein is a second hint on how the law is to be viewed. It alerts the reader, not only here but elsewhere, that the covenant is not a take-it or leave-it matter. Unfaithfulness by the covenant partner threatens forfeiture of land (Deut 29:28). The stance toward the individual laws, which is ultimately a stance for or against Yahweh, entails either life or death, and so the Deuteronomist calls for a decision (Deut 30:15). The law within the covenant, taking into account both the basic stipulation and the details, is either embraced into life or ignored or disobeyed unto death.[14]

To be sure, then, one part of the covenant formula incorporates a demand, an obligation. When God says, "I will take you to myself for a people," there is a particular kind of people which is in view. Specific legislation is prefaced by the reminder: "You are children of the LORD your God" (Deut 14:1).

3. The Covenant Community and the Promise

Israel is under obligation to Yahweh. As a "peculiar" people, God's possession, she had obligations to members within the community. Indeed, the summary of the law, love God, love neighbor (Deut 6:6; Lev 19:18) provides a succinct statement both about law, emphasizing commitment rather than slavish observance, and about covenant, highlighting loyalty. But the covenant formula, while it points to demand, also contains a specific promise: "I will be a God for you." This commitment by Yahweh is a very substantial part of the covenant. How does this promise square with the demand by God for a peculiar people? How are law and promise connected? It is a large question. Israel's disobedience will lead the prophets to speak to this issue; but the question can be broached, at least in theory, already here.

First, some observations. The promise "I will be your God" is a gracious promise. Israel had not asked, perhaps had not dared to ask, that Yahweh be her God. In fact, at the time the promise was enunciated, she could have had only an inkling of what such a God could mean to her. Then came the wonder of the exodus event. Now the gracious offer has meaning. Yahweh who promises this people to be their God, and in so doing in some sense links himself with their fortunes and misfortunes, is a most desirable deity. They will find in their wilderness wanderings that Yahweh is adequate. It is enough for them that Yahweh is their God. Enemy Amalekites who at once beset them are vanquished as Moses, supported by Aaron and Hur, raises arms to Yahweh (Exod 17:8–13). And when water is unavailable, then it is enough that Yahweh is their God, for he brings water from a rock (Exod 17:1–7). Manna is brought to them with a regularity and in a manner that is nothing short of astonishing (Numbers 11). The cloud of fire and shadow covers them in all their journeys, and the Jordan, like the Sea of Reeds, parts to give them admittance into the promised land (Joshua 3). Yahweh who is their god gives them their land and indeed works wonderfully with them. Experience teaches them that their god Yahweh is fully adequate. For them there could not have come a better word than this: "I will be your God."

But the promise, though clearly a promise of grace, sounds yet another note: that of exclusiveness. Paraphrased, one might read: "I, and not another, will be a God for you." The note, even if subdued in the covenant formula, is clear and unmistakable in the first of the Ten Words: "You shall have no other gods before me' (Exod 20:3). Israel's god Yahweh was not one who stood alongside other gods and competed with them for allegiance. Yahweh alone was Israel's god. The *š⁽ᵉ⁾maʿ* which till this day is repeated by descendants from ancient Israel, reads: "The LORD is our God, the LORD alone" (Deut 6:4). It was not uncommon for other peoples to identify various forms of Baal. It was quite unthinkable for Israel that this one God should be multiple and appear elsewhere as Baal or Osiris. For Israel, God was single.

It may be too much to say that Israel was from the first monotheistic. By definition monotheism refers to the affirmation of one God to the universal exclusion of other gods. However, other gods are recognized, e.g., the Egyptian gods or the Moabite god Chemosh. This recognition may be no more than an acknowledgment that other people worshipped other gods. Yet, however matters stood for others, for Israel itself there was one god. The name of that God was Yahweh.

Yahweh's rule over Israel, however, it might be noted in passing, did not mean a rule apart from human agents. These were persons divinely chosen, such as Moses or Joshua. In the post-Joshua period, the Spirit of God came variously upon Gideon and Samson (Judg 6:34; 14:6). These governed Israel as representatives of Yahweh. As for the pattern of governance, Moses established a hierarchical form of judgeship (Exodus 18). Yet over these men, and supremely over the greatest leader, was Yahweh, the God who alone was God over Israel.

Such claim to exclusiveness was indeed the claim of Yahweh over this people, but the claim was challenged in practice from the very first. Aaron at the bidding of the people made a golden calf, reminiscent of Apis, the bull in Egyptian worship (Exodus 32). In trying times in the wilderness, the people were ready to return to Egypt and to the gods there. Once in the land, they found Baal worship attractive, even irresistible; and later, as in Solomon's time, they erected temples to a variety of deities. The promise of Yahweh to be Israel's God, including as it did exclusive rights, presented Israel with some difficulties.

But to return to our earlier question: how does the promise fare if and when the people who are called to be God's people fail in their calling? The foregoing has already sketched the close intertwining between demand—"I will take you to me for a people"—and promise—"I will be a God for you." The demand portion is also promissory and the promise is partly obligatory. In the demand which can be heard in the "my people" of the formula there shines through the initiative of God in taking for himself a people. But that such an election entails responsibilities is also clear, as the further detail of the Sinai covenant sets out. In the promise "I will be your God" there is no explicit condition, represented for instance in an "if" clause. And yet while it is promise without strings attached, there is implicit also the demand that Israel recognize no God but Yahweh. The formulation is such, however, that one is not allowed to say that the failure to meet the conditions negates or automatically cancels the promise. As we have explained, the covenant is between persons and so ambiguity in details is to be expected. In a contract the failure by one party voids the obligations assumed by the other. But in a covenant, failure does not call forth an immediate judgment. The outcome is not as clear-cut, for it is contingent on the person offended. Given the disloyalty of a people and thus an infringement of the basic covenant stipulation, allegiance, what course is the covenant partner to take? Yahweh is entitled to disengage from the commitment, but it is conceivable that he would not, by virtue of his character and purposes. The golden calf incident already hints at a continuing promise despite a people's failure. In fact, such a god is Yahweh that the promise will be honored even if the covenant obligation is not met by Israel. The offer of God remains, so it seems, even if one covenant ceases and another is instituted (Jer 31:31–33). How the matter is worked out in history when clearly the question of law and promise is no longer theoretical is one of the stirring aspects of covenant theology. Amos and Ezekiel, separated by almost two centuries, speak to that problem.

4. The Covenant and Community

If after this survey on the meaning of covenant we step back from the Old Testament texts and look out, as from a mountain, upon a people spread out below and ask once more what it means to be Israel, a people of God, then several conclusions press in for consideration.

First, Israel is a community defined by a contemporary idiom, the covenant. With Israel in touch throughout her history with great powers, it is not difficult to think of her as familiar with the political treaties of the time. It is conceivable that Moses, trained at Pharaoh's court, would easily have become acquainted with the accepted form used when drawing up agreements. The covenant clarified the relationship between two parties, here Israel and her God. Such a definition of God and people is unique for the ancient East. The model of covenant itself was not unique, but use of this model to explain how a people was related to its God was novel. By the very use of the model there was suggested a personal, somewhat intimate relationship between deity and people. At the same time, taken as it was from diplomatic interchange with judicial and legal overtones, the covenant suggested orderliness, even rightness.

It was an appropriate model for a community, for in the political life of a people, covenant, though they were made between individuals, were on occasion arrangements with city-state populations as well. As given to Israel, Yahweh's covenant with his people at Sinai incorporated the traditional elements of treaty, and this made explicit the identification of Yahweh, the historical prologue to the covenant itself, which for Israel was the history of redemption. The covenant with Israel specified loyalty to Yahweh as a basic requirement and articulated in detail how this was to be understood. The seriousness of the arrangement was clear from the blessings and curses. Israel acknowledged that Yahweh was her overlord and sovereign. Israel regarded herself as the people of Yahweh, both by reason of redemption and by reason of the covenant. The covenant form made clear to Israel that she stood in a unique relationship to

Yahweh in which she was both recipient of Yahweh's promises, and obligated to be loyal to Yahweh as his people. The prophets, while still drawing on this model, were in addition to introduce other ways of speaking of the way in which Israel stood over against God. They were to use images from family experience: husband-wife, father-son. Or they employed agricultural images such as shepherd-sheep. But the model of the international treaty remained an important substructure.

Secondly, Israel as a community with a sense of solidarity generally was given an additional sense of solidarity and religious bondedness through the covenant. In the ancient world the clan and tribe, more so than the individual, was the unit of everyday life. So it was also for Israel. The blood kinship as descendants of Jacob brought a sense of togetherness; but to that was added, first the common experience of the exodus, and second the consolidation of a people through covenant. Tribes and clans, but also other people, non-Israelites, were incorporated within a people whose distinguishing mark was not primarily ethnic, but religious and spiritual. To be sure the descendants of Jacob made up its core. But that a pure blood line was not a prime consideration is already evident by Joseph's marriage to an Egyptian (Gen 41:45) and Moses' marriage to a Cushite (Num 12:1). Caleb and Othniel, though incorporated into Israel, were Kenizzites (Num 32:12; Judg 1:13) and so not from the line of Jacob. In Israel's history the incorporation of Rahab and her descendants is additional evidence that blood kinship was not determining for group cohesiveness (Joshua 2; Matt 1:5). Voluntary commitment, subscription to a group ethos, and almost certainly the worship of the same deity were determinants in group membership.

The expression "people of God," while not common in the Old Testament, is nevertheless found there. For instance, the tribal identification is not lost but submerged in the following: "The chiefs of all the people, of all the tribes of Israel, presented themselves in the assembly of the people of God" (Judg 20:2). The tone of the narrative can be heard from the very frequent mention of "congregation" or "assembly" in the

Pentateuch (e.g., Num 10:7; 20:4; Deut 5:22; 23:3). Whatever else these people held in common, and whatever else united them, the allegiance which they shared collectively to one God whose provision and direction they experienced collectively, and by whose covenant they were collectively bound to one another, was a high consideration, if not the uppermost consideration. It was through a failure to respond to the covenant God that the individual would be "cut off from the assembly" (Num 19:20). Israel's solidarity was cultural, to be sure, but not only so. It was spiritual solidarity.

Third, Israel was a community in covenant with Yahweh. Of the many ramifications of such a status, a decisive one was this: they were confronted in their experience with the person of Yahweh even more than by his laws. There is easily a tendency to read the Pentateuch as a book of laws and to think therefore that Israel must have been preoccupied with a host of detailed regulations. But scattered throughout these laws, whether cultic, ceremonial, or family, is the recurring statement, "I am the LORD your God." While this assertion gives motivation to these laws, it also gives perspective. Yahweh as the deity is the one to whom devotion is to be given. The covenant, with its stipulation of loyalty and its regulations, is one of the ways in which Yahweh distinguishes himself from the gods Baal, Anath, Mot, Re, Osiris, and the others. Yahweh is not, like those gods, a God of caprice, not arbitrary and insensitive to humankind. Instead Yahweh has made the divine will known. Israel is not left guessing about the will of her deity. Other gods are unpredictable. Yahweh is a God who acts in freedom; but also a God who is committed to an order and a rightness and who does not act out of whim or precipitous fancy. Israel is confronted with her God, not only at the exodus, but at Sinai.

Israel, aware of this awesome fact of God's presence, calls on Moses at Sinai to be the intermediary. "Go near, you yourself, and hear all that the LORD our God will say. Then tell us everything that the LORD our God tells you, and we will listen and do it" (Deut 5:27). It is not comfortable for sinful beings to be face to face in their nakedness before God. They naturally

seek a screen. Even the law, as so many words, offers a screen
from Yahweh. It is easier to be caught up with it—analyze and
justify it—than to remain outright in the presence of God. Luther captured it well: "He who studies *mandata Dei* (the commandments of God) will not be moved; but he who hears *Deum
mandatum* (God commanding), how can he fail to be terrified?"
But then one dare not live only in the commandment section of
the covenant. One hears again the preamble which proclaims a
God of grace to the weak: "I am Yahweh your God who brought
you out of Egypt." It is with Yahweh her Redeemer, rather than
mere law-giver, that Israel is bound up in covenant.

5

God's Design
Knowledge of God

The third aspect of God's design as set out in our keystone text reads: "You shall know that I am the LORD your God, who has freed you from the burdens of the Egyptians" (Exod 6:7b). This statement differs from the two before it and the one following in that it is the only one with the "you-I" sequence. The other three sentences are formulated in the order of "I-you": "I will bring you out"(RSV); "I will take you as my people, and I will be your God"; "I will bring you into the land." The interaction between God and people is constant, but in the third statement that interaction is described particularly as the expected activity of a people: they are to know that he is Yahweh. The ramifications of this part of God's design will become clear as we investigate in turn the Hebrew concept of knowledge, the knowledge of God through the world of nature and nations, through the exodus event, and through the cult, i.e., the religious practices.

1. Knowing God: The Possibility

The word "know" is so much at home in everyday language that it surely presents no difficulties. To know means to become aware of, to distinguish, to identify. Knowledge means information, data, facts. Knowledge pertains to one's cognitive abilities of reflection, memory, insight, and understanding. Such usage, basic for English, is also basic in Hebrew. To know is to have information. The patriarch Jacob speaks to his sons and says, "You *know* that my wife bore me two sons" (Gen 44:27). Joseph sets up a scheme whereby he will know whether or not his visitors are spies (Gen 42:23; cf. Exod 33:16). God says to Moses about Israel in Egypt: "I know their sufferings" (Exod 3:7). Through participation, through active investigation, and through observation one arrives at knowledge.

But there are two additional nuances to "knowledge" as used in the Bible, one of which links knowledge with experiential familiarity. In the English language we approximate to the biblical meaning of knowing when we speak of knowing people. At an elementary level, to know a person is to know about that person. At a more advanced level, knowledge of persons means firsthand contact, awareness of characteristics or individuality. For the Hebrews "knowing" is definitely not restricted to the cognitive and the intellectual but reaches into the emotional and experiential. These elements are most striking in the marital reference, "Now the man knew his wife Eve, and she conceived and bore Cain" (Gen 4:1). Sexual intimacy is described as "knowing." Lot offers his two daughters to the perverts in Sodom saying, "I have two daughters who have not known a man" (Gen 19:8). Among the spoils from Israel's battle with the Midianites were 3200 women who had not known a man by sleeping with him (Num 31:35). In this category of knowledge, meaning closest familiarity, must be classed statements that speak of skills. Thus Bezalel and Aholiab are able men who "know how to do any work in the construction of the sanctuary" (Exod 36:1).

The experience dimension of "know" is recognizable from its use in the Exodus 6 text: "By my name 'The LORD' I did not make myself known to them (the patriarchs)" (Exod 6:3). This does not necessarily mean that they were strangers to the name as such, for the mother of Moses is called Jochebed, a name that incorporates the Yah from Yahweh (Exod 6:20). But God's name Yahweh was not known in the sense that not until the exodus was it expounded. The usage of the word to signify "fully known" is illustrated also in the prophet's word: "You only have I known of all the families of the earth" (Amos 3:2; cf. Hos 13:5). Such a statement cannot mean that God is ignorant of other nations—Amos himself declares that it was Yahweh who brought the Philistines from Caphtor and the Syrians from Kir (Amos 9:7). God knew Israel in that he was emotionally involved with and personally attached to the people. Experience, if not equivalent to "knowledge," is at least an additional dimension in the Hebrew understanding of "know." It is this interchange between persons that figures significantly in the expression, "You shall know that I am the LORD your God" (Exod 6:7a).

If this nuance of "know" touches the emotions, then another understanding of "know" in the Bible touches the will. This is illustrated by Jeremiah's accusation against Jehoiakim (Jer 22:13–17). Josiah, the father of Jehoiakim, was remembered for his just rule and care for the people. Jehoiakim was self-seeking, using tax money for the elaborate decoration of his courts. He built a palace with spacious upper rooms, paneling it with cedar and painting it with vermilion. Jeremiah says:

> Are you a king because you compete in cedar? Did not your father eat and drink and do justice and righteousness? Then it was well with him. He judged the cause of the poor and needy; then it was well. Is not this to know me? says the LORD. (Jer 22:15–16)

Knowledge here is linked with action. Knowledge of God involves ethical action. The will to follow through is part of what it means to "know." In characteristic Hebrew fashion, the thought is holistic. The person as entire person enters into knowing.

The possibility of knowing God is present because God gives himself to be known, either in theophany, as often to the patriarchs, or through events such as the exodus, or as we shall see presently, through worship experiences. But knowledge of the kind we have described, consisting of information and also of an interior relationship arising out of experience, requires the knowing agent to be capable of receiving information and of integrating the experience. Despite God's making himself

known, an animal cannot be said to know God. Modern think-
ers may be catapulted into a net of philosophical questions by
the notion of knowing God; but it apparently was not thus with
the Israelites—not because they were unthinking persons, but
because their understanding of humankind and God was fundamentally different from ours. The difference is best illustrated through the Israelite belief in humans as being in the
image of God.

In Hebrew thought, persons are so constituted that they
can know God. The term "image of God" is descriptive of that
affinity which humankind has to God. The exact meaning of
that phrase has been much disputed. With primitive religions in
mind, some have wanted to see the phrase as meaning that people are physically like God. They will call attention to the way in
which God is described as having a powerful arm, as wrathful,
or as walking in the garden. But against this interpretation is
the command that one not make an image of God and explicit
statements that God is not as people are. Food, for example, is
not necessary to God (Ps 50:12ff). The physical resemblance of
a person to God is not what the "image of God" means.

Approaching the phrase from definitions of personality,
popular in psychology some decades ago, some allege that human beings, like God, have intellect, emotion, and will. While
these affirmations about God and humanity are true, it is
doubtful whether ancient Israel understood the phrase in these
abstract terms. The ancient Near Eastern practice of a ruler
putting his image in a remote province which he could not visit
in person is helpful. The function of the image was to represent
the king. The Assyrians' inscriptions carry the phrase: "I will set
up my statue in their midst." To destroy the image was equivalent to destroying the one it represented. One could make the
case that human beings are in the image of God in the sense
that they are God's representatives. Just as God rules, so they
are called on to exercise dominion, though in God's behalf.

While accepting this interpretation, one can add to it the
meaning, relying on the comparable statement in Gen 5:3,
"Adam . . . became the father of a son in his likeness, according

to his image," that to be in another's image and likeness is to be capable of dialogue and interchange. The affinity between two is such that significant communication can take place. A Jewish writer has made memorable the substance of the point in the expression, the "I-Thou" relationship.[1] Human beings, to put it in everyday language, are a near relative of God. As such they have the capacity, one which distinguishes them from other forms of life, to be in dialogue with God. It is this feature of humankind, namely affinity with God, that is presupposed in the biblical language about knowing God.

2. Knowing God in the Larger World: Nature, Family, and Nations

The earlier chapters of Genesis, known as the primeval history, disclose a particular portrait of God. Assuming that at the time of the exodus Israel had the narratives of the creation, the flood, Babel, and also the genealogies available to them, they could not but have understood that God was God of the larger world—a world that embraced both nature and nations.[2]

For a major question is: what experience of God is reflected in that primeval history? Clearly God is seen as the creator, but what kind of a creator? The answer is that he is a creator whose creation is good. A value judgment is offered in the first chapter of Genesis: "And God saw that it was good." Upon all that is made the estimate is given: "And behold, it was very good." We may still ask, good for what? But the question is not answered for us. We infer that in and of itself the creation was good, aesthetically pleasing. We may want to say more, namely that for God's purposes it was good. This, while true, is not explicit in the text. The world, as it leaves the hand of its creator, is unspoiled, unsullied, and free in any and all of its parts from evil.

While Israel confessed belief in God as creator, there is not sufficient evidence to believe that she, like the nations of the ancient Near East, elaborated the creation story into a separate cult ritual. In other ancient neighboring religions, elaborate stories or myths were told to explain the beginning of the world and the existence of mortals. According to the *Enuma Elish*, the famous Babylonian myth of the second millennium, the sweet water ocean, Apsu, and the salt water ocean, Tiamat, commingled to produce gods.

Sky and earth were created when one god, Marduk, slew another, Tiamat, and cut her body in half. The gods celebrated and created human beings in order that they might serve the comforts of the gods. The god Marduk had brought order out of chaos. To sustain the order in the universe, the Babylonians celebrated an annual festival, at which time the drama of creation was re-enacted.[3]

But Israel's worship ritual, though elaborate, did not occupy itself with creation. In the creed which the Israelite repeated upon bringing the first fruits to the temple priest he did not, as might be expected, recall God as creator, but rather as the deliverer who brought the people out of Egypt (Deut 26:5ff). None of the festivals or rituals in Israel was taken up with the creation idea.

This fact has been interpreted sometimes to mean that in Israel, history was all-important, whereas in surrounding pagan peoples nature rather than history was the active sphere of the gods. Certainly Egypt with its gods of bulls, cats and natural objects such as the Nile was nature-oriented. Canaan with its Baal, god of fertility, was preoccupied with season and cycles, vegetation growth and dearth. But Israel was not without interest in nature. The creation narrative testifies to that interest. And while the Psalms and Isaiah explore the creation motif most clearly, the idea of creation is not absent from the patriarchal stories. Melchizedek's blessing of Abraham reads: "Blessed be Abram by God Most High, maker of heaven and earth" (Gen 14:19). While in these early chapters creation is not a dominant theme, and is subservient to history, it is nevertheless clearly present. Israel's God, experienced as a delivering God, was God of nature as well as history.

But these preliminary chapters to Israel's story also present us with a God who has moral sensibilities. God is eventually impatient with evil and so works destruction as well as good; not indiscriminately or unaccountably, for in his initial acts God intends "good." Yet humankind, created good, does not remain so. People mar the harmony that exists throughout the created world by aspiring to be like God. In response to evil, developed in the world outside himself, God is moved to drastic action. This drastic action, while most obvious in the flood narrative, is apparent also in the expulsion of Adam and Eve from the garden, in the banishment of Cain, and in the confusion of tongues at Babel. God is provoked by evil; evil, committed by an individual or by an entire race, does not go unchecked in God's world. Thus the moral dimension, often absent from early ancient Near Eastern stories about deity, characterizes the God who is God of the world and of Israel.

It is important to repeat that the threatening God, the God of judgment, is also a God of grace. While these early chapters present the encroachment of sin in various spheres of life, as described in a preceding chapter (2), they also portray a God who in his response to sin acts in grace. Christians have recognized a messianic promise in God's statement following humankind's sin in Eden: "I will put enmity between you and the woman, and between your offspring and hers; he will strike your head, and you will strike his heel" (Gen 3:15). But aside from this word of grace, which may be heard in the proto-evangelium of Gen 3:15, the good news of God's grace, the gospel, may be heard in the material of Genesis 3–11. The successive threats to Cain of a fugitive existence, to Noah of a world deluge, at Babel of world-wide dispersion are each accompanied by a redemptive note, for Cain receives a mark, Noah's family is spared, and from the dispersion God calls Abraham. Already early on there are illustrations from a variety of spheres of the reality that where sin abounded, grace did much more abound.

When we proceed to the patriarchal narratives (Genesis 12–50), and inquire, how is God known, then several observations deserve attention. To begin with, God was known as one who crossed people's lives. God called Abram out of Ur; covenanted with him, listened to his prayer concerning Sodom and

Gomorrah, rescued Abram's wife, and tested Abram (Genesis 12–22). God intersected with the ways of people. God appeared to Abraham at Mamre (Gen 18:1), to Isaac at Beersheba (Gen 26:23ff), and to Jacob at Bethel and in Egypt (Gen 28:10ff; 46:2). God conversed with people, commanded them, entered into covenant with them. He was a God who, as in Jacob's experience, suddenly appeared blocking the way, or yet again as opening the way, as in Joseph's rise to leadership in Egypt.

Moreover the God of the Fathers was a God of promise. To Abraham, as well as to Isaac and Jacob, promises of descendants had been given, as well as the promise of land. But the promise was not indiscriminate. The promise centered in Isaac, not Ishmael. Hence the promise given to some but not to others denotes God's freedom and also his purpose, for election is not solely to salvation but to role and responsibility. Crucial to promise was the recognition of God as a god of performance. Obstacles, of a barren and aged wife Sarai, for example, were no hindrance to God. The patriarchs might blunder as Abraham did, when before Pharaoh he passed off Sarai his wife as his sister—Pharaoh's act of taking her into his harem spelled potential disaster for the promise. But the incident (Genesis 12) and similar ones later (Genesis 20, 26) showed that even human foolishness and sin could not in the end jeopardize the promise. The descendants became numerous, so numerous indeed that Pharaoh mounted a population control program.

The God of the Fathers was not a distant God. This God was present as a reality for Jacob when at Bethel he not only saw a ladder with angels ascending and descending, but heard God say, "Know that I am with you and will keep you wherever you go" (Gen 28:15). God's presence was forcefully experienced as Abraham offered Isaac, or in quite a different but no less real way when Eliezer was guided to Laban's house in his search for a wife for Isaac. The story of Joseph in which God does not directly appear to Joseph still gives evidence of God's presence, as the narrator reminds us (e.g., Gen 39:21) and as the turn of events in Joseph's life and that of his family demonstrates.

The theme of nations continues, however. While the patriarchal stories are basically family stories, and God's confrontation, promises, and presence are illustrated in family settings, the God of the patriarchs was not a localized deity or a family patron. Two stories illustrate a larger understanding of God. The first, the Sodom and Gomorrah episode, presents a God whose concern is broader than the Hebrew families. Moreover, God is morally sensitive, outraged at evil, and so acts in judgment to destroy wicked cities (Genesis 19). But God's action upon other peoples is not exclusively punitive. Yahweh protects people. The story of Egypt's preservation through Joseph's seven-year plan illustrates God's beneficent care for non-Hebrews. In each instance, a witness to the claims of God was not only present but was in a responsible position of leadership. Lot is described by New Testament writers as a righteous man (2 Pet 2:7), and his role in entertaining and defending the strangers as well as his being seated in the city gate bespeaks a leadership role in the city. Joseph, next to Pharaoh, gave forthright witness concerning God (Gen 41:25). Thus the patriarchal stories, for all their family character, do not portray a provincial deity, but rather a God whose jurisdiction extends to other peoples.

Through the primeval history (Genesis 1–11) and through the record about the patriarchal stories (Genesis 12–50), Israel confessed her belief in a Yahweh who was God of nature, but whose influence and control extended to families and to the world of nations.

3. Knowing God through the Event
The Exodus

If the creation story and the narratives about the patriarchs set the framework for the exodus, it is still in the exodus event itself that major contributions to the knowledge of Yahweh as God are placed. In the exodus Israel became aware of the identity of Yahweh above all as a salvation God. The exodus experience expounded the basic manner in which Yahweh was to be understood. The prophet, for example, sees in the exodus the paradigm for salvation (Jer 23:7–8). And when Hosea wishes to confront his people with Yahweh, the cry is, "I have been the LORD your God ever since the land of Egypt" (Hos 13:4).

Moses' message to the people, even though they refused at times to listen (Exod 6:12), was that a deity by the name of Yahweh (the LORD), the same as had appeared to the patriarchs, would be instrumental in bringing them out of the land. Granted that Israel had traditions about a deity guiding the steps of the forefathers, and granted that they held to a belief in God as creator, they were nevertheless cast upon a bare word that Yahweh would indeed free them from their plight. The support of "signs" was not unimportant, to be sure, but if we inquire how Israel experienced Yahweh we must say the obvious: Israel experienced Yahweh in the exodus as one whose word to them could be trusted.

Further, Israel knew Yahweh as the liberator. Bondage and cruelty, servitude and humiliation, were behind them. Yahweh had led them into freedom. In so doing, his power was proved, for the forces of the strongest people of that world, the forces of an army, political power, and religion, had not been sufficient to halt or frustrate Yahweh's liberation advance. The emotion with which they greeted this experience of deliverance is expressed in the Song by the Sea (Exod 15:1–18), to which attention has already been given.

The exodus was to bring knowledge of God to Israel, but not to Israel only. It must not be overlooked that while our immediate text statement from Exod 6:7 stresses the intent that through the exodus Israel was to know about Yahweh, the larger narrative of the exodus spells out God's greater design, namely that through the exodus complex of events, Egypt also was to know about Yahweh. Such knowledge was brought about in part through the presence of Moses, who on behalf of Yahweh requested that Pharaoh release his people. The power struggle which ensued between Yahweh and Pharaoh was anticipated in Pharaoh's comment: "I will not let Israel go" (Exod 5:2). The

more basic context emerges in the question, "Who is the
LORD?" followed by the assertion, "I do not know the LORD"
(Exod 5:2). More than information about Yahweh is at stake, for
Moses had supplied the necessary data. Not only had Pharaoh
not had an experience that put him in touch with Yahweh, but
Pharaoh did not acknowledge Yahweh.

But that state of affairs was to be altered. To this pagan king
there were given, not lengthy apologetic proofs through argument, but a communication which he could understand: signs.
These signs, first as wonders and then as plagues, were to remedy the lack in Pharaoh's experience. By these he was to know
Yahweh, and not alone he, but all Egyptians. It is as though
Pharaoh's protest "I do not know the LORD" is to be met head-
on, for what follows as signs and wonders is directed explicitly at
bringing Pharaoh to know Yahweh.

In the narrative preceding the first wonder of the rod becoming a serpent is the programmatic statement: "The Egyptians shall know that I am the LORD, when I stretch out my hand
against Egypt and bring the Israelites out from among them"
(Exod 7:5). The wonder of the Nile turning to blood is announced to Pharaoh: "By this you shall know that I am the
LORD. See, with the staff that is in my hand I will strike the water
that is in the Nile, and it shall be turned to blood" (Exod 7:17).
When the magicians fail to bring forth gnats from the dust, they
admit to Pharaoh: "This is the finger of God" (Exod 8:19). Another wonder, the hail, is prefaced by the statement to Pharaoh
given in the name of Yahweh the God of the Hebrews, "So that
you may know that there is no one like me in all the earth"
(Exod 9:14; cf. 9:29). The climax in this contest comes at the
Sea of Reeds, for now the might of the Egyptians, concentrated
in the pursuing army, is the foil that will demonstrate convinc-
ingly the supremacy of Yahweh. By Yahweh's action in which by
the collapse of the waters the Egyptians army is vanquished
"the Egyptians shall know that I am the LORD" (Exod 14:4, 18).

Pharaoh, it must be remembered, was a god-king. He was
the deity, not as in Mesopotamia where the king was the
adopted "son" of the deity, but in an even more intimate way by

being the personification of deity. It is not without reason that the plagues affected those areas held by the Egyptians to be under the power of this more-than-human figure. The plagues put into question the extent of the control which these Egyptian deities exercised. The signs and the wonder at the Sea showed Yahweh to be superior not only to the lesser animal and insect deities, but to the god-king Pharaoh himself.

Thus at the beginning of Israel's national history, account is taken of a nation other than Israel. This nation, Egypt, is to understand that Yahweh is at work. The plagues are sent for Egypt's benefit more than for Israel's, yet the evidence, though it might just as conveniently have been unrelated to Israel, comes in conjunction with God's covenant people. Whatever else Egypt may see in the incidents, they must be persuaded of the power of Yahweh, God of Israel. The impact of this demonstration of power could hardly have been lost on the Israelites, of course, and some of their boldness, even glee, is apparent in the instruction "that you may tell your children and grandchildren how I have made fools of the Egyptians and what signs I have done among them—so that you may know that I am the LORD" (Exod 10:2). The Egyptians understood that this power and Yahweh's employment of it were exercised in behalf of the unfortunate, the slaves. The "missionary" intent is hardly veiled. The Egyptians did not come to faith in Yahweh but they were not without an exposure to him—a witness about Yahweh was left them.

While directed immediately at the Egyptians, the witness extended to other people. Jethro, a Midianite, upon hearing what had transpired, said, "Now I know that the LORD is greater than all gods, because he delivered the people from the Egyptians, when they dealt arrogantly with them" (Exod 18:11). The prophets, Ezekiel in particular, will return to the theme that by God's action for Israel, nations will know "that I am the LORD."

But to say that knowledge of God comes through events is to be slightly misleading, for it suggests that the events as bare events made it clear that Yahweh was the agent behind them. Not so; for it can be plausibly argued that nothing in the wonders or plagues in themselves would have convinced Pharaoh that Yahweh was acting. The events, even those at the Reed Sea, are not self-interpreting. A modern newspaper reporter, had one come on the scene as it transpired, could hardly have been expected to say while walking away, "That was Yahweh." Pharaoh had reason to be persuaded that it was Yahweh because of the interpretive word which accompanied the events. Prior to the plagues, as well as at the Sea of Reeds, announcement of the act was not only made and the actor, Yahweh, identified, but the purpose was stated: the Egyptians were to know that it was Yahweh (5:2; 7:5; 14:4, 18). This combination of word with the event made it possible for the event to carry meaning. And had our hypothetical newspaper reporter been present *before* the event to hear the announcement that Yahweh was about to hand the Egyptians a resounding defeat in order that they might recognize him as God, the reporter, though he might have discounted the claim, would at least have been confronted with it in a straightforward manner. The events recorded in the Bible, while impressive, require interpretation in order to bear their message.

There is truth in the claim that the Bible presents God as the God who acts.[4] But the Bible is not a chronicle of nothing but the acts of God. Often, though it must be said in fairness not always, events are preceded or followed by an explanation. This pattern holds for the exodus, the fall of Jericho, the defeat of the Midianites at the hand of Gideon, the removal of Saul, the fall of Israel, and the devastation of Jerusalem. The pattern remains for New Testament events also, especially the crucifixion. Without clear enunciation about its significance, Christ's crucifixion could be dismissed along with other crucifixions as religiously unimportant.

Thus, much as we make and should make of the mighty acts of God as a vehicle for knowledge, we do violence to the biblical story if we neglect the word given by God through his servants. For though statistically the events are many, the divinely given words are just as frequent, perhaps more frequent. The writings of an eighteenth-century scholar give us pause when he calls attention to proportions as follows:

> God created the whole world in six days, but he used forty to instruct Moses about the tabernacle. Little over one chapter was needed to describe the structure of the world, but six were used for the tabernacle.[5]

In the Exodus-Sinai narrative complex the space given to the word of Yahweh at Sinai is more extensive than that given to the action of deliverance, and to it we turn.

4. Knowing God through the Word Cultic Worship

The exodus, an event played in the arena of international powers, represents a forceful medium for the experience of Yahweh. God's acts were decisive. But events in the frame of history do not exhaust the means by which God becomes known. In the cult, Yahweh was known, not in a physical display of power, but in the no less forceful practices of worship. In these worship prescriptions and practices Yahweh was known in a way different from a physical display of power, but no less forceful.

It is not as though in an arbitrary way we leave the exodus and dip into cult. A passage in Exodus which is taken up with prescriptions about offerings, priests, and furnishings concludes with: "And they shall know that I am the LORD their God, who brought them out of the land of Egypt that I might dwell among them; I am the LORD their God" (Exod 29:45–46). Here the deliverance from Egypt aims at the dwelling of Yahweh with his people, and that phenomenon cannot be understood apart from the cult. In fact another passage ties together the ideas of God delivering his people and dwelling among them: "I will place my dwelling in your midst . . . and I will walk among you . . . I am the LORD your God who brought you out of the land of Egypt, to be their slaves no more; I have broken the bars of your yoke and made you walk erect" (Lev 26:11–13).

We now turn to divine instruction and single out legislation about the cult: the tabernacle, cultic laws, and cult festivals. By the word "cult" we mean the observable actions of a people, singly or in community, in which people engage in conjunction with their religion.

The tabernacle can be described as a windowless wooden oblong structure with four layers of coverings: linen underneath, goats' hair, dyed rams' skin, and an outer coating of leather. Beneath this roof the structure is divided into two parts: the holy place where stood a table for bread, an altar for incense, and a lampstand; and a smaller and more sacred division where was placed the ark of the covenant. The tent was set in a fenced courtyard just inside the entrance of which stood the main altar and the laver. Priests were active in the courtyard section. Access to the holy places was limited, however, and entry into the most holy place was permitted only one day a year to the high priest. While the descriptions down to the details of posts and rings are many, the meaning of all these trappings is not given explicitly or at great length.

The meaning is given, however, though sadly it is often ignored and fanciful symbolism is given free rein instead. What did the Israelite, confronted in the wilderness by this structure in the midst of the camp, understand about its importance?

The Israelite understood three things primarily, if the designations for the structure are a legitimate clue. The structure was called a tent of meeting, a tabernacle, and a sanctuary. It was a tent of meeting (*ʾōhel mōʿēd*). The location of the tent of meeting outside the camp has led some to believe that there were two irreconcilable accounts of the tent, one in the middle of the camp and another outside. Possibly the tent of meeting described in Exodus 33 was a provisional tent used while the other was in the making. The name "tent of meeting" remained and was attached to the later centrally-placed structure. Here the people's representatives, the priests and Moses in particular, met with Yahweh and Yahweh with them. At the door of the tent of meeting the dispute between Aaron and Miriam and their brother, Moses, was arbitrated (Numbers 12:4). The

instructions about the daily offerings state that it is at the door
of the tent of meeting where the lambs shall be offered morning
and evening, and "where I will meet with you, to speak to you
there" (Exod 29:42). Moses' meeting with Yahweh, so the description runs, was accompanied by the appearance of the pillar
of cloud at the door of the tent. Yahweh spoke to Moses "as one
speaks to his friend" (Exod 33:11). But Yahweh met with his
people also: "I will meet with the Israelites there" (Exod 29:43).
The entire contents of the book of Leviticus are represented as
being delivered to Moses by Yahweh at the door of the tent of
meeting (Lev 1:1). From one reference it appears that individuals also could hear from Yahweh in response to their seeking after him at the door of meeting (Exod 33:7). As the name
implies, the tent of meeting was the place where Yahweh and his
people met.

But the structure had yet a different name which pointed to
yet another understanding of its significance: the name "tabernacle," which translates the Hebrew *miškān*, "dwelling-place."
Yahweh gave instruction: "And have them make me a sanctuary
[the following verses use the word *miškān*], so that I may dwell
among them" (Exod 25:8). "Dwelling" signifies an active sense,
"living with," and is not the word used of ordinary sitting or
staying. When the tabernacle was completed, the signal that
Yahweh had come now to inhabit it was the descent of the glory
cloud (Exod 40:34–38). Through their journeys the cloud had
been evidence of Yahweh's presence. Its covering of the tabernacle was a visible token that Yahweh both honored the construction and took up dwelling in it. Two pieces of furnishing
reinforced the concept of the deity residing there. One was the
ark, which was put in the holy place of the tabernacle not only as
the depository for the law but as part of the throne of God, as
represented by the cover. The second, the table of the bread of
the presence (Exod 25:30), on which were placed the twelve
loaves, was so named to indicate that the tribes were present before the LORD. Understood throughout is the assumption that
Yahweh is also present.

A third designation for the wilderness structure, much less used than the other two, is "sanctuary," a word which translates the Hebrew *miqdāš*. This term derives from "holy" (*qādôš*) and may have come into use because of the two parts into which the facility was divided: the holy place and the most holy place. The designation, like the name given to the rooms, reinforces the notion of holiness or separateness. The sanctuary testifies to the holiness of God not only by its structure; Aaron, the chief minister in its precincts, wore a diadem with the engraving, "Holy to the LORD" (Exod 28:36). God's instructions were, "You shall . . . reverence my sanctuary" (Lev 26:2). The designation *miqdāš* lends an aura of the unapproachable and the distant. Though God was accessible to the people there was enough, including the name, to remind them that this was no ordinary facility. It was set apart and special to Yahweh.

The understanding of the tabernacle as represented by the two terms *miškān* (tabernacle) and *miqdāš* (sanctuary) comes to terms with the knotty problem of divine transcendence as opposed to divine immanence. Christian theologies have fluctuated between a God who is transcendent and distant, and one who is immanent and present. Stress on transcendence means that God is so much above humans that it seems eventually he is beyond reach. By contrast, the view of God as immanent tends to make God so much here and now that it fails to distinguish deity sufficiently from creation. That tension between transcendence and immanence remains, for Israel affirmed both as true, contradictory as it may sound.

The manifestation of Yahweh together with his presence and holiness sums up the theological implications of the tabernacle. It has been tempting for writers to say more than this and to attach to the tabernacle furnishings, for instance, even if typologically, meanings for the separate fixtures. The laver, it has been maintained, demonstrating the necessity of purity for an approach to God, points to the washing of regeneration and sanctification in Christ (Tit 3:5; Heb 9:10). Bread of presence is said to symbolize the reestablishment of harmony and be a type and pledge of closer fellowship with Christ.[6] An immediate

problem in this type of interpretation is that there are no controls or check points to verify the interpretation.[7] The book of
Hebrews is sometimes cited in justification for the method, but
it must be emphasized how restrained the author is, for while he
enumerates the tabernacle divisions and the furnishings he
says, "By this the Holy Spirit indicates that the way into the
sanctuary has not yet been disclosed" (Heb 9:8). The author of
Hebrews views the tabernacle as such as a type, but he does not
see individual parts of it as having typological significance. He
mentions also the impermanence of the arrangement (Heb
9:9–10). In keeping with a more restrained approach we may affirm that the tabernacle has its New Testament counterpart in
Christ, who has come to dwell (tabernacle) among us. In Christ,
God meets the world and its people.

The tabernacle conveys a message about God; so do the
laws. The laws, which went far beyond the cultic, were means by
which Israel might know her God. Frequently, especially in Leviticus 17–26, the so-called Holiness Code, the instructions are
punctuated with "I am the LORD your God." The precise implication of this statement is given: "Speak to all the congregation
of the people of Israel and say to them: You shall be holy, for I
the LORD your God am holy" (Lev 19:2; cf. 11:44; 20:7, 26).

Holiness is sometimes equated with purity or cleanness.[8]
While such an equation is not to be dismissed, it does not gather
up the essential meaning of the word "holy"—for prostitutes
were also said to be "holy." The Hebrew root (qdš) is the same
for "sanctuary" and for "harlot" or temple prostitute. This is
understandable only if we know what lies behind the words.
Scholars are agreed that a key idea wrapped up in "holy" is the
idea of separation, not initially separation from, but a separation to. Someone or something was separated, that is, distinguished from the common, by reason of its specified separation
to deity. Prostitutes at the sanctuary were designated as holy in
the sense that they were consecrated to a deity (1 Kgs 15:12;
2 Kgs 23:7). In the Pentateuch one first meets a form of the
word in Gen 2:3: "God blessed the seventh day and hallowed it"
(i.e., made it holy and separate). A distinction is given to the

Sabbath: it is not to be like the six days; it belongs in a special way to Yahweh.

Yahweh is not the only agent who sanctifies, for priests consecrated themselves and also tabernacle furnishing unto God. To sanctify oneself was to prepare, often by cleansing. Israelites changed their clothes prior to performing a holy act (Exod 19:10); priests bathed in water (Lev 16:4). Moses was told to remove his shoes because the place was holy (Exod 3:5). The tabernacle, the altar, and other objects were sanctified by anointing (Exod 40:9–11). Essentially such acts were preparatory to the formal act of consecration.

The notion of holiness is broadly applied. A catalogue of items to which the adjective "holy" is attached is illuminating. It is applied to everything that is connected with cult: the temple, the furnishings such as ark, table, candlestick, and altar (Num 3:31); priests (Lev 21:6–8); their clothes (Exod 29:29); the sacrifices; days such as the Sabbath and festival seasons (Leviticus 23) and the year of jubilee (Lev 25:12). The Nazirite through a vow separated himself to the LORD (Num 6:2), or is holy (Num 6:5). Even the people of Israel are designated as holy (Exod 19:6). The first-born is holy (Exod 13:12), as are the first fruits of the fields and vineyards (Lev 19:24). All that is given to Yahweh becomes holy (Lev 27:9, 30).

In every instance the idea of holiness is bound up with God, Yahweh. No thing or person is holy in itself. Its holiness derives from being placed in relation to God. Thus a people is holy in the sense that "the man whom the LORD chooses shall be the holy one" (Num 16:7). "For you are a people holy to the LORD your God; the LORD your God has chosen you out of all the peoples on earth to be his people, his treasured possession" (Deut 7:6).

If holiness was the prime message about God that surfaced in the cultic legislation, it was reinforced in the legislation that went beyond the cult. Divine regulation governed virtually every area of the people's life. Holiness was not confined to the tabernacle but extended to daily life, for even sexual regulations were weighted with the refrain, "I am the LORD" (Lev

18:6). What it meant to be holy, consecrated to the LORD, was specified. Sexual defilement came through intercourse with next of kin. Sexual relationships with a neighbor's wife were prohibited. Economic transactions, such as the wages of the servant (Lev 19:13), came into the purview of a holy God's regulation, as did just balances and weights, agricultural practices such as harvesting, customs, or cattle breeding or land use. Health regulations, as for instance those touching leprosy, and dietary rules were specific to the point of exclusion of certain meats such as pork, rabbit, etc. The large and encompassing range of human activities included in the Torah cannot escape even the most casual reader. Holiness reached into all compartments of living.

And yet, while so widely ranging, the legislation is clearly intended, not to provide laws for every possible situation, but to mark limits, borders. These limits are there to mark off a people separated to Yahweh, a people that is holy. The borders are marked off in part in the context of pagan practices: cuttings on the body or tattoo marks on account of the dead are taboo: "You shall not do as they do in the land of Canaan, to which I am bringing you" (Lev 18:3). The seriousness of violating these borders is emphasized by the degree of punishment: excommunication (*kārat*) from the congregation or permanent severance from it, through either ostracism or death. Certain infractions such as offering children to Molech are to be met with instant reprisal: death by stoning (Lev 20:2). Such drastic punishment is necessary because Yahweh's name has been defiled.

What holiness means and implies reaches beyond these two observations, to be sure, but a beginning is made by appreciating the extensive domain of human life governed by the call to holiness, and by recognizing that demarcation lines are intrinsic to the holiness concept.

Even the mention of holiness raises for most people a scene of sobriety, even melancholy. One conjectures that Israel lived with an ever-present consciousness of borders and limits, and that such a lifestyle was necessarily glum and gloomy.

The opposite, however, is true. Knowing Yahweh provided for joy; festivity and celebration were integral to a life with Yahweh.

After all, Israel was instructed to observe three festivals each year. Each, without exception, as will be explained in the next chapter, was an occasion for joy. The festival of unleavened bread followed the spring observance of Passover. Later in the spring or early summer came the festival of first fruits, also a week in length. The feast of booths followed the grape harvest in the autumn. The instruction concerning the last feast is typical: "You shall rejoice before the LORD your God seven days" (Lev 23:40). Knowing Yahweh through the cult must be interpreted, not as a dark and foreboding experience, but rather as joy-creating and joy-bringing.

Knowing God through the cult, namely through worship and religious practice, just as knowing him through historical events, was not an exercise of the intellect alone, for it was not qualities in the abstract that were known. Rather, in very concrete ways, such as in a building, the tabernacle, or through instructions, or in the social gatherings of a festival, Israel participated in life with Yahweh. From these settings she knew Yahweh as present with her, manifested, but always as the Other, holy. She knew Yahweh as a God whose interest penetrated all aspects of her life, but who had established limits, borders, not for the purpose of making life dull or tedious: the festivals testified to the mood in which Yahweh desired Israel to live—joy.

In summary, early Israel knew about God through his activity in nature and among nations. She experienced God more directly in his power and salvation at the exodus, and in an on-going fashion she was led into a life of intimacy with Yahweh in the religious practices enjoined for her.

God's Design: Land

T he Christian can readily identify with the first three statements of God's design as presented in Exod 5:22 – 6:8. It is not
hard to see how God's promise of deliverance of the people
from Egypt corresponds to the liberation of salvation in Christ.
Again, if God says to Israel, "I will take you as my people and I
will be your God," then the Christian applies this formula to the
church. If God's word to ancient Israel is, "You shall know that I
am the LORD your God," then even the less literate believer
may remember John's gospel and epistles which speak of
"knowing." The bridge between the Old Testament and the
New can be almost effortlessly constructed to this point; New
Testament counterparts of the Old can (whether correctly or
not) be identified.

But the Christian is puzzled as to how to identify with the
fourth aspect of divine design: "I will bring you into the land
that I swore to give to Abraham, Isaac, and Jacob; I will give it to
you for a possession" (Exod 6:8). A New Testament connection
can be made, if at all so it seems, only by resorting to fanciful
symbolism.

It is not our concern at this point to articulate the relationship between the two Testaments. Yet it is wholesome to anticipate the direction in which our discussion of land must
eventually go. The land promise is the most difficult of the fourfold aspects of design to relate to the New Testament, but close

attention to the meaning of land in the Old Testament will make the task easier.[1]

A little research will show that theological discussion about land is almost totally absent in the literature until recently. This scarcity of exposition is surprising because "land" is the fourth most frequent noun or substantive in the Old Testament: it occurs 2504 times. Statistically land is a more dominant theme than covenant. True, many occurrences of the word are in keeping with the Semitic practice of referring to another territory such as Egypt not simply as "Egypt" but as "land of Egypt." In this way the country of Egypt as territory is distinguished from its population. But even if these directive uses of "land" are discounted, there is left a large number of occurrences of the word, and that in contexts where its theological significance is unquestioned.

Limiting ourselves to the material in Genesis to Judges, three broad areas require discussion. Two of these surface in the design announcement of Exodus 6. Land is promised: "I will bring you into the land that I swore to give to Abraham, Isaac and Jacob." Land is a gift: "I will give it to you for a possession." A third theological dimension of land arises out of responsibilities, more or less cultic, which are associated with a life-style in the land and which are introduced in Deuteronomy as, "When you come into the land . . ."

1. Land as Promise and Fulfillment

The schema or plot of the literature from Genesis to Joshua is a promise-fulfillment schema. And in this schema, land is a major component. The story of Abraham opens with a promise of land (Gen 12:1ff). Repeatedly confirmed, both to him (13:14–16; 15:18–21; 17:8) and to his descendants Isaac (26:3–4, 24) and Jacob (28:3–4, 13–15; 35:9–12), the promise is taken up in Yahweh's speech to Moses in Exod 6:8 and elsewhere in the course of the wilderness journey (e.g., Exod 33:1). By Joshua's time the promise of land is no longer a promise but a reality (Josh 23:15). For convenience we can discuss land in the schema first as promise and then as fulfillment.

Certain promises to the patriarchs mention only land, whereas in others the land promise is combined with one or more promises. The most forthright promise of land is found in Yahweh's speech to Abraham: "To your offspring I will give this land" (Gen 12:7). Another statement is phrased like the exodus language: "I am the LORD, who brought you from Ur of the Chaldeans, to give you this land to possess" (Gen 15:7). The verification of this promise is supplied in an ancient ceremony: the slaughter and cutting in two of a heifer, a goat, a ram, and some birds, the parts being laid across from each other to form an aisle through which the torch, representing Yahweh, moves. The ritual, known to us from other ancient Near Eastern documents, signifies: "May the fate of the animals be the fate of the promise-maker if the promise is not kept." By such an oath God binds himself to the promise. The account concludes: "On that day the LORD made a covenant with Abram, saying, 'To your descendants I give this land . . .'" (Gen 15:18). It is a sworn promise. There is no specific word in the Hebrew language that means solely "to promise." The English "promise" is a translation in proper contexts of "to say" or "to speak."

The verb most frequently connected with Yahweh's intention to give the land to Israel is "to swear" (šbʿ), and so as one scholar says: "The 'sworn land' would be a more accurate rendering than the 'promised land.'"[2] Abraham refers to the promise when he says to his servant: "The LORD, the God of heaven . . . spoke to me and swore to me, 'To your descendants I will give this land'" (Gen 24:7). It is this promise of land, repeated to Jacob (Gen 48:4), which Joseph cites at his death and which sets the stage for the next act, the exodus, which in turn aims at the realization of the promise.

But the land promise, while sometimes given in isolation, is also interlaced with other promises, chiefly of descendants (Gen 13:14–16; 26:4; 27:3; 35:9–12). Typical of these is the report by Jacob: "God Almighty appeared to me at Luz in the land of Canaan, and he blessed me, and said to me, 'I am going to make you fruitful and increase your numbers; I will make of you a company of peoples, and will give this land to your offspring after you for a perpetual holding'" (Gen 48:3–4). Such a promise echoes the initial word to Abraham when he was called by God out of Ur, "I will make of you a great nation" (Gen 12:2). It is a promise that, in view of Sarai's barrenness and advanced age, is not readily believable, unless one also believes that with God all things are possible. Isaac, the carrier of that promise, is reassured by God, "I will make your offspring as numerous as the stars of heaven, and will give to your offspring all these lands" (Gen 26:4). The promise for descendants and the promise of land are complementary. Numerous descendants need living space; a land needs occupants. From the first, then, people and land belong together; both belong to Yahweh.

Occasionally the promise of blessing or of God's promise to be their God is found either in conjunction with the descendants (Gen 12:1–3; 22:17; 26:24) or with both land and descendants (Gen 17:4–8; 28:13–15). It is this combination of promise of descendants and land, and that within a covenant relationship with Yahweh, that distinguished Yahweh's act of bringing Israel into the land from that of bringing the Philistines out of Caphtor to their land and the Syrians out of Kir to their land (Amos 9:7). Both the Philistines and the Syrians were without divine promise of territory; whereas to Israel God committed himself in a promise.

The fulfillment of the promise is a climax in the story of the patriarchs and early Israel. Certainly entry into the land at Jericho, if not already the earlier takeover of the lands of Moab and Ammon, represents this fulfillment of the promise. With the conquest Israel as Abraham's descendants occupied the land which had once been promised to Abraham. The Israelite confessed that the promise had been fulfilled when, appearing at the sanctuary, the worshiper testified: "He brought us into this place" (Deut 26:9).[3]

Yet from another angle the precise fulfillment point is not so neatly established, since the descriptions of the land's border in the promise varied, and Israel during its occupancy of the land had control at different times over different land masses. In the ritual of the slaying of the animals, the extent of the land is given as "from the river of Egypt to the great river, the river Euphrates" (Gen 15:18). The river of Egypt is commonly held to be, not the Nile, but a wadi or seasonal river flowing into the Mediterranean midway between the mouth of the Nile on the west and the plain of the Philistines on the Mediterranean coast to the east. In another passage the boundaries are from the Red Sea to the Mediterranean and from the wilderness to the Euphrates (Exod 23:31ff). A detailed but smaller area is described in Num 34:1–10. Similar but defined more generally are the boundaries in Deut 11:24 and Josh 1:2–4: "From the wilderness and the Lebanon as far as the great river, the river Euphrates"; or the territory is referred to even more simply as the land of the Canaanites (Exod 3:17; Num 34:2) or Amorites (Deut 1:7). It appears that the land was never defined with geographical precision; one might even say it was to some degree an idea. Yet it was a territory.

Not only was the promise inexact as to boundaries and area, but the fulfillment of it took place by degrees. While with the earlier conquest under Joshua it could be properly said that the promise was fulfilled, it was only in the reign of David and Solomon that Israel possessed the large expanse mentioned in Exod 23:31—the additional territory later in Israel's history meant a more rounded or complete fulfillment of the promise. Perhaps the promise was so structured in the first place that an exhausting of the promise was not immediately likely. How can the exact fulfillment of blessings promised by God be calculated? How many descendants must there be for the promise of the multiplied descendants to be regarded as fulfilled? And perhaps the land boundaries were sufficiently indistinct that some flexibility was possible. While still in Ur, Abram was promised a land. His mere arrival in Canaan did not fill up the promise. The promise was reiterated and clarified, even though Abram could correctly claim (even if in a limited sense) that the promise was fulfilled. More compelling was Joshua's claim at a later time that the promise had been fulfilled and that not a word had failed of all that Yahweh had spoken (Josh 23:14). A still more complete fulfillment came in David's time, when the extent of conquered territory corresponded more exactly to the larger borders given in the promise.

The theological significance of the promise-fulfillment schema becomes apparent by making a threefold comparison of the land promise with (1) the ancient Near Eastern notions of deity and land-holding, (2) the promise for multiplied progeny, and (3) the larger promise-fulfillment schema in the Old Testament. Nations surrounding Israel described their relation to their land and deity in terms quite different from Israel. In Babylon the holy city was venerated because in its creation myth a group of lesser deities built a temple and temple tower in gratitude to Marduk for his victory in the divine struggle. Babylon was Marduk's city. As to the city's origins, its residents pointed back to myth. In imaginative ways, expressed poetically, they elaborated stories about beginnings rooted in neither territorial space nor time.

Likewise in Egypt, Thebes was the holy center because it was "the honorable hill of the Primeval beginning, the beneficent eye of the Lord of all, his beloved place."[4] But in Israel there are no such myth-like stories about the land. Here one does not base a claim to territory on a direct link with deity outside space and time. Instead it is a word by Yahweh, which in the course of time comes true, that causes Israel to occupy her land. A promise is given in the life of a people, in history. That promise is fulfilled in the life of the people in history. The link with the land is forged in the sphere of history, not myth.

A second comparison of the land promise is profitably made with the promise of descendants, to which it is closely associated. In each, because of obstacles, the promise faces difficulties on the way to fulfillment. For Sarai the obstacle is barrenness and so descendants are unlikely; as for the land promise, the obstacle in the way of fulfilling the promise is that Israel is a captive people in Egypt, and moreover, the Canaanites, Perizzites, Jebusites and others are in the promised land. It is not at once transparent how these obstacles will be overcome.

But on the way to the fulfillment there are miracles; the miracle of conception for Sarai who is beyond child-bearing age, and the miracle for Israel of the parting of the Sea and the river Jordan, as well as the defeat of the Canaanites at Jericho and elsewhere. Both promises are put in jeopardy by hasty or ill-advised actions: Abram takes Hagar, begets Ishmael and puts Sarai in danger at Pharaoh's court; the Israelites first balk at entering the land at Kadesh-barnea and then in ill-timed enthusiasm invade the land, only to be roundly defeated. But in either event, though the promise is jeopardized, it is not paralyzed. In each promise there is a time lag between the initial word (and in both cases it is nothing more at the beginning than a word) and the realization. Years elapse before Isaac, the son of the promise, is born; centuries pass before Abraham's descendants ultimately settle in the land. Both promises also, as we noted, are open-ended with respect to the precise points of fulfillment.

The promise of land, as well as other Yahweh promises, present us with an opportunity to track a promise from its initial word to its fulfillment. Such an exercise yields a variety of insights, among them the observation that frequent fulfillments of these promises punctuate Israel's history. Moreover, the components of a promise, even when given at a single point in history, teach fulfillment stages at differing rates. The accompanying table suggests how one might follow the trajectory of a promise. The last column in the chart is definitely not the last word about the promise.

In assessing the theological significance of the land promise and its fulfillment we must note that the promise of land is part of a larger promise-fulfillment schema in the Bible. God's promise to David of a dynasty is followed with interest by the author of the book of Kings. That promise of a perpetual set of rulers presupposes a territory over which they are to rule. Following the expulsion of Israel from that territory there are promises of a restoration. Ezra and Nehemiah tell the story of how this restoration came about. Beyond this the promise of a deliverer, the Messiah, took increasingly detailed shape: Bethlehem was a town in the promised land, the people walking in darkness who were to see a great light were in the land of Galilee (Isa 9:1ff). The New Testament often documents fulfillment of Old Testament promises. The land promise as a small circle takes its place within the larger circle of promise-fulfillment.

2. Land as Gift

The Exodus text which specifies that land is a promise also describes it as a gift: "I will give it to you for a possession" (Exod 6:8). The connection between the promise of land and the gift is a close one, of course (cf. Deut 1:7; 6:10, 23) for to the promise to bring Israel to the land there is added the statement that the land itself is a gift.[5]

In Deuteronomy, according to one count, assertions about the land as gift occur thirty times (e.g., 5:31; 9:6; 11:17; 12:1; 15:7, 20; 26:9). One reason for the recurrence of this theme, judging by the context, is that it emphasizes the free act of grace on Yahweh's part. Israel brought nothing to the situation that precipitated God's action. The initiative was with God and arose out of God's love for his people. Their election and the accompanying gift of territory is explained as follows: "He (Yahweh) loved your ancestors . . . to bring you in, giving you their land for a possession" (Deut 4:37–38). The land, its vineyards, its olive trees, its cities, came into Israel's possession without Israel on her part planting vineyards or olive trees or building cities (Deut 6:10). Israel could not say: "My power and the might of my own hand have gotten me this wealth" (Deut 8:17). Any hint of Israel meriting the land is discounted. The opposite is true: Israel deserved to forfeit even what she had. Israel's disqualification is singled out, in fact, so that against her unworthiness the gift aspect stands in bolder relief: "Know, then, that the LORD your God is not giving you this good land to occupy because of your righteousness; for you are a stubborn people" (Deut 9:6). The land is totally a gift.

But an associated idea is also present. Israel cannot take the land or grasp it. The land is beyond her power to acquire. It can

Tracking a Promise

Cluster of Promises Gen 12:1–3	Announced	Confirmed	Jeopardized	Fulfilled	Threatened/Lost	Regained
Land	Gen 12:1, 7	Gen 15:18	Presence of Canaanites, etc., Gen 15:19. Kadesh battle, Num 14:39–45	Josh 23:14	Exile 586 BC	Return under Zerubbabel, 538 BC
Posterity	Gen 12:2	Gen 15:1–17 Gen 17:1–8	Wife/sister incident, Gen 12; 20; 26	Gen 21:2 Exod 1:17	Isaac offered, Gen 22:1ff. Population control, Exod 1:15ff	Isaac spared, Gen 22:12; cf. Heb 11:17–19. A large "nation," Num 1–2
Blessing	Gen 12:3	Gen 14:19–20 Melchizedek's blessing	Shechem incident Gen 34:1ff.	Joseph's service in Egypt, Gen 37–50	Israel's disobedience, Judg 2:11ff.	Davidic/Solomonic empire Jesus Christ

be hers only as a gift. The land will be hers as gift or will not be hers at all. Two examples make this point emphatically. At Kadesh-barnea, Israel, rebuked for faithlessness, proceeds in willfulness apart from Moses and without the presence of the ark of the covenant to move into the land. But the enemies beat her down (Num 14:39–45). She is unable to seize the gift, but is fully dependent on the Giver, even as to the time when she may possess her gift. The second example, the attack on Ai, is further proof that Israel cannot secure her gift by her own power. There, as at other instances in the conquest, the victory is given by Yahweh. Disregard of basic stipulations spells paralysis. Even after the conquest her relationship to the land is dependent on Yahweh, for Yahweh remains the donor.[6]

Yahweh remains the donor because he was and remains the owner. The clearest expression of Yahweh as the title-deed holder is made in conjunction with the jubilee-year regulations that the land was not to be sold, "for the land is mine" (Lev 25:23). The implications for Israel of this claim are many, including concepts of stewardship, tithe, and appropriate lifestyle; but the fundamental claim is unmistakable even though the basis for Yahweh's claim is unspecified. Is the land his because of creation? The statement "the whole earth is mine" (Exod 19:5) seems at first to link Yahweh's ownership of the land to his creative act, but the term "earth" is there used with the meaning of populations rather than territory. Abraham responding to Melchizedek's blessing described the LORD God Most High as "maker of heaven and earth" (Gen 14:19). We assume the creation faith undergirded the right of land ownership (cf. Josh 3:11, 13), but specific statements are lacking. In the Bible the issue is not about Yahweh's right to own the land. The issue is one of Israel's right to dwell on the land. But that right is safeguarded for her because Yahweh is the divine proprietor. Israel is described as "strangers and sojourners with me" (Lev 25:23)—an assertion that follows directly after the claim, "The land is mine." Their sojourning status is not intended to minimize Israel's right to the land. "With me" may well mean "under my protection." The stranger who was with

the Israelite, possibly employed, was under the protection of
the Israelite (Exod 12:48; cf. Lev 25:35, 40; Gen 29:14; 1 Chr
4:23; and Judg 17:7–13). Israel's status with Yahweh was similar
to that of an alien with an Israelite. The security of the people in
the land is therefore underscored; they are not at the mercy of
some king or landlord.

Yahweh's gift of the land is further described in somewhat
legal language as an inheritance (*naḥ*ᵃ*lâ*). In one sense the term
"inheritance" refers to allotment. So, for example, the Israelite
tribes were given their territorial areas (Joshua 13–22). Or,
more broadly, the division of the land to each tribe through the
casting of lots is another reminder that Yahweh dispenses the
land. The entire land is Israel's allotment from Yahweh. And
this signifies more than that a portion of territory near the
Mediterranean was designated for Israel. The inheritance represents that which is inalienable, a land from which she cannot
be forcibly removed. Already within the tribes the inalienable
nature of the property was made clear. The special case of Zelo-
phehad's daughters brought this ruling: "No inheritance shall
be transferred from one tribe to another; for each of the tribes
of the Israelites shall retain its own inheritance" (Num 36:9).

The jubilee year in which the encumbered property was returned to the head of households illustrates this understanding
of inheritance as inalienable property. Naboth's refusal even at
the request of the king to sell his land is in keeping with this understanding of the inalienable right of property-holding
(1 Kings 21). It is an impressive fact, though an argument from
silence, that neither in the historical narrative nor anywhere in
the Old Testament is there a case of an Israelite voluntarily sell-
ing land beyond his family group. Levirate regulations account
for the transfer of land (Jeremiah 32 and Ruth); other transfers,
as in post-exilic times, were a mortgage for debt (Neh 5:3). As
yet there is no archaeological evidence of Israelite sale and pur-
chase of land, though there are many such transactions in Canaanite culture. And beyond this, there is not even a provision
in the Old Testament for the sale of land. Land could not be
transferred except to heirs.

In broader usage of the word "inheritance" (*naḥ^ₐlâ*), all of the land of Canaan was a collective inheritance. The entire land was legally secured to Israel from the time of Abraham onward. Scholars have noted that according to oriental law it was possible to transfer land to a man by showing it to him if alongside such gesticulations as pointing there was clear expression of intent.[7] Payment and transfer of deed could come later, but the land was legally in the possession of the beholder from the moment it was pointed out to him. Such a transaction of promise, pointing and viewing, is described in Gen 13:14ff. The inheritance passed by way of the promise to Abraham, Isaac and Jacob and his descendants. Israel might and in fact did lose the land, because of failure on their part to live in the land in loyalty to Yahweh. Yet the land was inalienable in the sense that it could not be forcibly taken from Israel by others.

Israel, however, through disobedience, forfeited the land. Prophets in the exile fell back on the inalienable right of Israel to the land, and announced a return from exile to the land, for, they said, it was rightfully theirs still (Jer 12:14–16; 16:14–15; Ezek 36:8–15). Whatever one may conclude about the relevance of these statements of inheritance and inalienability to modern Israel's possession of the land, it is true, as some have noted, that Theodore Herzel and early participants in the Zionist movement at the beginning of this century lacked theological insight in proposing Argentina or Uganda as a homeland for the Jews.[8] In the teaching of the Old Testament, the land to which Israel had inalienable rights was the land of Israel.

The land was a gift, totally so. Israel could not take it on her own, nor was she entitled because of some intrinsic merit to possess the land. Yahweh was the ultimate owner, and remained so. The land was Israel's as an inheritance and so was intended to remain permanently in the family of Israel.

3. Land as a Blessing

It may go without saying that a gift from the hand of God to his own people would be a desirable and good gift, a blessing. But since this theme is no minor theme in the promise of land, it is worth a closer look. In an earlier promise to Moses, similar to the pivotal text of Exodus 6, Yahweh says: "I have come down to deliver them from the Egyptians, and to bring them up out of that land to a good and broad land, a land flowing with milk and honey . . ." (Exod 3:8). The description of the land as "good" combines "fruitfulness, wealth, beauty—in short, the fullness of the blessing . . . it is the abundantly blessed glorious land."[9]

The meaning of this description of land as blessing can be discerned by looking at a select number of particulars: abundance and rest.

The promised land is a place of great abundance, a land of milk and honey (Num 13:27; Deut 6:3; 11:9). The expression "milk and honey" may hark back to some mythological story about these two products either as the special gifts of gods or else as the favorite, desirable diet of the gods. As used in the Bible the phrase refers essentially to the fertility of the land. In hymnic phrases the land is extolled as

> a good land, a land with flowing streams, with springs and under-ground waters welling up in valleys and hills, a land of wheat and barley, of vines and fig trees and pomegranates, a land of olive trees and honey, a land where you may eat bread without scarcity, where you will lack nothing (Deut 8:7b–9a).

For its richness and desirability it is compared with the land of Egypt, to which it is far superior (Deut 11:10–12). The land was a favored land for "the eyes of the LORD your God are always on it" (Deut 11:12). The land appears as a kind of paradise. It is praised with great enthusiasm. The report of the spies when sent from Kadesh-barnea to investigate the land is not only glowing about the land's productivity, but is accompanied by an exhibit of fruit, among which was a cluster of grapes carried on a pole between two of them (Num 13:21ff).

The promised land represents the blessing of rest. The type of rest is not primarily psychological peace of mind, but a physically oriented rest, a freedom from the harassment of enemies. "Rest" in conjunction with the land is hardly a spiritual rest, as though it were the result of the redemption event. Evidence for this view of rest as physical security, a home, a base, is found in Deuteronomy:

> You have not yet come into the rest and the possession that the LORD your God is giving you. When you cross over the Jordan and live in the land that the LORD your God is allotting to you, and when he gives you rest from your enemies all around so that you live in safety . . . (Deut 12:9–10).

The rest is freedom from harassment of enemies; it is the absence of wandering. The rest speaks of peacefulness and safety. Such rest was not possible in the wilderness where wandering was Israel's lot and where enemy peoples attacked. Such rest is possible only in the land. While some expressions suggest two gifts, the gift of rest and the gift of land, other formulations bring the two together: "Therefore when the LORD your God has given you rest from all your enemies on every hand, in the land that the LORD your God is giving you . . ." (Deut 25:19). Settlement in the land, though that settlement was not without struggle, was tantamount to rest in comparison with the earlier dislocation and refugee style of living (cf. Josh 21:43–44). Joshua recalled the word of Moses to the people: "The LORD your God is providing you a place of rest, and will give you this land" (Josh 1:13). The security from outside interference was a blessing, which while itself a gift, was a gift in association with land. Anticipating a later discussion, we need only now mention that the author of Hebrews refers to the gift of rest and makes an application to Christian experience (Heb 3:7).

4. Land as Demanding a Specific Lifestyle

Human conduct and behavior are understood to have a bearing on land, and conversely, land occupancy demands a particular quality of lifestyle. This association between lifestyle and land is found in scattered references through the books of Leviticus, Numbers, and Deuteronomy; but these references occur in sufficient number to command notice and have shown a point of view that is unique to the Bible. For a glimpse of this association between land and lifestyle we look in turn at moral and cultic responsibilities, specific rules relating to land use, and the cultic festivals which had an agricultural orientation. A discussion of these moral, economic, and cultic regulations will clarify the theological aspects surrounding land.

As to moral, civil, and cultic instructions, their association with the land needs first to be established biblically and then assessed. Various statutes are announced for observance at the time of entry into the land, often introduced by a general statement of which Deut 12:1 is typical: "These are the statutes and ordinances that you must diligently observe in the land that the LORD, the God of your ancestors, has given you to occupy"(cf. 11:31–32; 4:5, 14; 5:31; 6:1). From these statements it is obvious that a prescribed form of conduct is appropriate for life in the land. Thus the land is not only a promise or a gift; fulfilled responsibility is integral to land tenure.

These regulations range broadly. They deal with governance, for they speak to the possibility of the people's desire for a king and give direction for the establishment of a monarchy (Deut 17:14). Cities of refuge are to be established for murderers in the land as a part of the civil-law complex regulating blood revenge (Deut 19:7). Religious and moral instruction in the Torah is to be undertaken in a family setting, and Moses, visualizing a permanent residence, commands that "these words" are to be written on the door posts of the house and on the gates (Deut 6:9). Dietary instructions are also given (Deut 12:20ff). To occupy the land, as in modern occupancy of rental property, a willingness to submit to regulations of the owner is

required. Israel is not at liberty to set its own behavior guidelines. Residence in the land means paying attention to what is
fitting in the land.

But the case for law and land association is stronger than
the words "fitting" or "propriety" indicate. Wrong behavior, for
instance, is not only unbecoming but it defiles the land. Harlotry is forbidden, for example, "that the land not become prosti-
tuted and full of depravity" (Lev 19:29). Shedding of blood
pollutes the land and no expiation for it is possible, except the
death of the murderer (Num 35:29–34). A man who is hanged
for an offense is not to remain on the tree into the night—he
must be buried, for "anyone hung on a tree is under God's
curse. You must not defile the land that the LORD your God is
giving you for possession" (Deut 21:23). Divorce is permitted,
but not the remarriage of the husband to his divorced wife who
has already married another. Not only is such a practice an
abomination before the LORD, but it will "bring guilt on the
land" (Deut 24:4). Marriage and family ethics are not in themselves associated directly with land—yet violations of these
family-related moral and civil regulations are said to defile the
land. In what sense? In the sense that Yahweh dwells in the
midst of the land (Num 35:34). And in another sense also. Land
is the "middle term" between Israel and Yahweh. Land is a tangible symbol of Yahweh. It would not be conceivable that Yahweh could be defiled, therefore the negative consequence could
best be stated by saying that the land will be defiled. So close is
the association between Yahweh and land that an infraction
against Yahweh has the effect of polluting or defiling the land.
The land therefore symbolizes in a forceful way Israel's relationship with Yahweh.

Yet it is not only Israel, to whom the Torah belongs, who defiles the land: the Canaanites who are strangers to the Torah
have by their abominations defiled the land. Israel is cautioned
not to defile herself with such things as child sacrifice, for "by all
these practices the nations . . . have defiled themselves. Thus
the land became defiled" (Lev 18:24–25). Pollution of self and
pollution of land result from unlawful behavior. Even apart

from revelation the non-Israelite should know to abstain from such sexual perversion as bestiality and homosexual activity and from human sacrifice. These evils defile the land. Though they did not possess the Torah, peoples outside Israel are held responsible for their conduct in the land. It is not therefore that the land is rendered impure because of its relation to Israel. Again, it is defiled almost in its own right, or, perhaps more accurately, because of the close relationship of the land to Yahweh.

The case for the interdependence between moral behavior and land is even stronger than the preceding discussion has suggested. There is more to be said than that obedience to Yahweh is fitting in the land and that disregard of Yahweh's instruction defiles the land. Continued occupancy of the land is itself conditioned by observance of the law. This means on the one hand that by faithful adherence to the admonitions, Israel can continue in the land. Motivation for such observance of law includes the promise of continued residence: "This entire commandment that I command you today you must diligently observe, so that you may live and increase, and go in and occupy the land" (Deut 8:1). Moses says: "Justice and only justice you shall follow, that you may live and inherit the land which the LORD your God gives you." Obedience to the law brings blessings, which, as the catalogue of blessing indicates, are primarily prosperity and fruitfulness in the land (Deut 28:1–14).

But if blessing follows obedience, curse within the land and even deportation from it will result from disobedience (Deut 28:15–68). Lack of rain, defeat by enemies, internal confusion, and disease are only a few of the disasters which may be expected, and the ultimate disaster, apart from ruin, is that "you shall be plucked off the land . . . The LORD will scatter you among all peoples" (Deut 28:63–64). Again, such drastic treatment as removal from land is not reserved only for a people like Israel with a revealed Torah. It was because of the sinfulness of the Canaanites that they were expelled from the land (Lev 18:24). Indeed, so much are these infractions directly against the land that the land personified is described as vomiting out Canaanites (Lev 18:24). The threat for Israel too is that unless she keeps the statutes and the ordinances, the land may vomit up the people in it (Lev 20:22–26). By this one is to understand that violation of norms is so reprehensible that, quite apart from Yahweh's displeasure, the land itself cannot tolerate them: the land will spew out the population.

It may seem at first glance that the stipulations accompanying the gift of the land make the land not altogether a gift. A few passages indeed give the impression that obedience to God's ordinance was a condition of entry into the land (e.g., Deut 8:1). But these are not to be understood as qualifying people in a fundamental sense for the gift; rather they are to be taken, as are the many statements cautioning Israel lest through disobedience they forfeit the right to continue on the land, as accompanying the gift. To a gift, even a gift totally the result of grace, there is not inconsistently attached stipulation for its use. A British company director who at his death left £33,000, specified that £5,000 be given to each of his two grandchildren—provided they did not spend the money on motorcycles. This twentieth-century example, while not the norm for interpreting ancient Israelite practice, may still illustrate the basic principle that a gift may have conditions. The land gift was unique in that Yahweh remained the owner. Yahweh disposed of it, but not in a final sense by giving it over to Israel. As the proprietor of the land, Yahweh's right to make stipulations, along with his claim to Israel, is everywhere assumed. Life in the land can continue provided a certain lifestyle, one marked by obedience, is maintained.

The subject of lifestyle is far too large to survey with any depth, but the regulations about land use can move us from generalities to specifics and can illustrate the tenor of conduct pleasing to Yahweh.

Sabbath and Jubilee

Two regulations dealt with land use: the Sabbath and the jubilee. From Mount Sinai Moses issued this instruction: "When you enter the land that I am giving you, the land shall observe a

Sabbath for the LORD" (Lev 25:2; cf. 23:10–11). By this, as the explanation which follows shows, is meant that whereas for six years the land is to be sown and vineyards cultivated, in the seventh it is to be fallow. There is to be no seeding of the land, and vineyards are not to be pruned, nor is there to be reaping of that which grows by itself. The practice of leaving the land fallow for the purpose of rejuvenation was not uncommon among Israel's neighbors. The reason for such a practice in Israel, however, takes a decidedly different shape. The sabbatical year is for the benefit of the poor and for the benefit of wild life, "that the poor of your people may eat, and what they leave the beasts may eat." This purpose could be achieved if for individual farmers the seventh year came at different times. In Leviticus there is assumed a universal and uniform observance of the fallow year. But the purpose, while humanitarian, is not exclusively so. A religious motivation is announced in the terminology, "a Sabbath for Yahweh." The land, by being left fallow, bears witness to Yahweh's ownership. The direct link between Yahweh and land is left intact; the land's rest is not disturbed by human intervention of tilling.

It is argued by some scholars that Deut 15:1–3 couples a regulation about the release of all debts every seven years to the command to fallow the land. While complicated in details, Deut 15:1–3 is best considered not as a cancellation of debts generally but as a case where land was mortgaged to a creditor. In the seventh year the creditor was not to demand annual payment of the land's harvest. This provision, also humanitarian, allowed the debtor some hope of meeting his obligations. If a loan were taken in the sixth year and not fully paid, it would not be payable till after the harvest of the eighth year, thus giving the impoverished Israelite an extended period of credit. The Sabbath for the land was for Yahweh (Lev 25:2) and the practice of charity to the debtor was also performed before Yahweh (Deut 15:2). The Sabbath regulation, while clearly given as an obligation unto Yahweh, pointed two ways: to the land, and to the debtor whose land had been encumbered. Failure to observe these statutes is given as reason for drastic action of God's removal of people from the land (Lev 26:32–33, 43; 2 Chr 36:21).

A second ordinance that dealt especially with land use is the jubilee. The instructions about jubilee also require that the land be left fallow, not only every seven years but during the fiftieth year, namely after seven sevens of years (Lev 25:8ff). It was unlike the seventh fallow year in that in the jubilee year the land was to revert to the family that originally claimed ownership. An impoverished Israelite, once he had mortgaged his land and his crops, might find it necessary to "sell" the land to his creditor, and even if a relative redeemed it, the unfortunate Israelite would still in all likelihood be working it for the benefit of his kinsman (Lev 26:36ff). The purpose of the kinsman provision was to retain the land within the particular family of the clan; otherwise descendants of the unfortunate Israelite would be condemned to be property-less. The jubilee year, coming every

God and Israel's Land

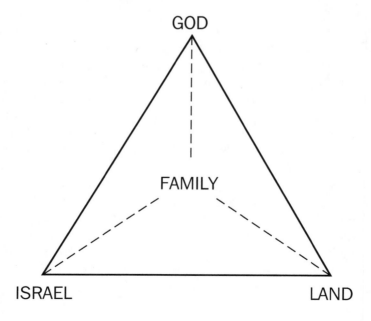

few generations, was to remedy this eventuality, for in the jubilee year, even had the land remained in the clan through redemption, it was now to be returned to the particular family within the clan.

The jubilee year also had provisions for the release of slaves. It is therefore clear that the regulations of the jubilee affected the economic life of a people by demanding magnanimous action by the well-to-do for the benefit of the less capable or unfortunate man. Without such a provision as a jubilee, territories of a clan could come into the hands of a few families, and the remaining clans people would be serfs. The jubilee aimed at the preservation of household units, ensuring their economic viability. The land belonged inalienably to the householder. This right of the household landowner to regain his property was not due to some belief about the right of property per se, but a belief in land as a gift from Yahweh, whose regulation stabilized the people's relationship with each other and with their God. It is not hard to see that in the Old Testament, land, Israel and Yahweh belonged together, and that in this triad the rights of the family were particularly safeguarded.[10]

Festivals

With such agricultural practices as the Sabbath year and the jubilee year, a lifestyle characterized by non-exploitation of land and of people was inculcated. A considerate and caring attitude was encouraged.

In addition a set of festivals, primarily agricultural, established yet another orientation and lifestyle attitude: thanksgiving and joy. Instructions about these festivals appear in each of the four law books (Exodus 23; 34; Leviticus 23; Numbers 28; Deuteronomy 16).

All of the three major annual festivals, each a week long, were held in connection with the harvest from the field. The festival of unleavened bread was held in the spring of the year immediately following the Passover observance. Scheduled for the beginning of the barley harvest in late April/early May, its important feature was the baking and eating of unleavened bread. The bread of the harvest was deliberately not prepared with yeast, so that the firstfruits would be eaten untouched by a foreign element. The second festival, called a feast of harvest in the book of Exodus but more commonly a feast of weeks (Deut 16:10), came fifty days after the sickle was first put to the spring grain. It was observed at the end of the wheat harvest, corresponding to our month of June. At this time the firstfruits of the farmer's labor were presented before Yahweh. Either the whole crop, the first of several in the agricultural year, or the firstfruits of the barley grain harvest preserved from their first cutting to the end of the season, were brought to the sanctuary. The third agricultural festival was the feast of ingathering, known also as the feast of booths or tabernacles, because of a provision that during the week people should live in tents. This festival followed the day of atonement in the month of October, and centered on the harvest of fruits, especially olives and grapes.

Though agrarian-based, these festivals were not pagan orgies. They were religious occasions. In all three, males of the country were to present themselves at the sanctuary. Although social in character, with feasting and celebration, these were more than social events. The festivals were festivals "to Yahweh." The religious orientation emerged in the presentation of animal offerings to Yahweh and also in the gift of firstfruits of the grain and fruit to Yahweh. The detailed instruction for such a presentation of agricultural produce is given in Deut 26:1, and, while given for the particular occasion of the very first harvest, the instruction may also have been ritually applied, especially at the feast of weeks and the feast of ingathering.

At these festivals the Israelite was not to appear before Yahweh empty-handed (Exod 34:20; 23:15). The worshiper with the produce in the basket would appear before the priest and say: "Today I declare to the LORD your God that I have come into the land that the LORD swore to our ancestors to give us" (Deut 26:3). After rehearsing the history of his people, with emphasis on Yahweh's grace to them, he concluded with the words: "So now I bring the first of the fruit of the ground that you, O

LORD, have given me" (Deut 26:10). The priest either set the basket before the altar (Deut 26:4) or waved the sheaf before Yahweh (Lev 23:10–11, 20). The character of the festival as a festival to Yahweh was safeguarded through this ritual at the sanctuary in which through word and act Yahweh was acknowledged. The worshiper expressed personal thankfulness and gratitude to Yahweh.

Now it is highly significant that the speech the worshiper made at the presentation of the offering is a rehearsal of the deeds of Yahweh in history. The dedication of the produce was motivated by recognition of Yahweh not so much as creator, but as deliverer. It was not as a creature who enjoys the yield of creation that the worshiper came before Yahweh, but as one who had experienced deliverance from oppression. One's personal history was a history of salvation, and here the land is remarkably in focus. The ailing forefather Jacob migrated to Egypt with but a small family and without land. The population in Egypt had no land they could call their own. But now, the worshiper concluded, Yahweh had brought them into the land.

The pagan worshiper by contrast addressed a god related to nature, from whom he expected the benefits of fertility in field, flock, and family. But in Israel these ideas of God so closely and so exclusively associated with nature are absent. While Yahweh is a God of nature, and is so celebrated in the Psalms, Yahweh is a God of history; and his connection with the land is not only or even primarily as a God who makes it fertile, but as one who in response to a promise has brought his people to enjoy the abundance that the land offers. To this God of history, the worshiper offered thanksgiving.

Judged by the instruction in Deuteronomy, the festivals, while foremost festivals for Yahweh, were also festivals for the people. The males appeared at the sanctuary but the festivals involved all—sons and daughters, servants and Levites. The fatherless and widow are singled out for special mention, but, more arresting from a sociological point of view, the sojourner was also to participate in the celebrations (Deut 26:11, 14). These celebrations were not to become exclusivist—the non-

Israelite was to be included. The festivals, related so closely to the land, display, as did the land use regulations, a humanitarian concern. Israel was to recall that she had been a slave in Egypt (Deut 26:12). Love to God and love to neighbor came to expression in the festivals.

Finally, the mood of the three-week-long annual festivals deserves mention. "Rejoice before the LORD your God" (Deut 16:11). "Rejoice during your festival" (Deut 16:14). "You shall rejoice before the LORD your God for seven days" (Lev 23:40). The imperative to rejoice, like the imperative to love, while strange, nevertheless indicates the basic posture for the Israelite. Philo, the Jewish philosopher-exegete of the first century AD, described even the day of atonement as the "feast of feasts." Israelite worship was a worship of joy and praise. In the light of the ancient Near Eastern record and practice, no doubt, one scholar has gone as far as to say, "There is hardly a word so characteristic of the Old Testament as the word joy."[11] Festivals, as ordered by Yahweh, were an expression of this joyful mood.

Land, then, is more than acreage or territory. It is a theological symbol, through which a series of messages are conveyed. It is the tangible fulfillment of the promise. Land is a gift from Yahweh, and Israel, through preoccupation with it, has her attention continually called to Yahweh. Land requires a specific and appropriate lifestyle. Responsibilities concerning social behavior are enjoined upon the people for the time when they will occupy the land, and they are warned that disobedience defiles the land and may result in loss of their privilege of tenancy. The specific regulations about land use, such as the sabbatical year and jubilee, take ecological and humanitarian concerns into account. Finally the festivals, associated with the production from the land, once again link land and Yahweh, point to social responsibilities, and portray the joyful spirit in which this people lives its life on the land, always before Yahweh.

But if land is more than acreage or territory and symbolic of promise, gift, blessing, and lifestyle, it is nevertheless still soil and territory. It has theological aspects, but it is not thereby an ethereal thing, nor should it be spiritualized. Land is real. Earth is spatially definable. Life with Yahweh takes place here and now. The quality of that life is all-embracing—it relates to Yahweh, to neighbor, to environment. Life with Yahweh cannot be compartmentalized, as though Yahweh's interest lies only within a small area. No, his interest extends to the total person and to the total society and to the total environment. Yahweh is misrepresented, and his people's life misshapen, if the wholeness of life is not emphasized. The promise of land and all that it signifies keeps the entire design rooted in history and is thoroughly reality-related. We shall find the this-worldly and earth-affirming aspect strong and marked once again in the wisdom literature, especially in Proverbs. In the New Testament, the concept of discipleship is equally all-embracing.

Part 3

God's Design Tested

The Era of the Monarchy

Prologue

Hos 2:14–23

Earlier chapters have described God's design for Israel as one which incorporated deliverance, covenant, experiential relationship, and the blessings of abundance. This fourfold purpose is clearly and programmatically stated at the beginning of Israel's national history (Exod 5:22 – 6:8). Whenever a design is implemented, whether from an artist's sketch or from a builder's blueprint, its workability is put to the test. From the vantage point afforded by history we may survey the implementation of God's design in Israel's life. Since God's design is one which gives people a good measure of freedom, the path of progress toward the goal is not uniformly paced or even straight. Rather than to follow step by step the history of Israel, we will content ourselves with a synoptic view of two periods: the monarchy and the exilic/post-exilic period.

From the standpoint of history, as presented by the Old Testament itself, Israel moved from Egypt after years of wilderness wandering into the land of Canaan. Under Joshua much of the land, but not all, was brought under the control of the Israelite people. The period of the judges was marked by repeated cycles of spiritual apostasy, crises of subjugation by an alien power, cries of desperation for help, and deliverance by God through the agency of a judge, or leader. Eventually the people called for a new system of governance; they wanted a king. With the inauguration of Saul as king, there began a new era in the nation's history. With the collapse of the divided kingdoms, Israel and Judah, in 722 BC and 586 BC, the story of the people continued in the context of exile. Later, however, Israel returned to her land, but not any more to be under the rule of kings.

Theologically, one can see the Old Testament as a drama in three acts. In the first the characters of the drama and their situation are presented. In the second act the developing conflict between God's purpose and the reality of a people's life is explored; and the third tells how the conflict is resolved. Having established in part 2 the cast of characters and the line of action, we will look in part 3 at the tension points which arise as God leads his people toward fulfillment of his purpose.

The period under review is the Israelite monarchy, which stretches for 400 years, from approximately 1000 to 600 BC. It encompasses the time of the united monarchy and the subsequent two kingdoms Israel and Judah, and thus includes kings from Saul, the first king, to Zedekiah, the last king of Judah. For Israel, prophets are as important during this period as are kings. Non-writing prophets, including Samuel, Elijah, and Elisha, confront kings, and so do the writing prophets Isaiah, Amon, and Jeremiah. In addition to the prophetic corpus, literary works by the wisdom teachers such as Proverbs belong to this period.

How does God's design fare in this significant era of Israelite life? Basically it is put to the test and challenged at several points. As first enunciated and demonstrated, deliverance came through Yahweh's activity in the holy war. But in the monarchy period, while Yahweh's help along the lines of holy war was occasionally apparent, the pattern of holy war was supplanted by the standing army. Under David, wars of conquest were waged in which skill and weaponry were factors larger than faith and reliance on God. As for the covenant, the relationships with Yahweh were strained, eventually to the breaking point. Instead of being a people of whom it could be said, "Their God is Yahweh," Israel fell victim to the temptation to give allegiance to Baal, and the prophets complained, "Israel has forgotten and forsaken Yahweh." God's intention was for Israel to know him, a knowledge which included the adventurous experience by Israel of God's presence and activity. The prophets lamented, "There is . . . no knowledge of God in the land" (Hos 4:1). The gift of the land, with its abundant blessings, was a gift which was suspended, so to speak, for Israel in 722 BC and for Judah, the southern kingdom, in 586 BC, when people were removed from the land and taken into exile. Yet between the pure ideal of God's design and the utter failure to realize the design there were times in the course of the four centuries when Israel, even if for a brief while, approximated to God's intention.

Before the checkered progress of Israel relative to the divine intention is surveyed in greater detail, it is prudent to anchor our approach textually to establish the elements of God's design toward which progress is to be made. As in part 1 we examined a key passage, Exod 5:22 – 6:8, so here the elements of God's design need to come into sharp focus before description and assessment of progress can be made. The scripture which further sets forth the divine intention is found in Hosea, who together with Amos is the first of Israel's literary prophets. Writings from earlier prophets have not been preserved, but these eighth-century prophets recall, among other things, the foundations of Israel's life.

> [14]Therefore, I will now allure her,
> and bring her into the wilderness,
> and speak tenderly to her.
> [15]From there I will give her her vineyards,
> and make the Valley of Achor a door of hope.
> There she shall respond as in the days of her youth,
> as at the time when she came out of the land of Egypt.

[16]On that day, says the LORD, you will call me, "My husband," and no longer will you call me, "My Baal." [17]For I will remove the names of the Baals from her mouth, and they shall be mentioned by name no more. [18]And I will make for you a covenant on that day with the wild animals, the birds of the air, and the creeping things of the ground; and I will abolish the bow, the sword, and war from the land; and I will make you lie down in safety. [19]And I will take you for my wife forever; I will take you for my wife in righteousness and in justice, in steadfast love, and in mercy. [20]I will take you for my wife in faithfulness; and you shall know the LORD.

²¹On that day I will answer, says the LORD,
I will answer the heavens
and they shall answer the earth;
²²and the earth shall answer the grain, the wine, and the oil,
and they shall answer Jezreel;
²³and I will sow him for myself in the land.
And I will have pity on Lo-ruhamah,
and I will say to Lo-ammi, "You are my people";
and he shall say, "You are my God."

In this passage, Hos 2:14–23 (vv. 16–25 in Hebrew), there is given an announcement of what God will do in the new age. It is a statement which recalls Exod 5:22 – 6:8, though it is given in different circumstances. These verses bring to a conclusion a diatribe or argument between God and Israel. Israel has been rebuked for her alliance with Baal, the Canaanite fertility God. Using the picture language of adultery, God has charged Israel with leaving her first commitment and going after Baal, in the delusion that grain, wine, and oil come as gifts from Baal (Hos 2:5–13). The poem describing the spiritual harlotry is sand-wiched between two narrative accounts of the marriage of Hosea and Gomer. Hosea has been instructed to take Gomer, a woman who eventually becomes a prostitute, for his wife. She bears three children whose names, symbolic of the message of God, are given in Hosea 1, but which reappear in the poem at the end of chapter 2, securely linking poetry and narrative, as interpretation is linked to parable.

In form Hos 2:14–23 consists of four segments. The first is a stanza of general announcements introduced by "Therefore" and thus linked to the immediately preceding verses of judg-ment. This opening announcement (2:14–15) with the use of participle is followed by three oracles characteristically marked with the formula "On that day" (vv. 16, 18, 21). Each of the four sections includes statements of Yahweh's initiative. The tense of the verbs is future, calling attention to what God will do. Each contains descriptions of that intervention. Except for the first statement of consequence (v. 15c, d), which is elaborated slightly, these statements, always at the conclusion of a segment, describe the result of God's action in a short, almost cryptic way, e.g., "And you shall know the LORD" (vv. 20; cf. 17b, 23d). In content these ten verses are dominated by the covenant idea presented under the imagery of a marriage. The announcements of salvation open with courtship language: "I will allure (literally, 'seduce,' 'persuade') her . . . and speak tenderly (literally, 'to the heart') to her" (v. 14). In a future day, the second stanza continues, Israel will call God her husband and no more "my Baal." While "Baal" can mean lord, and was used of a husband in a marriage relationship, the word referred basically to the rights of possession. Such formal, even legal language, was to be replaced by the expression "my husband," a speech form more intimate, reserved apparently for a man who had only one wife. Still, carrying forward the marriage imagery, the third announcement unit (vv. 18–20) singles out betrothal, by which the ancients meant more than "engagement" means in contemporary marriage practice. "I will take you for my wife forever" is equivalent to saying, "I will pay the bridal price and thus remove the last obstacle in the way of our marriage." Betrothal (cf. NASB) virtually seals the marriage. God's betrothal price will be made in the currency of righteous justice, love, loyalty and compassion and faithfulness. These are qualities which God brings to this relationship, though they are intended also to characterize the relationship as such. The final two lines of the announcement are in keeping with the marriage symbol, although formally they represent the formula of covenant, reminiscent of the Sinaitic covenant: "I will say . . . 'You are my people,' and they shall say, 'You are my God'" (v. 23).

A second intention is God's objective of bringing about a life of security and abundance in the land. In the first announcement God says, "From there I will give her her vineyards" (v. 15). The scene pictures the transition from the wilderness into which Yahweh has temporarily brought Israel, to the land of fertility with its vineyards. In the second of the "on that day" oracles, the security in the land is to be accomplished first by God's covenant with beasts, birds, and creeping things, thus averting internal disaster, and secondly by the abolition of bow, sword, and war; Israel will have security from external threats (v. 18). In the last oracle the land motif surfaces once more: "I will sow her (Israel) for myself in the land" (v. 23). This promise is preceded by a reference to prosperity, artistically presented as the result of a chain reaction. God in initiative will activate the heavens. They shall respond to the earth by supplying rain, the earth responds with fertility in producing grain, wine, oil—all for Jezreel, understood as the people of the valley in northern Israel located in the breadbasket area of Israel (2:21-22). A prosperous life in the land is clearly a major strand in the fabric of this announcement.

Two other themes, reminiscent of the design presented in Exod 5:22 – 6:8, are more subdued. Reference to deliverance is apparent in the expression, "And I will . . . make the Valley of Achor (trouble, misfortune) a door of hope" (v. 15). God's deliverance is also in view in the expression, "I will abolish the bow, the sword, and war from the land" (v. 18). The other motif, "knowledge of God," is mentioned but not elaborated: "And you shall know the LORD" (v. 20).

Thus all four design elements—deliverance, covenant, knowledge of God, and land—are represented in this set of announcements, echoing Exod 5:22 – 6:8. As in Exodus, the time of the announcement represents a new stage of God's relation to Israel. Hosea depicts judgment on Israel for its idolatry, but then looks beyond the judgment to a continuance of God fulfilling his design. The use of the covenant formula, modified here to fit dialogue, is similar to that of the Exodus passage. "I will take you to be my people and I will be your God." In Hosea, as in the Exodus passage, the anticipated result is for God's people "to know Yahweh." Reminiscent of the Exodus promise "I will bring you into the land" is the expression, "I will sow him for myself in the land" (v. 23).

Yet the Hosea passage is not an exact repetition of Exodus 6 even though all the motifs are present. Covenant is presented, not in the imagery of international treaty, but in the imagery of marriage. The intimacy of this relationship of Israel with God is especially highlighted. The order in which the design elements are introduced in Hosea differs from that in the seminal passage, but the event of exodus is clearly in the mind of Hosea, "There she shall respond as in the days of her youth, as at the time when she came out of the land of Egypt" (v. 15). It can hardly be accidental that the same four themes, and no others, are itemized for the listeners of the eighth century as the countdown, this time towards judgment, proceeds. With this affirmation of God's purpose given by Hosea we proceed to an analysis of the monarchical period, noting the fortunes of each component in turn.

7

Deliverance

Israel's history is punctuated by many marvelous incidents of divine intervention and deliverance. First and easily chief of these incidents is the exodus. In the period of the monarchy, too, there are dramatic occasions of deliverance (though none on as large a scale as the exodus), as for example the sudden departure from Hezekiah's Jerusalem of Sennacherib's army because of the plague (2 Kings 18–19). Salvation language is prominent during this period crystallized in two dominant motifs: the day of Yahweh, and messianic expectations.

The deliverance of which the prophets speak, using the model of the day of Yahweh and messianic language, is different from the earlier exodus model. The exodus experience of deliverance was historical; the day of Yahweh is primarily eschatological. The exodus experience involved external enemies: the Egyptians were physically oppressing a people. The deliverance of which the prophets spoke, while sometimes of a physical nature, was predominantly a deliverance from interior adverse characteristics and spiritual forces. Isaiah spoke of pride. Amos pointed to disregard of the poor by the affluent. Hosea described idolatry as spiritual adultery. Micah took businessmen, prophets, and priests to task for misuse of office.

Further, at the exodus, the man Moses, a leader and mediator, confronted a Pharaoh; the deliverance was a political event. The vision of the prophet, introduced with the familiar "on that day," did not always require an agent of deliverance. As Joel said, God would display "portents in the heavens and on the earth, blood and fire and columns of smoke. The sun shall be turned to darkness, and the moon to blood" (Joel 2:30–31). The prophets during the monarchy focused on a form of deliverance which was more multidimensional than was the exodus from Egypt. Larger spheres of human experience were being incorporated under the rubric of salvation. Most important, the prophets spoke of deliverance often as post-judgment. The crisis calling for deliverance was a crisis brought on by God's judgment against evil, Israel's evil. One cannot therefore speak of the salvation event without taking into account the judgment against sin which the Hebrew prophets insisted precedes talk about salvation.

1. The Day of Yahweh

The expression "the day of the LORD (Yahweh)" occurs first in Amos.

> Alas for you who desire the day of the LORD! Why do you want the day of the LORD? It is darkness, not light (5:18).

Amos fails to give an explanation of the meaning of "the day of the LORD." One must assume that his audience understood. Judging by Amos's question, the day of Yahweh was understood to be a day of salvation. Yahweh would come on the scene and deal decisively with Israel's enemy so that Israel would be spared. And more, Israel herself would experience the fulfillment of the glorious promises made to her. With such notions about the day of Yahweh, Israel welcomed the day. The message of Amos was that Israel had no reason to welcome that day.

Bible readers and scholars have puzzled about the background of the expression, "the day of Yahweh."[1] If we knew the origin of the concept, we could better appreciate the anticipation that this expression evoked. Out of what setting did it develop? Several settings for the origin of the day of Yahweh have been suggested. One is that the notion of the day of Yahweh derives from the creation account. At creation God was fully in command. Later humankind sinned and creation was marred, but even from the moment of the fall, hope for a change of conditions had been offered. The day of Yahweh would be a time, then, not limited to a twenty-four-hour day but representing a larger time block when the world would be restored to its pristine freshness, the original version as at creation.

A variation on this suggestion for the origin of the day of Yahweh is that the reflection about the Sabbath of the creation week gave rise to the expression, "the day of Yahweh." While the creation account refers to the six days as having evening and morning, the seventh day—the day in which God rested—has no such designation. The inviting prospect of a people experiencing the rest of the first Sabbath was caught in the phrase, "the day of Yahweh." Support for this position can be found in Isaiah where creation allusions (sun, moon, stars, man, beast) are used in conjunction with the day of Yahweh (Isa 13:9–16).

A second suggestion for the origin of the day of Yahweh comes from Scandinavian Old Testament scholars. They, and others too, propose that the worship experiences of Israel, its cult, accounted for the expectation of a future day of Yahweh. According to this view, Israel adopted a pagan festival in which the creation of the world, depicted as involving struggle and conflict, was re-enacted in drama form. In a climactic moment, the king, representing deity, having defeated the foe, was enthroned. The day of Yahweh, following this view, would incorporate the idea of victory for Yahweh in his enthronement and the consequent jubilation of the people, who would anticipate an age of increase and prosperity. Other scholars refuse to build much on the enthronement festival because of fragile documentation for its existence in Israel. They call attention to the cult experience, especially the theophanies, however, as the element that gave rise to the concept of the day of Yahweh. God's demonstrable presence, as in the coming of the glory cloud following Solomon's prayer (2 Chr 7:1), was indicative of the divine intervention. While that intervention could take different forms, including the prophet 's utterance, it signaled the awesome, overpowering presence of Yahweh God, at whose word entire situations could be reversed.

A third proposal for the origin of "the day of Yahweh" is that its background is divine war. In holy war the role of people, while of consequence, was not paramount. The battle outcome was clearly due to God's fighting for his people. Israel could proceed into battle with a small company of 300 men and, with such unlikely weapons as torches and trumpets, win the victory (Judges 7). There was only one hero: none other than God. The day of battle was the day of God, and that meant defeat of the enemy and victory for Israel. The most impressive model of such a war was the exodus. Israel had but to remain still (Exod 14:14). God was warrior (Exod 15:3), deliverer, and king (Exod 15:18). In Israel's tradition, then, reference to the day of Yahweh would evoke good and joyous feelings. While set in conflict and combat, the day of Yahweh was without question a day of victory. As one scholar has saliently put it, the day of Yahweh was "the day monopolized by Jehovah as his day of victory."[2] Of the three suggestions for the origin of the concept, the holy war is the most likely in view of the frequency of military language associated with the day of Yahweh.

The day of Yahweh was traditionally the day of salvation for God's people. Amos, however, by offering a fuller range of meaning, declares that the prospect of Yahweh's day is not a joyous one, but a fearfully ominous one. For Israel the day of Yahweh will be not a day of light, but a day of darkness. Indeed severe calamity will come. In graphic language, he compares Israel's experience to that of a man who flees from a lion, only to be met by a bear, or to one who side-steps the dangers outside his home, only to be bitten by a snake as he leans his hand against a wall inside the house (Amos 5:18–20). Gloom and not brightness is in store for Israel. Because of Israel's sin, which Amos forever emphasizes, the day of Yahweh will mean Yahweh's fighting *against* Israel and not for her. Amos exposes an entirely new wrinkle in the language of "the day of the LORD."

In subsequent prophets the emphasis on judgment rather than salvation continues. Isaiah announces that Yahweh will have a day of reckoning against everyone who is proud and lofty. People will seek out caves in the rocks and attempt to escape the terror of Yahweh (Isa 2:19–21). "The LORD alone will be exalted in that day" (Isa 2:17). More than a century later, the prophet Zephaniah announces Yahweh's fury against "those who have turned back from following the LORD, who have not sought the LORD or inquired of him" (Zeph 1:6). The day of Yahweh will be distress for people who will lose wealth, houses, and see all the earth devoured in desolation, "because they have sinned against the LORD" (Zeph 1:17). It is Zephaniah who particularly graphically writes about the day.

> The great day of the LORD is near,
> near and hastening fast . . .
> That day will be a day of wrath,
> a day of distress and anguish,
> a day of ruin and devastation,
> a day of darkness and gloom,
> a day of clouds and thick darkness,
> a day of trumpet blast and battle cry . . . (1:14a–16a)

Still the salvation and deliverance concepts are present in "the day of Yahweh" language. The judgment of God is dispensed on the basis of righteousness. When God's people persist in their evil, they become targets of God's destructive judgment. But the day of Yahweh, the day in which God comes on the scene, may still be a day of salvation, provided there is repentance. The prophet Joel, whose book has the day of Yahweh for its theme, puts it most eloquently:[3]

> "Yet even now," says the LORD,
> "return to me with all your heart,
> with fasting, with weeping, and with mourning;
> rend your hearts and not your clothing.
> Return to the LORD, your God,
> for he is gracious and merciful,
> slow to anger, and abounding in steadfast love,
> and relents from punishing." (2:12–13)

Joel glimpses the prospect of God's salvation, should repentance be forthcoming. He sees reason for Israel to rejoice.
"The threshing floors shall be full of grain, the vats shall over-
flow with wine and oil . . . and my people shall never again be
put to shame. You shall know that I am in the midst of Israel,
and that I, the LORD, am your God and there is no other" (2:24,
26b–27). There follows the significant passage about God's
spirit being poured out on all mankind: "Your sons and your
daughters shall prophesy, your old men shall dream dreams,
and your young men shall see visions" (2:28). The deliverance
note is clearly sounded: "Whoever calls on the name of the
LORD will be delivered" (2:32, NASB; cf. 3:18–21).

Whereas in Amos it is Israel that is primarily in view in discussions of the day of Yahweh, other prophets hint at a day that
will involve nations. "For the LORD is enraged against all the nations, and furious against all their hoards . . . For the LORD has a
day of vengeance" (Isa 34:2a, 8a). Zephaniah is preoccupied in
the main with the day of the LORD: "'Therefore, as I live,' says
the LORD of hosts, the God of Israel, "Moab shall become like
Sodom and the Ammonites like Gomorrah"" (Zeph 2:9). The
roll-call of the nations includes Philistia (Zeph 2:4–7) and
Ethiopia (Zeph 2:12–15). "For my decision is to gather nations,
to assemble kingdoms, to pour out upon them my indignation,
all the heat of my anger; for in the fire of my passion all the
earth shall be consumed" (Zeph 3:8).

In Joel also, the broader national aspect is heavily underscored especially in the final chapter. Tyre, Sidon and Philistia
are representative of the nations who gathered in the valley of
Jehoshaphat ('Yahweh judges,' Joel 3:2). Under this figure of a
gigantic war in which ploughshares are beaten into swords and
nations are aroused against Yahweh so that multitudes assemble
in the valley of decision, Joel pictures the great day when Yahweh roars from Zion, sun and moon darken and heaven and
earth tremble. The day of Yahweh is near in the valley of decision (Joel 3:14; cf. Obad 15). It is a day when God will deal decisively with the opposition: "Egypt shall become a desolation
and Edom a desolate wilderness" (Joel 3:19).

It is on a grand scale, then, that Yahweh shows himself in the midst of Israel as a victorious warrior. Even though nations are involved, they are involved in relation to Israel. The circumference of the day of Yahweh is extended by these prophets to include nations, but it is only later in Israel's history that the day of Yahweh is fully universalized.

The accompanying table will indicate some of the nuances for this expression as found in the pre-exilic prophets.

Since the prophets speak of "the day" as future, Bible readers have entertained the question of timing. When is the day of Yahweh to occur? As to chronology, there are at least four answers. Post-exilic prophets refer to the final disposition of all things, the end of history, as the day of Yahweh (Zech 12–14). In that ultimate divine coming God will be all in all. A second time referent is that of God's signal intervention in Israel's more distant future (Isaiah 34). A third time period spoken of is that of the imminent appearance of God: "The great day of the LORD is near," says Zephaniah (1:14; cf. Joel 1:15; 2:1; 3:14). A fourth indication of time is not future at all, but past. The locust plague described by Joel is within Israel's contemporary experience (Joel 1). Moreover, there have been days of Yahweh in the past. Isaiah refers to the fall of Babylon on conjunction with the day of Yahweh (Isa 13:19). While that event was future for him, it is now history, for Babylon fell at the hands of the Medes and Persians in 539/8 BC. It is not proper to regard one future event, and one only, as definitive of the day of Yahweh. Rather, as to time, several events, both future and past, qualify as "days of Yahweh."[4]

In fact—and here is a most significant consideration—the expression "the day of the LORD" has primarily to do with the *quality* of the day. Israel, not so bound up with time sequences as moderns are, asked about the *kind* of day rather than its date. The answer was uncomplicated. The day of Yahweh was a day in which God was clearly in charge. While Israel confessed God's sovereignty generally, the day of Yahweh was a time in which it would be obvious to all that God had come on the scene, that God had intervened, that it was God who was responsible for the defeat of evil and the triumph of good. The day of Yahweh was distinctly and qualitatively different from other days. While history ordinarily took its course under the watchful eye of God, the prophets announced a particular time when God was not distant but immediately present in power and victory. It was a day totally monopolized by Yahweh.

The Day of Yahweh in Pre-Exilic Prophets

Text	Subject	Character	Effect	Figure of Speech
Amos 5:18–20	Israel	Judgment	Fear Surprise	Darkness/light
Isa 2:12ff	Proud and idolatrous people	Judgment	Terror	Massive leveling
Isa 13	Babylon	Judgment	Terror Desolation	War
Isa 34–35	Nations (Isa 34:1–17) Israel (Isa 35:1–10)	Judgment Salvation	Desolation Renewal/ wholeness	Warfare Paradise
Zeph 1:1 – 3:7	Judah (1:4)	Judgment	Distress Desolation	Sacrifice (1:8)
Zeph 3:8ff	Nations (3:8) Israel (3:14)	Salvation	Worship Joy	Convocation (1:8, 18, 20)
Joel 1:1 – 3:7	Judah/Jerusa-lem Nations (3:2)	Judgment	Destruction (1:15; 3:13)	War (2:3–11; 3:9–11)
Joel 3:18–20	Judah	Salvation	Agricultural prosperity	Paradise

An understanding of the day of Yahweh as focusing on Yahweh is helpful in approaching Peter's reference at Pentecost. The prophet Joel spoke of the day of Yahweh and referred to the Spirit of God coming on all flesh. At Pentecost Peter proclaimed, "This is what was spoken through the prophet Joel" (Acts 2:16ff). To paraphrase, that which Joel saw as a time when

God would be wonderfully, even incomprehensibly, on the scene, is here. The day of Pentecost is not one person's day nor the apostles' day, but something beyond routine or ordinary experience: it is the day of God in our midst. Understood in this way, the designation of the day of Yahweh would be a fitting and accurate description of a variety of incidents in the life of the church through history, though historians would perhaps not readily agree among themselves on specifics. The New Testament writers could with propriety latch on to the expression. The second coming of Jesus Christ, for example, is the day of Yahweh—an event in which God demonstrably comes on the scene. As with the day of Yahweh in the Old Testament, that day will be a day of salvation for some but of judgment for others.

In summary, deliverance components loom large in the concept of the day of Yahweh, even though Amos and others stress judgment. The day will be one of judgment or salvation, depending on one's relationship to God. Hence God's messengers employ the language of the day of Yahweh as a call to repentance. While in the Old Testament the day of Yahweh has chiefly to do with Israel and her enemies, reference to nations, even "all nations," is not absent. More important than a date for the day of Yahweh is its quality. It is above all else a day monopolized by Yahweh, in which God bares his arm and brings victory.

2. Messianic Expectations

To speak of deliverance in the era of monarchy is to speak of messianic expectations, which, cast in language of rulership, rise to a crescendo as conditions worsen. Messianic talk has a background, of course.

Salvation from enemy powers was a theme prominent in Israel's history. The exodus from Egypt signaled liberation from an oppressive power. Almost at once, however, Israel was engaged in a wilderness battle with the Amalekites (Exod 17:8–16). Once settled in the land, Israel was subject to threats from external powers and invasions from neighboring

Philistines, with consequent loss of crop and possessions. Indeed, the pattern of government which developed came in response to these frequent threats. Judges such as Samson and Gideon became the leaders and, under God, the saviors of the people. Empowered by God's Spirit, these leaders became heroes since they restrained or expelled enemy forces. These savior figures were significant in that they made possible for Israel a time of peace and security.

The prospect of an age characterized by an absence of threat and conflict and by conditions of security and prosperity is older than the time of the judges. Since early times such prospects were associated with an agent through whom the blessings of a golden age would come. The *proto-evangelium*, God's message of hope to Eve in Eden, specifies the conflict but announces the outcome: the ultimate defeat of enemy forces (Gen 3:15). Destruction of evil powers implies, especially in that setting, a return to conditions of paradise.

Resolution of conflict and a new order among peoples are envisaged in Jacob's patriarchal blessing of Judah: "The scepter shall not depart from Judah, nor the ruler's staff from between his feet, until tribute comes to him; and the obedience of the peoples is his" (Gen 49:10). In what follows, the prosperity and the accompanying exuberance are painted in compelling pictures (Gen 49:11–12). Vines are now so numerous as to serve as hitching posts for animals, and wine flows in such abundance that people wash their garments in it rather than in water. Feasting and revelry are the order of the day. "His eyes shall be red with wine" (Gen 49:12 RSV). Gone is the age of thorns and thistles.

The same theme of victory over evil forces is struck in Balaam's oracles. En route to Canaan, Israel encountered Balak, king of Moab, who engaged a prophet, Balaam, to curse the invaders. But Balaam became a spokesman for God, and in speaking a blessing over Israel announced:

A star shall come out of Jacob,
and a scepter shall rise out of Israel;

> it shall crush the borderlands of Moab . . .
> Edom will become a possession,
> Seir a possession of its enemies.
>
> (Num 24:17–18)

Instead of Israel being subdued by neighboring tribes, Israel herself through her heroic leader shall subdue nearby Moab to the east and Edom to the south. The prophet Amos was later to pick up that theme when he announced a day in which the fallen booth of David would be restored and the people of Edom, representative of enemy forces, would be subdued (Amos 9:11–12). There would follow an age in which harvests would be so abundant and rich that "the one who plows shall overtake the one who reaps, and the treader of grapes the one who sows the seed" (Amos 9:13). Vineyards and gardens would yield abundant wine and fruit.

In Israel the coming good age is linked from the beginning with a person who is responsible for the restoration. He is one especially designated and who has distinctive leadership qualities. "The scepter shall not depart from Judah" (Gen 49:10). "A star shall come out of Jacob" (Num 24:17). Combat is necessary, as he brings about the obedience of the peoples (Gen 49:10) and crushes Moab and subdues Edom (Num 24:18). The divine-war motif familiar from the exodus is clearly present. While these early expressions of hope in Jacob's blessing and Balaam's oracle strongly hint at a kingly figure, it is in the time of the monarchy and by means of the institution of kingship that messianic hopes are given dominant expression. We may conveniently describe the messianic expectations in the period of Israel's monarchy (eleventh to sixth centuries BC) by examining the historical narrative as well as the poetic and prophetic materials related to that time.

Messianism: Intimations from the Historical Records

The term "Messiah" has come in the course of history to signify the expected, divinely sent deliverer. In the Old Testament, the word *māšîaḥ*,[5] which means "anointed," is not used as a technical term for the coming Savior (unless it be in Dan 9:26). The word "anointed" is used of Israelite kings, of course, as in Ps 2:2, which at a second level of meaning may anticipate Christ.

The word "anointed" is also used of foreign kings, such as Cyrus (Isa 45:1). Although kings were anointed (e.g., 1 Sam 15:17; 2 Sam 12:7), the word *māšîaḥ* was not limited in its use to royal occasions. Anointing with oil was used for induction into leadership positions generally. Priests were anointed (Exod 29:7; 30:30) and so were prophets (1 Kgs 19:16; Isa 61:1).

Theologically, the significance of anointing is fourfold. First, the ritual of anointing indicated an authorized separation of an individual for God's service. The king, for example, was anointed to Yahweh (1 Chr 29:22). While such a position represents honor, it also represents increased responsibility. Secondly, since these are anointed of Yahweh (e.g., 1 Sam 10:1), they are to be held in special regard. Indeed, they are inviolable (1 Sam 24:8ff). Thirdly, anointing is associated with divine enablement. Of both Saul and David it is said that "the spirit of God came mightily upon him" (1 Sam 10:6ff, RSV). Finally, the term anointed (*māšîaḥ*) is a reference to the coming one, for the New Testament writers apply to Jesus the statement about the anointed in Psalm 2 (Acts 13:32ff; cf. Heb 1:5). The term *māšîaḥ* came eventually to be applied to Jesus.

Since the messianic expectations were to crystallize around the kingly figure, it is of importance to examine the first anointed king, Saul. Now while it is true that David became the archetype for the expected future deliverer, Saul is not for that reason to be dismissed. Indeed, features of a messianic leader are found initially in Saul.

The choice of Saul and his coronation as king came as a response in part to the political threat of the Philistines. Now while Samuel had been effective as a leader and in the tradition of the holy war had routed the Philistines (1 Samuel 7), the people, troubled by Samuel's unruly sons, were apprehensive of future leadership and national security. The anointed king for which Israel asked was to function as deliverer. Specifically, it was the Ammonites at Jabesh-Gilead who threatened to impose their rule on the citizens of that Israelite city. Saul proceeded with dispatch against these enemy forces. The initial portrait of Saul as it emerges from this incident is not only positive, but may well be construed as messianic modeling, and that in three respects.

First, Saul is a charismatic leader. On him the Spirit of God comes (1 Sam 11:6). The biblical writer, while noting the empowerment of the Spirit on certain judges, is at pains to emphasize the coming of God's Spirit on Saul. Indeed a proverb is born: "Is Saul also among the prophets?" (1 Sam 10:11). Moreover, when the plight of the people of Jabesh-Gilead is presented, the "spirit of God came upon Saul in power" (1 Sam 11:6). The deliverance is kept to the fore in the story as the messengers sent from Jabesh-Gilead are told to return to their city with the message "Tomorrow, by the time the sun is hot, you shall have deliverance" (1 Sam 11:9). Charismatic endowment is given here not for prophetic utterance but for combat with the enemy.

A second characteristic of Saul, the anointed king, is his victory in the ensuing battle. The *māšîaḥ* is victorious over the opposing forces. The Ammonites are thoroughly routed. Saul has gathered a total of 330,000 men, whom he arranges in three companies. They fall upon the Ammonites in the morning watch, and before the day is over the enemy is so scattered that no two sons of Ammon are found together. Thus the beginning of Saul's reign is auspicious: he conquers. Does he not at least anticipate the star that shall rise out of Jacob to bring neighboring tribes into submission?

A third messianic trait is Saul's gracious action. Following the battle, the populace, impressed with their new leader, call for the earlier opponents to Saul's kingship to be put to death. Saul intervenes. "No one shall be put to death this day, for today the LORD has brought deliverance to Israel" (1 Sam 11:13). Here is an action of forbearance and tolerance. One who has every right to execute judgment and sentence of death extends an offer of grace and life. This is the portrait of Israel's first anointed king—a charismatic, victorious, and wonderfully gracious king.[6]

And yet because of disobedience, willfulness, selfishness, and an unrepentant spirit, this leader is later set aside by God. Not Saul but David becomes the chief model according to whom the messianic expectations are shaped. In the skirmish with the Philistines in the valley of Elah, David is the deliverer, and that quite along the lines of divine war. The contest with Goliath is not settled on the basis of strength or numbers but in terms of God's might. "I come to you in the name of the LORD of hosts, the God of the armies of Israel . . . This very day the LORD will deliver you into my hand" (1 Sam 17:45–46).

But the foremost reason for David's becoming the paradigm for messianic expectations is God's covenant with him. David wishes to offer a gift to the LORD by building a temple. Instead God offers a gift to David. That gift consists of (1) making David's name great, (2) guaranteeing future security for Israel, God's people, and (3) establishing an everlasting dynasty for David (2 Sam 7:8–16). This covenant holds out the hope of an age in which Israel will not be disturbed and in which the wicked will no more afflict them as formerly. The coming age of peace will, by inference, be linked to the kingship of a Davidide.

David's reign as king is not without serious blemish. As a ruler he arranged for a standing army. No longer is victory in warfare a matter of faith in Yahweh independent of numbers. The procedures for divine war have been jettisoned, military forces have been substituted for implicit faith. David's census of his army is an abomination to God and David is punished (2 Samuel 24). In his private life, David's affair with Bathsheba shows him up as weak and sinful. Yet for these and other transgressions David humbles himself before Yahweh (cf. Psalm 51). Despite his failures, David and his descendants cling to God's promise.

Subsequent kings, whether in Israel or Judah, never measure up to the people's expectations. Some, such as Hezekiah and Josiah, demonstrate their loyalty to God and more than others approach a rule characterized by righteousness. They are the exceptions, for the majority of rulers fall into one or more of the traps that face people in positions of power. The ideal of a king who functions as God's agent to bring in the new age lives on, unfulfilled. That anticipation can best be traced in the Psalms.

Messianism: Anticipation in the Poetical Literature

It is in the Psalms, particularly those described as royal Psalms, that the anticipations for a greater king are evident.

The second psalm is a royal psalm, and, according to the New Testament, a messianic psalm (Acts 13:22ff). In its cultural setting the psalm may well reflect a coronation event. As in the *proto-evangelium* (Gen 3:15) and in Baalam's oracle (Num 24:15ff), the combative situation is quickly sketched: nations are in an uproar, people devise a vain thing, the kings of the earth take counsel together against Yahweh and his anointed (*māšîaḥ*) (Ps 2:1–3). In the context the anointed one is the king of Israel.

The response by Yahweh to the threat of a worldwide monarchial coalition is amusement followed by anger. The threat is not sufficient to warrant his personal intervention. He announces, "I have set my king on Zion" (Ps 2:6). The king, depicted in total dependence on Yahweh, rehearses Yahweh's word of affirmation, "You are my son; today I have begotten you" (v. 7), and the word of promise, "I will make the nations your heritage" (v. 8). Confrontation of world powers with Yahweh's emissary is ominous for the world powers. The poet warns them that their fitting response is worship and submission; otherwise they shall be broken and shattered by a rod of iron.

This psalm envisages an Israelite king who is totally subordinate to Yahweh and is his representative, sure to be victorious in any conflict. God is king in the ultimate sense; yet there can legitimately be a place for a human king as a representative for him. The nations (compare Moab and Edom in Num 24:17–18) are this ruler's inheritance. Clearly the king in such a favored position can ensure the desired peace able quality of life for

Israel. But the claims for the Israelite king are exaggerated claims. To no king were all the kings from all the ends of the earth subservient. The psalm, while fitting for the royal coronation, reaches beyond the immediate Israelite experience. It was a messianic word. As the apostles were later to note, what God promised to their ancestors "he [God] has fulfilled for us, their children, by raising Jesus; as also it is written in the second psalm, 'You are my Son; today I have begotten you'" (Acts 13:33). The psalm was understood as a promise (Acts 13:32).

If Psalm 2 stresses the international scope of his conquest and rule, Psalm 72, while expressing the hope that the king's rule may extend from the river to the ends of the earth (Ps 72:8) and that all nations would serve him (Ps 72:11), lays greater emphasis on the character of kingly rule: "May he judge your people with righteousness, and your poor with justice" (Ps 72:2). As is customary in the Old Testament, righteous conduct is demonstrated in compassionate behavior to the disadvantaged. Righteous rule means defending the cause of the poor of the people (Ps 72:4). It involves delivering "the needy when they call, the poor and those who have no helper" (Ps 72:12). The righteous king saves the life of the needy and rescues their life from oppression. In reality, Israel's experience with their rulers was almost always the opposite. Solomon, through imposed labor, was oppressive. Others, such as Mannaseh, manipulated the people. Still, hope in a ruler characterized by righteousness lived on.

Psalm 72 also stresses the hope for an age of plenty and peace. Grain will be abundant. "May people blossom in the cities like the grass of the field" (v. 16). The name of the king will grow in reputation (v. 17); and the hope is voiced that the king will be good for the land, quite like rain and showers which are both pleasant and necessary. "In his days may righteousness flourish, and peace abound, until the moon is no more" (v. 7). In a line that recalls the Abraham blessing (Gen 12:2) the poet writes, "May all nations be blessed in him; may they pronounce him happy" (v. 17). It is to the king that people look for a righteous rule. It is on the king that they set their hopes for victory over encroaching enemy forces. More than that, Palestine will be the nucleus of the empire that is worldwide (72:8–11). It is because of the king that they experience a period of prosperity.

The psalm is a magnificent prayer for a king; its optimism and hope give it a delightful buoyancy. Great expectations are pinned on the leader and his enterprise. So great are the expectations that their fulfillment is not to be found in any Israelite monarch, but spills over beyond the possibilities of human attainment to another, the Messiah. Thus while the psalm is a royal psalm attributed to Solomon, possibly a prayer for his own reign or that of his son, it has quite fittingly been regarded as a messianic psalm, even though the New Testament does not draw on it for messianic support. The Targum, an Aramaic translation/paraphrase, adds the word *Messiah* after the word *king* in verse 1 and so underscores the Jewish understanding of the psalms as messianic.[7]

Messianism: A Delineation from the Prophets

Pointers toward a messianic age and a messianic figure are found most explicitly in the prophets. Yet it would be a mistake to think of the prophets as being occupied primarily with predictions of a coming deliverer. Indeed the earliest writing prophets, Amos and Hosea, although they include sections describing a new age, say little if anything about a saving figure. Their message is largely one of judgment. Two eighth-century prophets, however, Micah and Isaiah, touch on hope for a messiah more specifically.

Micah's reference to Bethlehem Ephrathah as the place from which is to come the ruler of Israel, whose goings forth are from eternity, is well known. Matthew emphasizes, quoting the Micah text, that the promise has been fulfilled (Matt 2:6). Scribes probably drew on this text in answering Herod's question where the king of the Jews was to be born. Yet the context in Micah is seldom examined. A descriptive lament in Mic 5:1, which sketches the plight of an Israelite army and its leaders about to become the victims of a humiliating siege, sets the stage for the promise of a victorious ruler who is to come from Bethlehem. As often happens, God brings forth his agents from the small and insignificant. Once more the scene is that of combat and struggle. The Assyrians threaten invasion of the land (v. 5). Indeed the lament of verse 1 may describe the incident of Sennacherib, the Assyrian who shut up Hezekiah king of Judah "like a bird in a cage," to use Sennacherib's own wording of the incident. The popular song of the day as described in Micah held that seven shepherds and eight additional leaders would be sufficient to ward off the Assyrians (Mic 5:5–6a). But the prophet points to a single ruler of obscure origin. "He will deliver *us* from the Assyrians" (5:6, NASB). Indeed, given an analogous situation in New Testament times with the Romans occupying the land, Matthew's citation of Micah's announcement is startling, to say the least. Deliverance from enemy forces continues to be a dominant function of the coming one.

It is also into a politically tense situation, one in which Ahaz is about to seek military help from Assyria, that Isaiah's announcement is made: "Therefore the LORD himself will give you a sign. Behold, a woman of marriageable age (*'almâ*) will be with child and shall bear a son, and shall name him Immanuel" (Isa 7:14, my translation). Isaiah emphasized this announcement as being a sign. Before the boy would know enough to discern good from evil, the political threat to Ahaz by the Israel-Syrian alliance would have disappeared. Because of this reference to the immediate situation, the mother of the promised son is best understood to be either Isaiah's wife (cf. the "sign" nature of his other children, 7:3; 8:3) or the queen. But, as is often true of Old Testament announcements, there is yet a fuller fulfillment. Thus Matthew can declare, particularly since the Greek translation of Isa 7:14 employed the word *parthenos* (virgin), that in Jesus' coming the ancient word of Isaiah has come true—a virgin, Mary, has given birth to one whose name is Immanuel, "God with us." The Isaiah context leads one to believe that "God with us" is introduced to call attention to God's presence in judgment (cf. 7:18). Deliverance from one enemy is imminent, but judgment by another power, Assyria, is not to be ruled out. For our purposes it is important to recognize the political setting into which the announcement is spoken.[8]

Bypassing another familiar announcement of the birth of a child who is to be ruler (Isa 9:6–7) we look at Isa 10:33 – 11:10. As in the earlier announcement, the inauspicious origin of the coming one is underlined. Great trees of the forest, symbolic of the nations, are to be felled; the lofty will be abased. Yet a shoot will spring from one stem, the stem of Jesse—quietly, without fanfare, initially unimpressive—but this branch shall bear fruit. Indeed it is no ordinary branch. A multifold spirit will rest on him.

> The Spirit of the LORD shall rest on him,
> the spirit of wisdom and understanding,
> the spirit of counsel and might,
> the spirit of knowledge and the fear of the LORD (11:2).

Characteristically his rule is described as just. His decisions will not be determined by bribes or questionable arguments, but he will "decide with equity for the meek of the earth" (v. 4). "Righteousness shall be belt around his waist, and faithfulness the belt around his loins" (v. 5). Combat with evil is not foreign to him. "He shall strike the earth with the rod of his mouth, and with the breath of his lips he shall kill the wicked" (v. 4). His deliverance from enemy forces will usher in a new age, one radically different from the present era: "The wolf shall live with the lamb . . . the lion shall eat straw like the ox . . . for the earth will be full of the knowledge of the LORD as the waters cover the sea" (Isa 11:6–9).

From a survey of these passages in the historical, poetical, and prophetic materials of the monarchy period, it is clear that, as earlier, the anticipated golden age is linked with a specific individual, an agent of God. Even though the outline is ambiguous in many ways, at least three summary statements about him are warranted. (1) The ideal ruler will be a deliverer. As background for the announcement there is either an immediate historical situation that calls for a resolution (e.g., 1 Samuel 11; Mic 5:1ff) or the more general picture of foes that will be subdued (Psalm 2; Isa 11:4). (2) The ideal ruler will rule in righteousness. Such a rule implies particular care given to the disadvantaged (e.g., Ps 72:12) but also equitable treatment (Isa 11:3–4). (3) The ideal ruler by repelling the external foes and through an eternal rule of justice will be the king of a radically different age (Isa 11:6–9; Psalm 72). Israel's hope for an ideal ruler was crystallizing, and increasingly during the later monarchy, he was in the image of King David.

Christians confess that in Jesus the day of Yahweh has dawned and the expected Messiah has come. He will some day totally fulfill the expectations of historians, poets, and prophets. He delivers persons now, and will eventually deliver the world from the power of evil. He is righteous, and will establish righteousness over the whole earth. In the coming of Jesus there has come, and will come, a new age. The kingdom of God is here now, and will some day come in its entirety.

The Covenant Community And The New Functionaries Kings, Prophets

Prior to the exodus of Israel from Egypt God declared his purpose: "I will take you as my people, and I will be your God." Confirmed at Sinai and repeated in the Mosaic literature (Deut 26:17–19), the covenant represented the relationship of intimacy which God desired. God, the instigator of the covenant, presented himself as Israel's God; the demand placed on the people consisted of recognition of God as the exclusive Lord. Implied in the phrase, "I will take you as my people," is the notion of a special kind of people, "a priestly kingdom and a holy nation" (Exod 19:6).

God's intention is clearly stated; but how did the covenant aspect of God's design fare in the 400–year period of the monarchy? The situation was different from that at Sinai. Now there were kings. There were also prophets. Early in this period a new wrinkle in covenant history is introduced in that God makes a covenant with David. New also for this period are the prophets, who are to be understood as speaking from the context of covenant, but the precise way in which they relate to covenant is still debated. The phenomenon of monarchy and the rise of the prophetic movement shape our discussion as follows: covenant and kingship; covenant and the prophets.

1. Covenant and Kingship

In the history of the covenant 2 Samuel 7 takes an important place, for this scripture records God's covenant with David, a covenant which colors the history not only of the time of David through to the last Davidic king, Zedekiah of Judah, but into the New Testament where Christ is identified for theological reasons as the Son of David (Matt 1:1–17; 2 Tim 2:8). A look at the content of the covenant statement will be followed by a look backward at the kingship model, then forward to the consequences of the covenant. We will conclude this section with comparisons of the Davidic covenant with the former Sinaitic covenant.

The Content of the Davidic Covenant

The giving of God's promise to David occurs when David, having finished his palace, expresses to Nathan his concern about the status of the ark, which is still housed within a tent (2 Sam 7:1–3). Nathan's "yes" to David, encouraging him, one gathers, to build a temple, is reversed the next day to a "no." This reversal is explained by some to center in the problem of misplaced initiative. God says, "Are you the one to build me a house to live in?" (2 Sam 7:5), suggesting, according to this view, that it was not for David but for God to make such a move. Others resort to accusing Nathan of momentary spiritual insensitivity. More likely is the explanation that God's oracle to Nathan, since it includes a discussion about God's dwelling, is a negative check on the notion that God dwells, as pagan gods do, in temples. Elsewhere the reason for a refusal of permission to build a house is that David is a man of war (1 Chr 22:8). From what we know of court etiquette, it may be that the initial "yes" is the expected response by a citizen to a king's wishes (cf. 2 Kgs 8:10; 22:15). While this may be the best explanation of the double answer, Nathan should certainly not be regarded as a "yes-man," for it is he who later confronts David concerning the king's sin with Bathsheba.

But when God withholds a particular blessing he grants another which is more glorious. To David God offers a series of promises (2 Sam 7:9–16), elsewhere described as a covenant. In the 2 Samuel passage the word "covenant" does not appear, but Ps 89:21–37, which reiterates the promises in poetry, designates these promises as covenant: "My covenant with him will stand firm," "I will not violate my covenant" (Ps 89:28, 34). These promises, while mostly personal, are not totally so. The people of Israel are also in view. "And I will appoint a place for my people Israel and will plant them, so that they may live in their own place, and be disturbed no more" (2 Sam 7:10). This dimension of peoplehood is incorporated in David's thanksgiving prayer of response in which the covenant formula is cited—the only instance where it is given in the past tense, rather than the future tense: "And you established your people Israel for yourself to be your people forever; and you, O LORD, became their God" (2 Sam 7:24).

The promises to Israel to plant them in the land are reiterations of a former promise. The new promises made to David are essentially four in number. (1) God will make David's name great (2 Sam 7:9). (2) God will give David rest from his (surrounding) enemies. (3) God will give to David a royal dynasty, descendants who shall occupy the throne forever (7:11–13). (4) Finally, the relationship between God and the members of the future dynasty will be one reminiscent of the covenant formula: "I will be a father to him, and he shall be a son to me" (2 Sam 7:14). Chastening will follow acts of iniquity, but God's loving-kindness (*ḥesed*), a term associated with covenant, will not be taken from David's descendants. Of the four, the most striking is the announcement of an ongoing dynasty of kings to sit on the throne of Israel.

The Context of the Davidic Covenant

Such a large-scale promise affecting numerous future generations is a magnanimous gift of grace, for as David is reminded and as he acknowledges in his response, he was taken from a shepherd's pasture, and it is God who has chosen to make his name great. Yet there is for the reader not only the surprise that such large promises should be given to a man of obscure background, but the greater marvel that with this promise God gives positive affirmation to the institution of kingship. In the light of several negative statements about kingship and God's apparent displeasure at the people's request for a monarch, this endorsement of kingship through the establishment of a royal dynasty must give one pause.

The chapters which tell of the establishment of monarchy are among the most difficult to interpret, for they incorporate a tension which is not easily resolvable. On the one hand passages such as 1 Sam 8:11–18 are a description of the coming evils of kingship. Essentially Samuel describes the tyrant-like actions of the king which will bring the people of the land into service of the king, largely in the interest of the king's personal vanity and egotism. In this speech kingship as an institution has no redeeming features. The negative outlook on kingship is reinforced through such statements by Yahweh as, "They have not rejected you, but they have rejected me from being king over them" (1 Sam 8:7). Samuel rebukes the people by rehearsing God's deliverance of them from Egypt: "But today you have rejected your God, who saves you from all your calamities and your distresses; and you have said, 'No! but set a king over us'" (1 Sam 10:19; cf. 12:12).

Yet within these same chapters there are indications of divine approval. The choice of Saul is by God; the anointing is given in detail. The Spirit comes charismatically upon Saul and his defeat of the Ammonites demonstrates that God is with him. The tension between kingship viewed positively and kingship viewed negatively is clearly evident in Samuel's farewell speech. Saul is referred to as the LORD's anointed (1 Sam 12:3, 5); yet Samuel reproaches the people, announcing that through a sign of thunder and rain "you shall know and see that the wickedness that you have done in the sight of the LORD is great in demanding a king for yourselves" (1 Sam 12:17). So large a place has monarchy in the Old Testament, not only in Israel's history but through the Davidic covenant, theologically, that the interpretation of kingship in Israel is of considerable importance.[1]

The interpretations have gone different ways. Three possible interpretations are presented here: (1) harmonizing the opposite views, (2) championing the view that monarchy was a detour in Israel's spiritual pilgrimage, and (3) espousing monarchy as positive.

Attempts to harmonize the viewpoints on kingship presented in 1 Samuel 8–12 have been made along two lines. Resorting to theological sophistication, some Bible interpreters have rationalized the installation of monarchy as being in the category of the permissive will of God.[2] Other scholars, resorting to source analysis, have suggested that two traditions, the one represented by 1 Sam 7:3 – 8:22; 10:17–27; 12:1–25, and the other by 9:1–10; 11:1–11, 15, and 13:2 – 14:46, were so strongly embedded in Israel that both were incorporated by the author; or (a variation of that theme) that an initial description of the events, perhaps positive, was later edited in such a way as to present a negative assessment of monarchy. Many critical scholars hold that these chapters, part of a larger so-called deuteronomistic history, were finalized in the exilic period and so were influenced by the course of history of Israel under the monarchy. Taking his cue from God's choice of David, R. E. Clements argues that the writers of this history were so captured by the blessing of God on David that they faulted, not kingship as such, but the choice of king precipitated by the people's request. God's choice, a choice of David, was pre-empted by the choice of Saul.[3]

Some feel that the negative assessment about kingship is the one that should carry the day. They point to the theocratic ideal, God's rule as king, an arrangement in which God ruled directly. They recall with approval Gideon's refusal to take up the monarch's throne (Judg 8:22ff) and point to Jotham's devastating parable against Ahimelech, Gideon's son, when he adopted the title of king (Judg 9:7ff) and conclude that Israel, who was indeed to be different from other nations through rule by God, by insisting on kingship compromised and came short of the ideal. Moreover, in holy war God delivered people who were often militarily unskilled. The institution of holy war was altered, if not abandoned, through the standing army which became standard for the king. Does not the rise of the prophets, which corresponds to the institution of kingship in origin, testify to the undesirability of monarchy, especially since the prophets by vocation often stood in judgment over the kings? Hosea, it is claimed, is critical of the institution of monarchy. His allusion to Gilgal (Hos 9:15) as the place of "every evil" is interpreted as a jibe at kingship, since Saul's coronation and the beginning of the monarchy took place there. At its most extreme the monarchy is considered a parenthesis between theocratic rule of the judges and the post-exilic return to theocracy.

Ranged in opposition to this negative evaluation of kingship is one that lets the full weight of the argument fall on the positive side. Monarchy, it is claimed, was quite within the purpose of God, and that for these reasons. The situation was previewed by Moses and the limitations against kingly action were already described in Deuteronomy (Deut 17:14).[4] The book of Judges shows the inchoate and troubled conditions that prevailed without a strong leader. The book therefore prepares the way for a change in the governing structure. The ruler was described in the earlier period as leader (*nāgîd*), rather than as a king (*melek*), apparently to avoid crass imitation of surrounding peoples, and perhaps also to define his place as a bearer of less than totalitarian power. The covenant of God with David and the establishment of an ongoing dynasty are proof of the legitimacy of monarchy. Any evil that attached to monarchy attached to individual kings. Good kings, such as David, Hezekiah, and Josiah, were instrumental by reason of their position to lead Israel in godly paths. That David should be a paradigm for the Messiah seems sufficient reason to give to the monarchy a positive interpretation.

The clean-cut white or black interpretation seems in each case not to account for the criticisms brought against it. A synthesis or form of harmonization is likely to do more justice to the data, but it must be a synthesis that resorts neither to casuistic explanations nor the ever-ready but dubious key of literary sources. The explanation here proposed proceeds under the rubric of grace, or to put it another way, a theology of change. The description, given over several chapters in 1 Samuel, allows us to see the change from one form of administration to another. The initiative comes from the people, for it is they and not God who initiate a move toward monarchy. The people address Samuel, the judge, leader, and representative of Yahweh—an action in which one may detect regard for Yahweh. The reasons they give for wanting the change to kingship include a desire for someone who will go out before them and fight their battles (1 Sam 8:20; cf. 9:15; 10:1). The disorganization in the time of the judges may justify the request in part, though just prior to the request the Philistines were routed under the leadership of Samuel the judge (1 Sam 7:5ff). Since Samuel's sons were evil in administering justice, the people's request that the king govern Israel is at least understandable.

While it is true that the texts state that Israel's action is a rejection of God as king over them, there are also statements by God that Samuel is to hearken to them and give them a king (1 Sam 8:9, 22), and God provides them with his choice—hardly the action in which God should be implicated if the request was totally at odds with his intent. But how then can we explain Samuel's call for repentance, "You shall know and see that the wickedness that you have done in the sight of the LORD is great in demanding a king for yourselves" (1 Sam 12:17)? The spirit in which the request was made, and the insubordination to, even rebellion against, Yahweh (cf. 1 Sam 12:15) were sinful. When the people acknowledge this, Samuel says, "Fear not," and encourages them to serve Yahweh with their whole heart (1 Sam 12:20)—a word spoken after the installation of Saul, which may be taken to mean that total service to God is not incompatible with monarchy.

A positive view of the monarchy is found in the Psalms. The view of a single kingdom in which the human king is an agent of God, the divine king, surfaces in Psalm 2, the installation psalm, where nations rage in vain against "the LORD and his anointed"

(Ps 2:2), and in Psalm 110, where the king takes his throne beside Yahweh. God remains the eternal king (Ps 10:16; Ps 5:2).[5] In short, later affirmation of the monarchy, especially to David, will not allow us to appraise monarchy negatively. The chapters 1 Samuel 9–12 allow us to see the repentance of the people, and, more important, the grace of God in affirming kingship even though it was established by a people with questionable motives. Just as the sale of Joseph to Egypt by Jacob's sons, though not right, was the means by which Joseph was propelled into a place of instrumentality for God; so the people's request for a king, while not laudable, even wrong, nevertheless is turned by God into a vehicle toward the accomplishment of his purposes.

Our theology of change must take into account changing circumstances, human initiative, and the sovereignty of God. The sovereignty of God is not such that man's freedom is negated. People are not censured for wanting to meet the new circumstance with increased efficiency. It seems that here human initiative, however, suffered from two faults: the proposal for kingship arose out of a less-than-trusting attitude toward God; and the request was ill-timed since God's hour for kingship had not yet come. But God's sovereignty must not be interpreted as inflexible. God takes the false starts of a people and even through these, though by circuitous routes perhaps, fulfills his purposes. If the wrath of people can praise God (Ps 76:10), then the demands arising from the uneven loyalty of his people can also praise him. Persons are not absolved from fault in their lapse of faith, but God is glorified in his creative work with people, even in human failure. Kingship, though introduced by people spiritually inept, is not a parenthesis in God's program. The Davidic king rules within the sphere of God's kingship; the rule of the Davidic king is God's instrument.

Consequences of the Covenant

If we follow the Davidic covenant forward in history, then several developments are of interest. The first is that covenant promises served to escalate a faltering hope. The promise for perpetual descendants occupying the throne was understood to be accompanied by an age of prosperity, but such an age did not materialize. The expectations for the new age rose with each accession of a new king to the throne, as the royal psalms show (Psalm 2 and 132). Justice and righteousness would prevail, and through unquestioned victory over all enemies shalom conditions would at last be a reality. But it never quite happened. After two hundred years, Isaiah the prophet points still to a royal figure, one from the stump of Jesse, but now a messianic person upon whom will come the several-fold Spirit of God and who will judge the poor in righteousness, and in whose time the earth will be full of the knowledge of Yahweh (Isa 11:1–9; cf. Isa 32:1–8). The messianic portrait elaborated by Jeremiah (23:5) and Ezekiel (34:23, 27) will occupy us in a later chapter; but it should be observed that hope focused on a kingly figure, a Davidide. The messianic expectations were couched in language about royalty. The future hope, though as old as kingship, was accentuated by repeated experiences of the shortcomings of kings and by the events of the exile.

A second consequence of God's covenant with David was the teaching about the invincibility of Zion. Following the time of David, the temple and the ark inside it led to beliefs about the security of Zion, used as an equivalent for Jerusalem, where the temple was situated. Both temple and ark were symbols of God's presence. Where God was present, defeat was quite unthinkable. Hence God's dwelling on Mount Zion is linked with victory in combat: "There he broke the flashing arrows, the shield, the sword, and the weapons of war" (Ps 76:3). Zion was unshakable, not only because of temple and ark, but because near it in this capital, selected by David, was situated David's throne, which was to continue forever. Moreover, one of the promises to David was rest from his enemies, a promise which suggests peace because of a strong position. One psalm places the election of Zion in tandem with the election of David: "For the LORD has chosen Zion; he has desired it for his habitation" (Ps 132:13). Isaiah speaks similarly: "The LORD has founded

Zion" (Isa 14:32). The narrative sections do not describe any circumstance when an oracle about the election of Zion was given. Such a belief was quite possibly an inference from Yahweh's approval of the building of the temple, together with the covenant which promised permanence to David's throne. Thus reinforcement for the strong belief in Zion's impregnability came both from the cult and from royalty.[6]

Isaiah is the prophet who gives most forceful expression to the idea that Zion has been secured by God himself and is unshakable. Several motifs of the Zion tradition, some found also in the Psalms, can be isolated from Isaiah. One is that at Zion, which is Jerusalem, or more accurately the temple area, God has defeated the enemy. In exuberant language Isaiah describes how the multitudes of all the nations that fight against Ariel (the place where David camped, Isa 29:1) shall be as a dream. "[As when] a thirsty man dreams of drinking and wakes up faint, still thirsty, so shall the multitude of all the nations be that fight against Mount Zion" (Isa 29:8b; cf. Ps 48:1–8). It follows from God's victory at Mount Zion that Zion is a place of safety and refuge for God's people. In graphic imagery Isaiah tells how like a lion growling over his prey "the LORD of hosts will come down to fight upon Mount Zion and upon its hill" (31:4), and then changing the imagery to make his point about protection, he says, "Like birds hovering overhead, so the LORD of hosts will protect Jerusalem; he will protect and deliver it, he will spare and rescue it" (Isa 31:5; cf. Ps 46:5; Isa 14:32). Even more wonderful than victory on Zion and protection is the stream of blessing that flows from Zion. "Look on Zion, the city of our appointed festivals! . . . there the LORD in majesty will be for us a place of broad rivers and streams" (Isa 33:20–21; cf. Ps 46:5; Ps 132:13–18). At the heart of this enthusiasm for Zion is the belief that nothing can shake this city.

During the eighth century and later that faith was fully vindicated. By Jeremiah's time a century later, however, the people, falsely secure in that faith, were virtually oblivious to the danger of an imminent Babylonian conquest, and fanatically claimed immunity from disaster, chanting "This is the temple of the LORD, the temple of the LORD, the temple of the LORD" (Jer 7:4). But the moral ground had shifted; and because of the people's disloyalty, God eventually permitted both temple and city to fall.

One interpretation of the covenant was positive in its results, for belief in a yet-to-come leader sustained the people of Israel in times of difficulty. A second consequence of the covenant, an interpretation of it to mean that Zion was invincible, became a false basis for a people's security.

Comparison of the Davidic and Sinaitic Covenants

The covenant with David invites comparison with God's covenant at Sinai. The Davidic covenant does not alter the covenant of God at Sinai with his people. The Sinai covenant is for the people; the Davidic covenant is made with one individual. The Davidic covenant therefore takes its place as one circle within the larger circles. The Davidic covenant, while clearly given at the initiative of Yahweh, is nevertheless occasioned by David's desire to build a house for Yahweh. The covenant at Sinai is in the context of Israel's deliverance by Yahweh and so is a continuation of God's gracious activity.

It is sometimes held that the Sinai covenant is conditional, and that the Davidic covenant is unconditional. This sharp contrast has been overplayed, partly out of a misunderstanding about the nature of covenant. A covenant is a relationship of mutuality. Unlike a contract, whose essential feature is "terms" and "obligations in writing," a covenant has loyalty as its essential feature and is established in speech, for the response is important. Loyalty is assumed; and where disloyalty has entered, the covenant is in disrepair, perhaps in jeopardy. Loyalty entails specifics, but the specific conditions, unlike those of a contract, are subsidiary to mutual loyalty. The condition of loyalty is not specified in 2 Samuel 7, although David's response represents his pledge to loyalty. A psalm, however, makes explicit what is inherent in the Davidic covenant: "One of the sons of your body I will set on your throne. If your sons keep my covenant and my decrees that I shall teach them, their sons also, forevermore, shall sit on your throne" (Ps 132:11–12; cf. 1 Chr 28:7). Loyalty would be expressed in observing God's testimonies. We can agree with one scholar who, while stressing the grace aspects, says, "It would be wholly misleading to characterize the grace of the royal covenant as unconditional."[7] Obligations of trust, humility, and obedience to God's laws are part of the king's covenanted responsibilities. Both the Sinaitic and the Davidic covenant, like all covenants, are conditional. The condition is loyalty.[8]

Thus from a covenant point of view the Abraham and Sinai covenants continue in force in the monarchical period, supplemented with a covenant to David the king—a covenant which endorses kingship by promising an unbroken line of descendants to rule from a throne. This promise is perpetuated later with messianic overtones and already early is tied together with the belief of the inviolability of Zion.

2. Covenant and the Prophets

The link between royalty and covenant has been sketched; we need now to elucidate the prophets' relation to covenant. The rise of prophets in Israel coincides with the rise of the monarchy. While Moses is called a prophet (Deut 18:18), as is Abraham (Gen 20:7), their role as prophet is not particularly differentiated. A distinct office of a prophet is accorded first to Samuel.[9] During his time, Israel was at a crisis point because of the external threat from the Philistines and the internal agitation for a realignment of leadership roles. In that unsettling time, Saul became king. One way of seeing the two roles of prophet and king is to see them as differentiations of roles formerly combined into one person, the judge. The judges were charismatic; they were leaders in the struggle for deliverance. The prophets perpetuate the charismatic quality associated with the judges; the kings perpetuate the military role. Such differentiation soon raises the question of the way in which the prophets related to kings and to priests.

The Role of the Prophets

Before entering upon the discussion of the prophets' relation to covenant, preliminary remarks situating the prophet within Israel's religious life are in order. Samuel, the first prophet, is a convenient covenant figure on whom to focus, while being aware of the line of prophets beyond him. As spokespersons for God, prophets addressed the king, who was the political power figure but the instrument also for executing God's rule over God's people. The theocracy was not displaced by the monarchy. The prophet, more nearly representing God than did the king, stood above the king on the hierarchical ladder. As the charismatic messenger from God, the prophet installed the ruler. Samuel anoints Saul and David; Ahijah anoints Jeroboam; the prophet Jehu anoints Baasha; and Elisha's representative anoints King Jehu (2 Kgs 9:1–10). The prophets also announced the rejection of kings. Samuel addresses Saul; Elijah confronts Ahab. Moreover the prophets directed kings through oracles, as Micaiah ben Imlah did for Ahab and Jehoshaphat (1 Kings 22), and as did Isaiah for King Ahaz (Isaiah 7).

The prophets confronted kings with demands for personal righteous conduct: two most dramatic examples are Nathan's rebuke to David for the murder of Uriah (2 Sam 12:1), and Elijah's denunciation of Ahab for the appropriation of Naboth's vineyard (1 Kings 21). Indeed Jeremiah's writings about kings illustrates the prophets' summons to kings and other public officials to exercise righteous rule. God defines this prophet's mission: "Today I appoint you over nations and over kingdoms . . ." (Jer 1:10). A full discussion of the intersection between prophets and kings, while intriguing and illuminating, is not essential here, but it would show to what extent the prophet's mission took him, like Samuel, into the presence of the king.

The prophet Samuel also illustrates the ministry of a prophet directed to the populace. Samuel made his circuits year by year from Bethel to Gilgal, to Mizpah, to Ramah (1 Sam 7:16–17). Though "to judge" means to render decisions, it means also "to act as leader." This leadership function is depicted in his farewell address in which he rehearses God's activity for his people and rebukes Israel for its action. He instructs them after their repentance to serve Yahweh (1 Sam 12:20). This call to the populace to align itself fully with Yahweh is clearly sounded by Elijah in the contest with the four hundred prophets of Baal at Carmel: "How long will you go limping with two different opinions?" (1 Kgs 18:21). Jeremiah, among others, calls on the whole of Israel: "Hear the word of the LORD, O house of Jacob, and all the families of the house of Israel" (Jer 2:4). While the prophets' address is made with surprising frequency to community leaders, including kings, it is also to the people as a whole that they direct their words in the name of Yahweh.

The prophet shared with the priests the responsibility for the spiritual well-being of the community. Samuel, functioning as a priest, performed sacrifices; but the performance of the ritual duties was later the virtual prerogative of the priest. Since the prophets in several instances spoke disapprovingly of sacrifices (Isaiah 1; Jeremiah 7; Amos 5), some have suggested that a hostility existed between prophet and priest. It is true that the prophets did not hesitate to denounce the priests for corruption, such as drunkenness (Isa 28:7ff) or for yielding to bribery (Mic 3:11). But then, it must also be remarked, the prophets in the same breath spoke harshly against their corrupt peer prophets. Jeremiah is energetic in taking to task prophets who prophesy falsely, live unrighteously, and, chameleon-like, give to the people what the people want to hear (Jer 23:9ff). Both the prophets and the priests were engaged in making the will of God known to the people, but with this fundamental difference: the priests were teachers, transmitting the teaching which was found in the law (Deut 33:7–11); the prophets were persons who received a clear and immediate message from God to take, as messengers, to king or people. This message was primarily directed to the immediate situation of the community, and might be a judgment oracle, a salvation oracle, a word to other nations, or even directives to an individual. The message was bound up with the contemporary scene. Within these prophetic speeches, prediction of future events could be a part, but the intention even of prediction was to influence the immediate course of action of the listener. The predictions were often conditional and so acted as incentives toward right action (e.g., Jeremiah 18).

Although the prophet can be sociologically placed, it is not easy to determine whether the prophets were understood as reformers or as revolutionaries. They challenged their hearers with the demands of God. They spoke about the coming day of Yahweh. They were firm in their belief about God's freedom, convinced that he would bring about something new for Israel. Thus they were not unlike revolutionaries. Reformers also look for change but call their hearers to earlier values, and proceed methodologically in ways that are less threatening. If one is to regard the prophets' ministry as reformatory in nature, then their stance to the covenant particularly needs clarification.

The Prophets' Use of Covenant

Did the prophetic message revolve around the covenant, or attach itself loosely to covenant notions, or proceed quite apart from covenant? The question is important in order to determine the connections of the prophet with Israel's former beliefs (some have maintained that the prophets preached novel doctrines), to provide clues on how to understand the prophetic ministry within Israel, and, from our standpoint, to follow the fortunes of covenant in Israel's history.

Judging by the occurrences of the word covenant ($b^e r\hat{\imath}t$) the prophets were not much preoccupied with past covenants. While a word count for the term $b^e r\hat{\imath}t$ as used by the prophets shows substantial occurrence (more than eighty times), an investigation of the specific contexts will show that references to the historic covenants of Sinai, Abraham, or David are remarkably infrequent. There is talk of a future covenant of peace (Ezek

34:25), of a covenant with day and night (Jer 33:20), of a covenant with the Levitical priesthood (Jer 33:20). The Sinai covenant may be in view in Jer 11:3. The covenant with David receives brief mention (Jer 32:30; 33:25; Isaiah 55). But the infrequency of the word *covenant* to describe God's relationship with Israel need not be conclusive proof that the prophets shunned covenant notions. One can speak about values of democracy, such as equality and freedom, and not use the word *democracy*.

Scholars have amassed considerable evidence to try to show that the proclamation of the prophet must be understood in the context of God's past covenant with Israel. For instance, the covenant formula, "You will be my people; I will be your God" is well represented in Jeremiah (24:7; 30:22; 31:33), and occurs also in Ezekiel (37:27) and Hosea (2:23). Other words such as "know" and even "love" are technical vocabulary in the ancient Near East within covenant language. Expressions such as "Holy One of Israel" have strong overtones of covenant-community. More of the prophetic literature might be oriented to covenant than first appears.[10]

More important than terms or formulae are the theological connections. The prophets held out an ideal for life in the community which corresponds with the covenant ideal. In this ideal Yahweh is acknowledged as God, the only God to whom Israel gives allegiance. Heathen gods such as Baal are no longer rivals. Indeed, Hosea says, "They shall be mentioned (remembered) by name no more" (2:17). Such language is in accord with the covenant, notably the first commandment: "You shall have no other gods before me" (Exod 20:3), or as formulated in the legal material: "You shall love the LORD your God with all your heart, and with all your soul, and with all your might" (Deut 6:5). The prophets also hold out the ideal of social harmony among men achieved on the basis of "righteousness" and "under God." Isaiah describes a future time when nations shall not learn war any more. Their weapons have been converted into peace-time implements for they have been taught the way of Yahweh at Mount Zion (Isa 2:1–4). Elsewhere, elaborating on the character of the coming ruler, Isaiah says, "Righteousness shall be the belt around his waist, and faithfulness the belt around his loins" (Isa 11:5). Such a vision is at least in keeping with "You shall love your neighbor as yourself " (Lev 19:18). Indeed that which Jesus identified as the two greatest commandments is also intrinsic to the prophet's message.

Related to those ideals but approached from another angle is the indictment of the prophets against Israel, an indictment hardly explicable except for the covenant. Thus the demand of the people's loyalty, so well represented in the covenant, is the presupposition for the pointed accusations that Israel has departed from Yahweh. Hosea ends his list of indictments with "and *forgot me*, says the LORD" (Hos 2:13). In this he is followed by Ezekiel, who charges that "you have despised my holy things . . . who slander to shed blood . . . one commits abomination with his neighbor's wife . . . they take bribes . . ." (Ezek 22:8–12), and concludes with what, as a gross evil, is father to all evils, "You have forgotten me" (Ezek 22:12). In even stronger language Jeremiah castigates his listeners: "For my people have committed two evils: they have forsaken me, the fountain of living water, and dug out cisterns for themselves, cracked cisterns that can hold no water" (Jer 2:13). Their actions of departure from Yahweh are deliberate and wicked: "She has rebelled against me" (Jer 4:17). Another set of indictments directed against the evils that exist among members of the community presupposes a people set apart: "You shall be for me . . . a priestly kingdom and a holy nation" (Exod 19:6). Against this demand, quite contrary to it, are the political maneuvers in which in unpriestly fashion Israel trots off to Egypt for political alliances (Isa 30:1–5). Contrary to the demand for holiness are the social behaviors of inhumane actions (Amos 2:6ff). Also contrary to the covenant summons for righteous living are such practices as bribery (Mic 3:8–11), extortion (Isa 58:3–4), avarice (Amos 8:5–6), and deceit (Hos 12:7–9a).

The prophets did more than charge Israel with failure. They told of judgment to come. These prophetic judgment speeches, to be described as to their form in the next chapter, are associated with the covenant in two ways. First, as in Hosea's judgment speech, the specifics of the charge are formulated, beyond question, to recall the Ten Words of the Sinaitic covenant. "Swearing, lying, and murder, and stealing and adultery break out . . ." (Hos 4:2). Secondly, the announcement of threat, a part of the judgment speeches, is in keeping with covenant curses, an element identified as integral to ancient Near Eastern covenants and also found in the biblical material (Deuteronomy 27–28; Leviticus 26). The threat of God's judgment which was to fall on the covenant breakers is announced by the prophets in their judgment speeches.

The judgment is exacting, especially in view of the covenant. Amos says, "You only have I known (a covenant word) of all the families of the earth; therefore I will punish you for all your iniquities" (Amos 3:2). Indeed it has been argued that the reason the oracles of Amos are included in the Bible is that his position concerning Israel was so drastic, namely that the covenant relationship was terminated because of Israel's sin (Amos 7:1 – 8:3). The historical verification through the exile of Amos's threatened judgment would be additional reason why his writing would be preserved and highly regarded. But at the time of Amos's speech, since it was delivered at a time of national prosperity, any statement about the end of God's covenant with Israel would have been received with disbelief. Not only did the prosperity of the moment make it appear as most unlikely, but the people's understanding of the covenant did not really include such a possibility. By their emphasis on a people's loyalty to Yahweh and the announcement of judgment in the offing, these spokespersons for God were reinterpreters of the covenant.

Prophets are often regarded in stereotyped fashion as predictors, both of judgment and future salvation events. Such a stereotype only partially corresponds with facts. Prophets were spokespersons of God who grappled with their historical situation. Yet it is true, they did foretell future events. From where has this eschatological aspect sprung? Various answers have been given, but among them is the pointer, quite believable and convincing, that promise of the future, like threats of judgment, were anchored in the covenant. For if God's promise was believable, then it augured good, even if that good was postponed and even if it was preceded by judgment. Among the announcements for the future is indeed a distinctly covenantal-oriented one. Jeremiah, recalling the old covenant, holds out a promise of the new covenant, one in which people will no longer teach one another to know Yahweh but each shall know him (Jer 31:31–32).

If the covenants of God with Israel inform the prophets to the degree that has been suggested above, it remains a curious thing that they should be hesitant to employ the term or to refer more directly to separate covenants. One reason for their reticence may be that the covenants had lulled Israel into a false security. Preoccupied with the gracious promise of God, they would not have "heard" the prophet's message had these prophets in more direct fashion spoken about covenant. For them covenant spelled safety, but the prophet's message was coming dissolution. The infrequency of mention of covenant is therefore deliberate.

But if they were reluctant to employ the term "covenant," they were insistent upon the intent of covenant. Whatever stresses new structures imposed, the covenant dimension was not forgotten. Samuel had declared, "It has pleased the LORD to make you a people for himself" (1 Sam 12:22).

3. Theological Reflections

The foregoing descriptions about a covenant community, viewed in the light of current agenda, evoke several reflections. The theology of community addresses every age with a word about world community generally and Christian community specifically.

The primary concern which arises out of the covenant formula, is that a select community will rightfully bear the designation, people of God. But the concept of solidarity of all peoples is broadly presuppositional to the notion of a "chosen" people. The genealogies, to use one piece of evidence from an earlier chapter, point to the solidarity of the human family. Current language about a world community or about a global village is recognition of the oneness of the human race. Technology has finally forced a realization of a fact propounded theologically millennia ago. If in ancient Israel it was held that the actions of a few could impact the "many," how much more is that insight evident in a technological society in which the threat of nuclear destruction is brought about by the fear of what one person or a few persons might do in an emergency. The fortunes of the groupings within the human race are interlocked more today than ever before.

Racial discrimination, too commonplace even in the twentieth century, is essentially a denial that the human family stands together in solidarity. If persons are set aside from candidacy for positions solely on the basis of race, or, worse, treated as less than human beings, then the biblical teaching of one human family is canceled out in practice even should it be preached theoretically. The solidarity of the human race is established biblically. Recognition of this fact, and certainly expression of this fact, is sure to bring healing in a world often divided because of discrimination.

If world community has been hindered through discrimination, Christian community has been thwarted through individualism. The cultural progress claimed in the last two hundred years can be traced in part to the freedom extended to the individual to "be himself." And God's people, unconsciously caught up in the move to independence, have stressed the importance of the individual, often to the neglect of the significance of the group. To be sure, salvation from sin is a personal matter. Yet God frees from sin in order that the person might be free of egotism and take his or her rightful place in the church, God's community. Any position which says either through attitude or action that the church community is unimportant is hardly expressive of the biblical principles. The summons to conversion and discipleship is a summons to participation in the life of God's people, the church. Such a focus is important for the church and its leadership to maintain. Given the penchant for individualism and personal success, evangelists, and ministers in Christian mass media, radio or television, can easily become more concerned with developing a clientele than with building a community of God's people.

The covenant formula, "You shall be my people," is a call for a particular kind of people. In the wilderness setting and later in the promised land, God was at work shaping a godly community. Jesus called persons to himself whom he made disciples and who, through his teaching and shaping, came to be persons more and more in his image. Spiritual formation follows a decision to yield to Christ. Spiritual formation occurs in the context of Christian community. To be part of God's community is to experience the support of that community and also the admonitions of that community. Christian brothers and sisters are often God's agents of change. A willingness by the individual to grow is presupposed in Christian community. For the individual as for the group that growth is in the context of God's promise: "I will be your God." It is that promise, not unlike Christ's "I will build my church," that not only provides a basis for optimism in the Christian community, but remains as a forceful reminder that it is a Christ-characterized community that is being shaped.

Stress on the community, while an antidote for individualism, is unfortunately not a safeguard for all possible evils. Israel's story shows how a community can seize upon a theological symbol such as the temple, and theologize upon it to the point of bringing blindness on themselves. Isaiah had spoken about the invincibility of Zion. With God present among his people, they need not fear an enemy. That word of comfort was taken by the people to be eternally true. Thus, more than a hundred years later in quite another religious and social situation, the people were reinforcing their sense of security with the chant, "the temple of the LORD; the temple of the LORD; the temple of the LORD" (Jer 7:4). Jeremiah's task was to uproot and destroy a tradition now no longer valid. He pointed to the moral disarray, as well as to the historical destruction of Shiloh centuries earlier, to underscore the flimsiness of the people's security in this time-worn doctrine. Jeremiah exhorted his hearers not to become spiritually numbed with orthodox belief. He said: "For if you truly amend your ways and your doings, if you truly act justly one with another . . . then I will dwell with you in this place" (Jer 7:5–7). In short, a doctrine, true and defensible and even "proven" in an earlier day, had come now as a screen or shield between the people and God. They related to the doctrine rather than to God.

The danger of misuse and misappropriation of church doctrines faces the church in every age. A teaching, right and proper in itself, becomes institutionalized. Baptism and the Lord's supper are examples from church life in the Middle Ages. But current examples are not lacking. The love of God is being emphasized, as it ought to be. Yet in some circles little is heard about the demands of God and the possibility of his judgment on sin. The teaching about the eternal security of the believer, while a teaching of Scripture, has been emphasized in some circles to the virtual neglect of the call to discipleship and holiness. Scripture, to cite yet another example, is defined as God-breathed and inspired, and even inerrant in its historical and scientific statements. Yet while there is great commotion about holding to the correct formulation of Scripture, obedience to Scripture seems a more optional matter. In any event the Scripture as an item of theological orthodoxy, quite like the temple in ancient Israel, comes to be of primary concern. And that concern, though largely legitimate, serves to shield believers from an immediate and direct confrontation of God. The result both for Israel and for moderns is a limited awareness of God's call upon his people to be a righteous and just community.

The privilege of being in a covenant relationship with God is a high privilege. But election to covenant, even for King David, includes more than election to privilege. Election is to responsibility as well as to privilege. Just as the prophets insisted upon responsibility within covenant, upon right and just dealing by the rich with the poor, upon compassion and mercy, so must church leaders insist upon obligation by the Christian community to act with moral uprightness, integrity, and compassion within its society.

Jeremiah charged that the house of God, though crowded with worshipers, was infested with robbers. Jesus likewise accused those within temple walls of making the place a den of thieves. Today's minister is not called to perpetuate a cozy club of Christians. He or she must remain clear about covenant prerogatives, but must also be perceptive and outspoken about covenant responsibilities.

The Experience of God

$\mathbf{K}$nowing God, like knowing another person, is an encounter, an I-Thou experience. To know God, we have explained earlier, is to know about God not only intellectually, but also emotionally and experientially.

What does Israel's four hundred years of experience under the monarchy have to say about her relationship with God? How did Israel know God? Several options are open to us as we proceed toward an answer. We might ask, as we did in discussing this design element during Israel's formative period, how did God make himself known?[1] How did God intend Israel to experience him? We choose, however, to follow a different, even opposite course, and ask rather, how did Israel give expression to her experience with God? How did she describe her relationship with God? By observing the nature as well as the variety of Israel's experiences with God, moderns may unlock doors in their experience of God.

For the period of the monarchy, there are open to us the following primary sources: a narrative that relates the fortunes and misfortunes of Israel, primarily concerned with her kings (1 and 2 Samuel, 1 and 2 Kings); a book of poetry, much of it dating from David (Psalms); a book of Proverbs attributed to Solomon and Hezekiah (Proverbs); a drama (Job); two major prophets (Isaiah and Jeremiah); and several minor prophetic books (including Amos, Hosea, Micah, Zephaniah, Habakkuk).

A technical expert will at once raise objections on dating. Some psalms are post-exilic, one could argue. Granted; but the majority of the psalms are now generally agreed to be earlier, even if not all are by David. Job's date is questionable; granted, for Job is a most difficult book to date. We concur with Andersen that while the book could be dated any time from Moses on, it quite possibly originated in Solomonic times and came into its present shape by the time of Josiah.[2] Although the dating of the texts in this period is not totally certain, the broad outline is clear.

A large percentage of the material before us is in poetic form, a suitable form in which to express intense experience. We commonly hear, and correctly, that God acts in history and that the Old Testament is a history of salvation (*Heilsgeschichte*). But the Old Testament is not history only. Much of it, including major blocks from the prophets and even entire books, is in poetry. It has been suggested that the poetic sections contain Israel's response to God's acts. Poetry makes an appeal to the emotions. With its symbolism and its rhythm it quickly stirs the imagination. By compressing the language, the poet achieves a particular vigor and forcefulness. Poetry, rather than prose, is a fitting vehicle with which to describe the experiences of the large and mysterious elements of life, especially God.

One may tell a story, for example, detailing how in a given situation God answered prayer. One may even describe the situation in detail and seek, in prose, to share the impact of the event: "I felt overwhelmed." But a poet, painting in brilliance on the wide canvas of imagination, far supersedes the storyteller for impact. One Spirit-inspired poet tells how God heard his cry for help:

> Then the earth reeled and rocked;
> the foundations also of the mountains trembled . . .
> He bowed the heavens, and came down;
> thick darkness was under his feet.
> He rode on a cherub, and flew;
> he came swiftly upon the wings of the wind . . .

And he sent out his arrows, and scattered them;
he flashed forth lightnings, and routed them . . .
He reached down from on high, he took me;
he drew me out of mighty waters. (Ps 18:7–16)

Such language is not to be pressed for scientific verification, just
as nobody summons a doctor because a lover laments that his
heart bleeds for his fiancee. No, deeply moving experiences, including the experience of God, defy the everyday ranges of expression. Poetry is a more fitting form to tell of the mysterious
and the inexplicable.

Our question is about a people's experience of God. Since a
large percentage of the relevant material for our period is in poetry and since selection is necessary, our investigation will turn
on poetic materials, with attention particularly to some major
literary forms. What do the Psalms, with their major forms of lament, hymn, and thanksgiving song, say to the subject of knowing God? What understanding of God undergirds the prophetic
judgment and salvation speeches? What testimony to an experience with God do Proverbs and Job supply? Some generaliza-
tions emerge, anchored, as they must be, in specific text studies.

1. The Experience of God
Expressed in the Psalms

A century ago the Psalms were studied as individual composi-
tions expressive of personal piety and devotion. Today the
psalms are recognized as part of Israel's collective worship. Indeed, quite like worship hymnals today, they originated over a
lengthy time period; single pieces were collectively as well as individually composed. Just as a worship hymnal contains different types of songs intended for various occasions, so also the
book of Psalms contains three major forms: lament, thanksgiving song, and hymn. Together these forms describe the full
range of a people's experience with God.

The Lament

Difficult situations and frustrations were as common for ancient Israel as for us. Extended drought jeopardized the food supply. Epidemics brought fear, misery, and sorrow. Marching armies from the east or the south threatened Israel's security, even her future. Individuals suffered reverses or were the victims of family or neighborhood intrigue. People fell sick. Such situations of desperation brought the pious in Israel, collectively or individually, before Yahweh. In studying the Psalms, scholars have identified the lament form as appropriate for such times.

The lament consists of several standard components and is basically a stereotyped format into which the supplicant could pour a specific complaint or request; or, equally likely, existing laments became the ready vehicle for the troubled person addressing God in prayer.

The lament psalm begins with a word of address, often with the vocative, "O LORD." The specific complaint is then detailed: an enemy is threatening havoc, or is already tormenting the supplicant. There follows a prayer for help or deliverance. This may be as brief as "LORD, save me," or it may be an extended petition, documented with reasons for God to hear and pleas for his early intervention. Next follows a statement of confidence, e.g., "The LORD does not bypass those who are humble and contrite of heart." The psalm concludes with a word of praise to the LORD.

To the modern reader the praise feature appears out of character considering the immediately preceding sketch of the petitioner's plight. Scholars have conjectured that in a worship ritual the supplicant would appear before the LORD in the temple area and officiating priests would give a word of divine promise to the troubled person. Hannah's experience illustrates the point; her earnest prayer, though at first misinterpreted by Eli, who thought her drunken, brought a divine assurance from God through Eli: "Go in peace; the God of Israel grant the petition you have made to him" (1 Sam 1:17). It seems reasonable to suppose that such a word from God, though not recorded in the lament, was the reason for the final stanza of praise.

Psalm 13 is a short but excellent example of a lament by an individual. This lament opens with *direct* address, "How long, O LORD? Will you forget me forever? How long will you hide your face from me?" The *complaint*, in including a reference to unanswered prayer, is couched in the phrase "sorrow in my heart," and more pointedly, "How long shall my enemy be exalted over me?" The *prayer* section of the lament opens with, "Consider and answer me, O LORD my God!" The *profession of confidence* is a bicola, a two-line statement with parallel ideas:

> But I trusted in your steadfast love;
> my heart shall rejoice in your salvation (v. 5).

The final *praise section* following soon upon the earlier complaint with its focus of "sleeping the sleep of death," is exultant in mood: "I will sing to the LORD, because he has dealt bountifully with me." The praise word is suggestive of the release from burdens that is experienced in prayer. Someone has said, "Prayer is the place where burdens change shoulders."

The lament form, we may note in passing, is not peculiar to Israel. One ancient Near Eastern lament begins, "How long, O my Lady, wilt though be angered so that thy face is turned away?"[3] The similarities in wording with Psalm 13 are quite striking.

Scholars have identified approximately fifty psalms in the category of lament. Sub-classifications apart from the individual lament include the communal lament and the penitential lament.

Individual lament	3, 4, 5, 7, 9, 10, 13, etc.
Communal lament	12, 44, 60, 94, 137
Penitential lament	6, 32, 51, 102, 143

Lament forms also appear outside the psalms, as in the prophets and in the book of Lamentations, which contains both individual lament (e.g., chapter 3) and communal lament (e.g., chapter 2). There is perhaps no more striking lament than Jer 20:7–13—striking because of its surprising boldness:

> O LORD, you have enticed me, and I was enticed . . .
> I have become a laughing stock all day long (v. 7).

True to the lament stereotype, this lament concludes, despite the opening description of agony of soul, with "Sing to the LORD; praise the LORD!" (v. 13).

An understanding of the lament form helps greatly to follow the thought sequence of a longer psalm such as Psalm 22. At first sight it appears quite jumbled. In reality the psalm closely follows the lament outline.

> Complaint: "My God, my God, why have you forsaken me?" (vv. 1–8)
> Confidence: "Yet it was you who took me from the womb" (vv. 9–10)
> Prayer: "Do not be far from me, for trouble is near . . ." (vv. 11–21)
> Praise: "I will praise you . . ." (vv. 22–32)

The lament psalms describe a specific situation, yet are not so specific that they cannot properly be the literary vehicles for other persons, even generations of later believers, to give expression to distress. When pressed into a difficult situation, who cannot identify with the writer's anxiety and desperation: "I am poured out like water, and all my bones are out of joint; my heart is like wax" (Ps 22:14)? Indeed, our Lord's word on the cross, a quotation from Psalm 22, "My God, my God, why have you forsaken me?" may be intended, as some suggest, to be shorthand for the entire psalm as an expression of Christ's own agony.

The lament psalms suggest that Israel, whether collectively or as individuals, experienced God as one who was involved in life with them. These psalms depict a people who believed their God to be present, ready to help. He was there for them. The personal, even intimate dimensions of the relationship are significant. The confidence statements are a study in intimacy, for they consist of confessional statements about God and testimonies to past experiences with him. Perhaps the most striking fact of all is that while one third of the psalms are in lament form, all but one (Psalm 88) include praise.[4]

The Thanksgiving Song

Closely allied to the lament form is another recognizably distinct form, the thanksgiving song. It too reflects the way in which Israel experienced God. Here, too, scholars have distinguished a communal form (e.g., Pss 75, 107, 124) and an individual form (e.g., Pss 18, 30, 34, 118, 138). The thrust of a thanksgiving psalm is to render thanks to Yahweh for his help in a specific incident in life. For his deliverance, Israel's fitting response, like Jonah's, is: "But I with the voice of thanksgiving will sacrifice to thee" (Jonah 2:9).

The thanksgiving psalm has three parts. In an introduction, the worshiper states his intention to give thanks: "I will extol you, O LORD, for you have drawn me up" (Ps 30:1). The main section usually describes deliverance from a distress. The conclusion frequently contains a vow to give praise: "O LORD my God, I will give thanks to you forever" (Ps 30:12). It is a characteristic of this type of psalm that its main section outlines a relatively concrete situation, such as illness or war, from which the LORD has granted deliverance. Psalm 30 is illustrative: "I cried to you for help, and you have healed me." Not only has the writer been ill, however; the poet has fallen on hard times: "You had established me as a strong mountain; you hid your face" (Ps 30:7). Dismayed that his religion was inoperative, the individual prays and argues from the standpoint of profit and loss that were death to come, God would lose a worshiper, much to God's disadvantage.

The thanksgiving form also is not unique to Israel. A votive stele from the fifth century BC shows the king before the goddess with a libation cup. He addresses the goddess Ba'alat, the female counterpart of Baal: "Yehaw-milk, king of Byblos, to my lady, Ba'alat of Byblos; for when I cried to my lady Ba'alat of

Byblos then she heard me and showed me favor."[5] Israel
claimed that her rescue came from Yahweh and not a Baal.

A communal thanksgiving psalm such as Psalm 107 is helpful in illuminating Israel's experience with God. First, it exhibits
a marked enthusiasm; Israel was joyful about her God.

> O give thanks to the LORD, for he is good . . .
> Let the redeemed of the LORD say so,
> Those he redeemed from trouble (vv. 1–2).

Secondly, Israel knows God as active in a people's life. God
is real, and has a concern for the welfare of his people. The
threatening circumstances are itemized: refugees were in severe
straits (vv. 4–9); prisoners were apparently doomed (vv. 10–16);
an illness brought extreme nausea (vv. 17–22); and mariners at
sea were caught in a terrifying storm (vv. 23–32). But in each instance God came to the rescue. Thirdly, Israel celebrates the
power of God. In each circumstance God turned the situation
from evil into good. God is the God of the great reversals. Israel
revels in the transformation which God brings about.

> He turns rivers into a desert,
> springs of water into thirsty ground . . .
> He turns a desert into pools of water,
> a parched land into springs of water (vv. 33, 35).

Finally, as is evident from the way in which the psalm is bracketed by references to God's kindness, Israel celebrates the covenant love (ḥesed) of Yahweh.

> His steadfast love (ḥesed) endures forever . . .
> Let those who are wise give heed to these things,
> and consider the steadfast love (ḥesed) of the LORD
> (vv. 1, 43).

Israel responded in thanksgiving to God in recognition of his
redemption, God's concern for a people in a "down" situation,
God's transforming power, and God's covenant loyalty. Their
response, expanded in the laments but touched on also in the
thanksgiving songs, took into account the pain of God's

hiddenness and the distress of feeling his absence (Ps 13:1; 44:23). All the more forceful then are the thanksgiving anthems which, subsequent to God's distancing, celebrate God's presence and provision in a time of need.

The Hymn

A third psalm form is the hymn, which, like the thanksgiving psalm, is in three parts. The shortest psalm, Psalm 117, exemplifies the hymn in its most abbreviated form.

> Introductory summons: "Praise the LORD" (v. 1)
> Main section: "For great is his steadfast love toward us" (v. 2)
> Summary summons: "Praise the LORD!" (v. 2)

Each of these three parts can be greatly expanded, as can be illustrated by the hymns in Psalms 103–104, Hab 3:2–19 and Exod 15:1–18.

In Psalm 113, the summons to praise is expanded to three verses (1–3). The main body of the psalm, characteristically given to reasons for praise, offers two reasons for praise to God. First, God's majesty: "The LORD is high above all nations, and his glory above the heavens" (v. 4). Rhetorically the writer can ask, who is higher than God? Secondly, Yahweh's condescension: "He raises the poor from the dust" (v. 7). In a domestic reference that is almost out of character with the earlier mention of God's grandeur, the psalm concludes, "He gives the barren woman a home, making her the joyous mother of children" (v. 9). In strange and rapid succession the writer moves from the glories of the universe to ash-heaps and children: he affirms that God is an exalted God over nature and nations, and yet one who takes note of a barren woman. What response is appropriate to a God of the heavens whose interest includes the happiness of a household? Answer: praise (v. 9).

Other psalms point to God's work in history as sufficient reason for praise. One such psalm recalls God's people, the plagues in Egypt, and the role of Joseph and Moses   in delivering God's people, the plagues in Egypt, and the abundant water supplies in the desert (Ps 105). Others celebrate the "creation" of Israel (e.g., Pss 111, 114, 149). Numerous reasons are offered in the hymns for glorious praise to God.

Like the lament and the thanksgiving psalm, the hymn form is also found among Israel's neighbors. The celebrated Egyptian hymn to the god Aton is not unlike Israel's hymn:

How manifold it is what thou hast made . . .
Thou didst create the world according to thy desire . . .
Thou settest every man in his place,
Thou suppliest their necessities.
The Aton of the day great of majesty.[6]

But such features as God's covenant with Israel and the promises to his people are peculiar to Israel's hymnody.

Psalm 8 is an important hymn because it regards people as the occasion for praise and, incidentally, explains the basis for the possibility of a person's experience with God. The psalm is divided into three parts:

An ascription of praise verses 1–2: "O LORD, our
            Sovereign, how majestic is your name . . ."
Reflection: vv. 3–8
            Questions: vv. 3–5 "What are human beings that
                        you are mindful of them?"
            Answers: vv. 5–8 "You have made them a little
                        lower than God . . ."
An ascription of praise verse 9: "O LORD, our Sovereign,
            how majestic is your name . . ."

The central question is a query about the worth of human beings. While the context for the question, namely rapture in beholding the heavenly bodies of moon and stars in the heavens, might lead to an answer emphasizing human insignificance, the actual answer is the opposite: persons are of great worth. The author plots the place of human beings with reference to God and creation. If one were to imagine a scale of 1 to 10 with living creatures such as beasts at 1 and God at 10, so high is the writer's estimate of human beings, one would have to put them at 8 or 9. "You have made them a little lower than God." It is God and not animals who is humankind's closest relative. But people do not have equality with God. The psalmist is not a humanist. Nevertheless, men and women are creatures crowned with glory and honor. Human beings are persons with dignity.

Human beings are also persons of responsibility. God has called humankind to rule over the works of God's hands, including domestic and wild beasts, birds and fish. C. S. Lewis remarked at the coronation of Queen Elizabeth in 1953 that "the pressing of that huge, heavy crown on that small, young head was a symbol of the situation of all men. God has called humanity to be His vice-regent and high priest on earth."[7] Human beings are persons of dignity because of their affinity with God and persons of responsibility because of their role in relation to creatures.

Two comments are pertinent to our topic. First, it is the human being in his or her person, quite apart from his or her performance, that confers dignity and gives rise to the paean of praise. Despite human fallenness, human beings are prime exhibits of God's majesty. Reflection on people evokes praise to God: "O LORD, our Sovereign, how majestic is your name in all the earth" (Ps 8:9). Not only the wonderful world of nature, nor alone God's acts in history, but human beings *as human beings* offer reason for praise to God. Second, experience of God is possible because human beings are God's next of kin. Experience of God is premised on this affinity between God and persons. Made in God's image, human beings are in a position to engage in dialogue with God, this hymn declares. The praise of God, for whatever reason, brings gladness. The hymn, along with the cult festivals, underscores the joyous element in Israel's religious experience. The frequent references to song and musical instruments (e.g., Psalm 150) emphasize the jubilant character of her worship. The imperatives to praise given in the plural, together with the exhortations for all people to take up the praise song, emphasize praise to God as given in a collective setting. The congregation praises God. Not a lone, isolated voice, but choirs and large assemblies lift up a chorus of praise (cf. Pss 146–149).

An examination of the psalms from the point of view of Israel's expression of its life with Yahweh forces the conclusion that God is not marginal but a vital reality in Israel's life. The Old Testament does not contain lengthy philosophical or theoretical essays about God. We hear about Israel's God not from the essayist but from the worshiper. An enunciation of God's attributes, even, is almost always in the context of prayer or praise.

To be sure, the vigor of a relationship with God as examined in the psalms is not uniformly characteristic of all Israel, and certainly not for all of her history, otherwise prophetic judgment speeches would have been unnecessary. Before we turn to this genre, however, we shall examine another range of literature that indicates the way in which Israel understood her relationship to Yahweh.

2. The Experience of God In Wisdom Literature

Had we only the Psalms, we might conclude that a people's experience with God is primarily a "spiritual" one, and that, though related to crises in life, it is nevertheless quite closely tied to temple and worship. That assessment would be inaccurate. There is another dimension of a people's experience with God, one that surfaces in the wisdom literature.

Wisdom for moderns represents sagacity, often learnedness or a computer-like accumulation of information. The technical word "wisdom" (*ḥokmâ*) in the Bible refers to skill, as for example the ability to do metal or woodcraft (Exod 31:3–5). As used in the book of Proverbs, wisdom is skill in living. Wisdom deals with mastery of life. If the psalms suggest the setting of temple and cult for an experience of God, the wisdom books (Ecclesiastes, Proverbs, Job) point us to the street and the school.

Debate continues among scholars as to the sociological "home" of wisdom. A strong case can be made that wisdom material, such as Proverbs, originated in the king's court. The proverbs are attributed to King Solomon (Prov 1:1) or King Lemuel (Prov 31:1); some were collected by the scholars of Hezekiah, king of Judah (Prov 25:1). Proverbs are also known to us from Egypt. There, learned sages, usually in a court setting, instructed courtiers in the acceptable way of palace and government. The references to kings in Proverbs (e.g., 22:9; 24:21; 30:28) support the contention that the proverbs were propounded and recorded among the learned of the day in the environs of the king's palace.

A second, somewhat differing, view is that the proverbs belong to the common people, and that the origin of the book of proverbs is to be found among the tribes-people of Israel. The proponents of this view point to the homespun wisdom circulated among primitive peoples today. In Israel's history, too, the wise person was someone in the local community who, like the wise woman of Tekoa, was respected (2 Sam 14:2ff). Some proverbs, such as the one about the irritability of a nagging woman, are folksy in nature (Prov 19:13).

Whether only one particular life setting can be determined for wisdom material is doubtful. It is possible that teachers in the court and scholars gathered and refined folk proverbs and added to them. Research on this problem will continue.

Research has, however, made it clear that wisdom materials were common in the ancient Near East and not peculiar to Israel. In fact there is a strong similarity between a block of Proverbs (22:17 – 24:22) and the Egyptian instruction of Amen-em-opet, which according to some scholars predates the Israelite collection. The Mesopotamian poem "A Dialogue about Human Misery" is reminiscent in many ways of the biblical Job. Such information raises interesting reflections. If the wisdom sayings of people outside Israel found their way into Scripture, what does that suggest about truth in other religions, the nature of revelation, and Israelite ethics?

While there are similarities between ancient Near Eastern wisdom and Israelite wisdom, there are major distinctions, and one above all. The wisdom materials of Israel are interlaced with the mention of Yahweh. This feature puts books like Proverbs and Job in a class by themselves. There may be folksy wisdom, but overall, the guidelines for living are viewed in relationship to Yahweh. In Proverbs the word Yahweh occurs eighty-six times. Obviously, not every saying about table manners or domestic life is grounded in a reference to Yahweh. But a religious presupposition, especially an understanding of Yahweh, is clearly apparent. Some examples:

Do not say, "I will repay evil";
wait for the LORD, and he will help you (20:22).

The hearing ear and the seeing eye—
The LORD has made them both (20:12).

Whoever is kind to the poor lends to the LORD,
and will be repaid in full (19:17).

Do not be afraid of sudden panic . . .
for the LORD will be your confidence (3:25–26).

When Israelites thought about wisdom—skills for living—they thought also about Yahweh.

Proverbs

The relationship between Yahweh and wisdom is a subject of frequent mention in Proverbs. It has been noted that two large blocks (10:1 – 14:25 and 16:16 – 22:16) are bound together by a middle block (14:26 – 16:15) which especially stresses the fear of Yahweh. The maxim "The fear of the LORD is the beginning of wisdom" is a programmatic statement for the book of Proverbs (9:10; cf. 15:33; 1:7; Job 28:28). The statement emphasizes reverence for God as the first plank in the platform for skillful living: Yahweh is the source from which skillful living derives. To put it negatively, there is no living of life skillfully without a recognition of Yahweh.

The book of Proverbs cements this understanding of wisdom to Yahweh in yet another way. Through much of the book the exhortations concerning conduct are spoken by Lady Wisdom; she is said to call in the streets crying for young men to follow her (1:20; 8:1). Her counterpart is Dame Folly, the "strange woman" who likewise invites men to enter her house (chapter 7). On the surface one might think that what is at issue is sexual purity of the younger generation—they are warned about the houses of prostitution; they are urged to keep themselves morally pure. But the admonitions are more basic. Dame Folly and Lady Wisdom represent two directions in life: the way of evil in whatever guise, and the way of righteousness.

The opening chapters of the book describe the two roadways, detailing the company on each road and describing the ultimate destiny. Dame Folly destroys her victims. "Her house is the way of Sheol, going down to the chambers of death" (7:27). In contrast, Lady Wisdom walks in the way of righteousness, bestows wealth on those who follow her, and offers safety: "those who listen to me will be secure and will live at ease, without dread of disaster" (1:33). Now this talk about Dame Folly and Lady Wisdom could be moralistic, except for an important consideration: Lady Wisdom is in Yahweh's company. She belongs to him. She was with Yahweh from the beginning of creation: "The LORD created me at the beginning of his work . . . I was beside him, like a master worker" (8:22, 30). The voice of Wisdom, then, is like the prophet's call—a voice from the court of Yahweh; Wisdom is the spokesperson for Yahweh.

Thus far we have made one basic observation about Israel's experience of Yahweh based on wisdom materials: Israel's wisdom, or skill for living, was Yahweh-oriented. This means that everyday life, including business transactions, life in the house, and emotions, are given a religious dimension.

The implications of such a stance need to be stressed. Religion was a this-worldly matter. Yahweh's will and instruction touched on life at its most down-to-earth level. For example, one refrained from revenge because of the conviction that vengeance was in God's hand (cf. 20:22). The proverbs have an

earthy, even crusty flavor. Don't be lazy; learn from the ant (6:6).
Don't flirt about; drink water from your own cistern (5:15). Ill-
gotten gain does not profit (10:2). Be honest: false balance is an
abomination to the LORD (11:1). Exercise self-control; don't go
with a hot-tempered man (22:24; cf. 25:28). Control your appe-
tite; at the last wine bites like a serpent (23:32). Be kind to animals (12:10). Choose your friends with care (1:10ff). Remember
that a beautiful woman who lacks discretion is as a "gold ring in
a pig's snout" (11:22).

The separation between the sacred and the secular would
have been quite foreign to Israel. The Song of Solomon is a
poem about human love within the context of sexual intimacy.
This book nevertheless is part of the biblical canon.

It is in the wisdom literature, though not only there (cf.
Ruth), that we glimpse the pervasive manner in which Yahwism
affected life. Wisdom literature cannot be accused of fostering a
mystical or *unpractical* notion about religion. Reading wisdom literature will keep one's feet on the ground.

The experience with Yahweh as pictured in the Proverbs is
clearly defined with respect to reward and punishment. Quite
simply, those with good behavior will be rewarded, those with
evil conduct will be punished. The rewards are not rewards in
the after-life, about which Proverbs has virtually nothing to say.
Large claims for well-being in this life, however, are often made.
"Riches and honor are with me, enduring wealth and prosperity" (8:18). Elsewhere it is maintained, "The LORD does not let
the righteous go hungry . . . Blessings are on the head of the
righteous" (10:3, 6); "The fear of the LORD prolongs life, but
the years of the wicked will be short" (10:27). The contrast between evil and good is black and white. Consequences of good
and evil conduct are stated in absolute terms—overstated, some
would insist. "No harm happens to the righteous, but the
wicked are filled with trouble" (12:21). God is clearly above all,
ensuring the outcomes of a personal life in accordance with
one's character and action. Self-interest then would dictate
shunning evil. The conclusion from Proverbs also is obvious.

Misfortunes in one's life are the result of foolish or sinful behavior or attitudes.

Thus one block of wisdom material (Proverbs and Ecclesiastes) depicts life with Yahweh as straightforward. From Israel's viewpoint, proverbial wisdom is integral to Yahwism. The involvement of Yahweh is definitely existential, this-worldly. Choices and consequences of ethical behavior are crisp and clean. The book of Ecclesiastes, given to the raising of questions more than offering of answers, nevertheless ends by maintaining:

> The end of the matter; all has been heard. Fear God, and keep his commandments; for that is the whole duty of everyone. For God will bring every deed into judgment, including every secret thing, whether good or evil' (Eccl 12:13–14).

Drama

But the whole story has not been told. The book of Job presents another facet of life with Yahweh. The book, while in the wisdom mode and replete with sayings and proverbs, is cast in its poetic section (3:1 – 42:6) in drama form. Argument among scholars will probably continue on the question of whether the book is a unity, or whether an early story was used by the poet for a series of reflections in dramatic form.

More critical than its unity, but as controversial, is the book's message. A variety of interpretations are offered, accounted for perhaps by the form, since drama, like poetry, evokes emotional responses, and touches on a variety of themes which may be differently interlaced to make for unity—but not an identical unity for every reader. One view, which has only a few supporters, is that the message of Job is sin-oriented. Job knew he was righteous (so the interpretation goes), but his righteousness became an occasion for boasting and pride, and so sin was the basic problem after all. More common is the view that since suffering launches the story, the book ponders the problem of theodicy: "How can a good God, capable of averting suffering, still allow it?" The same question is at the heart of the view that Job as a book is intended as a commentary on Israel's exile. In this view the key to the book is Satan's question, "Does Job fear God for nothing?" (1:9).

Another view is that the book deals with the bankruptcy of orthodoxy. Using the example of suffering, the writer shows that the old ethical mores espoused in Proverbs are inadequate, or at least do not embrace all possibilities. Experience demonstrates that the easy and simplified answer to morality, "Do good and you will prosper," is too easy and over-simplified. The three friends, and Elihu too, uphold and press the old answers. Each asserts the nexus between sin and suffering, but with varying nuances. Eliphaz argues that the innocent do not suffer, but then, since total innocence is hardly possible, some suffering may be necessary. The death of Job's children, argues Bildad, is no doubt due to sin, and so Job should take heed (8:5–6). Zophar suggests that Job needs to repent for sins he has committed (11:6c). Elihu adds the possibility that the suffering may be meant as a warning to keep Job back from sin (33:19–28).[8] Job's argument is that these answers are insufficient. The old doctrine and especially the old clichés no longer fit. Where is the Yahweh worshiper when one is forced to conclude that the formulations of Yahwism which one has known are no longer adequate?

Closely allied to the view that Job teaches the bankruptcy of orthodox wisdom is the view that the problem addressed by the book of Job is struggling with an understanding of the nature and ways of God. The general conception is that God is a righteous judge, and that this means that God always punishes wickedness (8:3). While Job subscribes to this view, there are moments in which Job charges that God is capricious (18–19), and that quite possibly his judgments can also be corrupt (19:20–29). The purpose of the friends' speeches is to expose a naive view of God. These men feel they know how God works, they have answers to the enigmas of life. Job himself is reaching for something or someone greater than the definition of God given by these friends. But he is hardly prepared for the awesome event of God's appearance. While Job may not have definitions of God, he is clearly up against a mystery, the mystery of a God whose ways are impenetrable and whose person is overpowering. The answer to the mystery of God's ways is still partial at the end of the book, but now for Job the answer is adequate.

So understood, our topic, experience with God, is given a distinctly fresh dimension. If the main-line wisdom school insisted on the involvement of God in business and domestic life and a straightforward view of reward and punishment, Job, while insisting on God's intersection with the everyday, challenges the clichés and affirms the mystery. God is inscrutable. As in other areas of Old Testament thought, tension surfaces. The modern believer, like the Israelite, also lives in that tension: the ways of God are transparent, but then again they are not.

3. The Experience of God From the Prophets

In investigating the knowledge of Yahweh we turn from poetry and proverbs to prophetic materials. According to the Hebrew arrangement of Old Testament books, the books of Samuel and Kings fall into the prophetic classifications. Here the non-western understanding of "knowing God" is apparent from an expression in the story of Samuel, who, so reads the record, was "ministering to the LORD under Eli" (1 Sam 3:1). Yet a few statements later within the same incident one reads, "Samuel did not yet know the LORD" (1 Sam 3:7). Clearly the writer does not mean that Samuel was informationally ignorant of Yahweh, for Samuel was already serving Yahweh; but "knowing" is not theoretical or even primarily informational. Knowing is experiencing. To paraphrase: Samuel had not yet had experience in the ways of God. Experience came soon enough, with God's call to Samuel by night with a message of judgment; and Samuel came to know, experience, the word of Yahweh.

The narrative sections that deal with the monarchy illustrate God's becoming known not through word only, but through event. An example comes from the life of Elijah. He calls Baal-worshipping Israel to Carmel in order that Israel might know who is God. After the rules of the contest are given and after the champions of Baal have admitted defeat, Elijah prays, "Answer me, O LORD, answer me, that this people may *know* that you, O LORD, are God" (1 Kgs 18:37). The irony of that incident is that Baal, who is the god of rain and who is depicted in ancient friezes with stylized lightning and a thunder mace in his hands, is unable to bring fire upon the altar. Yahweh, however, answers his servant Elijah: fire consumes the offering; people fall on their faces and acknowledge, "The LORD indeed is God." Through an event, they have experienced Yahweh. In the life of Manasseh an event, namely his release from Assyrian captivity, is the key to an experience of Yahweh. After God restored him to his throne in Jerusalem "then Manasseh knew that the LORD indeed was God" (2 Chr 33:13).

Scholars have argued about the relative place of word and event in the revelation of God and in a people's experience of deity. Out of that discussion has come new appreciation for the interrelationship of word and event. On the one hand, the word to Samuel is fulfilled historically in God's judgment on Eli and his sons. On the other hand, the event at Carmel was a compelling event for Yahweh's disclosure because of the accompanying interpretive word. There is truth in the claim that the Old Testament talks relatively little about believing God. Its stress is on knowing God, for it is knowledge of Yahweh that is the basic presupposition for Israel's existence. Knowledge of God, not speculative, theoretical knowledge but experiential knowledge through word and event, is foundational to an understanding of reality.

The place of knowing God is illustrated by David and Jeremiah. In David's speech to Goliath David announces that he is coming in the name of Yahweh, and he anticipates a particular consequence:

> This very day the LORD will deliver you into my hand . . . that all
> the earth may know that there is a God in Israel, and that all this
> assembly may know that the LORD does not save by sword and
> spear; for the battle is the LORD's (1 Sam 17:46–47).

The pinnacle of knowledge is asserted by the prophet Jeremiah:

> Thus says the LORD: "Do not let the wise boast in their wisdom,
> do not let the mighty boast in their might, do not let the wealthy
> boast in their wealth; but let those who boast boast in this, that
> they understand and know me, that I am the LORD" (Jer
> 9:23–24).

Believing God, while important, is premised in large part on
knowing God; this knowledge receives repeated emphasis in
the prophets.

Prophetic Judgment Speech

Prophets before Jeremiah's day highlighted the place of knowledge but in another way. Hosea, for example, remonstrated
with Israelites, citing them for their lack of knowledge. Within
the last several decades scholars have identified a literary form
described as a prophetic judgment speech.[9] In its classical pattern it consists of a word of address, accusation(s), messenger
formula, and an announcement. An important insight derived
from this form analysis is that the announcement of the impending future is not a detached crystal-ball gazing, but is
grounded in the current situation.

The accusation functions as the reason for the announcement or prediction. When one examines the list of accusations,
one finds that there is frequently a summary statement, either
at the outset or at the conclusion of a list. That summary statement in several instances has to do with knowledge of Yahweh,
as in the following, "Their deeds do not permit them to return
to their God. For the spirit of whoredom is within them, and
they do not know the LORD" (Hos 5:4). Similarly, in the court
case of God the plaintiff against Israel the accused, the LORD
itemizes a series of evils: "There is swearing, murder, stealing."

This list is preceded by a summary statement, "There is . . . no knowledge of God in the land" (4:1).

Such an indictment about the absence of the knowledge of God is serious because God puts high priority on it. People may even worship regularly, but God looks for something more. "For I desire steadfast love and not sacrifice, the *knowledge of God* rather than burnt offerings" (Hos 6:6).

The book of Isaiah likewise highlights the importance of the knowledge of God. The opening blast is stunning.

> Hear, O heavens and listen, O earth . . .
> The ox knows its owner,
> and the donkey its master's crib;
> but Israel does not know,
> my people do not understand (1:2–3).

Israel—like all people made a little lower than God—ranks below the dumb beast in intelligence! Underlying all other evils is failure to "know Yahweh."

Jeremiah, who stands in the tradition of Hosea, often touches on the theme of knowing God. Like Hosea, he sees Israel's failure at this point as the general reason for other failures. "My people are foolish, they do not know me" (Jer 4:22). Two accusation speeches charging adultery and dishonesty conclude with, "They do not know me" and "They refuse to know me" (Jer 9:3, 6).

One may learn a definition of knowing God from the series of accusations against individual kings (Jer 22:2 – 23:6). Jehoiakim is accused of extravagance at the expense of righteousness and justice. Jeremiah points him to his father Josiah: "He judged the cause of the poor and the needy; then it was well. Is not this to know me? says the LORD" (Jer 22:16). Knowing God, we learn, is not only an experience of him through word or event, but means practicing his will. Knowing God is associated with a particular lifestyle.

Salvation Speeches

The prophetic judgment speeches magnify the significance of the knowledge of God. The salvation speeches, though opposite, likewise reinforce that significance. Scholars identify a variety of salvation speeches, each with its own set of elements.[10] The ordering of these components is somewhat flexible. The assurance of salvation speech (Isa 43:1–4, 5–7) includes such components as a word of consolation with a substantiation and an elaboration of consequences. The announcement of salvation speech (Isa 41:17–20) may begin with an allusion to lament, proclaim salvation by defining Yahweh's stance or by describing his intervention, and conclude with the end in view. In the sections in which the positive results of God's intervention are announced the prospect of knowing God is a feature. Hosea may serve as an initial example. In one of the salvation announcements, the good news is couched in courtship and betrothal language.

> And I will take you for my wife forever; I will take you for my wife in righteousness and in justice, in steadfast love, and in mercy. I will take you for my wife in faithfulness; and you shall know the LORD (2:19–20).

Knowledge of God is not for Israel only. In Isaiah the knowledge of God extends beyond Israel to Egypt. "The LORD will make himself known to the Egyptians; and the Egyptians will know the LORD on that day" (Isa 19:21). The "new covenant" announcement from Jeremiah extends the prospect of knowing God to all; the law of God will be put in the hearts of the people: "No longer shall they teach one another, or say to each other, 'Know the LORD,' for they shall all know me, from the least of them to the greatest" (Jer 31:34). Nowhere is the ubiquitous knowledge of God more enthusiastically embraced than in Ezekiel, where salvation announcement upon salvation announcement culminates with, "Then they shall know that I am the LORD." But since Ezekiel is a prophet of the exile following the monarchy, a discussion of his usage belongs in the next section.

Thus the old Testament not only offers examples of people knowing Yahweh, but points forward to a time when with greater intensity and with greater depth men and women will know Yahweh.

To summarize: the knowledge of God is a subject in the Psalms where, especially in the lament but also in the thanksgiving and the human, knowledge as experience is illumined. In Proverbs experience of God takes on a down-to-earth dimension. In Job, clichés about knowing God are tested. The prophets criticize a people among whom there is an absence of knowing God, but in salvation speeches they also depict a new age which they characterize as a time when all shall know God. In this chapter, we have been alert to literary forms, and the emphasis has been on communicating about experiences with God. The standpoint from which we examined the literary material was primarily that of the believer giving expression to his experience. At points sober reflection and even wrestling with ambiguities characterize an individual's description of the experience of God. But the reality and importance of an encounter with God is not in doubt. Paul's assertion can be heard with greater clarity against the Old Testament background. He reiterated the goal, "that I may know him" (Phil 3:10).

10
Life and Land

God's design as stated in Exod 5:22 – 6:8 and repeated in Hos 2:14–23 included bringing Israel to the land. The books of Joshua and Judges describe how this intention came to fulfillment. But God's plan went beyond Israel's reaching the land to their taking possession of it and living in it. What can be said about the implementation of the plan for the good life for the period 1000–587?

In general, to anticipate our discussion, the story follows the stress patterns we have already noted. The good life in the land with Yahweh was severely put to the test and challenged, as progress toward an ideal goal almost always is. In some ways the challenge was admirably met, but in other ways life in the land went sour, so that toward the end of the period prophets issued dire threats and finally announced the loss of the land. The topics to be discussed are three: (1) the good life from the perspective of wisdom literature; (2) the good life and management of the land—the historians' view; and (3) the good life and loss of land—an assessment from the prophets.

The relationship of "life" to land and wisdom materials is not at first obvious. Land is turf, but very early it acquires a symbolic meaning. For Israel land is the promised land, the good land, and as such is symbolic of a rich quality of life. To be in the land is to be the recipient of the blessings of God. For the land is a "land flowing with milk and honey" (Deut 26:9), a land with blessings of security, a land free from molestation, and above all a land with the blessing of God's presence. It is almost axiomatic that the prospect of dwelling in the land involved more than substituting a Palestinian address for an Egyptian address. At stake was the quality of life, so that the word "I will bring you into the land" is only partially fulfilled when the people pass through the Jordan and set foot on the land. The promise entails more than a promise for survival; it is a promise of a vitality of life unknown to the people while living in Egypt. God wanted Israel to possess the land, but not to possess it meagerly, eking out a bare existence. "The LORD your God will bring you into the land . . . and you will possess it . . . Moreover, the LORD your God will circumcise your heart . . . so that you will love the LORD your God . . . *in order that you may live*" (Deut 30:5–6; cf. 12:1). For the Hebrew, "life" is more than remaining alive; it is existence with gusto and enjoyment. God says through the prophet Jeremiah at the end of the period: "I brought you into a plentiful land to eat its fruits and its good things" (Jer 2:7).

This abundant quality of life can be studied from three points of view, following the genres of wisdom, history, and prophecy. The good life is specifically the subject of wisdom literature; just as the subject of land has an earthiness about it, so wisdom, especially Proverbs, is oriented to everyday experience. The historical books Samuel–Kings describe how the kings conduct themselves; the behavior toward their trust, which included management of land, determined the quality of life of the people in their land. Finally, the prophets of the period, pointing to the misrule and defection of leaders and people, eventually announced termination of life in the land.

1. The Good Life in the Land
A Perspective from Wisdom Literature

Wisdom literature is devoted specifically to exploring and pontificating upon the subject of living. Strictly speaking wisdom literature comprises the books of Proverbs, Job, and Ecclesiastes, though the Song of Solomon is often included as well. Of course, these books are not the sole books in which the quality of life is a concern. The pentateuchal laws are intended to govern life; prophets such as Amos exhort the people to "seek good and not evil, that you may live" (Amos 5:14; cf. Isa 55:3–5). Yet the preoccupation with the quality of everyday living belongs to the literature left by Israel's sages. About the message of this literature one scholar says, "The kerygma of wisdom can be summed up in one word: 'life.'"[1] Support for the position is at hand: "Whoever finds me (wisdom) finds life" (Prov 8:35).

The object of God's salvific activity by bringing the people into the land, it will be remembered, was to make possible a new quality of life.

Upon entry into the land God's word to the people through Moses was,

> See, I have set before you today life and prosperity . . . then you shall live and become numerous, and the LORD your God will bless you in the land that you are entering to possess (Deut 30:15–16; cf. v. 20).

One hears the same motif of life from wisdom literature.

> Hear, my child, and accept my words,
> that the years of your life may be many . . .
> Keep hold of instruction; do not let go;
> guard her, for she is your life (Prov 4:10, 13).

It is at the point of "life" that the design of God about land and the message of wisdom intersect.

The Quality of Life According to Wisdom Literature

Wisdom literature is a literary fabric with several quite clearly colored strands. These include, apart from the themes of wisdom and life, rehearsals of creation, delight in nature, attention to moral rectitude, the fear of Yahweh, and skill in living generally. A brief look at each will give definition to "quality of life" and also show how wisdom is linked with land.

Wisdom literature plays on the theme of creation. God is the creator. The mythical background of chaos found in other ancient Near Eastern creation stories may find a poetic echo, perhaps, in Job: "By his power he stilled the Sea; by his understanding he struck down Rahab. By his wind the heavens were made fair; his hand pierced the fleeing serpent" (26:12–13; for the chaos theme cf. Ps 89:10; Isa 41:9–10). But instead of enlarging on the theme of chaos, the creation material dwells on the role of wisdom. God's role as creator is tied closely with wisdom as a quality or even as semi-person in Job and Proverbs.

In Job God is said to know the whereabouts of wisdom, since as creator God has full command of knowledge. At the time that God measured out the waters and ordered wind, rain, and thunder it was announced, "Truly, the fear of the LORD, that is wisdom" (28:23–28). A series of questions put to Job to probe his understanding return to God's creative and profoundly wise activity: "Where were you when I laid the foundation of the earth?" (38:4). "Do you know the ordinances of the heavens? Can you establish their rule on the earth?" (38:33).

In Proverbs the creative works of God, such as establishing the heaven, drawing a "circle on the face of the deep," establishing the fountains of the deep, marking the foundations of the earth, are enumerated; but the emphasis is on wisdom, an entity created prior to these, "the first of his acts of long ago" (8:22). "The LORD by wisdom founded the earth" (3:19). Not only wisdom's priority but her activity as his agent, one who is "beside him" (God) adds weight to her summons, "Listen to me . . . whoever finds me finds life and obtains favor from the LORD" (8:32, 35). The response which wisdom literature wishes to elicit from the reader is a sense of awe and amazement. It is God who does "marvelous things without number" (Job 9:10), who stretched out the heavens and "made the Bear and Orion" (Job 9:8–9). The works of God's hands, such as causing pillars of heaven to tremble, stilling the sea, or hanging the earth upon nothing, "are but the outskirts of his ways; and how small a whisper do we hear of him!" (Job 26:14). Job may well marvel at creation, for there is much he cannot explain (Job 38), but he is driven back to the incomprehensible one who made creation. After the description of Leviathan, one of God's creatures, Job replies, "I know that you can do all things" (42:2). By comparison there is in wisdom more reflection on creation than in Genesis 1–2. In wisdom literature one turns from awe at the complexities of nature to awe of the creator—a significant shift that affects a person's quality of life.

Still, in wisdom the world of nature is affirmed. Furthermore, to touch on a subject controversial in the church, the beauty of physical form is not dismissed or disparaged, but enthusiastically praised. Most striking, though always in good taste, is the discussion of the delight of lovers in each other's bodies in the Song of Solomon. Here the emotion of passion is both recognized and cultivated, and sexual interests positively assessed. Far from spiritualizing the sensuous speeches of the Song, as both Jews and Christians have done, we should take them at face value, as expressive of the joys of physical love.

Yet, for all the enthusiasm about nature, nature is never presented as a god to be worshipped, but as a gift from the creator.[2]

In wisdom the moral dimension of living is placed in the forefront. To live well one should be upright. Throughout there is contrast between the just and the wicked, the wise and the fool. The wise is the person who pursues righteousness; the fool is perverse. Stress is laid on ethical principles. The LORD hates pride, deceit, murder, foul imaginations, and dissension (Prov 6:16–17). The ideal individual, the wise one, is pictured as a person of self-control (Prov 17:27), charitable to the poor (Prov 19:17a), concerned about the widow and orphan (Prov 23:10–11), moderate with respect to riches (Prov 23:24), and respectful of parents (Prov 15:20). Job describes himself as a man who has followed the norms of righteous behavior. He disclaims behavior marked by falsehood or adultery. He has not withheld his hand from helping the poor, he has not been set on money, he has not been malicious or idolatrous (Job 31:5–37). Concern with morality is also indicated by the discussion about retribution. The righteous will be rewarded, the evil punished. "The good obtain favor from the LORD, but those who devise evil he condemns" (Prov 12:2). The righteous will walk straight forward in his way, but the wicked falls by his own wickedness (Prov 11:5).

This dogma of reward for the righteous and wrathful retribution for the wicked is put to the test in the experience of Job. The dogma, so it appears there, is inaccurate, for the righteous person is not rewarded but deprived; and a tension develops even within wisdom. We shall return to this later.

Great attention is given in wisdom literature to choice. One who lives well makes good choices. Particularly forceful are the appeals, set side by side, of Dame Folly and Lady Wisdom (Proverbs 7–8). Each asks the attention of the youths, each offers her attractions. The loose woman decks her couch and perfumes her bed; Lady Wisdom holds out her appeal: "My fruit is better than gold, even fine gold" (Prov 8:19). She claims rulers and kings as her companions and invites association with her. If Dame Folly is pictured as the harlot who entices youth, it should be noted that the invitation to physical cohabitation does not exhaust the meaning of her appeal, nor perhaps is it the primary meaning. More than calls to sexual looseness, her appeal is to all kinds of moral vice and even wickedness generally. Together the calls of the two women enforce the notion of choice, for the young man, hearing both, decides which shall be his companion. This emphasis on moral choice is comparable to Jesus' description of the two ways. The call to decision is ever present and the seriousness of that decision apparent: one way leads to death; the other leads to life. Good choices lead to a good quality of life.

The fear of Yahweh is prominent in the wisdom material, where it is heralded as the beginning of wisdom (Prov 1:7; 9:10; Job 28:28) and the means to life.[3] The fear of Yahweh is not terror but a reverence for God which expresses itself in positive responses to God and his Word. The fear of Yahweh, according to Proverbs and also Deuteronomy, has to do with keeping God's commands and serving him (Deut 10:12–13). Those who fear Yahweh walk in his ways (Prov 14:2). These shun, even hate, evil: "Do not be wise in your own eyes; fear the LORD, and turn away from evil" (Prov 3:7); "The fear of the LORD is hatred of evil" (Prov 8:13). Fear of Yahweh is urged by wisdom writers on the grounds that it will contribute to a high quality of life. "The fear of the Lord is a fountain of life . . ." (Prov 14:27). "The fear of the Lord is life indeed . . ." (Prov 19:23). "The reward for humility and fear of the LORD is riches, and honor and life" (Prov 22:4). Yahweh-fearers can expect security and protection (Prov 14:26; 19:23). Finally, "The fear of the LORD prolongs life" (Prov 10:27).

While we can thus show that the theme of the fear of Yahweh is related to living well, it is helpful to see how such an emphasis on Yahweh distinguished Hebrew wisdom from ancient Near Eastern wisdom. As developed in the ancient Near East, wisdom affirmed a cosmic principle of order, apparently rigid and unbending. In this view a principle rather than a person stood at the center of the universe, and the cosmos as such became a god toward which man's life was to be oriented. The quality of life was determined, in this view, by its conformity to the principle of order inherent in the cosmos. It is most instructive however to see how this potentially dangerous viewpoint is addressed.

In Hebrew wisdom the name of Yahweh is injected with vigor, especially in Proverbs and Ecclesiastes; less so in Job.[4] "The LORD gives wisdom; from his mouth come knowledge and understanding" (Prov 2:6). Yahweh is not trapped in inflexible rules but remains free as a person. He reproves whom he loves (Prov 3:12). "The LORD has made everything for its purpose" (Prov 16:4). "The human mind may devise many plans, but it is the purpose of the LORD that will be established" (Prov 19:21). Repeatedly the reader of wisdom is reminded, "The fear of the LORD is the beginning of wisdom." The wisdom-type of discussion of Job's friends ranges far and wide; but the book ends both in its poetry section and in the prose division clearly subordinating wisdom to Yahweh, who has the final word (Job 38:1). So also in Ecclesiastes, though the final verses (Eccl 12:13–14) have sometimes been considered the appendage of a later editor since they descend on the reader quite unexpectedly. The book has examined proposed solutions to the question of life's meaning, found most of them inadequate, and then without argument or proof declares this: "The end of the matter . . . Fear God, and keep his commandments; for that is the whole duty of everyone" (Eccl 12:13–14). But the abruptness of the final work makes the telling point that human life must be ordered over against Yahweh. Whatever principles of the cosmos there are, these are subject to Yahweh, who in his person and his action is free. The fear of Yahweh is the beginning of wisdom, and one might say its climax and conclusion also.

Wisdom literature thus occupies itself with skill in living. Wisdom (*ḥokmâ*) is not limited to an innate capacity for intellectual analysis. Essentially *ḥokmâ* is skill, as is clear from the word used for Bezaleel, the workman who was endowed with skill (*ḥokmâ*) in textile and metal craftsmanship (Exod 31:30). In wisdom it is not artisans' skill that is required of a human being, but the skill to live life well. The skillful person will know how to approach those in positions of power, and will have the capacity to deal with arrogance and anger in other people (Prov 17:27). The parent skilled in living will deal responsibly though firmly with children (Prov 13:24). The wise person will be courteous of speech, even-tempered and patient (Prov 19:11). Wisdom has about it an everyday ring. Work is valued and encouraged for it brings results: "Do you see those who are skillful in their work? They will serve kings" (Prov 22:29). The indolent person is rebuked and chastened (Prov 15:19; 24:30–34). Business pursuits are praised (Prov 13:11; 14:23–24; 31:10–19). Learning is discussed with approval. Guidelines are given for conversation. Sleep and even table manners receive attention (Prov 23:1–3). Caution and wisdom are urged in order that everyday life be positive and that living be skillful.

A review of the contents of wisdom as sketched above displays a most interesting fact, namely that at base the issue is one of quality of life. The world of nature is affirmed as good and contributes in a different way to a rich life. The blessing of Yahweh which comes through material things makes rich (Prov

10:22). The good life is more than material abundance; it goes hand in hand with obedience to God, the fear of Yahweh. The one who chooses wisely, that is, chooses wisdom, chooses life. "He who finds me finds life" (Prov 8:35; cf. 4:22). "By me (wisdom, skill in living) your days will be multiplied, and years will be added to your life" (Prov 9:11). "Lay aside immaturity, and live," advises the writer (Prov 9:6). The happiness of one who finds wisdom is described as finding something more precious than jewels. "Long life is in her right hand . . . She is a tree of life to those who lay hold of her . . ." (Prov 3:16, 18). As one Old Testament scholar has put it, "What this wisdom has to bestow is life, life, that is, in the grand sense of the Old Testament, as a saving blessing."[5]

The Salvation Design and Wisdom Literature

It should be obvious that with this description of the content of wisdom we have arrived at that in Israel's history toward which land possession aims: the blessings of a full life. A person is delivered *for* something. That something is a better life. The story of Israel's election, deliverance, and maintenance leads, via the mighty act of God, to the placement of people in the land, the place where life may be lived in its richness. Wisdom leaves aside the election, deliverance, the history of salvation, but brings its followers to "life." Wisdom is no cul-de-sac. Rather it represents a parallel traffic lane, according to the manner of the modern divided highway or dual carriageway, in which for an interval the wisdom route and the history-of-salvation route are shown parallel, leading toward the same goal. In Psalm 37, a wisdom psalm, those who do good, the righteous, the meek, the trusting ones, will dwell in the land (Ps 37:3, 9, 11, 22, 29). Such a passage indicates the harmony between the history of salvation and wisdom literature.[6]

In still another even more fundamental way wisdom literature dovetails with the subject of land. In both "design" is significant. The conviction underlying wisdom material is that there is design and order in the universe. In Proverbs the reader is encouraged to appreciate this order, to understand it in its fundamental structure and to orient one's life accordingly. Vocabulary of design is quite at home in wisdom. "It is the purpose of the LORD that will be established" (19:21). "The LORD has made everything for its purpose, even the wicked for the day of trouble" (16:4). In Ecclesiastes and Job the discussion penetrates to the heart of the matter: is there indeed such an orderly principle in the world that one may rely on it totally in the structuring of one's personal life? That question, put another way, is the question of design or purpose. In wisdom the issue is not so much what the design is but that design and order govern the universe. It is in the Israelite story of salvation that the precise nature of the design is explicated. Thus, as we have seen, the Exodus text sets out the specifics of that plan (Exod 5:22 – 6:8). Yahweh's purpose is underscored in Hosea (2:14–23), where, as in Exodus, the gift of land and the consequent abundant life are identified as Yahweh's purposes.

If we step up to look closer at wisdom material, we will find that the this-worldly, earth-affirming instruction in Proverbs is of a piece with land as turf and soil as presented in the Mosaic promise and its fulfillment. Though it appears to us less theological and more "secular" than "deliverance" or "covenant," "land" shares this secularity with wisdom literature. Everyday life is life in a land.

At one level, then, Israel's possession of land and the promise of the good life correlate with wisdom's emphasis of life. On another more basic level, the framing of the specifics in Exodus as design places design as the common denominator for both historical material and wisdom material.

This overarching bridge between Exodus (history of salvation) and wisdom material (non-history) as sketched above is not readily accepted by many as a valid one. Indeed the way in which wisdom material is incorporated into an Old Testament theology is a thorny matter.[7] It is commonly pointed out that the difference between Torah, the history of Israel's salvation as a people, and wisdom with its individualism, is very great. And so it is. Arguments supporting the difference are familiar. In the historical and prophetical books there is given an authoritative word: "Thus says the LORD." But such signals of divine revelation are absent in the wisdom material. We encounter instead something from the reservoir of human experience generally. The flavor in the bulk of the Old Testament is Israelite. Elect people are the subject. But in wisdom we are on an international stage, so much so that it seems likely that Egyptian wisdom sayings have been incorporated into Proverbs. One section (Prov 22:17 – 24:22) is modeled (some claim adopted) from the earlier wisdom of Amen-em-ope of Egypt.[8] This need not be surprising when it is remembered that experience can yield valid insights. Further, much of the Old Testament deals with God's intervention in the history of his people: God acts in behalf of his people. But in wisdom there are none of these salvific injections of God into the arena of world history. The form of the revelatory material is story, augmented by the prophetic word. Wisdom material is not story, but proverb, comparison, and sometimes parable. The purveyors of instruction on Israel's past were priests of the temple. The purveyors of the sage counsel, crystallized through the centuries, were the scribes at court. The distinction between prophets, priests, and wise men is traditional (Jer 18:18). Moreover the contents of wisdom, it is said, are so clearly different from the salvation history that, as one writer put it, wisdom is a cul-de-sac. The differences between wisdom material and the story of salvation (*Heilsgeschichte*) are there and are recognizable. But to see wisdom as a cul-de-sac with the main street continuing in the form of the salvation history is inaccurate, as we have shown.

2. The Good Life and Management of the Land
A Perspective from History

The wisdom material is directed largely to the individual, who is called to adjust to the cosmic order as directed by Yahweh. By and large wisdom deals with the practicalities of life for the individual. The historical sources, however, are concerned with community and therefore management of resources, particularly land. In ancient Israel, largely agricultural, the land was strategic in determining the quality of life, so that management of land and resources was a strong factor in determining whether or not the individual Israelite would live comfortably and would live well. The historians have something to say about management of land and the quality of life. An overview of land management requires more information than we are given in the Old Testament, but we may give attention at least to management by the monarchy, since Israel and Judah lived under a monarchy from Saul to Hoshea, 722 BC; Judah continued another 150 years until the monarchy ended in 587 BC with Zedekiah.

Land Management Guidelines

The pertinent material in Deuteronomy, after specifying that the King shall be an Israelite, "one of your own community," posits negative and positive directives (Deut 17:15). Negatively put, the king is not, like kings of other nations, to multiply horses to himself, nor wives, nor gold and silver. Israel's monarchy, while similar to that of other nations in form, was supposed to be different in character. Whereas other kings used the resources of land and people to private advantage, the Israelite king was forbidden to press for his personal advantage, either through acquiring property or other wealth, or through taking to himself wives. Since marriage was one form of making alliances with other powers, the prohibition may be calculated to leave the king dependent on Yahweh in warfare—neither military armaments (horses) nor alliances were to take precedence over Yahweh. But the prohibition was presumably given also for another reason: the king was to remain the equal of his subjects and not to be in a class by himself because of his wealth in horses, wives, and silver.

The king was directed to secure a copy of the Torah, which he was to read or even transcribe for himself (Deut 17:18–20). The reason for occupying himself with such religious matters in addition to his administrative chores is that the king himself should fear Yahweh his God and obey the statutes in the Torah. An additional reason for immersing himself in the Torah was to prevent him from "exalting himself above other members of the community" (Deut 17:20). The king was subject to the To-rah, as was every other Israelite. The temptation of a monarch to exalt himself above his brethren by becoming the law to them was, like the temptation to appropriate horses and silver, to be strictly avoided.

What should be noticed is that the king's management of resources was to be in the interest of all, not in the interest of the egotistical appetites of the ruler. Understandably the quality of life of the citizens would be diminished by the self-assertion of the king, and the result of such pagan behavior would be more drastic still: a loss of land for king and people. The king who managed according to the Torah would, with his descendants, "reign long over his kingdom in Israel" (Deut 17:20).

The threat of land loss, implicit in the Deuteronomy text, is quite explicit in a word from Yahweh to Solomon. Following the completion of the temple, God affirms this word to the king: if Solomon will keep Yahweh's statutes and ordinances, then God will establish his royal throne to Solomon forever; but if he de-parts from this law, and particularly if he forsakes Yahweh for other gods, "then I will cut Israel off from the land that I have given them" (1 Kgs 9:7). Either the kings obey the Torah, man-aging land and kingdom by God's rule, with the result of life in the land; or they disobey the Torah, mismanage, and forfeit the gift.

Land Management Practice

Solomon will serve as an example of the king at work in manag-ing the land given by promise of God to his people Israel. The historian who records the achievements of King Solomon does so initially in a most favorable light. The prosperity which accompanies the king's reign is undeniable and wonderful. The historian, with an eye to the welfare of the people of the land, records: "Judah and Israel were as numerous as the sand by the sea; they ate and drank and were happy" (1 Kgs 4:20). And is this not how it had all been anticipated? God was bringing them into a good land, so ran the word at the border, "a land where you may eat bread without scarcity, where you will lack nothing" (Deut 8:9). And now under Solomon this rich quality of life was a reality. After the temple dedication people went to their homes in a joyful mood (1 Kgs 8:63; cf. 2 Chr 7:10). The historian adds, "During Solomon's lifetime Judah and Israel lived in safety, from Dan even to Beer-sheba, all of them under their vines and fig trees" (1 Kgs 4:25). The queen of Sheba sums up by saying, "Happy are your wives! Happy are these your servants" (1 Kgs 10:8–9).

Such a good state of affairs does not endure even to the end of Solomon's reign nor can it be found later, except rarely in the monarchy period. Following the end of his reign Israel pleads with Rehoboam, Solomon's successor, explaining, "Your father made our yoke heavy" (1 Kgs 12:4). Indeed as the historian relates, Solomon had employed forced labor for the building of the temple, of his house and the Millo and the fortifications of Jerusalem, Hazor and Megiddo (1 Kgs 9:15). Already early he had a Department of Labor (more correctly Department of Forced Labor) over which Adoniram was appointed (1 Kgs 4:6). Although the record says that of the Israelites he made no slaves (1 Kgs 9:22), the situation can have been but little better than slavery; their yoke whether by taxation or forced labor was heavy. Solomon accumulated wealth from which he built a royal palace that took almost twice as long to complete as the temple; he also built for himself an elaborate throne of ivory overlaid with gold (1 Kgs 10:18). He had chariots totaling 1,400 and horsemen numbering 12,000 (1 Kgs 10:26). He loved many foreign women, and counted 700 wives. He followed other gods, devoting himself to Ashtoreth, Milcom, Chemosh, Molech. In short, he violated the command to worship only Yahweh; he did not remain as one among his brethren but through wives, goods, and houses lifted himself up above them, and, for that matter, at their expense.

The evils against which Samuel had warned (1 Sam 8:10–18) are the evils that attend Solomon's reign. Solomon appointed Israel's sons to be horsemen. He taxed the harvests. He regarded men and women as commodities and put them to forced labor. Elaborate household bureaucracy had become necessary (1 Kgs 4:1–6). The further disregard of God's law is evident in Jeroboam, who became his own law; he set up altars and exceeded a king's normal right by appointing priests (1 Kgs 12:32–33). Ahab, in disregard of the brother's rights as well as the laws of inheritance, appropriated Naboth's vineyard; Ahab neither understood nor desired to follow the prescribed way for Israelite kingship. Far from experiencing a full life, the average Israelite, such as Naboth, stood in danger of losing his land and his life.

3. Loss of Land and the Good Life
A Perspective from the Prophets

The glorious part of Israelite history is the way in which, relying on the promise, she received the gift of the land. The tragedy of Israel's story is that the gift of the land was forfeited. Warnings that loss of land could become a reality were already given prior to entry into the land (Deut 30:17–18); they were repeated in the course of the four hundred-year history, towards the end of which the ominous word was announced that loss of land was imminent.

Enumeration of several warning signals will indicate the concern of the prophets with the possibility of loss of land. Samuel's farewell speech concludes by exhorting people and king to serve Yahweh, but warns: "If you still do wickedly, you shall be swept away, both you and your king" (1 Sam 12:25). To David and Solomon, so it is reported by the historian, who notes Manasseh's evil in setting up an image of Asherah in the temple, God had said, "I will not cause the feet of Israel to wander any more out of the land that I gave to their ancestors, if only they will be careful to do according to all that I have commanded" (2 Kgs 21:8). Continual occupancy of the land, Israel's kings knew from the outset, was contingent on their compliance with God's commandment.

But before long threats of loss of land are replaced by firm announcements that Israel will go out from her land. Ahijah delivers a message through the queen to Jeroboam I, the "king who made Israel to sin" by setting up bull calves at Dan and Bethel. To him the prophet who only a little earlier promised him ten tribes now says that not only will Jeroboam's dynasty be cut off, but "the LORD will strike Israel, as a reed is shaken in the water; he will root up Israel out of this good land that he gave to their ancestors, and scatter them beyond the Euphrates" (1 Kgs 14:15). Several generations later during the reign of another Jeroboam (eighth century) the prophet Amos responds to Amaziah the priest, who was presumably attached to the royal sanctuary at Bethel. Amaziah had excommunicated Amos from Bethel, not taking seriously or even tolerating the prophet's rebuke. Amos replied, "You yourself shall die in an unclean land, and Israel shall surely go into exile away from its land" (Amos 7:17). Thirty years later the northern kingdom came to an end and the historian records: "So Israel was exiled from their own land" (2 Kgs 17:23).

In Judah it was Micah who announced in a word addressed to the heads of the house of Jacob and rulers of the house of Israel, "Zion shall be plowed as a field; Jerusalem shall become a heap of ruins" (Mic 3:12). The prophet nearest to the historical fulfillment of that word was Jeremiah, who lived through the set of sieges of Nebuchadnezzar against Jerusalem. He announced that Yahweh would bring calamity from the north (Jer 4:6), a reference not necessarily to a power located geographically in the north but to one which, like Babylon in the east, followed the trade routes and invaded from the north. Of Jehoiachin (also known as Coniah), the last recognized king of Judah (Zedekiah the last ruler was appointed by Nebuchadnezzar and apparently not fully recognized as king), Jeremiah says, speaking in the name of God, "I will hurl you and the mother who bore you into another country" (Jer 22:26). Then in poetic reflection, "Why are he and his offspring hurled out and cast away in a land that they do not know? O land, land, land, hear the word of the LORD!" (Jer 22:28–29).

As W. Brueggemann notes, Jeremiah 2 is a history of Israel given in terms of land.[9] The starting point is Israel's devotion to God in the wilderness, "in a land not sown" (v. 2). Yet later generations disregarded the God who led Israel through the wilderness "in a land of deserts and pits, in a land of drought and deep darkness, in a land that no one passes through, where no man lives" (v. 6). God rehearses the further developments: "I brought you into a plentiful land" (v. 7). Israel's response was unworthy of the gift: "But when you entered you defiled my land, and made my heritage an abomination" (v. 7). The future is sketched, a future in which lions "have made his land a waste" (v. 15). So while the story of Israel's past could be told with the use of covenant language, Jeremiah can tell it in terms of land.

4. Theological Reflections

Of the many issues which the subject of "land" in the Old Testament raises, two which have current relevance are the secular/sacred dichotomy and the issue of lifestyle.

A common way of viewing life even by Christians is to compartmentalize experience. A part of one's life and experience is religious in nature. Included in the religious compartment are such items as worship, Christian doctrine, prayer, and acts of charity. But the routine of life, including day-to-day work, pleasures, recreation, investments, socializing, and friendships are relegated to a non-religious or secular compartment. God is in the individual's consciousness in Sunday worship, to be sure. But the work in the kitchen, office, or industrial plant is perceived to have a different, non-religious quality. One may want to ascribe this dichotomy to a Greek philosophical viewpoint which differentiated sharply between matter and spirit.

But whatever the reasons for this kind of divided thinking, the Old Testament calls for a reassessment and a realignment. The assertion, particularly of wisdom literature, is that work and pleasure, toil and sex, and emotions of anger or impatience as well as of love are all included in the realm of faith. It will not do to disparage these areas as "non-spiritual" or to isolate them as though they were outside God's reach. God is not to be put at arm's length in the everyday work arena. God is not uninterested in business or sex. Indeed, God cannot be excluded from any area of life. Wisdom literature asserts that this-worldly concerns and pursuits are totally within the Yahweh compass. The division of life into things secular and things sacred is a convenience, no doubt, but if propounded as a Christian view, is a distortion of biblical teaching.

One illustration of the dissection of reality into matters sacred and matters secular is the management of natural resources, including land. Rarely, until recently, have issues of environment and ecology entered significantly into the thinking of clerics and the people of God. Use of energy resources such as oil has been left to the jurisdiction of business firms. Chemicals, pesticides, or the treatment of industrial wastes are subjects for discussion in laboratories and city halls, but hardly in the church. But when one studies all that the Bible teaches about land and related subjects, one comes to see that use of natural resources and the moral quality of a people are interlocked.[10] Hosea indicts his listeners for violence, lying, stealing, and faithlessness, and declares that it is their sinful condition that accounts for the coming ecological imbalance: "Therefore the land mourns, and all who live in it languish; together with the wild animals and the birds of the air; even the fish of the sea are perishing" (Hos 4:3).

Attention to natural resources is an integral part of a concern for stewardship generally. Humankind, so prophets and wisdom teachers affirm, must see the natural resources of land and energy sources as gifts of God. These are not to be exploited, but are to be managed in a responsible manner, not only in view of pragmatic concerns, such as supplies for future generations, but especially in view of accountability to God. The legislation in the Torah about the jubilee year in which the land was to be fallow points to specific practices of conservation and non-exploitation that are premised on God's demand and human accountability. The jubilee year put a restraint on monopoly and greed. "Honor the LORD with your substance and with the firstfruits of all your produce" (Prov 3:9). Use of natural resources, whether those of an individual or those of a country, are religious concerns and not to be relegated to arm's-length distance as secular.

Related to the subject of the use of natural resource is the topic of economic lifestyle. Modern attitudes, fed by compelling advertisements, are marked by grasping. The enterprising seek to get all they can, often by whatever means. The name of the game in life is acquisition, whether acquisition of things, influence, or power. But Old Testament literature speaks to the quality of life in such terms as fearing the LORD. It exhibits a large interest in the quality of a person's life, but underscores, as in the case of land, that security and abundance, even life itself are gifts. God's people are to live from a stance of gift, not grasp. They receive from God's hand the gifts he offers them. They do not, or should not, seize with their hand all that they can humanly accumulate. They remember, or should remember, that one does not live by bread alone.

But more is at stake than a warning against grasping and acquisition. Is it justifiable, even if one is able to do so, to live extravagantly? The pattern established by God for the king was essentially that he should not follow the ways of kings who multiplied wives to themselves and horses and chariots. While this stipulation was intended no doubt to restrain preoccupation with military strength and the securing of alliances, and to emphasize trust in Yahweh for times of military threat, it also offers a caveat against extravagance and acquisition for purposes of display and self-vaunting. Ahab wishes to extend his extravagance and luxury by acquiring Naboth's vineyard. Such action

is contrary to the covenant stipulation and the divine instructions which forbade land sales. Taking the jubilee instructions
about land into account, it is clear that while individual enterprise was not discouraged, the evils of social stratification,
brought about by large land holdings, was prevented. One must
ask whether the biblical view of prosperity and lifestyle does not
call into question consumerism, at least its excesses.

There is little doubt that the self-indulgence, the planned
obsolescence of consumer goods, the wastefulness of goods and
resources which often accompanies a high standard of living,
stand under the judgment of God. A high quality of life defined
biblically corresponds much more with an economically simplified lifestyle than with indulgence in luxury.

While this is not the place to elaborate on the ethical dimension that arises out of a study of such subjects as the good
life in the land, it should be clear that the historical materials on
the subject of "land" augmented by the wisdom literature, not
to mention the prophetic books, address a large set of problems
in current society. Theologically a review of the so-called "secular" is necessary. Practically, expositions on lifestyle for an affluent people are overdue.

Part 4

God's Design Reaffirmed

The Post-Monarchy Era

Prologue

Ezek 34:17–31

Our survey of the Old Testament is in three giant steps. The first step includes a time period from the formation of Israel at the exodus to the time of Samuel, approximately four hundred years. At the threshold of that period God announces a master plan through his servant, Moses (Exod 5:22 – 6:8). That design includes his intention to bring deliverance to his people, to form them into a unique community, to lead them into an experiential relationship with himself, and to bring them into the land of promise, the land of abundance. The books Exodus to Judges help us to see the progress in the implementation of that plan.

During the second step, which includes the time period of the monarchy, this master plan is put to the test in a variety of ways. Israel eventually falls to the Assyrians, and Judah to the Babylonians, so that instead of deliverance there is captivity. By the end of the period the prospect of a people destined to be peculiar to Yahweh and an exemplar to the world appears badly vitiated. Yes, Israel has experienced Yahweh, but it is his discipline and judgment and bitter medicine rather than sweet enjoyment. Israel has had a taste of the good land; but by the end of the period she is taken away from the land, no longer to enjoy the richness of milk and honey. An observer might have concluded that God's design, grand and overarching though it was, was essentially in shambles and inoperative.

But such pessimism is unwarranted because of who God is. The next large step into Israel's history is a step that stretches time-wise from the exile through the post-exilic period to the dawn of the New Testament era. This period, which begins with Israel in exile, covers more than five hundred years (587–4 BC).

The third large period puts us in touch with prophets such as Ezekiel, Obadiah, Haggai, Zechariah, and Malachi. Isaiah 40–66 is descriptive of this period, so whether authored by Isaiah in the eighth century or by someone in the exile, it belongs in this section.[1] Canonical books from the hands of administrators such as Ezra, Nehemiah, and Daniel give us historical information. In this period too, the book of Chronicles was written. Non-canonical books, whether of a historical nature (e.g., 1 Maccabees) or of a wisdom character (e.g., Ecclesiasticus) or similar to novels (e.g., Tobit and Judith), illumine the later part of this period. In terms of national achievement it is certainly not Israel's most glorious hour, but God's work in her and through her is still ongoing and shines with particular brilliance.

What has become of God's design for Israel? A preview of the period suggests that God's design has not forever folded but that out of the ashes, so to speak, there arises a vision model which is recognizable for its familiar motifs: deliverance, community, relationship, abundant life. Some alteration in details occurs; nevertheless the overall purpose is intact. Deliverance is held out to Israel with apocalyptic overtones . . . and also, strangely, through a servant who suffers. Community, God's people, can no longer be defined nationally; prophets now speak about a remnant. The prospect of "knowing" God is given a fresh and prominent nuance by Ezekiel, who maintains that all nations shall yet know God. Israel is back in the land and "the land" functions more than ever as a symbol for the abundant life. All in all, God's design is reaffirmed.

In this period it is Ezekiel who gives a concise statement of God's fourfold purpose. He writes from Babylon, outside the land of Israel, where he is in exile. Just as Hosea during the monarchy asserted God's intention, so Ezekiel, now in the midst of a disorientation brought about through national disaster, affirms that God's design for his people and the world remains unchanged. That affirmation is found in Ezek 34:17–31.

In Ezekiel 34 the prophet takes up the theme of Israel's disqualified leadership, indicting the shepherds for their failure to be true shepherds and assuring them that God himself will be the true shepherd (Ezek 34:1–16). There is a continuation of the shepherd-sheep metaphor as the prophet takes up the theme of the flock (vv. 17–31). Broadly speaking the section about the flock is in two parts: a judgment section (vv. 17–21) and a salvation message (vv. 22–31). It is in the latter announcement of salvation that the four familiar motifs of God's design appear.

The divine stance toward an unruly flock in which the strong trample the weak is given in crisp, programmatic fashion: "I will save my flock" (v. 22). As is often the case, the general statement is followed by more specifics. In this instance deliverance is in conjunction with one shepherd whom God will set over his people—his servant David. This promise was spoken in the context of the exile. It is most unlikely that Ezekiel had a resurrected David in mind, nor is it likely that the reference was to an immediate king from the Davidic line. Ezekiel avoids the word "king" because of the tragic end of Judah's last kings, Jehoiachin and Zedekiah: there was little reason for hope from that order. Christians of course have regarded Ezekiel's reference to David as fulfilled in the Messiah, Jesus Christ. With this promise for deliverance Ezekiel affirms God's design for his people as announced already in Exodus 6.

The salvation announcement proceeds next with a reference to land, an element in fourth position in the Exodus passage. Ezekiel elaborates on the security and prosperity which Israel can anticipate in the land. Security is assured because harmful beasts will be eliminated (v. 25; cf. v. 28, Hos 2:18). A picture of prosperity is presented in phrases such as "I will make them and the region around my hill a blessing and there will be 'showers of blessing'; The trees of the field shall yield their fruit" (vv. 26–27). Both security and prosperity aspects are brought together in the assertion that God will establish Israel in the land as a renowned planting. This phase of the announcement has continuity with Amos 9:13–15, "The mountains shall drip sweet wine" and anticipates Zech 8:12, "The ground shall give its produce."

The motif of knowing God is expressed as follows: "And they shall know that I am the Lord when I break the bars of their yoke, and save them from the hands of those who enslaved them" (Ezek 34:27).

The community dimension of God's design or purpose, already present in the entire section by virtue of the reference to the flock, is given more specifically: "They shall know that I, the LORD their God, am with them, and that they, the house of Israel, are my people, says the LORD God" (v. 30). The final statement, "I am your God" (v. 31) echoes the familiar "You shall be my people and I will be your God." This "covenant of peace" (v. 25) is fourfold in its specifics: deliverance, community, knowledge of God, and abundance (represented by land).

This third scripture (Ezek 34:17–31) defining God's purpose invites comparison with the earlier two discussed above (Exod 5:22 – 6:8; Hos 2:14–23). One could say that each of these statements is programmatically given at the outset of an era: theocracy (Exodus 6), monarchy (Hosea 2), the post-exilic experience (Ezekiel 34). These statements, or better restatements, each take up what has preceded historically. In Exodus there is a reference to the God of the fathers; in Hosea, written during the monarchy, there is a reference to exodus, and in Ezekiel, written in the post-exilic period, there is a reference to the monarchy. Both restatements employ a figure of speech: in Hosea, marriage, in Ezekiel, shepherd-sheep. While God's initiative is emphasized in all three, the mention in each passage of God's name and the specific formula "I am Yahweh" mentioned in Exodus, Hosea, and Ezekiel underscore God's initiative and sovereignty.

Standing at the threshold of the exilic/post-exilic era, Ezekiel announces God's design: deliverance, community, knowing God, and a rich quality of life—a design unchanged from that given in Exod 5:22 – 6:8.

God's Fourfold Purpose: A Summary

	Exod 5:22 – 6:8	Hos 2:14–23	Ezek 34:17–31

God's purpose
1 Deliverance
2 Covenant/
  community
3 Experience with
  God
4 Land (blessing)
	Articulated	Restated	Affirmed

Emphasis	Deliverance	Covenant/ community	Land (blessing)
Dominant figure of speech		Marriage	Shepherd/sheep
Linkage with pre- vious era	God of the fathers	Exodus	Monarchy
Threshold state- ment for the historical era	Theocracy 1400(?)—1000 BC	Monarchy 1000–587 BC	Post-exilic era 589–4 BC

11

Deliverance

Ever since the exodus from Egypt, "deliverance" had been a sweet-sounding word for Israel. In the period of the judges and many times during the monarchy, God's power to deliver had been put to the test. In Israel's worship, as reflected in the Psalms, Israel had extolled God's power to deliver. But then in Hoshea's reign (732–724 BC) Samaria was attacked and after two years of siege fell to the Assyrians. God had not delivered his people. More than a century later Jerusalem fell at the hand of the Babylonians (587 BC). In these two national crises, Yahweh had not delivered his people at all.

How was Israel to deal with God's failure to deliver his people? Were the gods of the Assyrians and Babylonians more powerful than Yahweh? Whatever the popular explanations, God's servants the prophets kept insisting on two things. First, despite Israel's prosperity, they had announced an impending judgment on Israel because of her social injustices and her disloyalty to Yahweh. When defeat came it was not therefore to be ascribed to Yahweh's powerlessness but to his holiness and righteousness. Secondly, God was still even now a God of deliverance. Despite the defeat in the exile Yahweh could and would bring salvation.

Deliverance from exile did come in 539 BC when Cyrus the Persian issued a decree allowing peoples within his rule, including Israelites, to return to their homeland. Under Sheshbazzar certain ones, but not all, made their way to Jerusalem. There, despite adversity, they succeeded by 516 BC under the leadership of Zerubbabel and the prophets Haggai and Zechariah in rebuilding the temple (Ezra 6:15). Much later, under the leadership of Nehemiah, the city wall was built (Neh 2:17ff). Repeatedly this struggling group, beset with adversity from the officialdom of Samaria and the neighboring Edomites and Arabs, experienced the deliverance of their God. Indeed, still later, in the second century BC, as the books of 1 and 2 Maccabees relate, God wrought deliverance in conjunction with Hasmonean leadership.

In the exilic and post-exilic period the emphasis on God's deliverance took two forms. Earlier prophets had frequently and forcefully called attention to the power of God, but now the portrait of God's power and deliverance was painted in colors more brilliant than ever. The deliverance motif was heightened to large proportions; in the hands of the apocalypticists it was treated most imaginatively and compellingly. God's might, greater than the world's kingdoms, even if all at once were arrayed against him, assured the final triumph of his people.

The alternative portrait was totally opposite. It too asserted unquestionable deliverance for the righteous but it refrained from talk of strength and grandeur. Instead it sketched a suffering servant. In language that turned on concepts of meekness, suffering, even death, the prophets held out the prospect of deliverance, even if through the most unlikely means. God's design for deliverance of his people and all those who trust Yahweh was affirmed, to be sure, but in a way that made for tensions then and on into the New Testament period. Both portraits will now be examined.

1. The Apocalyptic Vision: Deliverance

The literature which depicts the gigantic, world-impacting, cataclysmic deliverance which God will eventually effect is technically known as apocalyptic literature. The word "apocalyptic" ('unveiling," "uncovering") refers both to a distinct body of literature and also to a mood.[1]

Apocalyptic literature born out of hard times flourished in the inter-testamental period. It includes such non-canonical books as 1 Enoch, 2 Esdras, and Baruch, which, while not "Scripture," nevertheless illumine the direction apocalyptic literature took. Within the canon of the Old Testament, scholars have identified proto-apocalyptic sections which are precursors of full-blown later apocalyptic literature: Isaiah 24–27, Ezekiel 38–39, parts of Daniel and Zechariah. These do not in every case necessarily exhibit all the characteristics of apocalyptic literature, but they do represent the flavor of apocalyptic more than that of the prophetic.

One feature of apocalyptic shared in part by proto-apocalyptic is a series of discourse cycles revolving around vision. Unlike prophetic literature, in which one finds "Thus says the LORD," apocalyptic literature introduces an angelic interpreter as part of the vision report (compare Dan 8:16ff, Zech 4:1ff). Apocalypticists relate their own reactions of inward turmoil and physical faintness as they are confronted by the Word of God. Whereas the prophets were essentially speakers, the apocalypticists are authors. When they write they may not identify themselves but instead write in the name of a former Israel hero. The book of Enoch, which dates from the Maccabees in the second century BC and later, is written in the name of and from the perspective of the antediluvian saint.

A further contrast between the prophets and the apocalypticists is that whereas the former used symbolism mildly (e.g., Isaiah 5; Ezekiel 19), the latter use it profusely. In Daniel, one reads of beasts, seals, or stars, and elsewhere of rivers and mountains, each of which represents persons. Why symbols? Some hold that this tactic was a verbal camouflage in the interests of the safety of the readers. Others think that the subject of God's intervention was too staggering to present in ordinary words. Since the symbols are in strong use in Daniel, Isaiah 24–27, and Zechariah, some scholars suggest that these sections may not belong to the ascribed author but may already be presented, as in later custom, in the name of a hero.

Aside from these literary distinguishing marks, apocalyptic material is characterized by a clearly defined mood, and that mood is also distinct from the mood of the prophets. The coming catastrophe is far more than a large, even national disaster; it is cosmic. An entire world is implicated in God's coming, and his action will affect all the earth and the heavens, sun and planets as well. A graphic description is given in the non-canonical books; Isaiah is also forceful.

> And it shall come to pass that whoever gets safe out of the war shall die in the earthquake, and whosoever gets safe out of the earthquake shall be burned by the fire, and whosoever gets safe out of the fire shall be destroyed by famine (Bar 70:8).

> Then shall the sun suddenly shine forth by night and the moon by day; and blood shall trickle from the wood and the stone utter its voice (4 Ezra 5:4).

The Isaiah apocalypse (24–27) is an earlier precursor of global catastrophe.

> Now the LORD is about to lay waste the earth and make it desolate, and he will twist its surface and scatter its inhabitants . . . The earth is utterly broken, the earth is torn asunder, the earth is violently shaken . . . Then the moon will be abashed, and the sun ashamed . . . (Isa 24:1, 19, 23).

The coming action by the Almighty will be huge in its devastation.

And the devastation is inevitable. True, there is continuity with history, but now one speaks of epochs and of periods yet to come prior to the end. In the Testament of Abraham, for example, human history is said to total 7000 years. Numbers such as 4, 7, 12, 70 and their multiples become important. The times allocated and the end of all things are predictable because divinely determined even from long ago (e.g., seven of the ten weeks of world history have elapsed, 1 Enoch 91:12–17; cf. 93:1–10). The canonical materials are not so explicit, but even in Daniel the sequence of kingdoms depicted by the image which Nebuchadnezzar saw—gold, silver, bronze, and iron (Dan 2:31)—follow one another in a particular order.

The final cataclysm is imminent. There is no longer much time.

> The pitcher is near to the cistern,
> And the ship to the port,
> And the course of the journey to the city,
> And the life to its consummation (2 Bar 5:10).

The controversial seventy weeks of Daniel suggest not only a predetermined time but a relatively short time until the end.

The nature of the upheaval at the end time, while memorable for its fire and earthquake, is conspicuous for the part the demons and angels play in it. The classical prophets of the eighth century and even those of a later period were virtually silent about spirit beings. In 1 Enoch considerable preoccupation with angels leads to elaborate descriptions of angels' names, function, and hierarchy. In 1 Enoch a discussion of sin in the world centers on Gen 6:1–4 and spirit beings in general. Demons are also identified by name, Belial being the chief. In comparison with the later apocalyptic literature, the biblical material is very restrained. Daniel does make mention of Gabriel (9:21). The contest between the angels and opposing forces is suggested in the note that the Prince of Persia, presumably a demon force, withstood God's messenger for twenty-one days but was overpowered with the help of the Prince (angel?) Michael (Dan 10:13). The pre-Christian Qumran materials elaborate on this motif of spirit beings in *The War of the Sons of Light against the Sons of Darkness*. Since the New Testament Gospels and even the book of Acts frequently mention angels and demons, one can ask whether they breathe the apocalyptic spirit.

Moreover, apocalyptic as an outlook is marked by a clear-cut dualism: good and evil, light and darkness, this age and the age to come. It is as though wicked persons have been hardened to become totally wicked. The righteous by contrast are easily identifiable.

Following the ominous global devastation, the age to come will be an age of new salvation, notably different from the present age.

Apocalyptic then is a kind of eschatology. Prophets had spoken about the future, to be sure, even about the latter days, but their context had been the world as they knew it with nations and the ongoing flow of history. Within this history God would bring salvation. The judgment and salvation were definitely this-worldly. The apocalypticists saw God's cataclysmic judgment outside history, trans-history as it were, terminating history. No longer were nations God's tool. All nations were opposed to the Almighty. The setting was not this-worldly but other-worldly.

The apocalyptic writers are successors to the prophets, though some scholars have traced their spiritual ancestry to wisdom or even to priestly material. As a British scholar affirms, "That Apocalyptic is the child of prophecy, yet diverse from prophecy, can hardly be disputed."[2] It has been said that prophets were in touch with current reality but nevertheless had a vision. In apocalypticism, the vision was divorced from the reality and in itself became the primary focus.[3]

With this background on the nature of apocalyptic we can more fully appreciate the shape of salvation presented in this literature. Two sample passages, one from Daniel and one from Zechariah, will serve as illustrations of deliverance seen from the vantage point of apocalypticists.

Deliverance Depicted in Daniel

It is generally held that Daniel's vision of the image (chapter 2) depicts the same sequence of kingdoms as the image of the beasts (chapter 7). There is less agreement about the interpretation of the particulars, specifically the symbolism of the materials in the image (gold, silver, bronze, iron) or the beasts that arose out of the sea (lion, bear, leopard, and the fourth beast). That these represent kingdoms is explicitly stated and that minimally Babylon, Media, Persia, and Greece are intended is undisputed; but while some list only the four kingdoms, and that in the order Babylon, Media, Persia, and Greece (e.g., H. H. Rowley), others include Rome and defend the sequence Babylon, Media/Persia, Greece, and Rome (e.g., Edward J. Young).[4] Besides, according to one school of thought, the four kingdoms have already come and gone. Another holds that the visions are intended as a panorama of world history. In some circles there is talk of a revived Roman empire which will precede the coming establishment of the kingdom of God (Dan 2:44–45; cf. 7:13–14). "The correct view can only be so that these representations (ten toes) can be true in the manner depicted: ten contemporary kings."[5] Virtually every view raises its own set of problems.

Westerners are frequently exercised about the "timing" of these two visions. Calendaring of future events is not the primary stress of the texts, however; the main stress is to point to the kingdom of God as an entity quite different from worldly kingdoms, and to assert the assured triumph of God's kingdom over the worldly kingdoms. The stone cut without hands will pulverize the kingdoms represented by gold, silver, bronze, and iron; or, in the language of the second vision, the Son of Man, totally unlike the four beasts that rise out of the sea but fully adequate to their challenge, will establish his kingdom forever.

In these two visions there is a forceful statement about salvation and deliverance. The language about kings and kingdoms sets the salvation on a broad plain. Not Israel or even her nearby neighbors, but the kingdoms of the world are in view. The opposing forces are the political structures of nations, depicted in the image as strong and even attractive; but from God's vantage point as beasts, strong to be sure, but menacing and ugly. Great boasts are made by the fourth beast particularly (Dan 7:8). But looking into another direction the seer sees thrones set up with the Ancient of Days taking his seat: his "clothing was white as snow, and the hair of his head like pure wool" (Dan 7:9). The throne, ablaze with flames, is also the source of a river of fire. The court attendants are in readiness. A gigantic power struggle is in the offing. The apocalyptist pictures the conflict between God and enemy human forces on a grand scale.

Ultimate victory moreover is ensured. God triumphs, even effortlessly. A rolling stone cut without hands from the mountain deals the smashing blow to human kingdom pretensions. Or, to change the figure, the Son of Man is presented to the Ancient of Days and to him is *given* a kingdom and dominion which is not temporary, nor shall it be destroyed, but is forever. It appears that this kingdom is given in turn then to the "holy ones of the Most High" (Dan 7:18) with whom the fourth beast has made war and who we were, so it momentarily appeared, about to be overpowered. Judgment is passed by the Ancient of Days in favor of the "holy ones of the Most High," and the fourth beast, dreadful and destructive, was "taken away, to be consumed and totally destroyed" (Dan 7:22, 26). The triumph of the Almighty is total. It is a triumph in conjunction with the Son of Man. It is a triumph in which the saints of the Highest One, possibly Israelites,[6] share the dominion and greatness, for "the greatness of the kingdoms under the whole heaven shall be given to the people of the holy ones of the Most High" (Dan 7:27).

The role of the Son of Man in this victory scene and his identity particularly, have occasioned much discussion.[7] There is little in other canonical literature about the Son of Man, though he appears in 1 Enoch. The Son of Man comes with the clouds of heaven (Dan 7:13). He is presented to the Ancient of Days, who is God himself.

> I saw in the night visions,
> And behold, with the clouds of heaven
> there came one like a Son of Man,
> and he came to the Ancient of Days
> and was presented before him.
> And to him was given dominion and glory and kingdom,
> that all peoples, nations, and languages should serve him;
> his dominion is an everlasting dominion
> which shall not pass away,

and his kingdom one that shall never be destroyed
                                    (7:13–14 RSV).
To the Son of Man are given dominions as well as glory so that
all peoples and languages might serve him. In function, then,
he is a king. That portrait of royalty continues in 1 Enoch, a
book that dates from the second century BC to the first century
AD where the Son of Man is said to be named in the presence of
the Lord of the Spirits by a name already assigned him prior to
creation. The Son of Man, also called an Elect One, is placed on
a throne of glory (1 Enoch 61:10). "All who dwell on earth shall
fall down and worship before him" (1 Enoch 48:5). He judges
kings (1 Enoch 46:4–5).

In Enoch, then, as in Daniel, the Son of Man is a celestial
figure. Daniel's language is cautious: "He is like a Son of Man";
in Enoch he is known only by the title "Son of Man." It has been
suggested that if one is to describe a heavenly being one can
best do so by making a comparison with a human being (cf.
Ezek 1:26). Hence deity is compared to humankind. If, however, one writes about a human being who seems to be more
than human, then comparison is made with deity. If this interpretation is correct, then the term "Son of Man" is clearly a reference to a celestial or heavenly figure. Our Lord's
self-designation as "Son of Man," while it might be understood
as representing an identification with humanity, was, strictly
speaking, a reference to his deity.

The language of deliverance is now the language of the
kingdom of God, of thrones, of dominions, and of the Son of
Man. The story of deliverance is told with a heavy use of symbol.
The time of salvation, though future, is certain.

Deliverance Depicted In Zechariah

Of the many portraits and models of deliverance which one
might review from the exilic and post-exilic period, in addition
to Daniel, an apocalyptic-like chapter in Zechariah 9 warrants
attention. The chapter is little known except for the quotation

from the New Testament story of Jesus' entry into Jerusalem on
Palm Sunday.

> Rejoice greatly, O daughter Zion!
> Shout aloud, O daughter Jerusalem!
> Lo, your king comes to you;
> triumphant and victorious is he,
> humble and riding on a donkey,
> on a colt, the foal of a donkey (9:9).

Yet the entire chapter is an interesting statement on God's salvation, framed, as some believe, on the pattern of an ancient
warrior hymn.

At first or even at third reading the chapter seems to lack
coherence. More than one scholar has suggested that certain
verses are later additions. If one checks modern English translations, the confusion is only compounded, due to the various
conjectural Hebrew text readings adopted in the opening
verses. Rather than translate "The capital city of Aram is the
LORD's," it is preferable, for reasons that cannot here be elaborated, to retain the more difficult Hebrew idea and render, "For
the LORD has his eye on all people, as on the tribes of Israel"
(9:1, my translation). The general direction the chapter takes is
clear, however. The Lord Yahweh is on the march from the
north southward. The northern city Hadrach, mentioned only
here but known from ancient history, first comes into view.
Then he, the army general Yahweh, arrives at Damascus. The
Phoenician cities along the Mediterranean and the Philistine
cities of the southern coastal plain all fall, and Yahweh takes
possession. Ekron, the northernmost city in Philistia, is ab-
sorbed into Judah, just as were the Jebusites at the time of David
(9:7). The "house," either the temple or the entire land, is now
made safe (9:8). The enemy cities have been conquered, and
the warrior rides triumphantly into the city (9:9) and establishes his dominion "from sea to sea, and from the River to the
ends of the earth" (v. 10). Yahweh's rule will be a rule of peace.
Chariot and horse will no longer be in use; the warrior speaks
peace to the nations. A war skirmish may ensue (9:13–14), but

God will intervene. "On that day the LORD their God will save
them" (9:16). Deliverance then is assured. Prosperity follows,
for "grain shall make the young men flourish, and new wine the
young women" (9:17).

For our purposes we single out two observations for emphasis. First, this passage depicts a time of salvation. Some
scholars have tried to pinpoint the salvation period historically,
which on the face of it should be possible, since various cities are
mentioned; but particulars in earlier history do not align with
the description given here. Almost certainly the time question is
not primary. The traditional enemies of Israel were listed, and
that in the context of a warrior hymn, to emphasize the grandeur of God's victory. He would also be Jerusalem's safeguard:
no oppressor would pass over the land again.

Secondly, the form in which the poem is cast is that of an
ancient warrior hymn. Paul Hanson identifies the parts as
follows:[8]

Conflict-victory	1–7
Temple secured	8
Victory shout and procession	9
Manifestation of Yahweh's universal reign	10
Salvation: captives released	11–13
Theophany of divine warrior	14
Sacrifice and banquet	15
Fertility of restored order	16–17

Hanson shows that there are other warrior hymns from the ancient Near East, dating from early periods. He finds the ritual
pattern (threat, combat, manifestation of universal reign, salvation) in numerous psalms (2, 9, 24, 46, 47, 48) and also in
prophets (Isaiah 34–35). The Isaiah apocalypse is arranged in
its first part to correspond to the same ritual pattern (combat,
24:1–13; victory shout, 14–16; combat-victory, 18–22; manifestation of Yahweh's universal reign, 23; victory-shout and ban-
quet, 25:1–8).

The apocalyptic elements of the warrior hymn in the Zechariah 9 poem include the concern about nations and God's victory, a victory in which an arrow will go forth like lightning as Yahweh marches "in the whirlwinds of the south," is reminiscent of divine war familiar from the exodus.

The warrior hymn of Zechariah 9 harks back to Israel's early divine war. In earlier narratives God's deliverance was described historically as Israel fought against the Canaanites and the Midianites. Now in Zechariah the same model of war and combat is emphasized to depict God's deliverance of weaponry but through faith, so in Zechariah's poem victory is assured, not because of a people's armaments but because of the appearance of Yahweh. In our discussion about deliverance which started with the exodus, we have at the end come full circle.

Even so, though Zechariah reaches back into time for his model, he points into the future. From early times both in Israel and the ancient Near East, the donkey was an appropriate mount for royalty (Judg 5:10; 10:4; 12:14; 2 Sam 16:2). The expression "ass's colt" is attested from the second millennium at Mari outside Israel, where it signifies "pure-bred." When Jesus rode into Jerusalem on his mission of peace mounted on a donkey, those knowledgeable about the Old Testament would recall Zechariah's poem, not only as a summons to joy but as descriptive of a warrior king and therefore announcing the imminent prospect of salvation.

2. The Suffering Servant: Deliverance

Deliverance may come from the strangest quarters and in the most unusual ways. That is the message of Isaiah's servant songs.

Ever since Bernard Duhm, the German scholar of the nineteenth century, four passages in Isaiah have been known by the title "servant songs." Since the four have a similar theme and, according to scholars, did not fit properly into the context, there has been speculation about their origin and also about the

literary limits of each song. It may be, as one British scholar
suggests, that the songs were something of a separate composition at first but later fitted into the prophet's writing. The "fit"
was improved by some bridge statements. These connecting
verses continued the thought of the song and contained echoes
of it.[9] According to this approach the four songs are found in
the following texts; the suggested bridge statements are noted
in brackets.

> 42:1–9 (5–9)
> 49:1–13 (7–13)
> 50:4–11 (10–11)
> 52:13 – 53:12

Many chapters, even entire books have been written in response
to the nagging question: "Who is the servant?" One answer is
that the servant is an individual, either Moses or Job from Israel's past, or Isaiah himself, or someone future, the Messiah.
Another answer is that the servant is the nation of Israel—the
entire people, or a portion, either historically or ideally. The solution may even lie in a multiple of answers. Reading back from
the New Testament enables one to give a "Christian" answer. As
Philip explained to the Ethiopian cabinet minister who was
reading one of the servant songs (Isaiah 53), the servant par ex-
cellence was Jesus. Whether Isaiah's audience had any inkling
of a messianic reference could be debated, but the whole question of the servant's identity as of first priority detracts from the
more crucial question, what is the servant's role?

   An answer to that question leads us directly to the subject of
deliverance. Three songs particularly assert that the servant is
to be God's instrument bringing deliverance; they describe in
greater detail the way that deliverance is brought about. It is not
through war and might.

   The first song sets the stage. "Here is my servant, whom I
uphold . . . he will bring forth justice to the nations" (Isa 42:1).
The word "justice" is much more encompassing in the original
than "legal decision," for, as has been well said, it can stand here
for "true religion." The theme of justice, true religion, appears

three times in four verses. The servant will establish justice in the earth (v. 4). The succeeding "bridge" verses stress the deliverance dimension of that assignment, "to open the eyes that are blind, to bring out the prisoners from the dungeon, from the prison those who sit in darkness" (v. 7). The deliverance extends to individuals.

A bruised reed he will not break,
and a dimly burning wick he will not quench (v. 3).

The servant deals gently with those whose hope, if not also their life, is almost snuffed out.

God has appointed him also as a "covenant to the people, a light to the nations" (v. 6). A similar oscillation between the individual and the nation can be found in Isaiah 49 and also in Isaiah 61, which some designate a servant song. The servant, here identified as Israel (49:3) or possibly the remnant, is to bring Jacob back to God. But restoration of Israel's loyalty to Yahweh is only part of the job description. "I have given you as . . . a light to the nations" (49:6). In Isaiah 61, the same double focus—the intimate group, nation—is apparent. The servant, God's anointed, is sent to work in the smaller circle "to bind up the broken-hearted;" and in a larger circumference, his work "shall be known among the nations, and their offspring among the peoples" (Isa 61:9). It is not always clear in what way the nations are involved in the day of salvation, but at least as spectators they will witness the work of God's deliverance as he will "cause righteousness and praise to spring up before all the nations" (Isa 61:11).

Just as the Zechariah warrior-hymn in the exilic period recalled Israel's ancient traditions of holy war, so the servant songs tapped the traditions of the exodus. Israel in exile is promised a return after the pattern of the earlier exodus.

In a time of favor I have answered you,
on a day of salvation I have helped you;
I have kept you and given you as a covenant to the people,

to establish the land,
to apportion the desolate heritages (49:8).

The word comes to the captives as once it came to the slaves in Egypt, "Come out" (49:9). As the exiles return, "they shall not hunger or thirst" (49:10), for Yahweh will bring them to springs of waters and feed them. One remembers the wilderness provision of manna and water. The scorching sun will not strike them. As at the exodus, Yahweh will have compassion on his afflicted (49:13; cf. Exod 6:3).

The prophet presumably describes a physical return from the exile, but something more than a physical journey is at stake. The phrase "those who are in darkness" (v. 9) is symbolical. The servant delivers from a captivity which is more than physical. As Henri Blocher helpfully notes, a similar use of the exodus to typify a spiritual experience is made by Micah, who wrote in the eighth century: "As in the days when you came out of the land of Egypt, show us marvelous things" (Mic 7:15): The miracle of which he speaks is introduced by "Who is a God like you?" (Mic 7:18)—an echo of the famous song of Moses at the Sea of Reeds (Exodus 15)—but here consists of pardoning iniquity, treading it underfoot. The deliverance has to do with sin . . . better still, casting all Israel's sin into the depths of the sea (Mic 7:18–19). "In the first exodus it was the Egyptians and their chariots that were cast into the Red Sea. Now God is going to deal in an equally final and devastating way with our sins."[10] The exodus, always a paradigm for deliverance, now almost a millennium later becomes the image both for Micah and Isaiah by which to speak of deliverance from sin.

Salvation, though many-faceted, is secured through the suffering of the servant. This message, strange and almost unbelievable, is most straightforwardly proclaimed in the fourth song (Isa 52:12 – 53:12), although the third already speaks of God's servant being humiliated (50:4–11). There are those who strike his back, pluck his beard, spit on his face (50:6). The servant's self-description depicts one who is obedient, experiencing the sustaining hand of God. It is to suffering that this servant is called! In the fourth servant song, the suffering, entailing sorrows, acquaintance with grief and being smitten even of God, is not for his own guilt but is laid on him by God for others: "But he was wounded for our transgressions, crushed for our iniquities" (53:5). He himself was innocent (53:9), but he carried the sins of all of us who like sheep had gone astray. "The righteous one, my servant, shall make many righteous, and he shall bear their iniquities" (53:11).

In his brief but valuable study of the servant songs Blocher points to repeated use of "the many" in the fourth song and claims quite plausibly that it is a technical term (52:15; 53:11; 53:12).[11] "The many" refers to the beneficiaries of sacrificial suffering. These included Israelites but not only Israelites. The Qumran community a century before Christ uses the term "the many" as a regular official title. Blocher holds that Jesus "freed the term from national exclusivism when he spoke of himself as 'a ransom for many' (Matt 20:28)." Both Jews and Gentiles are the recipients of salvation made possible by the sacrifice of the servant.

The question of the suffering servant impels one quickly into the New Testament, where one sees so clearly that all that was spoken of concerning the suffering servant is fulfilled in Jesus. But by stressing the fulfillment we may miss a large part of the message of the servant songs. In the servant songs the servant is essentially anonymous. More important than the name is the role. The servant is God's agent of change. The servant is sensitive and brings help; is obedient to God, prepared to suffer. The servant's suffering can be redemptive for others. Here is a description of God's servant—any servant. A Christian who analyzes the servant portrait rejoices in the fulfillment which has come in Jesus, but is personally confronted with the question, To what extent am I God's servant?

Salvation, deliverance, described in the apocalyptic period of Israel's history, is obtained in two totally opposite ways. On the one hand, there is the power of the victor on the field of battle; on the other, the meekness of the victim on an altar of sacrifice. Both develop different themes from the exodus. Both issue in a description of deliverance—deliverance from external peril, perhaps, but a deliverance also from the corruption of sin. Deliverance is as big as God.

As a divine warrior, Jesus showed himself victor over demonic powers. His was a greater power than the political power of Rome. As a suffering servant Jesus laid down his life on the cross. In retrospect one can see how the kaleidoscope of deliverance requires both divine warrior and suffering servant. In view of these facts the religious leaders of Jesus' day may be judged less harshly, for they seized upon the apocalyptic image of a political war hero and disregarded the image of a sheep led to the slaughter. The tension between the two images remains even now and will into the future, for as John, the revelator, saw the overcomer, he was the lion from the tribe of Judah, the lamb slain (Rev 5:9).

3. Summary

A look at the terrain over which we have come in talking about deliverance as part of God's plan makes certain way markers loom large. Two kinds of deliverance have occupied us from the first.

The one deliverance model takes shape at the exodus. It is deliverance from the enemy through a Yahweh war. In the pre-monarchy period divine war is prominent both in Israel's march to the land and in her conquest of the land. During the monarchy the prophets, apparently drawing from the paradigm of Yahweh war, speak about the day of Yahweh. Like the war of Yahweh, the day of Yahweh puts Yahweh center stage. The day of God's coming spells judgment for some and salvation for others. In the exilic and post-exilic period, the day of Yahweh was universalized, so to speak, by the apocalypticists. The cataclysmic coming of Yahweh would mean worldwide judgment of evil. The age of bliss would be then ushered in at last. From the exodus in the second millennium to the apocalypticists of the intertestamental time, the theme of God's deliverance was constant, though the nuance varied in different time periods.

The second kind of deliverance is structured initially around sacrifice. It too has to do with freeing persons from evil. The evil is defined as sin—it is alienation from God that is the issue. In the worship rituals, and in the sacrifices particularly, Israelites acknowledged their sin and claimed the forgiveness God extended to them. Sacrifices continue in the monarchy of course, but the prophets urge the importance of right relatedness to God which extends beyond the habitual offering of an animal. The messianic expectations which center on a king-like deliverer are also described by other language such as "Immanuel," "God with us." In the later periods of Old Testament times the suffering servant motif climaxes in sacrifice-type language.

> But he was wounded for our transgressions,
> crushed for our iniquities . . .
> Like a lamb that is led to the slaughter,
> and like a sheep that before its shearers is silent,
> so he did not open his mouth . . .
> yet he bore the sin of many,
> and made intercession for the transgressors (53:5, 7, 12).

Here is a word of deliverance but in another key. The New Testament will elaborate on deliverance according to the sacrifice model, but laced throughout its pages is the assurance of victorious deliverance over all contrary forces.

Covenant and Community in the Post-Exilic Period

The covenant formula, "I will be your God and you shall be my people," punctuates the Old Testament like a refrain. A harbinger of the covenant formula occurred in God's communication with Abraham (Gen 17:7). Its classic form is given in Exod 6:7 and in the Torah generally (Lev 26:12; Deut 26:16–19). We meet the expression again in the monarchy period as God establishes covenant with David (2 Sam 7:24), and as the covenant relationship is put to the test through Israel's misbehavior (Jer 7:23–26; 11:4). The tragic incidents of the fall of both Israel and Judah and the captivity of the peoples would put an end, one would think, to such covenant talk. But no, the opposite is true. The greatest frequency of the covenant formula is found in the period surrounding the debacle of the exile, 600–520 BC (e.g., Ezek 11:20; 14:11; 36:23; 37:27; Zech 8:8; 13:9). Through the tragedy, the shambles of war, and even the dispersion, the clarion call to covenant is sounded, "I will be your God and you will be my people." The original design remains: "My purpose shall stand, and I will fulfill my intention" (Isa 46:10).

Are the assertions of the covenant realistic and credible in the face of the hiatus between Israel and her God as evidenced through the exile? Israel had strained the covenant relationship to its breaking point. God had said, "I will be your God," but Israel, led by her kings, had gone after other gods. God had said,

"You shall be my people," but, as the prophets kept insisting, Israel's action belied such an identity. What are the dynamics and the developments that account for the old refrain to be heard again, strangely at first, in a distant land? We must investigate.

1. An Interpretation of the Exile
A Broken Covenant

We shall need to understand, as Israel had needed to understand, that the covenant made with her had been broken. Already Hosea and Isaiah, eighth-century prophets, had alerted Israel to her fragile relationship with God. Unless there was an early turn-about on the part of Israel, they said, the covenant relationship would terminate. Hosea employed his personal marriage and his subsequent difficulties to picture the covenantal situation between Israel and God.

The waywardness of a covenant partner could indeed result in God's verdict, "Not my people," in which case the covenant was no longer in effect. In a covenant lawsuit Isaiah identified the strained relationship, charging that Israel had "forsaken the LORD" (Isa 1:4), but still invited the wayward covenant partner to "come now, let us argue it out" (Isa 1:18). Hosea, also in a covenant lawsuit, had been more threatening.

> My people are destroyed for lack of knowledge.
> Because you have rejected knowledge,
> I reject you from being a priest to me.
> And since you have forgotten the law of your God,
> I also will forget your children (4:6).

In courtroom language, the indictments were systematically laid before the people. The verdict was all but certain. Finally Jeremiah, who ministered, as we know in retrospect, just prior to the fall of the nation of Judah, says, "The house of Israel and the house of Judah have *broken the covenant* that I made with their ancestors" (Jer 11:10).

There it was in unambiguous language. The covenant was in ruins. As treaties go this breach was not unusual. One historian who investigated treaties between 1500 BC and AD 1850 has noted that some 7,500 "eternal" treaties lasted an average of two years each.[1] But whether commonplace or not, covenant-breaking is serious.

What results from a broken covenant? One thing is clear, the covenant partners must bear the consequences. For Israel the consequence was to experience, even if for a little, the justified anger of the covenant partner. Judgment on her evil came in the form of enemy invasions and deportations.

Israel found it difficult to appreciate such a turn of events. Nor is the reason far to seek. For her, God's guarantee of faithfulness was written so large that an unwarranted feeling of security had developed. True, God's promise in Isaiah's day was that Zion would stand. To that promise Israel clung despite her later disloyalty to Yahweh. But God's promises have qualification. The immediate situation, not to mention the attitudes of a people, was determining. That which was a guarantee for Israel when Hezekiah feared the Assyrians was no longer a guarantee a hundred years later when in judgment God was bringing the Babylonians against Israel. Israel had capitalized on the promise half of the formula "I will be your God," without paying sufficient heed to the demand half, "You shall be my people."

It is critical, as has been argued earlier, to understand that a covenant differs from a contract. In a contract violation of certain demands is at once cause for invalidating the agreement. Failure to comply cancels the contract. In a covenant, this solution is not so clear-cut—for it is not conformity to code but loyalty to person that is basic. But dissolution of covenant is definitely possible, because loyalty is demonstrated through obedience. Israel had not been obedient. God had been forbearing with Israel's flirtations with other gods and her injustices to one another, but a breaking point had now been reached. If an explanation for God's judgment is needed, it is given in the book of Isaiah, who points to the rupture of the relationship: "O that you had paid attention to my commandments! Then your prosperity would have been like a river" (48:18).

The obvious consequence for Israel of a broken covenant was to experience God's judgment. But there was another possibility: God would still fulfill his desire. A new covenant structure at his initiative was possible.

2. Affirmation of Covenant Formula I Will Be Your God

The covenant formula has two parts. In the literature of the exilic and post-exilic period both parts are emphasized, sometimes together but more often separately.

The people of the exile heard the reassuring word: "I will be your God." Judging from the material in the second half of Isaiah there were two points on the agenda, both fully understandable.[2] First was the question, "Is God really, as claimed, sovereign Lord of all gods?" The collapse of national life raised the issue whether other gods were perhaps more powerful than Yahweh. Assuming that Yahweh was all that he claimed, and recognizing that the covenant was broken, the second question was, "Would God take up with Israel again? Would Yahweh still own her as his people?"

"Is Yahweh Truly God?"

It is through Isaiah especially that an answer to this twofold agenda is not only given but propounded and argued. Yahweh is indeed God. This assertion is boldly proclaimed: "Your God reigns" (52:7; cf. 62:8). But mere table-thumping will not suffice as a reply to the doubters. The argument for God's sovereignty over all competing deities is established through several supporting arguments. Yahweh is creator. In majestic rhetoric, the prophet asks, "Who has measured the waters in the hollow of his hand and marked off the heavens with a span, enclosed the dust of the earth in a measure, and weighed the mountains in scales and the hills in a balance?" (40:12). It is Yahweh who sits above the circle of the earth, who reduces rulers to nothing (40:22–23). Look beyond the earth to the heavens and see that the one who created the stars "brings out their host and numbers them, calling them all by name; because he is great in strength, mighty in power, not one is missing" (40:26). The doctrine of creation, important in the hymnic literature of the Psalms, functions nowhere else as dominantly as here where it underscores Yahweh's uniqueness, his incomparability, and his supremacy.

Yahweh, the creator, is also Lord of history. Testimony is given in the hearing of the coastlands that the God Yahweh has aroused someone from the east, presumably Cyrus, who will deliver up nations and subdue kings. That development in the world of nations, so runs the argument, is in keeping with earlier action in which God has called forth the generations from the beginning. God appeals to history, to "the former things" (41:22; 42:9; 43:9, 18; 46:9; 48:3). The identity of the mover of history is declared once more: "I, the LORD, am first, and will be with the last" (41:4). A God who moves the course of nations is unlike the idols of the heathen.

The prophet now takes the offensive. The heathen idols are impotent. In unabashed sarcasm the prophet mocks the production of an idol. He describes how the craftsmen, the goldsmith, the silversmith, or the woodcarver make the figurines, ensuring that the fragile images "will not topple" (40:20). The man who uses his tools to fashion the idols is nothing but a man, for he becomes hungry and his strength fails (44:12). What he makes will be inferior to himself rather than stronger. Moreover the idol he fashions is in his own image. As if to compound the stupidity a man will take a tree, use some of it to fashion an idol and with the remainder make a fire for baking bread—part of that lumber serves to keep him warm, the other part is his god before which he falls down and worships. "He prays to it and says, 'Save me, for you are my god!'" (44:17). But the images fashioned by human hands are powerless, futile, claims the prophet. They are *tōhû* (44:9), a word used in the creation account to describe the waste and uninhabited earth (Gen 1:2).

How different from the product of human hands is Yahweh. "Thus says the LORD, the King of Israel, and his Redeemer, the LORD of hosts: I am the first and I am the last; besides me there is no god. Who is like me? Let them proclaim it, let them declare and set it forth before me" (44:6–7).

The argument for Yahweh's sovereignty over other gods includes the ability to predict the future—a benefit the heathen gods cannot supply. The setting is the court. "Set forth your case, says the LORD; bring your proofs, says the King of Jacob. Let them bring them, and tell us what is to happen . . . or declare to us the things to come" (41:21–22). The gauntlet is thrown down to all who would claim to be gods: "Tell us what is to come hereafter, that we may know that you are gods" (41:23). When challenged in a court controversy the gods, who cannot declare either the former things or the things to come, are silent and so lose the court case by default. Hence the verdict, "You, indeed, are nothing" (41:24).

The argument is subtle in this sense: it is before nations that God offers proofs of his supremacy, but in providing these proofs God is at the same time answering the misgivings of Israel. The argument for fulfilled prediction has a further interesting facet. God says to Israel, "You are my witnesses" (43:10). The nations along with their deities are unable to attest to "the former things," namely events in the past, now fulfilled. But Israel is a witness to Yahweh predictions. As Israel gives witness to Yahweh's ability to foretell the future, she will "know and believe me and understand that I am he. Before me no god was formed, nor shall there be any after me" (43:10). Through her own witness as God's advocate in this controversy between God and nations, Israel will know that Yahweh is God.[3]

These four arguments—God's role in creation, in history, in prediction, together with the impotence of the heathen gods—represent the chief evidence the prophet marshals for the superiority of Yahweh. The prophets were faced with the crucial question from their people and from the Gentiles: is the God of Israel the God of gods? The experience of the exile had put the answer in doubt. The prophets replied, yes. There were reasons for that answer, and by following the format of a legal court controversy they sustained an appeal to their hearers to consider the evidence.

"Will God Own Us as His People?"

Before Israel was prepared to appropriate God's promise "I will be your God," she needed the assurance in the exile context that God would indeed own Israel as his people. To this question, verbally posed or not, the material in Isaiah 40–66 speaks repeatedly.

The lawsuit form was used as a vehicle to supply an answer to the earlier question; here various forms of salvation speeches are used to communicate the assurance of God's relationship with Israel.[4] The "assurance of salvation" is one type of salvation speech. It is characterized by its formal "Fear not." Then follow reasons why Israel should not be anxious. One of these reasons is, "I have redeemed you; I have called you by name, you are mine" (43:1). In another assurance-of-salvation oracle the affirmation of God's ownership of his people comes in the so-called "consequences" section: "This one will say, 'I am the LORD's,' . . . yet another will write on the hand, 'The LORD's'" (44:5). In yet another salvation oracle the assurance of God's ownership of Israel is elaborated extensively and impressively in conjunction with the "addressee" section, "But you, Israel, my servant, Jacob, whom I have chosen, the offspring of Abraham, my friend; you whom I took from the ends of the earth . . . saying to you, 'You are my servant, *I have chosen you and not cast you off*'" (41:8–9). God's willingness to continue with Israel is most impressive.

A second type of salvation speech is the "announcement of salvation." It is characterized among other features by a lament nuance. God, addressing the afflicted, announces his help and defines the relationship: "I the LORD will answer them, *I the God of Israel* will not forsake them" (41:17).

Assertions of God's readiness to continue a divine purpose with Israel occur also in conjunction with family-oriented language in which God is pictured as either a parent or a marriage partner. The parental attachment is highlighted by Yahweh's rhetorical question given in reply to Israel's complaint: "But Zion said, 'The LORD has forsaken me, my Lord has forgotten me.' Can a woman forget her nursing child, or show no compassion for the child of her womb? Even these may forget, yet I will not forget you" (49:14–15).

The same thought of God having forsaken his people is taken up in 50:1, but now under the figure of a marriage relationship. "Where is your mother's bill of divorce, with which I put her away?" The expected answer is that it cannot be produced. Israel's separation from God occurred because of her sin and not because of a divorce decree issued by her partner. The metaphor of matrimony surfaces again. As a youthful woman who is forsaken and grieving is recalled by her husband to be his wife, so the LORD recalls Israel into the relationship that once existed (54:6; cf. Zech 10:6). And then as if to leave no doubt about God's willingness to take Israel as his partner, the prophet declares,

> For as a young man marries a young woman . . .
> and as the bridegroom rejoices over the bride,
> so shall your God rejoice over you (62:5).

The parent will not disown the child. The bridegroom is not expected to disown the bride. So the LORD will not disown Israel.

In the second half of the book of Isaiah a double movement centers around the first covenant formula: "I will be your God." On the one hand it is necessary to articulate clearly "I am God." On the other hand it is not immediately self-evident that God will still be identified with Israel following the exile and the brokenness of the covenant. Hence the many attempts to clarify the simple statement, "I will be your God."

3. Affirmation of Covenant Formula You Shall Be My People

The second part of the covenant formula "You shall be my people," as heard by the exilic population, contains things old but also things new. There were the familiar sounds: a people, *one people*, and also a certain kind of people, God's people. With each of these components there were now new nuances: the word *people* was given an enlarged definition; the demand to be God's people had new, even exciting dimensions.

"You Shall Be One People"

Even the familiar word "You shall be my people" was not without its problems, for Israel and Judah were two distinct entities, separated for 150 years in their history by the downfall of the respective capital cities Samaria and Jerusalem. The citizens of each were in strange lands, Assyria and Babylon, large distances apart. On the surface, the call "You shall be my people" had a hollow ring, for they were not even a people, quite apart from being called "my people."[5]

The promise looked into the future. Ezekiel underscored the reunification of Israel and Judah in a memorable way. Two sticks were in the prophet's hand; one was labeled "for Judah," the other "for Joseph." In Ezekiel's hand the two rods were then held together on end, so that to an observer it appeared that there were not two sticks but one. The explanation which accompanied this symbolic action was straightforward: God would take Joseph, who represented Ephraim and the northern tribes of Israel, and put them with Judah, that "they may be one in my hand" (Ezek 37:19). The prospect was one of a people once more united.

For reunification to become a reality the regathering of the dispersed was necessary. The explanation of the two sticks takes up this subject at once: "I will take the people of Israel from the nations among which they have gone, and will gather them from every quarter, and bring them to their own land . . ." (Ezek

37:21–22). The promise for a regathering is repeated often in
Ezekiel (e.g., 11:17; 20:34; 36:24; 37:12) and in the book of
Isaiah also (14:1; 51:11). Further investigation of this prospect
will occupy us in a later discussion about land, to which the regathering is closely linked, but the description of the anticipated trek, more unusual even than the earlier exodus, is highly
lyrical. "So the ransomed of the LORD shall return, and come to
Zion with singing; everlasting joy shall be upon their heads;
they shall obtain joy and gladness, and sorrow and sighing shall
flee away" (Isa 51:11). The guarantee for the regathering is Yahweh, creator of the heaven and earth and of Israel. Just as the
exodus from Egypt aimed at the formation of a people, a community (Exodus 6), so the regathering from the lands of the dispersion is aimed at community. "I have . . . hidden you in the
shadow of my hand, stretching out the heavens and laying the
foundations of the earth, and saying to Zion, 'You are my people'" (Isa 51:16). God's work of deliverance, whether of the exodus or the regathering, has a clearly stated objective:
community.

"You Shall Be God's People"

The post-exilic regathered community, like the earlier post-
exodus community, was to be a marked community, *God's people*.
The promise "You shall be my people" contained a demand
within it for a unique quality of people. The prophets, both during the exile and later, pressed home the religious and ethical
demands entailed in living as God's people.

To be God's people—how often Israel had heard it—meant
to have a single loyalty to Yahweh. Ezekiel, for instance, reminded his people, those in the land and those dispersed, that
God would deal swiftly in judgment with any who set up idols
and then came piously to inquire of the LORD through his
prophet. The prophet and inquirer would bear the punishment
of their iniquity "that the house of Israel may no longer go
astray from me, nor defile themselves any more with all their

transgressions. Then they shall be my people, and I will be their God, says the Lord God' (Ezek 14:11).

Ethical behavior for God's people was not optional; it was mandatory because of who God was: "For I the LORD love justice, I hate robbery and wrongdoing" (Isa 61:8). Did Israel fast? Well and good. But Yahweh would not hear when the businessmen were driving hard all their workers (58:3). The acceptable fast, Israel must learn, is not without moral dimensions such as loving one's neighbor; specifically, loosening the bonds of wickedness, dividing bread with the hungry, bringing the homeless poor into the house, and clothing the naked (58:6–7). To the returned Jews Zechariah (c. 518 BC) reiterates the teaching about the fast, correcting what seems continuous misunderstanding: "Render true judgments, show kindness and mercy to one another; do not oppress the widow, the orphan, the alien, or the poor; and do not devise evil in your hearts against one another" (Zech 7:9–10). Zechariah, recognizing that a quality of lifestyle was appropriate to God's people, told of the coming refinement in which Israel would be "refined as silver is refined." Israel's purification, then, would anticipate the covenant. "They will call on my name, and I will answer them. I will say, 'They are my people'; and they will say, 'The LORD is our God'" (Zech 13:9; cf. 8:8).

The small, often beleaguered community, occupied with rebuilding the fallen Jerusalem walls and the temple, was encouraged toward appropriate ethical behavior by leaders such as Ezra and Nehemiah. Both instructed the people in the statutes of Moses (Neh 8:8; 13:1; cf. Ezra 7:10). In keeping with the Mosaic law various reforms were instituted: foreigners were excluded (Neh 13:3); sales on Sabbath were disallowed (Neh 13:15–22); and those who had married foreign women were asked to put them away (Ezra 10:3ff). The implementation of God's demands by such hard action as the separation of marriage partners seems to us to border on racism. Whatever we may think of this action, the fact remains that God had chosen a people, but this people had not chosen God, and therefore was but a sad exhibit of God's people (Nehemiah 9).

An Old Formula with a New Ring

Neither of these emphases—a united people, and an upright people—was new to the exiles. But there were overtones for each in the prophets' announcements that were definitely different from and shattered earlier stereotypes. One fresh note added to the promise of a united people was that not all exiles but only a remnant would constitute the returned united Israel. Another note, sounded more clearly than ever, was that Gentiles would be a part of God's people. A third note in the triad added to the call for an upright people was that with the demands of the covenant there were now new resources available.

The new community of God's people would contain an ethnic core of Jews, specifically a remnant. The direct teaching about a remnant is already found in Isaiah (4:3; 6:13; 17:6; cf. 30:17). Prior to the fall of Jerusalem, Zephaniah, who had announced the day of God's wrath against Judah, had predicted that only a remnant would later return to inhabit the land, and these would be the humble and lowly, those spiritually qualified (2:7, 9; 3:12–13). Ezekiel, who ministered during the exile, made it clear, although he did not use the word *remnant*, that not all of Israel would be restored to the land but only a small group (14:21–23; cf. 11:14–20). Ezekiel pictures an exodus of God's people from the lands to which they were scattered, but states that before they are brought into the land they will be judged in the wilderness, and the rebels among them shall be purged (20:34–38).

Jeremiah, like Ezekiel, speaks of a spiritual renewal which will characterize the remnant. In the earlier passages in Jeremiah the repentance of the people apparently precedes the physical return to the land and their unification (31:15–20). Other passages describe a spiritual renewal of the people *after* their physical return to the land (32:7ff; 37:23). The post-exilic community identified itself as the faithful minority, the remnant that remained (Hag 1:12–14; 2:2; Zech 8:6, 11–12; Ezra 9:8, 14–15; Neh 1:2–3). The remnant was not identical with the political or ethnic definition of Israel, a point that the apostle Paul was later to stress (Rom 2:28; 9:6).

Even more consequential for Israel's understanding and life is a further new element, namely the announcement by the prophets, Isaiah especially, that Gentiles will be numbered among God's people. The call, "Turn to me and be saved, all the ends of the earth!" (Isa 45:22) was a repetition of earlier universal strands (cf. Gen 12:1–3; Ps 68:31). But God's purpose with the Gentiles was more explicit, as Isaiah will describe. Israel, clearly bereaved of her children, as well as barren, now was to find herself in the land with many "children." "Who has borne me these?" she asks (49:21). Are these but dispersed Jews from an unexpected quarter, or is there a veiled hint that Yahweh is making a place among her for the Gentiles? Indeed, the association of other people with Israel is described: "See, you shall call nations that you do not know, and nations that do not know you shall run to you" (55:5).

Foreigners were not to be shunned, but to be welcomed. Yes, they did have "a place": "And the foreigners who join themselves to the LORD . . . these I will bring to my holy mountain . . . for my house shall be called a house of prayer for all peoples. Thus says the Lord GOD, who gathers the outcasts of Israel, I will gather others to them besides those already gathered" (56:6–8). Isolated Gentiles such as Rahab the Canaanite, Ruth the Moabite, and Ittai the Hittite, had joined Israel as God-fearers to be part of God's people, and now the prospect was for a wave of non-Israelites to be incorporated into "my people." Through a faith commitment expressed through observance of sacrifice and other requirements foreigners would become members of the community in full standing. Isaiah is bold indeed when he tells of Egypt's future when Yahweh will make himself known to Egypt, and the Egyptians will know Yahweh (19:21). Then Yahweh's blessing will sound, "Blessed be Egypt *my people* . . ." (19:25). The term "people of God" is wider certainly than ethnic Israel.

A further wrinkle in the covenant formula which, if not totally new, was definitely more prominent in the exile than earlier, was the promise for new resources. Through Ezekiel and Jeremiah God was offering a new covenant,[6] and offering also the resources of his Spirit, so that this time the covenant partner would remain faithful, would exhibit the loyalty essential to covenant. Loyalty is essential for covenant. Ezekiel put it graphically: the heart of stone would be removed from Israel, and by divine transplant a new heart and a new spirit would be supplied (Ezek 36:24). The purpose for this radical spiritual surgery is to "make you follow my statutes and be careful to observe my ordinances" (Ezek 36:27). That purpose in turn is directly related to the covenant: "and you shall be my people, and I will be your God" (Ezek 36:28). Jeremiah had likewise linked the newly promised provision of God's grace-act, putting his law within them and writing it on their heart, with the covenant formula, which follows immediately: "I will be their God, and they shall be my people" (Jer 31:33). God's law put within the human heart ensured that they would both know the LORD and follow him in obedience.

The frequent occurrence of the covenant formula in exilic and pre-exilic literature testifies to the anxiety about covenant, perhaps, but more important, it testifies to the durability of God's design, especially his eagerness to establish a fruitful relationship with a people. The earlier covenant had been broken. Beyond judgment, which that brokenness entailed, God now affirmed the covenant basics. He was God, ready still to be Israel's God; they in turn were to be uniquely his people.

Israel, though in exile, had a fresh word of hope. God would enter into covenant with her as he had in the past. But that new covenant would be unlike the covenant of the past. The new arrangement would include the Gentiles in a way more pronounced than before. The new community, though consisting of a spiritually vital Israelite remnant, would embrace more than token Gentiles. The new community would be distinguished by the resource of the Spirit of God, by which they would be enabled to be truly God's people.

4. Summary

The shifts in covenant content are most obvious in Jeremiah, who nevertheless reaches back into history as he makes a contrast. Jeremiah contrasts the new covenant with the old, for the new covenant will be "not like the covenant that I made with their ancestors when I took them by the hand to bring them out of the land of Egypt . . ." (Jer 31:32). With that statement Jeremiah points forward to the Christ event, as the author of Hebrews explains (Heb 8:6–13). But in giving the promise, Jeremiah also harks back to the beginnings of Israel's story, to the covenant at Sinai.

Having come to the end of our Old Testament survey of the covenant strand in God's purpose we may profitably look back and discern both the constants and the variables in the covenant relationships which God established with his people. The covenant, in a nutshell, is always "I will be your God, you will be my people," whether that be with Israel at the exodus (Exod 6:7) or with David in the monarchy period (2 Sam 7:14) or with the remnant in the exile (Ezek 14:11), or with the new covenant described by Jeremiah (Jer 31:31), or for that matter in the end time depicted by John the apostle; "He will dwell with them as their God; they will be his peoples, and God himself will be with them" (Rev 21:3). Always, whether implicit or expressly stated, loyalty on the part of each covenant partner is central. In the sense of a requirement of loyalty, every covenant is conditional, whether it be with Abraham or David, or whether with the Levites or Israel. Each of the covenants represents God's initiative in grace. No covenant recipient can boast of merit. Covenants, even those given to individuals, Abraham, and David, aim predominantly at descendants, at peoplehood, at community—not just any community but one in which the will of God is understood and obeyed.

But the differences between the covenants should not go unmentioned. Most obvious is the fact that a covenant is made at times with individuals such as Abraham or David and at other times with groups such as the Levites or Israel. Schematically

one may think of the sequel to the Sinai covenant being both exclusive and inclusive. The covenant with David is appropriated
later by Israel (Isa 55:3). Certain covenants such as the Abrahamic and the Davidic are weighted in favor of God's promises,
while others, such as the Sinaitic covenant, are more detailed as
to the stipulations. The new covenant, most striking of all, offers the promise of regenerated persons who will desire to do
the will of God.

Summary of Covenants in the Old Testament

		Pre-monarchy	Monarchy	Post-monarchy
Constants	Covenants	Abrahamic, Sinaitic	Davidic	New Covenant
	Covenant formula	I will be your God, you will be my people	I will be your God, you will be my people	I will be your God, you will be my people
	Initiative	God	God	God
	Basic stipulation	Loyalty	Loyalty	Loyalty
	Intention	Peoplehood	Peoplehood	Peoplehood
Variables	Setting	National deliverance (Sinaitic)	Personal commitment	National bankruptcy
	Partner	Group (Sinai) Individual (e.g., Abraham)	Individual	Group
	Features	Land, etc. (Abraham)	Royal dynasty, etc.	An "interior" law, etc.

The Experience of God

O_{ne} of the components of God's design according to our pivotal text, Exod 5:22 – 6:8, is that people may know God. Knowing God entails experiencing God. The often repeated phrase in Ezekiel, "Then you (they) shall know that I am the LORD," is already sufficient evidence that God's earlier design is reaffirmed. Yet within this reaffirmation fresh directions are discernible. In our initial discussion the knowledge of God was explored along the lines of cult, event, and the wider world. In the exilic/post-exilic period the same rubrics are appropriate.

1. The Experience of God within the Cult

Cult, defined as those external, often ritual acts in which people engage in the practice of religion, may in the Hebrew religion look in two directions.[1] For the Hebrews worship is premised on divine revelation. God the LORD gives himself and his will to be known, whether in divine appearance, in a theophany, the Urim or the Thummim, or the prophets' word or some other means. The people in turn respond to the divine self-revelation. Knowledge of God thus involves both revelation and response. This chapter will give attention to prayer as a form of response and to the temple as the revelation of God.

Prayer

The prayers of individuals are given in more detail and in greater number within this time frame than in earlier periods. Omitting the Psalms, some of which were certainly exilic (e.g., Psalm 74), one finds in the narratives from this period at least three lengthy prayers by individuals: Ezra, Nehemiah, and Daniel (Ezra 9; Neh 1:4–11; Dan 9:3–27). Each is a private rather than a public prayer, though Ezra's prayer attracted public attention. Furthermore, Chronicles, a rewrite of Israel's history dating from 400 BC, includes a public prayer by David in prose which the earlier histories in Kings did not incorporate. In addition to these lengthier recorded prayers, the narratives include short notices such as Nehemiah's "So I prayed to the God of heaven" (Neh 2:4), and the story of Daniel in the lion's den, an incident precipitated by Daniel's illegal prayer. The prominence given to private prayer by the narratives of this period is impressive.

The prayers give witness to the personal relationship between Yahweh and the worshiper. The directness is noteworthy. Ezra and Daniel pray, "My God" (Ezra 9:6; Dan 9:18). It has been argued that whereas in Israel's earlier history the group is primary, later periods in Israel's history are characterized by individualism. A prime example of this doctrine of individual responsibility is the series of hypothetical instances described in Ezekiel 18, each of which underscore individual responsibility. "The person who sins shall die" (Ezek 18:20). That principle is different from principles obtaining in earlier stories, that of Achan, for example, where the entire clan was punished by death for the sin of one man. Whether the difference between early Israel and post-exilic Israel on this doctrine is as pronounced as is claimed can be questioned, but the reports of the individual prayers lend support to the increasing importance in the exilic period of individual piety.

The freedom, even spontaneity, of these prayers, as well as the emotional intensity they exhibit, is impressive. The prayers contain historical allusions, even historical reviews, but they hardly follow a rigid or prescribed form. They represent intense emotional involvement. Ezra prostrated himself and wept (Ezra 10:1). He had begun his prayer by falling on his knees and stretching out his hands to the Lord (Ezra 9:5). Daniel reiterates his plea, "O LORD, hear; O LORD, forgive; O LORD, listen and act" (Dan 9:19). He is wearied, even exhausted following his prayer (Dan 9:21).[2]

In content the prayer is petition. Recognition of God's greatness is not absent (Neh 1:5; Dan 9:4), but the three prayers of Ezra, Nehemiah, and Daniel are essentially requests to God to look with favor and with forgiveness on his people. They urge God's response on the basis of various considerations. The speaker may acknowledge the divine commands which his people have transgressed (Ezra 9:10–12; cf. Neh 1:8–9), or he may interpret the present evil circumstances (Dan 9:14), or he may lay claim to God's favor on the basis of God's work in history or his quality of compassion. "Look at our desolation . . . forgive . . . act" (Dan 9:18–19). "Give success to your servant today" (Neh 1:11). In the face of personal and national difficulty on the one hand, and God's greatness and compassion on the other hand, the fitting response is to pray. Even leaders are dependent persons, and dependent persons pray.

To follow the sequel of these prayers is to be intrigued with the outworkings of prayers and to be led into the unexplainable but wonderful reality of divine responsiveness to prayer. Through prayer God is known and experienced; and the grandeur and the condescension of God are observed.

One may concede that prayer has its subjective elements. Such subjectivity in religious experience is balanced however in the Hebrew religion by the more objective aspect of cult—the temple, for example.

The Temple

The importance given in the post-exilic period to the temple, its reconstruction and rituals, is astonishing. The Chronicler, in retelling the story of David and Solomon, expands considerably on David's plan for the temple, the preparation of materials and the construction and dedication (1 Chronicles 17, 22, 28–29; 2 Chronicles 2–8). The priestly and levitical service, including the ministry of song, is described (1 Chronicles 23–27). Since a considerable part of this material is not found in the earlier account in Kings, it is likely that these materials deliberately contributed to the Chronicler's purpose, which in one way or another concerned the temple. Ezekiel devotes several chapters to the subject, down to the details of temple measurements and prescriptions about offerings (Ezekiel 40–46). Upon their return from exile the civil and spiritual leaders devoted their energies to the actual building of the temple (Ezra 3:10ff; Hag 1–2; Zechariah 1, 4). The vessels of the temple received frequent mention also (Ezra 6:5; 7:19; 8:25; Zech 14:20). The book of Malachi takes up the question of priestly qualifications and service in the temple. The temple was undoubtedly of prime importance, and the post-exilic community's concern for cultic matters was strong. Since the appropriate rituals could have been resumed in Jerusalem by the regathered community quite apart from the temple structure, one must ask about the exilic understanding of temples.

Dimensions and building progress aside, what is the theological significance of the temple? First, it speaks of Yahweh's presence. Ezekiel describes the way in which the glory of God leaves the Jerusalem temple prior to the city's destruction: the glory cloud representing God's presence is lifted from the cherubim, stands momentarily at the threshold of the temple, then moves to the courtyard and proceeds from the midst of the city eastward to the mountain (Ezekiel 10–11). This background is important for the new temple vision which Ezekiel later describes, for the glory of God now returns from the east and rests upon the temple (Ezek 43:2ff). It is Ezekiel's way of stating that God is present. There are those who hold that Ezekiel's vision is predictive of a future temple in the millennium.[3] Whether it is or not, the chief point of the concluding chapters of Ezekiel's book is a vigorous assertion that with the new temple God will once again be present among his people. Any hesitation toward adopting this conclusion is dispelled by the final sentence of the book: "And the name of the city from that time on shall be, The LORD is There" (Ezek 48:35). The temple, quite like the tabernacle before it, was a symbol of the LORD's presence.

Yet this belief was not to be interpreted to mean that God was physically limited to the temple. Jeremiah had taught the exiles that God's presence among them was not dependent on the temple (Jer 29:13–14). Ezekiel more than other prophets insists on the transcendence of God (but compare also Ezra 1:2; Neh 1:4–5; 9:12–13, 27–28). And Isaiah's word, whether spoken in the eighth century or in this exilic period, must not be forgotten. Indeed, some consider his word to be a protest against temple building:[4] "Thus says the LORD: Heaven is my throne and the earth is my footstool; what is the house that you would build for me?" (Isa 66:1). Still, the temple functioned as a symbol of the message that God was among the people.

Secondly, the temple bore witness to the honor of God, and that in a double sense. For Israel the temple was a witness to the values to which they as God's people ideally subscribed. Haggai the prophet put it to the people unambiguously, "Is it a time for you yourselves to live in your paneled houses, while this house lies in ruins?" (1:4). Construction of the temple represented a testimony by the believing community to the importance of their worship of Yahweh. Haggai challenged the people to proceed with construction, not that their limited resources would be extended as they put God first. He promised blessing in response to their immediate obedience: "Build the house, so that I may take pleasure in it and be honored, says the LORD" (Hag 1:8). The honor of God was at stake in another way, for the building of the temple was important for the sake of the nations. They had profaned Jerusalem which God had chosen (Ezek 7:21). By implication Yahweh's name and reputation were besmirched. Ezekiel had insisted that nations would know that God sanctified Israel when the sanctuary would be built (Ezek 37:28). God's honor, put in jeopardy because of Israel's disgraceful exile from the land, would be vindicated when the sanctuary would stand once more in the city.

Thirdly, the temple was the focal point for the community and facilitated worship. The temple was like pagan temples in having three sections; it was unlike pagan religious structures in that Israel's temple did not contain an idol or an image. Yet for Israel the temple was the acknowledged place for communal worship. Earlier prescriptions called for the males to gather at the central place of worship three times a year for extended festival and celebration (Exod 23:14, 17; Deut 16:16). The message of the Chronicler, according to one scholar, is a call for people in the post-exilic period to "rally round the temple."[5] Solomon's dedication as quoted by the Chronicler assumes that the temple is the place where people will come when they are making their supplications. When grief-stricken people spread forth their hands "toward this house" (2 Chr 6:29), then as Solomon petitions, "May you hear from heaven . . . in order that all the peoples of the earth may know your name and . . . that your name has been invoked on this house that I have built" (2 Chr 6:33). The temple was the place from which God would answer prayer.

Like the tabernacle before it, the temple was a place of meeting—a meeting with God. Zechariah's warrior hymn describes the climax of the warrior's coming as God's coming "to my house" (Zech 9:8). And Malachi announced that the LORD would suddenly come to his temple (Mal 3:1). There was an eschatological reason for the building of the temple. The temple was necessary for the messianic age to arrive; then would come about the ultimate meeting of human beings and God.

Fourthly, the temple built initially in conjunction with the offer of covenant, never lost the overtones of covenant. The temple was the visible symbol of the continuity of that covenant.

Symbols such as the temple are helpful. Those who view the Old Testament as a movement toward spiritualities more and more detached from "physical crutches" need to look more closely at the developments of the post-exilic period with its strong concern for the temple. To the extent that the symbolic value was understood, to that extent the symbol was preparatory for the coming of Christ in whom (1) the presence of God was demonstrated, (2) the honor of God was revealed, (3) the contact with God was established (John 14:6), and (4) the covenant was fulfilled.[6] At the same time, to the extent that the temple was a substitute for genuine active life with God, or became an object of false security as it had earlier in Jeremiah's day, to that extent the anti-temple mood by the Qumran community and by Stephen was justified (Acts 7:46ff).

God could be experienced apart from the temple, for as Haggai noted even before the rebuilding had begun, God was with his people (Hag 1:3). But God would be experienced also in conjunction with the rebuilding of the temple for, as Zechariah promised to Zerubbabel who was about to build, "Not by might, nor by power, but by my spirit, says the LORD of hosts" (Zech 4:6). The vision which immediately follows makes clear that the community experienced the power of God's Spirit flowing through the two anointed ones. We need to emphasize that experience with God was not restricted to the temple and that the Jews knew as much, namely that God was with those of humble and contrite heart. Nevertheless the temple was a way of preserving the importance as well as the awe and wonder of God revealing himself to human beings.

2. Israel's Experience of God In the Event

The prophet Ezekiel is distinguished from other prophets by the refrain "and they (you) shall know that I am the LORD." With variations this phrase occurs seventy-eight times in Ezekiel. Walther Zimmerli has provided several studies of this formulaic phrase.[7] The expression is applied to Israel in about forty instances; in about twenty the statement has other nations in view. In tracing the history of this expression, Zimmerli observes that the formula is now a combination of two phrases: "You shall know" and "I am the LORD." The phrase "you shall know" appears in different settings, but in particular incidents such as the sequel to Abraham's question, "How shall I know?"

the formula is associated with a sign, something observable or experiential (Gen 15:8). The experience of the firefall on the sacrifice on Mount Carmel is introduced in Elijah's prayer by "Let it be known this day that you are God in Israel" (1 Kgs 18:36)—a setting which shows that the expression "you shall know" is in the context of demonstration or proof, usually by an event or sign.

That the knowledge of God is brought about through events is abundantly evident from Ezekiel's discussion. For the moment we will focus on Israel's experience of God through event, following which we shall give attention to the nations' experience of God through event.

While God's object that Israel should know him surfaces repeatedly, Ezekiel 20 is most relevant as an anchor text because it makes connection with Exodus 6, our pivotal text. The elders of Israel came to Ezekiel in the exile to question him. God answered through the prophet in a lengthy tirade which, by reviewing Israel's history from the time of the exodus, scored the point that Israel had repeatedly rebelled against Yahweh. In spite of God's initial wrath he had acted in their favor for the sake of his name. The exposition begins with, "On the day when I chose Israel . . . *making myself known* to them in the land of Egypt, I swore to them, saying, I am the LORD your God" (Ezek 20:5). Here the allusion to the book of Exodus is apparent. Both the identification of Yahweh and the statement about the knowledge of God are written large in the pivotal text, Exod 5:22 – 6:8. This opening statement with its two parts prepares for the expression "that they (you) might know that I am the LORD," found six times in this speech (Ezek 20:12, 20, 26, 38, 42, 44).

For our purposes Ezekiel's survey of the history of Israel can be summarized in two propositions. Israel was to know God through the events of judgment. Israel was to know God also through the intervention in salvation.

God cites two instances of rebellion—their failure to eliminate idols in Egypt and the profaning of the Sabbath. Furthermore God's command was clear, this time to the descendants of those who left Egypt; yet "the children rebelled against me" (Ezek 20:21). At that point Yahweh swore that Israel would be scattered among the nations and dispersed among the lands. Yahweh brought difficulties upon them "that I might horrify them, so that they might know that I am the LORD" (Ezek 20:26). Elsewhere the prophet sets the traditional positive image of Israel as the vine (Isa 5:1; cf. Ps 80) on its head by describing the uselessness of the wood on the vine and consigning it to the fire: "Although they escape from the fire, the fire shall still consume them; and you shall know that I am the LORD, when I set my face against them" (Ezek 15:7). The fall of Jerusalem, also depicted symbolically through the death of Ezekiel's wife, is an event which aims at Israel's acknowledgment of God. "Thus Ezekiel shall be a sign to you; you shall do just as he has done. When this comes, then you shall know that I am the Lord God" (Ezek 24:24). God's acts of judgment were intended for Israel to know God.

Specific acts of salvation by Yahweh, no less than the acts of judgment, were also to lead Israel to a knowledge of God. Following the tally of judgmental acts against Israel, the speaker turns to developments yet future. The day is described in which the whole of Israel will serve Yahweh in the land. God in turn will accept them as a "soothing aroma" (Ezek 20:41). Bringing the people out of the land, God will be proved holy in the sight of the nations, but the effect on Israel shall be the positive acknowledgment of God. "You shall know that I am the LORD, when I bring you into the land of Israel, the country that I swore to give to your ancestors" (Ezek 20:42). Elsewhere, as in the prospect of repopulating the mountains of Israel and rebuilding the ruins, the stated objective as well as the means employed to reach that objective are given: "I will multiply human beings and animals upon you. They shall increase and be fruitful; and I will cause you to be inhabited as in your former times . . . Then you shall know that I am the LORD" (Ezek 36:11). The vision of the valley of dry bones, the Spirit's quickening and resultant mighty army, is a visual picture of Israel's new lease on life and the land. "I will bring you back to the land of Israel. And you shall know that I am the Lord" (Ezek 37:12–13; cf. 3–7). The new exodus from the lands of the dispersion, a distinct act of salvation, has as one of its goals Israel's acknowledgment of, and indeed her "interior experience" of, Yahweh.

Initially at the exodus God had declared his purpose: his people should know him. Ezekiel, centuries later, reaffirmed this component in God's design. In various ways, but specifically through events of judgment and salvation, his people shall come to know Yahweh.

3. The Experience of God In the Wider World

Humanly speaking the major actor in the Old Testament is the nation Israel. But from the divine standpoint the wider world of nations is also within purview. The opening chapters of Genesis display on wide canvas the movement of the world's peoples. Beginning with Genesis 12, the spotlight turns to one family, and later to one nation; but the context, the world of nations, remains. The major prophets are ample proof of the importance of other nations, for each includes a major segment of both judgment and salvation oracles directed at other nations (Isaiah 13–23; Jeremiah 46–51; Ezekiel 25–32). Ezekiel, deported to Babylon, is as sensitive as any prophet, not only to the reality of other peoples, but also to God's purpose with them, a purpose expressed in the formula, "Then you will know that I am the LORD" (Ezek 25:5, 7, 11, 17; 26:6; 28:22–24, 26; 29:9, 16, 21; 30:8, 19, 25, 26; 32:15).

Ezekiel 36 is pertinent to the issue of the knowledge of God in the wider world. In this chapter Israel is told how God's anger against her for her evil ways had resulted in God's dispersal of Israel among the nations. That action in turn had led to the nations' negative assessment of Yahweh. The nations profaned God's name, for they had concluded, "These are the people of the LORD, and yet they had to go out of his land" (Ezek 36:20). The inference was hardly veiled. Yahweh, the God of Israel, was not sufficiently strong to keep his people from attack and defeat by the enemy. While the nations rightly recognized that Israel was indeed Yahweh's people, they were in error in their interpretation of the exile, in that they cast aspersions on the God of Israel and profaned Yahweh's holy name.

Ezekiel explains that God is concerned for his holy name, for his reputation is at stake. The assessment of the nations must not go unchallenged. God will be vindicated, and that by means of an action. While his action will involve Israel, his people, God is acting now not for her sake but for his own name's sake (Ezek 36:22).

The divine act which is calculated to reverse the assessment of the nations is the return of Israel to her land. Yahweh will prove his holiness; the nations will know "that I am the LORD . . . when . . . I will take you (Israel) from the nations, and gather you from all the countries, and bring you into your own land" (Ezek 36:23–24). Yahweh will act on the point at which the disgrace was incurred—Israel's expulsion from the land. People and land, like the chemist's litmus paper used to identify acids or bases, are two entities by which God is revealed. For Israel, her removal from the land as well as her return to it both function to bring about an acknowledgment of God (Ezek 20:35–38). As for the nations, it is especially the return of Israel to her land which is to lead to the recognition of God (Ezek 36:23–24).

From the first, namely from the time of Israel's exodus from Egypt, God dealt with his people in such a way as to instruct nations about himself. When Pharaoh protested, "Who is Yahweh?" God declared that he would bring out his people, the sons of Israel, from the land of Egypt, "The Egyptians shall know that I am the LORD" (Exod 7:4–5). One of the purposes of the plagues was that Egypt acknowledge Yahweh (Exod 7:17; 8:22; 14:4, 18). As it was with Egypt, God's goal, now a millennium later with the nations, remains unchanged; and the method now as then involves his people.

The second half of Isaiah, like Ezekiel, underscores God's concern for the nations. There too Israel's role in providing a witness to the nations is underscored. Her mission is to the peoples of the world, not in the New Testament sense of going forth to them with the message about Yahweh, but in the sense of being a people of God whose life shall draw nations to inquire after Yahweh (cf. Isa 2:1–4). God's word to Israel at a time when all nations have gathered together is "'You are my witnesses,' says the LORD, 'and my servant whom I have chosen, so that you may know and believe me and understand that I am he . . . I, I am the LORD'" (Isa 43:10–11). It has been claimed that mission and witness in the Old Testament is centripetal: nations are drawn magnet-like to Israel; by contrast mission and witness in the New Testament is centrifugal: the church is commanded to move out to the nations with the gospel. The Old Testament key word in this conjunction is "Come." The New Testament word is "Go." But in both Old and New Testaments God's concern extends to the nations.[8] The Isaiah texts, and the Ezekiel texts no less, reiterate the phrase familiar from the exodus, "I am the LORD." At the exodus the significance of that name was exposed: Yahweh was a salvation name. And now, so the post-exilic prophets affirm, Israel, and the nations also, shall "know that I am Yahweh." As it was in the beginning, so it is still. People are invited to experience Yahweh.

4. Summary

The subject of knowing God has occupied us in each of the three broad eras of Israel's history: Pre-monarchy, monarchy, and post-monarchy. Admittedly, the subject raises issues.

How is God known? The answer includes some attention to the relationship of word and event. Thus, at the remarkable crossing of the Sea of Reeds, the explanation was given that it was Yahweh who, as warrior, had made possible Israel's deliverance from the Egyptians. During the monarchy, Elijah called down fire on the alter. Fire fell, and, given Elijah's prior statements, the people understood that it was Yahweh who had acted. In yet another and later era, the return of the exiles was

the means by which both Israel and the nations were to acknowledge that it was Yahweh who had acted. Revelation of deity is through word, but not word alone. It is through event, but
not event only. Revelation comes, though not always, through
word wedded to event.

Where may one experience God? Israel's answer is that
God may be recognized through divine actions in history. These
activities may occur within the compass of family life, as is made
clear in the story of the patriarchs. Individuals too—here David
and Job are examples—may experience God. Nations such as
Egypt at the exodus, or Edom at the exile, are to know God also.
Experience of God comes on the stage of history.

Where may one experience God? Ritual performances are
important throughout Israel's history. Officiating personnel,
such as priests, serve in a teaching function. Sacrifices and festivals are vehicles of communication between a people and God.
And objects and structures too are part of the "knowing" process. The ark in the wilderness, the Solomonic temple and the
restored temple in the sixth century BC, each speak of the presence of God. Through communal worship persons enter into
experience with Yahweh.

And how does one communicate experiences with deity?
The Psalms demonstrate ways in which one may meaningfully
express oneself concerning deity. The hymn gives expression to
adoration of Yahweh, who has intervened and brought deliverance. The thanksgiving song appropriately recounts the experience. But there are difficult experiences: Yahweh has not always
intervened, nor always answered prayer. When the worshiper
experiences God as distant, he or she resorts to lament. But always, as Job and Israel learned, one does not understand or
fully know. "I am Yahweh" is his self-identification. People are to
know God, and they do, through salvation and through judgment too, but even as they know God and acknowledge him as
sovereign Lord, they acknowledge that God is incomparable
and that they can penetrate but slightly into the mystery of the
one who asserts: "I am Yahweh."

5. Theological Reflections

A discussion of the experience of God that includes references
to prayer, temple, judgment, salvation, and the world's peoples
triggers a variety of issues for reflection. To note some possibilities: piety and spiritual formation for leaders, the function of
symbol, the role of sacred space, God's discipline through judgment, or the relationship of Israel to the larger entity, the
world's peoples. It is to the last item, the problem of the Old
Testament concern for humankind universally, that the following remarks are directed.

The problem is this: to what extent does the concern for
peoples everywhere surface in the Old Testament when its subject on the human plane is Israel? Or, put another way, what relationship is there between the particular (Israel) and the
universal (all peoples)? Proceeding from a New Testament base
the situation is clearer. The church (a particular) has for its mission the spread of the knowledge of God to the nations (universal). Is Israel's mission similar to, or even identical with, the
church's mission?

Especially when one stresses the covenant as the significant
cohesive of Old Testament materials, is there likely to be an exclusivist note. The argument easily runs: God chose a nation for
himself. Upon this people he bestowed marked privileges. He
summoned them to a preferred relationship with himself. Thus
a preoccupation with Israel as the particular can put any concern for the non-Israelite people on the periphery. And yet, the
Old Testament will not permit one to think in parochial or exclusivist terms.

The argument for a universalist concern in the Old Testament can begin with Ezekiel's refrain: "They (the nations) shall
know Yahweh." Following the collapse of a nation and at a time
when significant numbers of Hebrews were scattered among the
nations, this prophet articulated a perspective announced long
ago but stifled, and often obscured: nations should come to
know Yahweh. Of course, prophets other than Ezekiel had also
envisioned God's universal rule. Isaiah had explained that

God's purpose extended beyond Israel. "The LORD will make himself known to the Egyptians; and the Egyptians will know the LORD on that day" (19:21). Isaiah had cried out that the call for a turning to Yahweh was not restricted to Israel :"Turn to me and be saved, all the ends of the earth! For I am God, and there is no other" (45:22). Indeed one could ask whether a monotheistic faith does not necessitate a universalist concern. So Israel had in fact understood. "It is too light a thing that you should be my servant to raise up the tribes of Jacob and to restore the survivors of Israel; I will give you as a light to the nations, that my salvation may reach to the end of the earth" (Isa 49:6).

To these vision statements of a universal concern must be added the prayer from the Psalms: "May God be gracious to us and bless us . . . that your way may be known upon earth, your saving power among all nations" (Ps 67:1–2; cf. Ps 2; 96:10). According to one count there are 175 references to universalism in the Psalms. There can be little doubt that Israel understood Yahweh's concern and offer of salvation to extend to all peoples.

Aside from these vision statements there is historical evidence to show that Yahweh's people are not to be defined narrowly as an ethnic group, even though an ethnic group is its nucleus. After all, a mixed multitude joined the Hebrews at the exodus (Exod 12:38). Even if their commitment to Yahweh was not uniformly strong, one must take account of the Kennizites, Caleb and Othniel (Num 32:12; Judg 1:13), and a Moabitess such as Ruth, not to mention "believers" beyond Israel such as Melchizedek, Jethro, Job, Balaam—all of whom support the argument that Yahweh's concern extends beyond Israel to other peoples. Indeed, as Moses explains, God has strategically placed Israel geographically among the nations (Deut 32:8). Amos reminds his Israelite listeners that they have no monopoly on Yahweh, for as God led Israel from Egypt, so God has led the Philistines out of Captor and the Syrians from Kir (Amos 9:7). Two prophetic books, Obadiah and Nahum, deal exclusively with Gentile nations, and Jonah represents a witness to Yahweh brought to Assyrians, Israel 's archenemy. History confirms that God's concern for a witness to himself reaches beyond the borders of Israel.

Moreover a geographical review of Israel's story shows how she or certain of her number were put into contact with other peoples at important moments of history. Abraham was called from the east out of Ur of the Chaldees and in the course of his journeys came to the Egyptian Pharaoh's court in the west. Later Joseph in Egypt brought from the Pharaoh the acknowledgment that God was with him (Gen 41:39). Moses witnessed to the Egyptian authorities of the power and purposes of Yahweh, as did Daniel and Esther in Babylonian and Persian courts almost a millennium later. Since the network of political relationships during the Davidic and Solomonic empire were extensive, a witness to Yahweh, as at the visit of the queen of Sheba, was no doubt not uncommon (1 Kgs 10:1ff). With Abraham and Joseph in Egypt, Elimelech and Naomi in Moab and the deportees later in Babylon, one might even raise the question of population displacement as a strategy for acquainting non-Israelites with Yahweh. If one traces the Old Testament story by means of an atlas, one is impressed with the geographical range of Israel's contacts. The center of the circle is the land of Palestine but its circumference embraces the then known world.

Even the literary structure of the canonical Scripture impresses on one the universalist concern of Yahweh. The story of the Hebrews may be said to begin with Abraham in Genesis 12, but that story is given a universalist context in Genesis 1–11, which, apart from the creation material, lists two genealogical tables (chapters 5, 10), as if to indicate that though the story of the Old Testament will be concerned with one people, it is the entire world that is encompassed in God's design. And if further substantiation for the inclusive nature of God's compassion is needed, then it is supplied in the call to Abraham in which God specifies, "In you all the families of the earth shall be blessed" (12:3).

With that statement our query about the universal and the particular receives an answer. God's election of one person,

Abraham, is the means whereby God's blessing shall be extended to all nations. Walther Eichrodt has commented on the phrase, "They shall know that I am Yahweh," noting that it

> implies a great deal more than a mere theoretical recognition of the truth of the prophet's message. Rather, it expresses how the light of the new fellowship with God bestowed upon Israel also shines out over the Gentile world. The reason why this is not worked out fully is connected with the central importance of the chosen people whom God has destined to be the carriers of his saving purposes and the witnesses of his redemptive power.[9]

There will always remain the "scandal of the particular." Why should Abraham be singled out to be the instrument of blessing for the world? Why should one man, Jesus Christ, a Jew by birth, be the God-man to be the world's redeemer? From a philosophical standpoint one might argue that talk about universals is possible only if one can speak about particulars, but theologically one is left with a mystery of election. Yet election is not totally mysterious, for the *purpose* of election is sufficiently disclosed. Through Abraham God's blessing shall come on *all people*. And Israel is to be a light to the *nations*. And Jesus is the Savior of the *world*.

We may debate God's instruments and agencies of mission, comparing the Old Testament with the New, and we may discuss the enigmas in the universalist-particularist problem, but the missionary purpose expressed in Ezekiel's refrain, "They (the nations) shall know Yahweh," itself remains unambiguous.

14

Land

The three components in God's design examined thus far have been affirmed in the exilic/post-exilic period. The fourth component, land, is no exception. Israel had been tested at the point of land during the monarchy. She had failed the test and lost the land. But the last word had not yet been said; Israel was to return to the land. During the exile Israel heard again what it heard already at the exodus, that God's design, including his intention to give them the land, was still in force. Interest in the land component did not wane in the exilic time, but instead came to be of foremost importance for Israel.

Before long Israel did indeed return to her land. Theological considerations emerge both from the historic return to the land and also from the increasing use of land as symbol.

1. Historically: Land Recovered

When driven from their homeland in the early decades of the sixth century BC, the dispersed had been counseled by Jeremiah to settle down in the foreign land (Jer 29:4–7). Such counsel contradicted the advice of other prophets. Hananiah, for example, prophesied that Israel would return after two years (Jer 28:1–4). Jeremiah stated that seventy years would elapse for Babylon before the return would be possible (Jer 25:12; 29:14). Hananiah was a false prophet, and, as Jeremiah predicted, died within a year. Yet whether by false prophets or by true prophets, the hope for a return had been kept alive. Exiles returned to the land of Palestine following the decree of Cyrus in 538 BC in which he permitted enslaved peoples, including Israel, to return to their homelands (Ezra 1:2–3).

The Announcement of Return to the Land

One can easily count more than a dozen announcements in Jeremiah and Ezekiel that speak of Israel's anticipated return to the land. In Jeremiah some hope announcements are juxtaposed with earlier announcements that Israel will be hurled out of the land (Jer 16:13, 15; cf. 12:14–15; 24:1–10). Two representative announcements of salvation oracles follow.[1]

> For there is a reward for your work, says the LORD;
> they shall come back from the land of the enemy (Jer 31:16).

> Therefore say: Thus says the Lord God: I will gather you from the peoples, and assemble you out of the countries where you have been scattered, and I will give you the land of Israel (Ezek 11:17).

In the Ezekiel passage especially, the promise of return to the land is cast, with some variation, in a three-member statement, the most usual form of which is:

(1) I will bring you from the people
(2) I will gather you from the lands
(3) I will bring you into the land of Israel
    (cf. Ezek 20:34, 41–42; 34:13; 36:24; 37:21; 39:27–28).

One sees a rhythmic, somewhat stereotyped manner in the announcement for a return. Indeed in Jeremiah and Ezekiel the announcement for return to the land might well be examined from formulaic expressions.

One formula that recurs often in Jeremiah is, "I will restore the fortunes," which in Hebrew is a combination of cognates, šûb šᵊbût. Of the more than twenty occurrences of this phrase in the Old Testament, half are in Jeremiah. The "Book of Consolation" (Jeremiah 30–31) opens with the phrase attached here, as in most other instances, to the promise of return to the land.

> For the days are surely coming, says the LORD, when I will restore
> the fortunes of my people, Israel and Judah, says the LORD, and I
> will bring them back to the land that I gave to their ancestors and
> they shall take possession of it (Jer 30:3).

Earlier translations such as the AV rendered the expression *šûb*
šᵉbût as "restore the captivity." For linguistic and usage reasons
such a translation is unacceptable. Judging from certain occurrences of the formula in Aramaic, it is likely that the formula
had not to do with captivity but with economics.[2] The expression was used to indicate recovery of loss sustained through economic depression or enemy incursion and then subsequent
restoration to an earlier favorable position (cf. Jer 30:18;
33:11). The expression is associated with land, not only in Jeremiah (33:10–11; 32:42ff) but elsewhere (Deut 30:3; Amos
9:14–15). Moreover, the expression is not limited to Israel but
appears also in conjunction with Egypt. "And I will restore the
fortunes of Egypt" (Ezek 29:14). Elsewhere, while not linked to
land, the phrase is applied to nations such as Elam (Jer 49:39),
Moab (Jer 48:47), Sodom (Ezek 16:53), and Ammon (Jer 49:6).
"To bring about restoration" (*šûb šᵉbût*) is indicative of divine favor of which return to the land is a specific illustration.

A second formulaic phrase found in the prophetic literature is that of "planting" Israel in the land. The root "plant"
(*nāṭaʿ*) is found twenty times in Jeremiah and Ezekiel. Most of
these uses have a metaphorical meaning and several have Is-
rael/Judah and the land in view as in "I will plant them in this
land" (Jer 32:41; cf. 24:6; 42:10; 45:4; Ezek 36:36). One scholar
who has studied the word pair "build and plant" believes that by
Jeremiah's time the combination was firmly established in the
language. The subject of these verbs in the Bible is always Yahweh, and the object, where it is given, is a people, part of a
group, or even several groups. While one of the terms, "plant,'
may have a culture setting since it is used in conjunction with Israel's history of salvation (Ps 80:9), originally "build and plant"
were used as an expression of well-wishing for success at the
time of the birth of a child. The wish was for the child to marry,
build a house, and plant a vineyard.[3]

In the mouth of the prophets these words are theologically colored, however. The terms "build and plant" are an attempt to present salvation history in picturesque language and to capture the familiar tones of Yahweh's saving acts. One should add that more specifically the expression deals with land. Jeremiah announces,

> I will set my eyes upon them for good, and I will bring them back to this land. I will build them up, and not tear them down; I will plant them, and not pluck them up (Jer 24:6).

The word "plant," in contrast to "uproot," suggests firmness and establishment and more indirectly "to make secure." The force of such an expression as "I will plant them in the land" is to call attention to the initiating action by God, the solicitude for success, and the prospect of security and firmness. The promise "to plant and build Israel in the land" evoked emotional feelings of warmth, of hope, of security.

The biblical record preserves the announcements for a return; it also reports the return itself. Cyrus edict in 538 BC paved the way for the exiles to come back to the land of Palestine. Ezra and Nehemiah report the vicissitudes of the group in getting established in the land. Thanks to determination, good leadership, both by religious leaders such as Haggai and Zechariah and later by civil leaders such as Nehemiah, and the good favor of God upon the returnees, the temple was rebuilt and the walls of Jerusalem were restored. The community, though small, could live eventually in safety. Of their economic fortunes we know little, for the period following the return is without much surviving literature. Some scholars claim that the elaborate promises were never realized. The announcements suggest developments on a larger scale than was represented by the diminutive colony in Jerusalem. Still, the group flourished in some measure despite initial opposition from surrounding neighbors.

Motivations for the Return to the Land

Of greater interest than the historical developments for our purpose is the question—why was it important for the remnant of the people to return to the land at all? If God's interest is for Israel to give witness of him to the nations, then might not the dispersion be a means to that goal? Besides, there was a remainder of the population left in the land of Israel. Yet the announcement by the prophets promised a return, a return not only politically but also theologically motivated.

The theological reasons for the return are complex, but two observations are of significance. It was not, as popularly supposed, that God's promise to Abraham necessitated a return of Israel to the land. Some understood the Abrahamic covenant to mean that God was committed to return Israel to the land once he had removed her. While this interpretation of covenant may have logic on its side, it does not take into account the nature of covenant nor of the fact that Israel on her part broke the covenant. If one examines the announcements of the return in the books of Jeremiah and Ezekiel and asks for the motivations of the return, one discovers that not once is the earlier covenant with Abraham cited as a reason for the announcement. Now it is true that the land is identified as the land God gave to Abraham and his descendants. This is a theological way of speaking about the land, but one will not find an argument for the return that bases itself on the Abrahamic covenant with its promise of land. This is not to say that covenant as such is unimportant in promises of the return (cf. Neh 1:8–9) but it is to deny a simplistic view of the Abrahamic covenantal stipulation about land.

One of the reasons for return is threaded back in the discussion to the nature of Yahweh. Yahweh is compassionate. Yahweh's concern for his people is reason for returning them to the land. In Jeremiah's letter to the exiles, the exiles are told that God's thoughts towards them are thoughts of well-being (*šālôm*) (29:10–11). The Book of Consolation (chapters 30–31), punctuated with promises of the return, is also punctuated with affirmations of God's compassion: "I have loved you with an everlasting love; therefore I have continued my faithfulness to you" (31:3). The father-son metaphor is used in discussing the return: "I will surely have mercy on him" (31:20; cf. 31:9). Apparently Jeremiah draws on the Isaianic tradition, for the statement "I will grant you mercy . . . and restore you to your native soil" (42:12), strongly echoes a text from Isaiah: "The LORD will have compassion on Jacob . . . and will set them in their own land" (Isa 14:1). If it is suggested that Yahweh's compassion is directly related to covenant, then the discovery that God promises other nations a return to their homeland (12:15) rules out the notion that God's compassion is to be explained only out of his covenant relationship with Israel.

In our earlier discussion, Ezek 36:16–36 was noted for its relevance to the subject of experiencing God. The text is essentially an answer to the question, "On what basis can Yahweh act for Israel now that the judgment for the sin of that nation has taken place?" The question has a negative answer: it is not for Israel's sake (vv. 23–32). But the question also has an immediately positive answer: I will act "for the sake of my holy name" (v. 22). The focus on Yahweh's name is also evident from the structure of the passage. The historical section (vv. 16–21) terminates with a consideration of Yahweh's name. The predictive section (vv. 22–36) opens with the concern for Yahweh's name as the mainspring of action, the thought with which the unit ends (v. 32).

Profaning of Yahweh's name has occurred among the nations and has been occasioned by Israel's removal from the land (v. 20). By concluding that Israel's defeat in war means the inability of Yahweh to deliver a people, nations have slandered and besmirched the divine name. The concept of profaning the divine name occurs in the Holiness Code in conjunction with commands about not devoting children to Moloch (Leviticus 18–21). There one finds the instruction: "You shall not profane my holy name" (Lev 22:32). Similarly Ezekiel talks of cult in connection with profaning Yahweh's name (Ezek 20:39). He, however, refers, as do no other prophets, to the profaning of Yahweh's name in the political arena. It is not through

misconduct as much as it is through an adverse political condition that God's name has been profaned.

Sanctifying the name, the opposite of profaning it, is a concern for which Yahweh himself now takes responsibility (Ezek
20:31; 36:23). In Ezekiel, every statement about sanctifying
Yahweh's name occurs in conjunction with nations, for it is in
their sight that Yahweh will be sanctified. The concrete way in
which the injury done to Yahweh's name will be undone is
through the return of Israel to her land. Not the covenant, but
the personal reputation of Yahweh, is the motivation for salvation action in this instance. Ezekiel removes the ground for
hope from covenant or merit or even sympathy for a languish-
ing people. "All human arrogance and all human security are
thus guarded against; no appeal to the covenant at Sinai is possible any longer."[4] Ezekiel especially anchors Yahweh's future
action in Yahweh alone. In doing so, he reaches beyond utilitar-
ian or covenanted reasons to that which is now foundational, to
God, Yahweh.

More could be said about the way in which the theology of
Yahwism functions as the reason why Israel is to return to the
land. Enough has been said however to underscore the fact that
the prophets were concerned not merely to make dogmatic
statements about Israel returning to the land, but to offer reasons why this announcement was credible. One reason was Yahweh's compassion. Another was his reputation among the
nations. Other reasons were linked with the land, and with what
it symbolized. To the symbolism we now turn.

2. Theologically: Land as Symbol

Over the centuries of Israel's history the land of Palestine as
homeland had become more than the turf which Israel called its
own. Certainly by the post-exilic period, speech about the land
of Israel evoked a variety of emotions, for land symbolized
much more than living space. Specifically land was a cipher for
a gift, a promise, a blessing, a lifestyle, and even revelation.

The land was gift; so it had been understood from the first. The tradition is rich with assertions about Yahweh's ownership and richer with affirmations of land as gift, especially from the book of Deuteronomy (1:8, 35; 6:10, 18, 23; 7:13; 8:1, 10; 11:9, 21; 26:3; 28:11; 30:20; 34:4). All told, the expression "to give" with reference to land is found about 150 times in the Bible. Gift language is still current in the post-exilic period. The land is a land which Yahweh gave to "the fathers" (Ezek 20:28, 42; 25:5, 15; 28:25; 36:28; 37:25; 47:14). From other contexts one concludes that "fathers" refers to ancestors generally (Jer 3:24–25; 16:11; Ezek 20:36). Land, so the people of exile affirm, was an ancestral gift.

What is the function of the phrase, "which Yahweh gave to your fathers"? Its position is customarily in apposition to land. This place for the phrase points to its function of identifying the land or of recalling Yahweh's former favor (Ezek 20:28; 36:28; 37:25; 47:14). The phrase "which I have given them" seems superfluous when it follows such expressions as "their land" (Jer 16:15; Ezek 20:15) or even "land of Israel" (Ezek 20:42). The formulaic usage of the phrase becomes particularly evident here where it is not really needed but where force of habit accounts for the addition. One wonders whether the positive statement about land as gift to the ancestors is a deliberate counterpart to Ezekiel's negative statement, "countries among which you were scattered" (Ezek 11:17; 20:34, 41) or Jeremiah's "the lands where I have driven them" (Jer 23:3, 8; 32:37).

As noted earlier, the phrase, though frequently in conjunction with the announcement of return to the land, nowhere functions as the reason for that return. In Solomon's prayer, recorded in both Kings and Chronicles, the theoretical possibility is noted that Israel may be taken into captivity. Here, where one would expect the gift nature of the land urged as reason for return, one finds only a request that God would hear when they "pray to you toward their land, which you gave to their ancestors" (1 Kgs 8:48; 2 Chr 6:38). A careful check of the numerous announcements of return to the land in Jeremiah and Ezekiel shows that despite the many motivational clauses introduced by "because" (ya'an) or "therefore" (lākēn), nowhere is the gift of land a reason for the return.[5] But the gift nature of the land has become part of customary vocabulary so that the amplifying clauses about gift even appear following a judgmental word of destruction: "until they are utterly destroyed from the land that I gave to them and their ancestors" (Jer 24:10; cf. 2 Chr 7:20). Land perhaps more than any other factor is synonymous with gift.

The promise aspect of land, like the gift aspect, is integral to land symbolism. In the exilic period the earlier covenant promises are quoted and—important for land theology—are identified by the exilic writers as fulfilled. Nehemiah mentioned God's promise of land to Abraham and declares, "You have fulfilled your promise, for you are righteous" (Neh 9:8; cf. 9:23). One can agree with W. M. Clark, "The mention of the land promise after its fulfillment serves not to guarantee the continued possession but to testify to what Yahweh has done in the past."[6]

The patriarchal promise of land and its fulfillment was a fact of history. Yet in the exile the prophets announce a return to the land. The land was once more the subject of a promise. As earlier, so now, the promise of land was heard. But the two promises have at least one significant difference. In the promise of land to Abraham, land was constitutive of the covenant. In the exilic announcement, return to the land was preliminary to covenant (Ezek 34:25ff; 36:24ff). But in either case the promise involved land. To speak of land was to evoke association of promise.

In addition to symbolizing gift and promise, the land for Israel was the place of blessing. Abundance and rest, both dimensions of blessing, were motifs long associated with the promised land. Nehemiah surveys God's gracious acts and recalls how Israel came into the land with vineyards, olive groves, and fruit trees in abundance: "so they ate, and were filled and became fat, and delighted themselves in your great goodness" (Neh 9:25). For it was a land which God had given to the fathers "to enjoy its fruit and its good gifts" (Neh 9:36). As God had once intended for Israel to enjoy the blessing of abundance, so he still intended it for Israel, as Jeremiah reported: "I thought how I would . . . give you a pleasant land, the most beautiful heritage of all the nations" (Jer 3:19). The land was a choice land, God's inheritance with which he had now endowed Israel (Jer 12:14).

Returning people could anticipate fruitfulness and abundance. Yahweh as shepherd would feed his people in good grazing ground. "They shall feed on rich pasture on the mountains of Israel" (Ezek 34:14). Moreover he would make the places around his hill a blessing and send showers of blessing, and the "trees of the field shall yield their fruit, and the earth shall yield its increase" (Ezek 34:27; cf. 36:8). Yahweh would call forth the grain. Israel would not have famine, for the fruit of the tree and the produce of the field would be multiplied (Ezek 36:30). Prior to Ezekiel's announcement, Jeremiah had struck the same chord. God would rejoice over his people to do them good (Jer 32:41) and Israel would be radiant over the bounty of Yahweh—"over the grain, the wine, and the oil, and over the young of the flock and the herd" (Jer 31:12). God would fill the soul of the priests with abundance and "my people shall be satisfied with my bounty" (Jer 31:14). Once back in the land, Israel could expect prosperity. Indeed the land, now as earlier, was a cipher for abundance.

The land was to be a cipher also for rest.[7] Since the nations round about desired control of Palestine, there was continual unrest. The material wealth of the land could be enjoyed fully, however, only when the "international" situation was stabilized. The earlier ideal had been that upon entry into the land Israel would cease from her wandering and enjoy rest (Deut 3:20; 12:10). Now in the exile Ezekiel had the most to say on the subject of rest. Dangers to peaceful living, whether from beasts within the land or enemy nations without the land, would be removed (34:28), for God would make a covenant of peace (37:26). Israel will also live securely (39:36; cf. 28:6; 34:28). The mountains will not be relieved of their inhabitants (36:12), but God will feed the flock, and "make them lie down" (34:15). The land of Israel is synonymous with a good life, for here one may enjoy the abundance of the land without fear or worry.

The land of Israel became a symbol in still another way. A specific kind of moral and religious life was appropriate to the land. Here also one may observe something familiar and something new. The familiar note is that a certain purity is necessary for life in the land. Jeremiah in his temple sermon had pleaded with the people to amend their ways, to cease from oppressing the alien and orphan, to refrain from walking after other gods. It was promised that upon compliance with these moral and religious demands, Yahweh would let the people continue in the land (Jer 7:1–7). Similarly, Ezekiel in offering a rebuttal to those still back in Israel who now claimed a possession of the land, stated the moral requirements important for continuing existence in that land: if you "lift up your eyes to your idols, and shed blood; shall you then possess the land? You depend on your swords, you commit abominations, and each of you defiles his neighbor's wife; shall you then possess the land?" (33:25–26). The answer was "no," because certain behavior was inappropriate to life in the land.

Upon returning, Ezra recognized that the land was unclean by reason of the abominations and impurities with which the people of the land defiled it (Ezra 9:11). It was important therefore to stress that upon entry into the land people in Israel would "remove from it all its detestable things and all its abominations" (Ezek 11:18). Part of the hope included the prospect that, once upon the land, purification of heart would occur so that Israel would no longer defile itself with detestable things (Ezek 37:23). That hope was echoed by Zechariah, through whom the LORD said he would save his people from the land of the East and from the land of the West, bring them back to live in Jerusalem, and "they shall be my people and I will be their God, in *faithfulness and in righteousness*" (Zech 8:7–8). Nor was it a strange word, for the association between upright living and the land was well established in the tradition.

Ezra's reform is built specifically on his perception that life in the land is possible when premised upon genuine morality.

For Ezra the land is unclean, that is, unacceptable for covenantal life (Ezra 9:11). The purification requires action which will define the moral boundaries. Israelites are not to intermarry (Ezra 9:12). The result will be ". . . so that you may be strong and eat the good of the land and leave it for an inheritance to your children forever" (Ezra 9:12). The reformers regarded marriage, Sabbath-keeping, and land distribution as decisive, since it was because of failure in these areas that land had been lost in the first place (Neh 5:3–5a).[8]

The new note sounded by Ezekiel was that God himself would spiritually qualify the people to live in the land by giving them a new heart. Having affirmed that God would give them the land of Israel (Ezek 11:17), Yahweh continued, "I will give them one heart, and put a new spirit within them; I will remove the heart of stone from their flesh and give them a heart of flesh, so that they may follow my statutes and keep my ordinances and obey them" (Ezek 11:19–20; cf. 36:26–27). Jeremiah also spoke about people being spiritually qualified, but for the most part construed that qualification as coming about through a repentance by the people *prior* to coming into the land. In this respect he stood in the tradition of Amos, Micah, and Isaiah. But Ezekiel broke with the line of prophetic tradition by promising a return of the people to the land *following* which God would specifically qualify them by giving to them a new heart. "Israel will return to its God not *before* the redemption but *after* it, after it has returned to its own land."[9] In either case, however—and this point is crucial—there was insistence that conduct in the land be God-approved. Land had come to signify a particular lifestyle appropriate to it.

There remains at least one other significant dimension in the multifaceted symbolism of land: divine revelation. The foregoing aspects of land theology are affirmations of earlier positions and tradition, though with some variations to be sure. Ezekiel, however, introduced a new note when he maintained that God's action of returning Israel to the land would serve as a demonstration before the nations of Yahweh's identity. The land would be a tool for Yahweh 's self-revelation. In the

foregoing pages we have already had opportunity to observe
how the nations belittled Yahweh's name since his people had to
go out of the land. Yahweh redresses this poor judgment by asserting that when Israel returns to her land, that event shall
bring to the nations an acknowledgment of Yahweh (Ezek
36:18ff). The land becomes a medium whereby Yahweh can
make something clear about himself in a concrete way. Land,
whether in conjunction or disjunction with Israel, has a revelatory function. Of course it is not the turf which by itself bears
witness to Yahweh, but land functions as a grid in reference to
which Yahweh's moves with his people become both discernible
and significant. Land is a tool, a visual aid in the educative process of the nations. It is more, however, for that which is to be
known about Yahweh is to be made clear through the destiny of
the people with respect to land. Remove land from the salvation
message of these prophets and they are left one-armed.

> In the texts that depict the life in the land Yahweh is shown as a
> God of nature whose blessing means fruitfulness and increase.
> But of the texts that tell of the reasons for return, Yahweh is
> shown as a God of history, who by means of something as tangible
> as land can be identified. The land holds both the God of history
> and the God of nature together as one.[10]

It was in various ways that God throughout history was revealed.
Educative tools in this process include the holy war, the tabernacle, theophany, and the temple; but to this list must be added
"land" also.

Land is indeed significant as living space. But as the foregoing discussion has shown, "land" took on symbolic nuances
such as gift, promise, blessing, and revelation.

3. Theological Reflections

Given that richness in symbolism one may ask how the theme of
land functions in the New Testament. It is frequently noted that
there is little mention of "land" in the New Testament. Jesus
does state in the beatitudes, "Blessed are the meek, for they will

inherit the earth" (Matt 5:5), and one might make a connection
between "land" and the promise of the new heavens and the
new earth. In a more abstract way, as W. Brueggemann has
noted, there is in the Gospels a constant inversion. Those
grasping land lose it and those who receive the gift have it (Luke
9:24; 13:30; 14:11).[11] The land of Palestine, however, is not a
major theme in the Gospels or in the epistles. But may it not be
on the level of its symbolism that the bridge between the Old
Testament and the New Testament on this theme must be built?
In the New Testament Jesus has much to say about the kingdom
of God. It is not to be defined in earthly terms, and yet it, like
land, has been promised; it is a gift. Like the land, it is to be
characterized by a specific lifestyle by its citizenry.

Central to the kingdom of God is God's revelation in Jesus
Christ. Is it not apparent, to take another perspective, that the
theological significance of land finds its counterpart precisely
in the person of Christ himself? In this chapter we have identified the theology of the land as comprising a set of symbols including gift, promise, blessing, lifestyle, and revelation. Initially
the land is turf, a physical reality. Beyond that physical entity
land functions in history as promise, not once to Abraham but a
second time in the exile. Similarly Christ is the figure of promise, as repeated statements and the anticipating tenor of the
New Testament signify. Speaking of Heb 11:13–16, W. Brueggemann said, "It is sobering for New Testament exegesis to recognize that the single central symbol for the promise of the
gospel is land."[12] Land is a gift. So clearly also is the Savior, Jesus Christ (John 3:16). Land signifies the good life with its
abundance and rest. Did not our Lord declare, "I came that
they may have life, and have it abundantly" (John 10:10). The
writer to Hebrews likens the rest made possible in the land to
the rest to be enjoyed by the Christian (Hebrews 3–4). Occupation of the land called for a definite lifestyle; so does following
Jesus call for a singular lifestyle. Land was something of a reve-
lational medium. Jesus was the last and greatest word in God's
revelation to humankind. There may even be some echo in the

language usage between being "in the land" and being "in Christ." Thus in different ways land anticipates Jesus Christ.

Since land is a place, a geographical entity, the question has sometimes been posed: will the land of Israel figure uniquely in future Jewish history as it has in the past? Evangelical scholars differ as to the answer. The possibility must not only be left open but perhaps underscored, and that for several reasons: if God will deal with the nation Israel in the future in a singular way, then the importance of land is at once clear (Rom 9–11). Moreover, there remains a surplus of promises, even granting that Jeremiah's and Ezekiel's announcements were fulfilled in the return from the exile under Joshua and Zerubbabel. Specific promises such as the restoration of Judah and Joseph/Ephraim are foretold in Zech 10:6–7. In context this must be a future gathering, for the return under Zerubbabel is for Zechariah an event in the past.

The subject of land is a major subject in the Old Testament, not least of all because of the themes that come to be affiliated with it. Those themes, along with the overarching divine plan, are brought into sharpest focus in the New Testament.

Part 5

Framing God's Design

Framing God's Design: Creation

Much of the foregoing material has been a presentation of a salvation history (*Heilgeschichte*). The Old Testament is heavily tilted toward history, specifically that of Israel. Yet it is not a political history as we generally think of it, but history with a twist, a redemptive history in which God is demonstrably active. Despite God's periodic judgments, the story of Israel shows that God's intent is for a people to live in a deliverance mode, having physical and spiritual sufficiency. Even more, the story of Israel, from the exodus through the exile to restoration, is a story which, so to speak, leans forward toward something of importance still to come: the Christ event as reported in the New Testament. This kind of history is not only marked by events of salvation but culminates in salvation.

In following that story, we have paid minimum attention to the context in which it is set. Two dimensions of that context are crucial. The first, creation, is treated in this chapter. The second, the beyond-Israel theme, is examined in the following chapter. Both concerns, creation and the beyond-Israel motif, are highlighted in Genesis 1–11, a literary section that precedes Israel's story.

1. Starting with Creation

The preceding chapters took their cue from a Yahweh speech given to Moses prior to the exodus of Israel from Egypt, an event historically as well as theologically foundational to all that follows. But the question sometimes posed is a legitimate one: what if the starting point for an Old Testament theology were creation rather than the exodus? Why not start, as the Bible does, with creation? One answer is that the bulk of the Old Testament is built around Israel's story, so that a strong case can be made for occupying oneself with it. Another answer is that the early chapters of Genesis, even the entire book, is a prologue to the story of God's people, Israel. It has been claimed that Israel first experienced God's deliverance; only then did God's role as Creator become clear.[1]

It is, of course, possible to start with creation.[2] This chapter takes the view that the opening chapters of Genesis are in the nature of a prologue or narrative frame. The function of a frame is to set a story, or series of stories, into a larger unifying context. In Chaucer's *Canterbury Tales*, for example, the tales are told in the context of a pilgrimage to Canterbury. The book of Job brackets an extended dialogue between Job and his friends with a prologue set in heaven and an epilogue; the context becomes cosmic. The frame provides more than a setting, however; it adds to or alters the meaning of the smaller units. Chaucer's folk are on a religious journey, which adds considerable irony to the tales. The knowledge that Job's suffering is imposed to settle a wager in heaven modifies our view of the whole action.

Recent literary approaches call for sensitivity to the role of prologues. They are there for compelling reasons. That the creation prologue functions as a frame or bracket is clear when one observes that the larger biblical story begins with creation (Genesis 1–2) and concludes with a new creation (Revelation 21–22). In a study of Old Testament theology, Israel's story is of paramount importance with its own meaning, but the creation frame can be expected to nuance or extend that meaning. Therefore, the final stage, theologizing, must not ignore the "spin" that the prologue will give.

The intent of this chapter is twofold: to point to the way creation language permeates the larger story, and to indicate,

though sketchily, how the creation motif is related to the redemption motif.

The story of God's fashioning of the world is told in Genesis 1–2. Certain theological motifs extend, like fingers, into
other parts of the canon.

- The word *Elohim* (God) is an implicit challenge to
  polytheism.
- The seven-day pattern suggests a cult-orientation.
- The systematic description points to an ordering.
- There is an air of the mysterious in the account.
- Despite the importance given to humankind as the
  apex of creation, the account gives considerable
  attention to the inanimate and the animate.

These observations are elaborated in Israel's prophetic, cultic,
and wisdom literature. The first two observations are amplified
in the prophetic and cult-oriented literature, the last three in
the wisdom literature.

2. The Creation Motif
From the Prophetic Perspective

Any talk of creation is sooner rather than later talk about Elohim, and talk about one God. For that matter, creation is a more
dominant topic in Isaiah than it is in Genesis. The monotheism,
implicit in Genesis, for example, is made very explicit by Isaiah,
who leaves no room for dualism. The claim to an unqualified
monotheism rings out in the startling assertion:

> I form light and create darkness,
> I make weal and create woe;
> I the LORD do all these things (45:7).

The naming of opposites (light and darkness, heaven and
earth), a technique known as hendiadys, conveys the meaning
of "totality." Even darkness and calamity, so Isaiah affirms, are

within Yahweh's jurisdiction. God brooks no rival. The arguments from God as the Maker of all that exists, God's acts in history, and God's prescience (his knowledge of coming events; cf. Isa 41:21–29; 46:10; 48:3–6) lead to the declaration: "I am the first and I am the last; besides me there is no god" (44:6; cf. 44:8; 45:5–6; 46:9). That conclusion reappears in the majestic descriptive sweep in which Isaiah identifies Yahweh as he "who created the heavens . . . who formed the earth and made it; I am the LORD, and there is no other" (45:18).

The link between creation and redemption, between prologue and story, is made in various ways. Isaiah seems not to be interested in creation as a way of explaining the origin of the world. Rather, the doctrine of creation, if one may use the expression, functions in particular ways. Ben Ollenburger has identified the way in which for Isaiah the security of Zion was expounded in terms of creation. The one who is enthroned in Zion is the Maker of heaven and earth, by virtue of which Isaiah is "able reliably to declare that the unprecedented events of Israel's experience are God's own acts, and thus God's own creation."[3] Moreover, the argument is made from creation that God holds a position of supremacy over the nations. Hezekiah prays, "O LORD of hosts, God of Israel, who are enthroned above the cherubim, you are God, you alone, of all the kingdoms of the earth; you have made heaven and earth" (37:16: cf. 40:12–31). "It is the language of creation that is best suited to express the universality and irresistibility of God's dominion."[4] Creation theology functions to buttress the role of Zion and also to establish Yahweh's supremacy over nations. In both instances creation theology and history intertwine.

In other ways, too, God's creative work is linked to redemption. God's creation extends beyond the world of nature to the creation of a people, Israel (43:1a, 15; 44:24; 45:9–13; 54:5; cf. Ps 95:6–7; Hos 8:14). Creation language is ubiquitous in the disputation passages in Isaiah 40–55, where the purpose is to persuade Israel to take the next step: leave Babylon for her homeland. Repeatedly the argument pivots on God as Creator. God did a new thing at creation; he will do a new thing now in

Israel's history. "Do not remember the former things, or consider the things of old" (Isa 43:18–19; cf. v. 15; 4:9). Creation theology functions to inaugurate a new era in Israel's history. Even more, creation language is appropriate to describe the eschaton, which will entail a renewal of heaven and earth (65:17). In some sense the new creation is the object of salvation history (55:12–13). Redemption, therefore, is not only the redemption of a people, but is envisioned as having effects on a cosmic scale. B. W. Anderson is correct: "Creation and redemption belong together, as the obverse and reverse of the same theological coin."[5]

3. The Creation Motif from the Cultic Perspective

That recognition of God as Creator was a major element in Israel's cultic expression is readily substantiated, especially from the psalms (cf. also liturgies in the prophets, e.g., Amos 4:13; 5:8–9; 9:5–6). The psalms frequently offer God's work in creation as reason for worship. Psalm 8 is a clear example. With the mention of the heavens, sun and stars, flocks and herds, birds of the air, and whatever passes through the seas, there is a clear echo of Genesis 1. The litany of creation in Psalm 8 is bracketed first and last by the ascription of praise: "O LORD, our Sovereign, how majestic is your name in all the earth!" Other examples of exhortation to worship based on creation themes are:

> Come into his presence with singing . . .
> It is he that made us, and we are his (Ps 100:2b–3a).
>
> By the word of the LORD the heavens were made . . .
> He gathered the waters of the sea as in a bottle . . .
> Let all the earth fear the LORD (Ps 33:6–8a).

God was there before ever there was a world (Ps 90:2); therefore, worshipping God is fitting. Praise is due the Creator from the world of humans as well as from the inanimate world (Psalm 148).[6]

We may select several psalms as a way into our second question: how is creation linked with salvation? In Psalm 136, for example, the first several verses speak about creation with clear echoes of Genesis 1; the next verses detail God's acts in Israel's history. G. Von Rad commented about this juxtaposition and independence of the two themes: "Verses 5–9 deal with the creation of the world, and at verse ten the psalm abruptly changes its course in order to recount the mighty deeds of Yahweh in history. In this psalm, therefore, the doctrine of creation and the doctrine of redemption stand side by side, yet wholly unrelated the one to the other."[7]

More recent assessments, of which Richard J. Clifford's is typical, move in a very different direction. Clifford holds, drawing on examples from the ancient Near East, that a people resorted to cosmogony to narrate how they came into existence. The purpose of a creation narrative was not to satisfy the curiosity about the origin of the world; cosmogonies were concerned with the origin of a people. The story of creation was important, not for what it might declare about the past, but for what it stated about the present. Given that perspective, Clifford advances the view (drawing on communal laments and hymns) that the telling of the creation is part of a national story. In Israel that story could be said to begin with the exodus, or with Abraham, but it might also be narrated on another level, beginning with God creating the world. Put in Clifford's typology, the story could be told from the "historic" perspective where the emphasis is on the human characters, or from the "suprahistoric" perspective with an emphasis on heavenly beings.[8]

Clifford finds this linkage between creation and redemption not only in hymns, such as Psalm 136, but also in communal laments such as Psalms 44, 74, 77, and 89. Here one may find a historic perspective (e.g., Ps 74:1–11), but also a suprahistoric perspective in which God's work of dividing the sea and crushing the heads of the Leviathan is inserted in the lament (Ps 74:12–17). "In Psalm 89 the defeat of sea is cosmogonic, it is part of the founding event that includes establishment of the Davidic king."[9] The lament can move between the "historic" and the "suprahistoric" levels, for both belong to the same story.

A basic chord is struck: the God of creation is the same Yahweh who is Lord of Israel's history. Israel knows that her helper is the Creator. "Our help is in the name of the LORD, who made heaven and earth" (Ps 124:8). "We are to assume a reciprocal relationship between the themes "creation" and "history," because one and the same God is the liberator of Israel and the creator of heaven and earth."[10] The prophets, then, were not alone, likely not even the first, who made the association between creation and history.

4. The Creation Motif
From the Wisdom Perspective

The sages, in reflecting on creation, underscored the ordering and the rhythm which exist in nature. Such ordering, especially in Psalm 104, echoes the original ordering of the days of creation (Genesis 1). The poet of Psalm 104 revels in the harmony which is found between creatures and the environment. Here, spatially speaking, geographical turf and its inhabitants of animals and plants are wonderfully compatible ecologically (Ps 104:11–12, 16–18); and here, temporally speaking, coordination exists between creatures and time (day and night, vv. 19–23). There is meaningful order in the world: boundaries have been set; forces toward chaos are kept at bay (Ps 104:6–9; cf. Job 38:11; Jer 5:22). Even so the poet is aware of the dark side (vv. 20, 26, 29, 32, 35).[11] A wisdom-oriented parable in the prophets stresses that the world is so ordered that actions can be judged appropriate inasmuch as they correspond to the natural cycle (Isa 28:23–29). The Preacher says there are appropriate times to everything under the sun (Eccl 3:1). Even the ethical-social dimensions of society are connected to an original ordering.

> The LORD has made everything for its purpose,
> even the wicked for the day of trouble. (Prov 16:4).

Thus, both the natural and the social world are perceived as ordered by God.

A second theological reflection by the sages on the subject of creation centers on its mysteries. A poem in honor of Lady Wisdom elaborates the role which wisdom, virtually hypostatized, had in the creation process (Prov 8:22–31).[12] Still, aside from the assertion that wisdom was present at creation as a "master worker" (8:30), the manner in which the world came into being remains a mystery. God's monologue in Job makes the same point (Job 38–39). Here question upon question is posed by God to press to the limit the understandings mortals have of nature's processes: how is one to explain the formation of clouds, the track of lightning, or the possibility of birds flying? Even if a partial answer to the enigma resides in wisdom, one is not really helped because wisdom itself is enigmatic (28:12–28). The observer is left, not with answers, but with mystery.

Thirdly, the importance of the world of nature is affirmed, for example, in Job and the psalms. God's reply to Job's complaint has an extended section on Behemoth and Leviathan, monstrous land and sea creatures (40:1–24; 41:1–34). These are clearly creatures of value, not because they can be harnessed for energy or eaten for food, but in their own right. They are God's prime exhibits. Indeed, if this speech by God is to be an answer to Job, it is puzzling that animals and not human beings should figure so largely in the speech. Here one has not the impression, frequently given, that the world of nature exists for the benefit of humankind, but that the world of nature is itself of worth. The book of Proverbs, for its part, lends a kind of dignity to the nonhuman world. From animals—ants, rock conies—one can learn wisdom (6:6). Wild life is to be respected (30:24–28). Animals are not to be mistreated (12:10). Wisdom literature adds its voice to Genesis 1 in attributing importance to the natural environment. The implications for modern ecology are far-reaching.[13]

The Hebrew sages, then, highlighted the striking ordering apparent in creation, the mystery of creation, and the intrinsic worth of the nonhuman creation.

The wisdom material in Job, Psalms, and Ecclesiastes, since it does not take account of God's once-for-all acts in redemption history, can leave the impression that creation is a motif independent of redemption history. But that is not so. C. Westermann has rightly noted that salvation in broader terms consists not only of divine interventions, as in Israel's history, but also of God's sustaining activity of blessing. Only a narrow definition of salvation would wrench apart the motif of creation and salvation. It is part of God's saving work that creation is stable.[14]

Rolff Rendtorff has called attention to the interplay of God's covenant with Noah (Gen 8:22; 9:8–17) and history. God binds himself through covenant to guarantee the regularities of nature such as day and night, seed-time and harvest. The world is stabilized through grace. When Israel later finds herself in exile, God's word to her recalls the covenant with Noah (Isa 54:7ff). The creation motif is thus invoked to bear on a circumstance in salvation history. The link between creation and covenant is also made in Jer 5:22–25; and Jer 14:20–22, where now Israel's sin against God has a negative effect on the rain and on the environment generally (cf. Hos 4:1–3).

Rendtorff delineates the connection between creation and salvation history from still another set of texts. When Israel in exile complains that justice has been withheld from her (Isa 40:27), she is directed to consider God's word of creation as establishing a certain rightness, an ordering. Any question of justice, whether for corporate Israel in exile or for an individual such as Job (19:7), has an ultimate answer in God's justice discernible in creation (Isa 40:28; cf. Job 38:1–33). For "their [Israel's and Job's] righteousness and their redemptive history . . . are embedded in the world which God has created, and in his dealings with that world."[15] Creation, then, furnishes something of a bedrock or ultimate event by which warrant is provided that God's action with his people can be expected to be just. The Creator God characterized by justice is also the Savior

God who is characterized by justice. If canonical wisdom literature does not explicitly connect creation and redemption, it
nevertheless implicitly provides a compelling theological un-
derpinning for salvation history.[16]

5. The Creation Motif
And God's Design

In several ways the theology about creation in the prophetic,
cultic, and wisdom literature validates, but also extends, the
thesis that God's fourfold design is the heart of the Old Testament.

Design and order as a preoccupation of wisdom literature
correlate well with the concept of divine design articulated by
Moses. The sages maintained that there was a time and place
for every event (Eccl 3:1–8). The prophets capitalized on the
name of Yahweh as the guarantor for what they announced.
Their "Thus says Yahweh" echoed Exodus 6, where the assertion "I am Yahweh" bracketed the announcements to Israel of
deliverance, covenant, knowing God, and land (blessing). The
prophets were clearly in sync with the seminal word in Exodus
6. And so were Israel's poets, when, as in a reflection on creation, they reveled in the order discernible in the interrelation-
ships of the animate, the inanimate, and the human. "In wisdom you have made them all" (Ps 104:24).

But the literature that reinforces the notion of divine design also qualifies the notion in several ways. The presence of
wisdom material, with its numerous pointers to creation, qualifies the importance one might otherwise give to the rubric of
history. Wisdom literature, certainly not detached from the design to which history gives witness, has, not history, but the
natural and social world for its subject of reflection. Given the
inclusion of wisdom in the canon, and wisdom literature's preoccupation with matters of nature and creation, it is necessary
that an Old Testament theology not be limited to history, despite its dominance in the Hebrew Scriptures.[17]

Creation theology expands the horizons of a salvation history approach by insisting on God's initiative in the cosmic realm. The inauguration of Israel's history in the call of Abram, "Now the LORD said to Abram" (Gen 12:1ff), must be heard against the inauguration of the cosmos, "And God said, Let there be . . ." (Gen 1:3). With a word God spoke the world into existence, and with a naked word the history of God's people was launched. The creation of a history was a sequel to God's creation of the cosmos. Israel's poets understood this complementarity of creation and history. In extolling God's faithfulness they cited both creation (Ps 136:1–9) and Israel's history (Ps 136:10–24; cf. Pss 19; 135). Prophets and poets will not let us forget that the God who brought about Israel's history was the same God who brought the cosmos into being.

The creation motif is thus not an independent motif, but is integral to redemption in the following ways. Salvation occurs because God takes creation seriously. The prophets argue from creation for a recognition of God's supremacy over nations, as well as for God securing Zion. The cultic material deliberately combines affirmations about creation and redemption (e.g., Psalm 136). The story of creation (suprahistoric) and the narrative of human actors in history (historic) are both valid perspectives on the world. The Creator God is also the Covenant God. This assertion is buttressed by wisdom, which underlines the reliability of God's ordering, his justice. That datum in turn, when hooked to Noah's covenant, is foundational to the interpretation by the prophets of Israel's exile. Eventually, the Book of Wisdom joined creation and redemption in a tight knot by explaining that Wisdom, present at creation, was also the agent superintending Israel's history.

The major Old Testament story of salvation, then, takes on additional coloring when it is heard over against the prologue. The thesis that divine design is a theological magnet according to which the Old Testament is oriented is reinforced by the prologue. The element of "design" in Israel's story echoes the design and ordering in God's creation.

The God who is committed to a people despite the corruption of their way is the same God who is committed to the maintenance of the natural order, even when, as prior to the deluge, the earth is corrupted by the environment. "Salvation history finds its context in creation theology and is the context for it."[18] Goldingay discusses four facets of the relationship between creation and redemption: (1) the world God redeems is the world of God's creation; (2) the world God created is a world that needed to be redeemed; (3) human beings are redeemed to live again their created life before God; (4) the redeemed humanity still looks for a final act of redemption/re-creation. Creation and redemption stand in continuity. Still, the concept of design should not be construed in terms of exactitude, for as with creation, so with salvation history, the element of the mysterious remains.

Framing God's Design
The World's Peoples

God's fourfold purpose becomes explicit in the history of one nation, Israel. The bulk of the Old Testament is taken up with the story of this one people. Yet it would be a serious error to conclude that God's purpose is restricted to an ethnic group. Just as God is not the God of one people, Israel only, so God's design is not for one people only but for the world's peoples. More than a hint toward an interest in all peoples is given in Genesis 1–11. This frame for Israel's story has an inclusiveness about it. After following closely Israel's own story as we have done, when we return to Genesis 1–11 which frames the story, we see there more than an introduction.[1] Just as the center section in the book of Job, when pitted against the prologue, is sharply nuanced toward wider theological horizons, so the intent of Israel's story, when put against the Bible's prologue, leads to wider horizons. The significance of the particular (Israel) is seen in the perspective of the universal.

The tension between the particular and the universal is one with which Gabler (1787), the so-called father of biblical theology, occupied himself. His understanding of biblical theology entailed two steps. Working with the particulars of the Old Testament it would be possible, he maintained, to establish how the ancients understood God, people, and world. As Gabler saw it, these understandings would then be sifted in the sieve of rationalism to identify the universally applicable truths.

The tension between the particular and the universal can be stated, not only in philosophical terms but as questions of dynamics. The particular is the story of one people. The "universal" (as with Genesis 1–11) is the story of other (all) peoples. Is there a connection between the particular and universal, and if so, what is it? What dynamics function between these two polarities? Is the story of God and his people intended to embrace the world's people? Are there rubrics other than history in which this tension can be understood and analyzed?

This chapter intends to show, by giving attention to the canon, how pervasive the "international," even universalistic motif is. God elected Israel, but God's horizons of activity were more broad-based by far than a single people. The argument here is that the arrangement of the canon imposes an interpretation of Israel's story such that the constant reach toward the universal is kept to the fore.[2] The objective of highlighting the "beyond-Israel" theme begins, then, with a look at the Torah.

1. The Torah and the "Families Of Nations"

The first identifiable section of the Hebrew canon is the Torah, which counts five books: Genesis, Exodus, Leviticus, Numbers, and Deuteronomy. The term "Torah," which is a transliteration of the Hebrew, refers to "instruction" and so is broader ranging than the meaning of "law" usually assigned it. These five books of "instruction" consist of story as well as precepts. The major story, beginning with Gen 11:31, is the story of a particular clan whose chief figures are Abraham and his descendants Isaac, Jacob, and Joseph (Genesis). As for the rest, God's many precepts (Exodus–Numbers) to the elect people Israel were interlaced with the story of their escape from Egypt and their journey to Canaan (cf. Deuteronomy).

The "Families Of Nations" In Genesis 1–11

The story of the Hebrews must be read against its story frame (Genesis 1–11) and with attention to the canonical ordering. The primeval cycle is characterized, beyond the initial creation and fall stories, by a rhythm in which narrative alternates with genealogy. As with a camera with options of a zoom and wide-angle lens, the sequence in these chapters is that of a close-up picture (e.g., story of Cain and Abel, Genesis 4) followed by a panoramic picture (the genealogy of Genesis 5). This genealogy is followed by the close-up story of the one family of Noah and the great flood (Genesis 6–9), which is followed in turn by the wide-ranging genealogy (Genesis 10). The incident of the tower of the Babel (Gen 11:1–9), a close-up, is followed by a further genealogy (Gen 11:10–30), and then comes the story of yet another family, Abram (Gen 11:31). Whatever else the genealogies of peoples other than Israel may convey (e.g., human solidarity), their position at the outset of the canon signals an awareness of people groups and their importance. These genealogies, an ancient method of history writing, form more than a background or even the context for Israel's story. As the frame for the story, they are an invitation to cast Israel's story into certain theological motifs. The opening chapters signal a theological theme of inclusiveness, which is especially apparent in retrospect.

The call of God to Abram, with its promise of Abram being a blessing to all nations, immediately links the particular Hebrew story with the more universalist subject matter of Genesis 1–11. God's interaction with a select people is for the benefit of all peoples, for in Abram "all the families of the earth shall bless themselves" (Gen 12:3). God's purpose with one people is not restrictive but is inclusive eventually of peoples beyond the Hebrews. Melchizedek (Gen 14:17–24) and Jethro (Exod 18:10–12) are harbingers of larger things. The story of Joseph dealing with famine in Egypt is one clear example of a Hebrew bringing blessing physically to a people otherwise consigned to famine (Genesis 37–50).

Tensions in this motif of Israel relating to nations should not be overlooked. The motif of Israel as a blessing is problematic in certain texts (e.g., Gen 34:25–31) and can be appreciated only if taken long range. The Balaam oracles emphasize a flourishing people of Israel; these texts also speak of them devouring other peoples (Num 24:8). How in these circumstances Israel was to be a blessing is not so self-evident. Still, paradoxically, the ruler to come from Israel, traditionally interpreted as the Messiah, would indeed bless all people. In history (as with Joseph) and through prophecy (as in Balaam) the intersection between Israel and the nations is kept in view. The Torah is testimony to a beyond-Israel concern.

Literary Facets and the "Family of Nations"

If now, in addition to these periodic glimpses of the wider scene, the larger literary arrangement of the Torah is taken into account, the "internationalist" motif gains in luster. Not only does the Torah begin in Genesis on a world stage; the Torah also concludes by calling attention to peoples other than Israel. The Song of Moses near the end of Deuteronomy, while acknowledging the preferred role of Israel, identifies a divine strategy. When God assigned nations their respective places, he did so "according to the number of the Israelites" (Deut 32:8, Hebrew text; other versions read differently). The geographical location of God's people at the intersection of East/West and North/South travel routes can be interpreted as a divine strategic ploy. Such a location gave opportunity for Israel to exercise her priestly vocation of teaching others the way of Yahweh (Exod 19:6; for the teaching function of priests, cf. Deut 33:10 and Mal 2:6–7).

The song of Moses ends in an amazing, if somewhat enigmatic, way. "Rejoice O Gentiles, his people" (Deut 32:43, literal translation). The text is often amended (see commentaries). Other manuscripts read, "Rejoice O heavens," but the expression "his people" is then awkwardly orphaned unless one supplies a line as in the Septuagint, "worship him, all you gods."

The text is dense; three Hebrew words—"rejoice," "Gentiles," "his people"—occur serially without indication of relationships. The reading, "Rejoice, O nations, his people," is straightforward. On this interpretation the nations are designated as "his people" (cf. Ps 47:9). "In the end . . . God's judgment of Israel and the nations leads to a broader understanding of the concept of the people of God—not just Israel but the nations as well are called to praise God as 'his people.'"[3] Ridderbos explains: "This appeal to the nations is in the first instance a rhetorical device to express the greatness *of* Israel's salvation (*heil*). But in the light of the revelation as a whole, statements such as these require a deeper meaning and significance, namely that in the *heil* that befalls Israel the entire world is involved."[4] However much the song is taken up with Israelite matters, it does not lose sight of the beyond-Israel dimension. Even if "his people" is a phrase grounded in creation, the expression nevertheless has an inclusive cast.

The beyond-Israel theme may also be sounded in Moses' blessing in Deuteronomy 33. In the opening stanza the subject is God's theophany and kingship and the giving of the law (vv. 2, 4–5). Between these repetitive assertions is the statement, "And he (Yahweh) loves peoples" (v. 3, my translation). While most interpreters believe "peoples" refers to Israel, the possibility cannot be excluded that peoples other than Israel are in view. If so, by the very positioning of verse 3, an implied linkage between God's revelation to Israel and the nations is suggested.

While both references to peoples beyond Israel's borders (Deut 32:8, 43; 33:3) are not expanded, their very existence in these closing chapters of the Torah division echoes the theme of nations in Genesis 1–11 and so forms a veiled inclusio or bracket with that initial section. The theme of nations will be much developed in subsequent divisions of the canon, but it is already apparent in the Torah.

2. The Prophets and the Beyond-Israel Motif

The Hebrew canon's second division consists of prophetic books in two collections. To the four books of the Former Prophets (Joshua, Judges, Samuel, Kings) are added the four books of the Latter Prophets (Isaiah, Jeremiah, Ezekiel, and The Twelve). The two collections have their own distinctives. The Former Prophets are largely in prose; the subject matter is the vicissitudes of a people and its leaders. The Latter Prophets are characterized by poetic oracles, of which a significant number deal with oracles addressed to other nations. While Israel's interests are never far removed from these oracles, the oracles against other nations sweep up concerns that are more generic. In these oracles the nations are subjects in their own right and not only as they relate to Israel's story.

Each of the four Latter Prophets devotes a significant block of material to God's address to nations other than Israel. Isaiah's oracles are against Babylon, Assyria, Philistia, Moab, Syria, Ethiopia, Egypt, Edom, Shebna, and Tyre (Isaiah 13–23), and even more generally to the entire earth (Isaiah 24–27). Jeremiah, while repeating Egypt, Babylon, Philistia, Moab, Ammon, and Edom, adds Damascus, Kedar, Hazor, and Elam (Jer 46–51). Ezekiel devotes major oracles to Egypt and Tyre but adds Sidon to the roster (Ezekiel 25–32). In the Book of the Twelve, two books are given exclusively to other nations: Obadiah (Edom) and Nahum (Assyria).

Judgment and Salvation

Theologically considered, these oracles make several points. First, God acts, for the most part, in coming judgment against these nations. Egypt, for example, is shown as badly beaten. Pharaoh stumbles into Sheol to take his place with the uncircumcised (Ezek 32:31–32). In a rhythmic war song, a sword is said to swing against Babylon so that that large empire is virtually annihilated (Jer 50:35–37). One basic reason for such judgments is arrogance and self-exaltation. The king of Tyre is quoted as saying: "I am a god" (Ezek 28:2; cf. Jer 48:42). Accountability is rooted, then, in a sense of obligation God-ward.

For all the monotonous sets of judgment oracles against other nations, there are occasional surprises. Salvation comes to nations. Jonah's judgment speech to the Ninevites results in a spiritual turn-around by that city's populations. The city, including its little ones and animals, is spared (Jonah 3:10; 4:10–11). Isaiah 40–55 envisages the salvation of nations who will turn from their idolatry to confess the living God (45:14, 23; cf. Mic 4:1–4; Zech 14:16), and will live aligned with God's justice (Isa 51:4–5). "Although the appellations of God . . . already disclosed a 'universalistic' tendency, it was especially under the influence of the message of the prophets, and above all, that of Deutero-Isaiah, that the worldwide dimensions of the relation of Israel's God became apparent."[5] The tension between nationalism and universalism is somewhat alleviated, even if, as D. W. VanWinkle explains, the prophet does not envisage the co-equality of Jew and Gentile. The prophet envisages Israel as God's agent in exercising just rule, a rule for which the nations wait and to which they will submit.[6]

Acknowledgment of Yahweh

Second, the goal of God's actions is acknowledgment by the nations of Yahweh. Nowhere is that made more clear than in Ezekiel, where in oracles against the nations (Ezekiel 25–32) there are twenty-five occurrences of the recognition formula, "And you (they) shall know that I am Yahweh." Part of this acknowledgment is that nations recognize their accountability to Yahweh. The baseline for that accountability is not the Torah as it is for Israel, but an awareness of what is humane (Amos 1:3 – 2:3). So Ammon is scored for violating human decency by cruelly killing pregnant women (1:13–15). Tyre is punished for its slave trade and for breaking treaty (1:9–10). God has a claim on these nations in that they have reason to acknowledge him because of the witness of their conscience (as Paul would later say, Rom

2:14–15). God will yet be acknowledged by the world's people (cf. Ezek 25:11, 17). And so, while these oracles are, according to tone, oracles against the nations, they are, according to goal, oracles asserting the eventual acknowledgment of God by all peoples.

Inclusion

Hints of including some of these peoples within the covenant community are found in several prophetic books. Isaiah, for instance, despite a scathing word against Egypt, concludes that oracle with a scenario of Israel as one of the world's top three nations, along with Egypt and Assyria. The Lord's blessing is placed on all three. The Egyptians, the long-time enemies of Israel, are designated by the Lord of hosts as "My people" (Isa 19:25). Isaiah very self-consciously forbids the foreigners to disparage themselves with respect to the covenant community. Instead:

> And the foreigners who joint themselves to the LORD . . . their services . . . will be accepted on my atar; for my house shall be called a house of prayer for all peoples (Isa 56:6–7).

Perhaps not coincidentally the book's final chapter speaks about God's glory being declared among the Gentiles (66:19; cf. 42:6–7; 49:1–7).

The book of Amos, preserved among The Twelve, ends with a message of hope that affects other peoples. This message is that the dynasty of David, now in shambles like a torn and collapsed booth or kiosk, will be raised up and repaired. What is more, the remnant of Edom (LXX reads "humankind") will come under the restored Davidic umbrella, "and all the nations who are called by my name" (Amos 9:12; cf. Hos 1:10).[7] The New Testament understood this announcement, as interpreted by James, as a warrant for including the Gentiles, the uncircumcised, in the covenant of faith (Acts 15:13–18).

The Nations and Their Land

God's blessing (e.g., land or return to the land) is announced to select Gentile nations. Egypt is to be delivered into the hands of Nebuchadnezzar, but beyond judgment for Egypt is a measure of salvation. Its land shall be reoccupied. "Afterward Egypt shall be inhabited as in the days of old" (Jer 46:26). Similarly, Moab, against whom Jeremiah rails and whose destruction is vividly described at length, received this promise: "Yet I will restore the fortunes of Moab in the latter days, says the LORD" (48:47). A similar announcement for prosperity and restoration greeted Ammon (49:6) and Elam (49:39).

These four assertions about deliverance, covenant, knowledge of God, and blessing are obviously an expansion of the paradigm of God's design specifically articulated for Israel. That paradigm is quasi-functional also for nations. The sovereign God will intersect with the nations even in deliverance. God's acts of judgment on the nations as also God's judgments on Israel are punitive but also salutary. A fundamental consideration for both is God's justice. Very remarkable are those passages that envision peoples other than Israel as participants within the covenant community of faith. Ezekiel leaves no doubt but that the acknowledgment of Yahweh by the nations is the goal of Yahweh's activities with other nations. Even the theme of land (not now the land of Israel) surfaces in the announcements for select nations. The fourfold paradigm becomes transparent, even if not strongly so, in God's dealing with peoples beyond Israel as well.

Yahweh's salvation history is inclusive of more than Israel. The very ordering of the books within the prophetic corpus, whether or not deliberate, supports this conclusion. The Former Prophets occupy themselves with Israel's story; the Latter Prophets take their position on the world's stage with a word from God to those "beyond Israel."[8]

3. The Writings and the World of Peoples

The third division of the Hebrew canon not only begins with a book whose window is open to the nations, but the division is punctuated throughout with books characterized by a more universalist outlook.

The first book in the division of the Writings is Psalms. The first two psalms, some hold, are thematic for the entire book. The "torah" or teaching in which the godly mediate (Ps 1:2) may be a reference to what follows in the psalms and not primarily, if at all, to the formal Torah of Israel's previous writings. That is, the book of Psalms, for all its cult and liturgical orientation, is a book of teaching that includes such subjects as Israel's history (e.g., 78), sin and the reality of forgiveness (e.g., 32, 51), and theodicy (73). The second psalm sounds another note, an eschatological one, in which Yahweh's sovereignty over the world's people is asserted. The references to nations (gôyîm) in the psalms are arresting for their number. The imperative for nations to praise Yahweh occurs frequently (e.g., 67:3–6; 117:1). The prospect that Yahweh's rule will be truly exercised in justice over all people is stated repeatedly (82:1–8; 98:2, 9).[9] Yahweh's salvation is to be made known to all peoples (9:11; 96:3; 105:1). "All the peoples behold his glory" (97:6).

The Internationalist Note in the Wisdom Books

The internationalist note is heard even more sharply in the book of Job, where the cultural and historical trappings associated with Israel are removed. Job, whose residence was outside Palestine in the land of Uz, and whose book is silent about Israel's salvation history, is representative of humankind, as Everyone or Anyone. The book raises urgent questions about the way a human being experiences God. The dialogue between Job and his friends eventuates in Job's oath-like challenge to Yahweh (27). Yahweh answers that challenge through a theophany (38–41). The upshot is that Job has apparently been misguided in his assumptions and conclusions, but he has not committed sin. The book is an intense case study of experiencing God—not by an Israelite with access to historical traditions, but by a God-fearer outside the mainstream of God's revelation to Israel.

A similar internationalist flavor appears in Proverbs and Ecclesiastes. In these books one is not outside the provenance of Yahwism (how were that possible, given who Yahweh is?), but outside Israel's own story. The maxims on behavior, the sayings about home and society, the proverbs about industry and greed, the instruction about wisdom and folly have a universalistic texture. Parts of this literature have a strong affinity with Egyptian writings (e.g., Prov 22:17 – 24:22), and may even have been derived from the Egyptian Instruction of Amen-em-ope. These directives about ethical behavior and lifestyle, while they comport well with directives in the Torah, are not rooted in divine revelation as are the Mosaic directives, but arise out of the common experience of living one's life.

Internationalism in the Books of Ruth, Esther, Daniel

The books of Ruth, Esther, and Daniel, all of which are grouped in the section known as The Writings, burst any notions that Israelite faith was parochial, as though it could be walled in by Palestine's borders. The book of Esther follows the fortunes of adherents to Yahweh in a sometimes hostile environment of Persian power politics. The book of Daniel portrays Nebuchadnezzar, the most powerful world ruler of his time, acknowledging Israel's God as sovereign and universal (4:34–35). The book of Ruth urges yet another variation on the beyond-Israel theme. Repeatedly, Ruth is identified as the Moabitess, as if to keep her non-Israelite ancestry to the fore. But before long she is no longer an "outsider," and by the end of the book she as a non-Israelite has been incorporated into the community of faith and has become the ancestress to David. All three books give a high profile to non-Israelites in their religious and political interaction with the people of God.

These several canonical books with their beyond-Israel flavor, weight the third section of the Hebrew canon heavily in a more "universalist" direction. Only the books of Lamentations and Chronicles are occupied with solely Israelite concerns. Ezra and Nehemiah make an explicit connection with the outside world. The books of Daniel, Ruth, and Esther detail that dimension even more. The books of Proverbs, Ecclesiastes, and Job put the reader in a universe of religious (Yahwistic) discourse without invoking the particularist story of Israel.

Overall then, in following the trajectory set by the threefold arrangement of the books in the Old Testament canon, the movement is from the Torah (largely occupied with matters Israelite though the world's people are noted in inclusio fashion) to the Prophets, where oracles addressing nations are common, to the Writings, where several entire books are of an "international" flavor. The umbilical cord which ties Yahweh to Israel initially does not disappear in the canonical books, of course, but is much less pronounced in the Writings than in the Torah or the Prophets. Following the theme of particular/universalist via the literary composition of the canon, it is clear, given the ordering of the biblical books, how Israel's story is nested in the story of the world's people, how that story is a paradigm for God's relationship to the world's people generally, and how the trajectory is clearly from the particularist Israelite to the universalist, the families of the earth.

When these observations about the canon are rehearsed in the light of the story frame (Genesis 1–11), the initial universalistic note is recognized as part of the melodic theme. The Hebrew ordering of books offers an increasingly universalistic outlook, one which opens easily into the New Testament books of Acts and Romans. Brevard Childs is no doubt correct to say that "The New Testament is directed primarily to the nations."[10] Our survey shows that canonically that development was not alien.

17
Divine Design and the New Testament

The foregoing chapters attempt to provide a coherent description of Old Testament faith around the central theme of God's design. That design consists of God's intention for a people's freedom, their formation into a community, their experience of God, and their enjoyment of blessing in the land. The design is fixed but it is not rigid. One may discover in each era a variety of nuances and emphases, a partial kaleidoscope, though the design is never out of focus.

The New Testament period represents a historical advance over the three eras sketched in previous chapters. Our purpose now is to test the results of our Old Testament research in two New Testament books, Matthew and Romans, in order to see whether the pattern of God's design is exhibited in the New Testament. Both the gospel of Matthew and the epistle of Romans are books with numerous references to the Old Testament, and are books which have a particularly Jewish cast to them. We shall be able merely to sketch the lines along which a full treatment of our theme would proceed. The following comments are in the nature of hints. That our exploration is preliminary must be emphasized.

1. The Divine Design and The Kingdom of God in Matthew

In the New Testament Jesus Christ holds center stage. In his person he was unique; in his message, striking. He declared that the kingdom of God was present in him. Both he and his disciples came preaching the gospel of the kingdom (Matt 4:23; 9:35; 10:7). That kingdom is not so much a realm as it is the rule of God.[1]

The New Testament expression "kingdom of God" has its conceptual antecedents in the Old Testament. Yahweh, the creator of all, is the King of glory (Ps 24:7ff); "For the LORD, the Most High, is awesome, a great king over all the earth" (Ps 47:2); "The LORD is king" (Ps 93:1; cf. 95:3; 96:10; 97:1). The herald who announces a new exodus also announces, "Your God reigns" (Isa 52:7). Of the Son of Man to be presented to the Ancient of Days it is said, "His dominion is an everlasting dominion that shall not pass away, and his kingship is one that shall never be destroyed" (Dan 7:14b). The statements in the Psalms about the kingdom express a reality about Yahweh's lordship, but in Daniel 7 one leans forward to a future time when the intention of God's rule will be more fully established.

One of Jesus' emphases is that in him there is the fulfillment of the Old Testament hope. He declares: "But blessed are your eyes, for they see, and your ears, for they hear. Truly I tell you, many prophets and righteous people longed to see what you see, but did not see it, and to hear what you hear, but did not hear it" (Matt 13:16–17). Jesus quoted Isa 61:1 in his inaugural statement and concluded, "Today this Scripture has been fulfilled in your hearing" (Luke 4:21). But as Jesus makes clear to the messengers from John, fulfillment is not synonymous with consummation (Matt 11:4–6).[2] In Jesus God has come, but it is not yet his ultimate coming in eschatological judgment and salvation.

The tie-in between Matthew and the Old Testament occurs at several levels. Matthew's "formula   quotations" about fulfillment from the Old Testament are his trademark.[3] On another level Willard Swartley has shown how the geographically organized material in the Synoptics, i.e., Jesus' ministry in Galilee, his journey to Jerusalem, and his ministry in Jerusalem, is shaped by the Old Testament story. In these "movements" of Jesus' story are contained the themes of Israel's story: exodus/Sinai, way/conquest, temple and kingship. For example, the Jerusalem segment of Jesus' life is told self-consciously by Matthew in keeping with temple and kingship symbols from the Old Testament (southern) traditions. Swartley accounts for this distinctive shaping of the Gospels by positing a need in the early church for a cycle of lectionary readings about the life of Jesus, which was then shaped according to Israel's major themes and traditions.[4] If so, then the connection between Matthew and the Old Testament is even closer than the formula quotations suggest.

By focusing on genre, C. Talbert identified four kinds of "Jesus material" in the Gospels, Matthew included: miracle stories, sayings, portrayals of Christ as revealer, and the passion story. Each of these, Talbert notes, lends a distinctive understanding to the divine presence made manifest in Jesus. For example, the miracle stories display Jesus' power and the sayings give moral guidance and stress discipleship as a response to Jesus' lordship. In Jesus God is present and arranges for deliverance on a grand, even cosmic scale.[5] It would be artificial to equate this fourfold material in Matthew with the fourfold design in the Old Testament, but even here it is a matter of curiosity that there are some correspondences.[6]

Such tantalizing suggestions about Matthew's theological connections with the Old Testament prepare the way for a brief sketch on how the fourfold themes of God's design are incorporated in Matthew's work.

Matthew's gospel picks up on the deliverance motif at the outset when Jesus is announced as one who shall deliver his people from their sins (Matt 1:21). But the deliverance theme extends beyond "his people" to larger, even cosmic dimensions. Following the exorcism of a demon—one of the most characteristic of Jesus' activities—Jesus enters into discussion with the Pharisees and states: "But if it is by the Spirit of God that I cast out demons, then the kingdom of God has come to you." G. R. Beasley-Murray comments: "The kingdom promised for the world is the divine sovereignty that delivers and transforms humanity in the entirety of its relations, extending to cosmic transfiguration."[7] The exorcisms, by pointing to a cosmic struggle, bring to mind such motifs as the Old Testament Yahweh wars against Israel's enemies, and the wars of the day of Yahweh (Joel 3:9–15). Jesus explained that the coming of the kingdom of God meant the destruction of the very principle of evil (Matt 12:29). G. E. Ladd states: "Whether or not the modern man feels he must 'demythologize' it, an inescapable element in the biblical concept of redemption is that man must be saved from spiritual powers which are beyond his ability to conquer."[8]

The covenant-community aspect of God's intention is underlined in Matthew most forcefully in the saying of Jesus: "I will build my church" (Matt 16:18). The divine identity statement, "You are the Christ, the Son of the living God," precedes Jesus' word about the church just as "I am Yahweh" precedes the declaration "I will take you for my people and I will be your God" (Exod 6:7). The church, like Israel, is to be a distinct people, a people of God. Many are the instructions of Jesus on the subject of discipleship (e.g., the Sermon on the Mount, Matthew 5–7), as he defines what it means to be the people of God. Indeed, the community nature of such discipleship is also given in Matthew where the church as a group functions in the interests of the brother who has sinned: after personal confrontation, the recalcitrant person is to be disciplined by the church. The church has binding and loosing powers (Matt 18:15ff). Furthermore, Matthew's gospel looks beyond an ethnic people to an inclusion of Gentiles as members of the people of God. Jesus' word, "Go, therefore, and make disciples of all nations," makes that clear (Matt 28:19; cf. The Jewish mission in 10:1, 5 with the reference to a Gentile mission in 10:18). Jesus represents the hope for Israel (1:17), but also for the nations (28:19).

The disciples and those who do the will of God (Matt 12:46ff) are the nucleus of this new community, which, like the Old Testament community, is a community in covenant.

God's intention, following the cue of the Old Testament pivotal text, is captured in the statement: "You shall know that I am the LORD your God" (Exod 6:7). The knowledge of God which includes the experience of God is a constituent part of kingdom-of-God language. Jesus speaks of entering into the kingdom of God (Matt 18:3), which is another way of inviting persons to know God, for as G. Gloege has written, "The Kingdom of God (*Gottesherrschaft*) is never something which can to some extent be separated from God, but is only a more pregnant expression for God himself "[9] Jesus held out the prospect that the pure shall see God (Matt 5:8). Indeed, in Jesus God is present to be known. Matthew emphasizes that presence at the outset of his gospel: the child's name is Immanuel, God with us (1:23). The closing words of the gospel are the words of the resurrected Jesus, "I am with you always, to the end of the age" (Matt 28:20).

The transfiguration account (Matt 17:1ff) and the display of God's power reported in the miracle stories represent ways in which the disciples "know" or "experience" God. Beyond these incidents Jesus speaks about the kingdom of God in metaphors of eating and banqueting (cf. Matt 8:11–12; 22:1–14; 25:1–12). These metaphors, which depict the restoration of communion between God and humankind, add substantially to the claim that the intimate fellowship of believers with God is an integral part of the kingdom message.

The fourth component, that of land, is at first sight virtually absent from the message of Jesus. The beatitude "Blessed are the meek, for they shall inherit the earth" (Matt 5:5) appears as a lone example of interest in the subject.[10] A closer look however yields an interesting insight. In the Old Testament, we have maintained, "land" comes to be a symbol for gift and especially for "blessings of a good life." While this blessing was often defined as material abundance and security, it was not restricted to the physical dimension, since spiritual sensitivity, especially loyalty to God reflected in obedience to God in a distinctive lifestyle, came to be associated with occupancy of the land. The agenda to which God's promise of land refers is the agenda of a rich and full life with Yahweh. While the subject of land as such has been largely jettisoned in the Gospels, the agenda of the rich quality of life is clearly a priority in kingdom language. Jesus speaks of living not by bread alone but by every word of God (Matt 4:4). Jesus refers to salvation as eternal life (life with God) (Matt 25:46). In Mark 9:43–48, as Beasley-Murray notes, "The life is equated with the individual's participation in the kingdom of God."[11]

Jesus speaks of the joy of the Lord (Matt 25:21, 23). The metaphors of the wedding feast picture abundance (Matt 22:1–14; 25:1–12). Indeed, the joyous nature involved in Jesus' message surfaces in the opponent's accusation that Jesus lived in abandon, like a drunkard and a glutton. Life in the kingdom, like life in the land, is one characterized by fullness and a certain richness (Matt 6:33).

The gift nature of salvation, the "rest for your souls" (Matt 11:29), the rich quality of life (cf. the new-wine metaphor, 9:17), the lifestyle in the kingdom (cf. The Sermon on the Mount, Matthew 5–7), are all motifs that we have noted are affiliated with land. Thus, though the subject of land as soil and turf fades, the agenda of life here and now and forever is the agenda of the kingdom of God.

The affinity between the facets of the divine design in the Old Testament and Jesus and his message of the kingdom in the New is a close one. The newness of Jesus is not to be minimized, but the continuity of his message with that of the Old Testament is particularly obvious when seen against the background of divine design.

2. The Divine Design and Righteousness In Romans

Romans commends itself as a summary statement of the Old Testament, primarily because of its theme but also because it, along with Hebrews and Revelation, contains concentrations of Old Testament quotations. Apart from direct quotations Paul refers often to the Old Testament. He specifies the "law and the prophets" as witnesses to righteousness (Rom 3:21b). It is through the "prophetic writings" that the gospel is made known to all the nations (Rom 16:26). Indeed, "whatever was written in former days was written for our instruction" (Rom 15:4).

Romans is commonly regarded as the most systematic and extended treatment of the meaning of God's coming in Christ. Some have suggested that Romans is intended to encapsulate the Old Testament. One can agree with William Tyndale's prologue to Romans which appeared in the 1534 edition of his English New Testament: "Wherefore it appeareth evidently, that Paul's mind was to comprehend briefly in this epistle all the whole yearning of Christ's gospel, and *to prepare an introduction unto all the Old Testament*. For without doubt whosoever hath this epistle perfectly in his heart *hath the light and the effect of the Old Testament within him*."[12] Romans may well be a choice key for the understanding of the relationship between the two testaments.

If one were forced to choose a key text for the New Testament era as we have for the three Old Testament eras, then that text would be the book of Romans. Like Ezek 34:20–31 or Hos 2:14–23, Romans as a whole echoes the message of Exod 5:22 – 6:8.

A full exegesis of Romans would be necessary to explicate the way in which this book gathers up and expands themes of the Old Testament.[13] The suggestion here is that the fourfold divine design familiar from the Old Testament is present in this epistle.

The sense of purpose in God's actions is evident from the first. The opening sentence delineates the far-ranging and purposeful activity of God. Paul describes the gospel as one which "he (God) promised beforehand through his prophets in the holy scriptures" (1:2). The two doxologies both revolve around the idea of purpose. The first highlights the wisdom and knowledge of God: "How unsearchable are his judgments and how inscrutable his ways!" (Rom 11:33). Isaiah is quoted: "For who has known the mind of the Lord, or who has been his counselor?" (v. 33; cf. Isa 40:13). The overarching and far-reaching salvation explicated in the early chapters of Romans is demonstration of a continuity with the Old Testament events and so evokes this doxology. Another doxology also refers to the large time-span of God's operations and to the programmed way of his actions; the mystery kept secret for long ages past has been manifested, and glory belongs to the only wise God through Jesus Christ (Rom 16:25–26).

Apart from the doxologies a cluster of statements in Romans 8 stresses the purposeful nature of God's work. "We know that all things work together for good for those who love God, who are called according to his purpose" (Rom 8:28). The doxology-like material which follows almost immediately is prompted by the consideration of God's foreknowledge, his predestination, and his purpose in Jesus that Christ might be the firstborn among many brethren (Rom 8:29). That purpose, as Paul argues, embraces both Jews and Gentiles. One scholar comments: "What is the Epistle of Romans about? It is about God's plan for the world and about how Paul's mission to the Gentiles fits into that plan."[14]

Thus the notion of design or program underlies Paul's writings in Romans. The particulars of that design, familiar now from the foregoing chapters, can be traced, even if briefly, in order to indicate the theological cohesiveness of the two testaments.

The theme of the epistle, which is the righteousness of God (Rom 1:16–18), echoes the Old Testament deliverance theme. Since Martin Luther's experience and his exposition of the book, the term "righteousness" has commonly been given a forensic cast. One then asks about the quality of righteousness within a legal, even law court setting, and analyzes the way in which a God with this quality can justify a sinner. While this line of reasoning is not absent from Paul, it has been urged that the term "righteousness" (*dikaiosynē*) be studied against the backdrop of the Old Testament "righteousness" (*ṣᵉdāqâ*). To do so is to be brought up against a term that means "conformity to a norm," but a norm defined in terms of the demands of a particular relationship. For Israel, the supremely important relationship was with Yahweh. "Righteousness" in that relationship, as far as God was concerned, was above all an unquestioned faithfulness to his people.

This faithfulness was demonstrated in his acts of deliverance and also in his chastisement of a people when her response made such punishment necessary. An example of the use of the term "righteousness" may be taken from early Old Testament literature, the account of the conflict between Israel under Deborah's leadership against the Canaanites. In the triumph song, it is said: "There they shall recount the *righteous deeds* of the LORD, *righteous deeds* for His peasantry in Israel" (Judg 5:11, NASB). God's signal intervention in behalf of his endangered people is defined as his righteous deed. God had remained true to his commitment. His righteousness consists in his faithfulness to his covenant relationship in the face of challenge.[15]

When Paul claims that in the gospel the righteousness of God is revealed (Rom 1:17), he can explicate this in two directions. First, there is the revelation of the wrath of God against universal unrighteousness (1:18 – 3:20). The circle of discussion is drawn to encompass the entire human race. The relationship between humankind and God is of such a nature that his creatures are to honor him as God. But the story of the human race is that it did not honor Yahweh as God. Hence God, true to that intrinsic demand, acted in wrath against the creatures by giving them over to the lusts of their own impurity (1:24). On the other hand, his righteousness is revealed through the faithfulness of Jesus to those of faith (3:21 – 8:39). That theme is announced in Rom 3:22—"the righteousness of God through faith in Jesus Christ for all who believe. "The

theme "those who believe" is illustrated through the life of
Abraham (4:1–25), and the "faithfulness of Jesus Christ" is discussed in 5:1 – 8:39. It is in Jesus that God has demonstrated his
faithfulness to the human race. In God's act in Jesus Christ, to
put it another way, there is another of his "righteous deeds" (cf.
Judg 5:11).

There is a ready parallel, therefore, between the deliverance of the Israelites from Egypt and the coming of Jesus
Christ. Both are in the context of God's covenant commitment.
Both represent his clear-cut intervention. Both declare his
power: Egypt, the world's strongest power, was routed, and Jesus was "declared to be Son of God with power according to the
Spirit of holiness by resurrection from the dead" (Rom 1:4).
Both bring a deliverance from bondage; both events are decisive in the formation of a people of God.

The covenant community—the second component in
God's design—is of prime concern for Paul in Romans.[16] There
are now scholars who maintain that the apostle's chief reason
for writing the book was not to set out a doctrinal treatise but to
help the community at Rome understand God's intent to weld
out of Jew and Gentile a people for his name.[17]

Such a view of the book of Romans means that chapters
9–11, in which Paul discusses the relationship between Jew and
Gentile, are not an uneasy parenthesis in the book, but rather
lie at the heart of the book. In these chapters Paul argues that
there is not a distinction between Jew and Greek, for the same
Lord is open to all who call upon him (10:12) as the Old Testament also witnesses: "Every one who calls upon the name of the
Lord shall be saved" (Rom 10:13; Joel 2:32). Attention to the
Gentiles does not mean that God has rejected his people
(11:1ff). Admittedly there is the factor of Jewish unbelief, but
there is also a remnant. Thus the Gentiles are now in the fore-
ground; but beyond the "fullness of the Gentiles" Paul sees a
time when "all Israel will be saved"—a position which he documents from Isaiah 59:20 and 27:9 (Rom 11:26–27).

Throughout this discussion it is abundantly clear that both
Gentiles and Jews are in the purview of God's salvation. This

position is most concisely stated by drawing on Hosea which Paul quotes as follows, and which, let it be underscored, turns about the familiar covenant formula:

> Those who were not my people I will call "my people," and her who was not beloved I will call "my beloved." And in the very place where it was said to them, "You are not my people," they will be called "children of the living God" (Rom 9:25–26).

Of course, the theme of covenant community is touched on elsewhere in Romans. Paul's discourse on the Christian life stresses the gifts that each has for the benefit of the "body," namely the body of Christ's people (Rom 12:3ff). In that discussion Paul returns repeatedly to the concern for mutual interdependence and community (Rom 12:1ff). Injunctions such as "Welcome one another, therefore, as Christ has welcomed you, for the glory of God" (Rom 15:7) are significant because of Paul's view of the church. The final chapter with its list of names underscores the camaraderie and the family dimension that people of God feel for one another, and that is who they are—people of God. The key discourse on the covenant community, however, is centered in Romans 9–11, chapters which more than others link up with the Old Testament.

The third component of God's design is his intention for people to know him. As explicated earlier, according to the Bible, knowledge, while it includes information, is essentially experience-oriented. This theme of experience, even intimacy, is writ large in Romans. When Paul describes the righteousness of God, he does not do so for academic reasons alone. That revelation of the righteousness of God is revealed "through faith for faith" (1:17). One might say that the New Testament stress on "believing" is equivalent to "knowing" in the Old Testament. The objective righteousness of God, as described earlier, is related to the subjective righteousness. God's righteousness is demonstrated in the redemptive work of Christ in order that God might be "righteous and that he justifies the one who has faith in Jesus" (3:26). God's righteousness involves setting things right. The one who embraces Jesus (believes in him, "knows" him) is put right with respect to God. Such a person is righteous before God.

The theme of experience is in focus in chapters 5–8 but even more directly so in chapters 6 and 7. Having explained the way in which Jesus Christ was delivered up because of our transgressions and was raised for our justification, Paul explains the identification with Christ which is now the prerogative and privilege of a believer. "We have been united with him . . ." (Rom 6:5). The intimacy between a believer and his Lord surfaces in Romans 8. Those who are led by the Spirit of God are the sons of God (Rom 8:14). Because of the spirit of adoption, believers cry out "Abba! Father!" (8:15). Stress is repeatedly laid on the closeness of the relationship which exists between a believer and God, made possible by the Spirit of God. Indeed, Paul says of the believers that they are "in the Spirit" (8:9), and again, "Christ is in you" (Rom 8:10). In these statements there is expressed the meaning of the Hebrew "to know," namely "to be intimately involved." So close and intimate is the believer with Christ that Paul concludes by saying, "I am convinced that neither death, nor life . . . nor height, nor depth, nor anything else in all creation, will be able to separate us from the love of God in Christ Jesus our Lord" (8:38–39).

Finally, we ask, is there evidence of what might be called "land theology" in Romans? Since very little if anything at all is made of "land" in the New Testament, it appears at first sight that this aspect of the design is truncated or abrogated with the coming of Christ. The pervasiveness of "land" in its various Old Testament settings is astonishing. What of the New Testament? Walter Brueggemann in a monograph on the subject has gone as far as to say, "Land is a central, if not *the central theme* of biblical faith"[18]—biblical faith, not Old Testament faith. Has he overstated the case?

Before a hasty answer is given, it should be recalled that land in the Old Testament became a symbol for life. God's gift to his people was the abundant life in the land. In turn, he called on them to live according to a prescribed order.

It is not hard to demonstrate that these two facets of "land theology" are broadly displayed in Romans. The first eight chapters deal with the gift of a new kind of life. "The wages of sin is death, but the free gift of God is eternal life in Christ Jesus our Lord" (Rom 6:23). In Romans 8 Paul elaborates the kind of life possible for those who have embraced Jesus Christ and who walk after the Spirit. "To set the mind on the Spirit is life and peace" (Rom 8:6). A new quality of life is made possible in Jesus Christ and his gift of the Spirit. The gift aspect is indisputable. It is quite as though land in the Old Testament were a prelude in symbolic terms of a new age in which the gift, the promise, the blessings—in short, a quality of life enriched by the God-dimension—would be the possession of the believer.

One of the themes associated with land discussion in the Old Testament, apart from gift, is that of a people's lifestyle. Not infrequently one reads of instruction, the introduction to which is, "When you come into the land you shall . . ." These instructions deal with worship (Deut 12:1), with behavior towards Levites (Deut 12:19), with right behavior generally (Deut 12:28), even with foods (Deuteronomy 14), and with government (Deut 17:14). It is something of a curiosity that in Rom 12:1 – 15:7 Paul should be discussing the same subjects: "spiritual worship" (12:1), conduct towards one another involving charity and hospitality (12:10, 13), right behavior involving humility and tolerance (12:16–21), a relationship to civil government (chapter 13), and clean and unclean foods (14:13–23). This general correspondence between a section of Romans and sections of Deuteronomy does not necessarily argue for a self-conscious discussion in Romans patterned according to Deuteronomy, but it surely emphasizes that the gift of salvation entails righteous living, just as the gift of the land came together with requirements for obedience.

Essentially then, while land as such does not receive attention in Romans, the agenda raised by living in the land of promise is the agenda addressed in Romans.[19] The great act of God's faithfulness, his righteousness, is not to be divorced from faithfulness, yes, righteous living, on the part of his people. The

themes which are affiliated with "land" in a distinctive way in
the Old Testament are themes found again in the New Testament (Romans, for example), though not now linked immediately to the subject of "land."

It is necessary and helpful to distinguish the two meanings
of "land." Land is soil. For Israel the "land" is the territory of
Palestine. But land is also a symbol. It is on the wavelength of
symbol that the connection regarding land is best made between the Old and New Testaments.

In some Christian circles there is discussion of Israel's future possession of the land—land meaning the geographical
area of Palestine. This discussion often leads to the book of Romans. There is reason to believe, judging from Paul's discussion
of Israel in Romans 9–11, that the national history of Israel will
indeed be resumed by God in salvation history. Whether such a
position has credibility depends to some extent on whether the
church is viewed as a distinct "new" people of God, or whether
the church is seen as the anticipated outgrowth of ethnic Israel,
thus abrogating any further salvation significance for Israel.
This writer holds to the position that the church does not re-
place Israel. Even though the New Testament hope is on the
church, the promise to Israel, while transmitted in large measure to the church, is not for that reason exhausted but may quite
conceivably find fulfillment on a historical plane. Whatever the
conclusion of the relevance of land as *turf* for Israel, the corresponding blessing of being "in Christ" as one might physically
be "in the land" is one which opens larger horizons, when seen
against the Old Testament background of land as *symbol*.

Enough has been said to suggest that the book of Romans,
while not consciously written according to a table of contents
dictated by Exod 5:22 – 6:8, nevertheless reiterates the purpose
and design of God indicated there. From the standpoint of an
Old Testament theology, Tyndale was quite right: Romans was
written to be an introduction to the Old Testament. In broad
outline Romans is a commentary on God's design: deliverance
(chapters 1–5), experience of God (chapters 6–8), community

(chapters 9–11), and blessing (land), including lifestyle (chapters 12–15),

Romans with its stress on righteousness as well as Matthew with its focus on the kingdom of God are both books which carry forward the fourfold design identified from Exod 5:22 – 6:8. These two books are not organized mechanically around the fourfold purpose, but their central themes resonate with the themes familiar from the Old Testament. New overtones are found in the New Testament, to be sure, but the basic theme, as in a musical composition, gives coherence to both Testaments. It is reasonable to propose that divine design summarizes the New Testament, where its richness is revealed through Jesus Christ.

All four components of divine design—deliverance, community, knowledge (experience), and land (life, blessing)—receive a particular fulfillment to Christ. But the design has not yet come to full realization, for man's deliverance from sin's forces, while decisive through Christ, is not immediately total. The association in community with God's people, while wonderfully satisfying, is not without its negatives, even its pains. The knowledge of God we confess is partial, for we see through a glass darkly. Life abundant, of which land is a symbol, is available for the Christian, but is not his in perfection. In Jesus Christ, God's design through the ages is caught and concentrated, as if in a prism, in history; but beyond history is eternity. That design will be not only fully plain, then, but fully realized.

Appendix

A Place to Stand
Issues in Old Testament Theology

The investigation and exploration of the Christian faith takes many forms, one of which is biblical theology. Put simply, biblical theology, as the combination of words suggests, is a formalized statement about God (theology) derived from the Bible. Given human limitations, not to mention the large scope of the subject, any statement will have its shortcomings; yet the very idea of working toward such a statement is exhilarating and holds large promise. But first our elemental and incomplete definition of biblical theology must be clarified, and some issues about method examined.

1. Doing Biblical Theology: Setting the Markers

Biblical Theology as Overgrown Exegesis

Biblical theology is exegesis of the Bible at a macro level. At the micro level, one studies the Bible chapter by chapter, or pericope by pericope, or even verse by verse. In such explorations key terms are defined, traditions are investigated, and rhetorical techniques are identified. Attention is given to atmosphere, and certainly to the relationship that exists between the component parts of the passage. The exploration of a text unit concludes with a summative statement in which the essence and the significance of the passage are articulated: a good summary statement encapsulates the gist of the passage, "pulls it all together."

That which exegesis does for a single text, biblical theology seeks to do for the entire Bible. Biblical theology makes a summary statement of the entire Bible. Old Testament theology, therefore, has as its goal seeing the Old Testament "whole." The goal is to offer a summary statement of the Old Testament which will capture what is at the heart of the literature, and will in the restatement not skew or distort its foundational message. Somewhat simplistically put, Old Testament theology tries to answer the question, "What is the Old Testament all about?" To answer the question well, one must live with the Old Testament, give attention to its parts, and listen carefully to hear what it is that is being said. As it is important to the exegesis of a single text to look at the component parts, to analyze well, and to listen for the message, so too in Old Testament theology one examines the text blocks (now within large parameters), analyzes, though within a larger horizon, and listens well.

A biblical theology, then, will, like an exegesis, offer a restatement of the material.[1] An Old Testament theology will lay bare the theology of the Old Testament.[2] Biblical theologians are a special breed of theologians. They, and others too, differentiate between biblical theology and the closely related discipline of systematic theology.

Biblical Theology as Distinct from Systematic Theology

The discussion about the differences between the two disciplines, biblical theology and systematic theology, is more than three centuries old. Customarily, and perhaps too simplistically, the discussion takes as its point of departure the programmatic lecture by J. P. Gabler in 1787 in Germany.[3] Gabler, decidedly under the impulse of Enlightenment thinking, tried to free up the study of the Bible from the dogmatic system which, while necessary for the church's development, was then holding Bible study hostage. Investigation of the Bible had become, to overstate the case slightly, little more than documenting already formulated doctrinal positions; the biblical texts were used as proof-texts.

While Martin Luther and the Reformers generally had broken the hold of such thinking and championed the authority of the Bible as greater than the authority of dogmatic systems, the method of inductively studying the Bible had lapsed. Elaborate systems of doctrine, like heavy blankets, stifled open-ended Bible investigation. Among other things Gabler, 250 years after Luther, proposed that one determine what biblical writers thought about divine things, quite apart from the dictates of current doctrinal systems. According to Gabler, a rationalist, the positions of biblical writers would need further testing, largely at the bar of reason, to determine which positions were to be universalized as "pure truth." Critical for Gabler was the unfettered description of the biblical content, so that one might from that vantage point continue toward the universally applicable norms. After Gabler the notion became widespread that biblical theologians should hand over the results of their study to the systematic theologians, who would use the data to address the pressing issues of the day.

The distinctions between a biblical theology and a systematic theology have been charted elsewhere.[4] The intent here is to mention key differences with a view to profiling more sharply the specific task of biblical theology. First, biblical theology lays bare the theology of the Bible. It works within the covers of the Bible. Systematic theology, though with an eye trained to examine the Bible, takes its cue from philosophy and the issues inherent in religious faith. For example, systematic theologians establish the grounds on which given religious claims can be validated. Moreover, employing tools of philosophical analysis, they reach into the issues of the day, such as abortion, to inquire how a religious faith might address these.

Secondly, while both biblical theology and systematic theology resort to some kind of systematization in offering their conclusions, each proceeds along a different route. Biblical theology uses categories drawn from the Bible. So, for example, if the Old Testament in telling its story relies heavily on the category of "land," then biblical theology in shaping its statement will highlight the rubric of land. Biblical theology does not have primarily an interest in derived abstractions or attributes. Systematic theology (as the designation is used here and generally in the academic world) is more self-consciously allied to philosophy. So, for example, Paul Tillich as a systematic theologian sees his task as bridge-building between philosophy and theology, and proposes "correlation" as a possible approach. Process theologians, such as John Cobb, are clearly beholden to process philosophers, pace-setting among whom is Alfred North Whitehead. By contrast, biblical theologian Walther Eichrodt adopts a biblical category "covenant" around which to set forth the biblical faith.

Another graphic, though simple example of the difference between biblical and systematic theology arises from an exercise I put to students: list the words descriptive of God. Seminary students around the world, I have found, can be expected to furnish a list that includes terms like: loving, just, merciful, omnipotent, omniscient, omnipresent. Beneath this answer lies an Aristotelian philosophy which held that definitions require the enumeration of characteristics (e.g., a table is wooden and brown). But descriptors of "table" need not be characteristics; they could describe role (e.g., a table is a raised platform on which to place objects). The descriptors of God, following this kind of category, would include Creator, Redeemer, Father, King, Good Shepherd. The category of role and function is more closely biblical, I would argue, than is a set of abstract characteristics (cf. Isa 33:22). To be sure no analysis is without some philosophical grid, but the example delineates a fundamental distinction between biblical and systematic theology.

Biblical and systematic theology each perform an important service for the faith community, but in different ways. Just as a medical doctor and a political health lobbyist are each in the health profession but with different roles, so the two types of theologians, biblical and systematic, have traditionally assumed quite different roles. However, rather than demarcate the two disciplines so sharply, one might better see them on a continuum.[5] The line of this continuum stretches from the biblical text to the current situation. On this continuum the biblical theologian stands closest to the text, although the meaning he or she discerns there is not remote and archival but in some sense normative for the current contemporary situation. It is because of this conviction that biblical theology bears upon the faith and life of the church that sections entitled "Theological Reflections" are included in this book. The systematic theologian, on the same continuum, stands nearer to the current situation. He or she is also interested in the biblical text but gives greater energy to analysis of the immediate agenda or contemporary problem in society. The specializations of each, while distinct, are also complementary.

2. Tasting the Fruit
The Values of a Biblical Theology

The effort to formulate a biblical theology, though demanding, is rewarding. Its benefits consist both of aiding comprehension of the faith, and of shaping the practical outworking of that faith.

A Sense of the Whole

Biblical theology's synoptic view offers orientation. Not uncommonly people—and not newcomers to the faith only—approach the Bible only to throw up their hands in frustration. Without a table of contents that indicates subject matter, and without a clearly stated thesis (as may be expected in academic books generally), the Bible is a foreboding mass of material. The story of God creating a world as well as a people has its own dynamic and fascination. But the story from Abram to Ezra is supplemented with the poetry of Job and Psalms, as well as with prophetic oracles. The timeline for the whole can be sorted out, given a little diligence and some help from experts. But that leaves unanswered the question, What is the Old Testament essentially saying? Assuming a conceptual unity, what is one to make of such a diverse collection of stories, psalms, and oracles? The questioner asks for more than the meaning of each literary segment individually. Fortunately, biblical theology provides a sense of meaning for the whole. It offers itself as a guide which, while noting the details, keeps providing the "big picture." So, for example, while examining God's promise or God's laws, or the experience of Job, or the strident call by Amos for justice in economics and politics, the guide will show how components fit as pieces to the whole. The guide will forever be stressing the connections of the parts, and/or the direction in which a theme is moving.

A Help in Interpreting Smaller Text Units

By highlighting the Bible's major emphases and keeping visible the large markers, biblical theology serves another function. It assists the interpreter in the exegesis of the smaller text units, the single passages. It is inductively that one moves from the exegesis of the single passage to an umbrella formulation. But the direction of flow is also opposite. One draws from the umbrella statement a sense of the meaning of the whole, which then aids in capturing the meaning of the smaller constitutive parts. As in music where the melodic theme helps in appreciating a single musical bar, so the sense of the whole which biblical theology gives helps interpret a single text. A symbiotic relationship exists between exegesis and biblical theology. Exegesis is important in framing a biblical theology; biblical theology, in turn, can help in the understanding and situating of a single text.

The exodus story, for example, can be treated on its own as a model of political liberation. While the story is clearly set up in a political arena—a point that must be heard—the larger story of God and God's people shows how the event is critical in what it tells about God and the paradigm for redemption. In the "big picture," the Passover story is the theological cradle for the institution of our Lord's last supper and the ordinance of communion. A grip on the overall message of the Old Testament, to give another example, will aid in interpreting, say, Mic 6:1–8. The call to do justice and to walk humbly with God is not an arbitrary piece of moral obligation, but stands in the context of covenant, a key feature of which is the initiative and past action of God, the covenant partner. Thus biblical theology, in providing a scheme of the whole, helps ensure greater accuracy in the interpretation of a single text.

A Bridge to the New Testament

One of the driving forces for Christians to formulate an Old Testament theology is the need to relate the Old Testament to the New Testament. An Old Testament theology can become a set of columns for the bridge that will connect the two testaments theologically. It is only partially satisfying to connect the two testaments historically by pairing quotations in the New with the Old, or by identifying similar motifs. There is something at a fundamental level that holds the two testaments together in an inextricable linkage. Even to say that the Someone is God, who is presented in both testaments, is still to leave unanswered the way in which the theological continuity is to be articulated and explicated.

One logical first step is to prepare a summary statement of the Old Testament. The statement should initially be apart from any coloring imported from the New. A second step would be to formulate a theological statement for the New. The two statements would almost certainly, assuming the unity of the Bible, point to a common denominator. Walther Eichrodt, a pioneer in the renaissance period of biblical theology in the 1930s, contended that an Old Testament theology must at some stage connect with the New Testament. His own formulation of covenant as the centerpiece for the Old Testament helped admirably as a way of setting columns in place for the bridge to span the two testaments. Walter Kaiser Jr., in highlighting the promises of the Old Testament which looked for fulfillment in the New, was similarly interested in spanning the two testaments.[6]

A Barometer for the Church's Life

The discussion so far about the benefits of an Old Testament theology has been about intellectual comprehension. One more benefit—perhaps the most important—is that biblical theology helps the church live out its life as a faithful church. biblical theology is not only an intellectual exercise for the curious; it is important for the church. Biblical theology, it has been said, is the health department of the church. What a clinic in administering periodic checkups is to a patient, biblical theology is to the church. Biblical theology provides a monitoring service. Theological checkups enable early diagnosis of possibly troublesome developments. Correctives can then be put in place. From this vantage point one need not be so dismayed if over the past 60 years a range of syntheses in biblical theology have been espoused. Together they put before the church the question whether or not it, the church, is on course. That is, by confronting the church with a summary statement of Scripture, biblical theology poses for the church the question whether or not the church still adheres to its founding document and functions in keeping with it. To change the figure of speech to the world of higher education, biblical theology is a standard by which the church maintains its accreditation.

3. Navigating the Bumps
Hurdles in Doing Biblical Theology

In road building it is good to know where one is going and why, but in the process obstructions such as trees and hills are likely to be encountered. So also in working at a biblical theology, hurdles are inevitable. Only a few of them will be mentioned here. Such a listing will help explain how theologians have made different decisions on methodology and why, therefore, a variety of worthwhile synthesis statements exist. The debate and exploration of these issues can be pursued in detail in other sources.[7]

How Do History and Theology Relate?

One major decision involves the notion of history, which is so large a factor in biblical faith, but which, from the vantage point of theology, becomes hard to negotiate. Theologians have taken differing positions.[8] The difficulty consists in moving from history to theology. How do the events described in Israel's story yield valid theological insights? That is, how can we from God's actions in a particular situation, even from such a well-known event as the exodus of Israel from Egypt, draw conclusions of a theological nature? Are such conclusions primarily about God's power, about political liberation, or about ecology? And of the three, is one more valid than the others? If so, why? Sometimes, as in the event of the exodus, the Bible itself points the way toward a theological reading (cf. the song celebrating Yahweh's victory, Exodus 15). At other times, as in David's succession narrative (2 Samuel 9–20; 1 Kings 1–2), the move to theology is more hazardous.

A vexing question has been to determine which history should serve as the grid for an Old Testament theology. The story line of the Bible is well known and is punctuated by such events and eras as creation, exodus, monarchy, exile, and restoration. The question is, is this story line to be adopted uncritically? The traditional view is that the Pentateuch, written by Moses, records events as they transpired. The critical view depends on source analysis, which ascribed the Pentateuch to traditions (formerly considered authors) designated J(ahwistic) (ninth century); E(lohistic) (eighth century); D(euteronomistic) (seventh century); and P(riestly) (sixth century). Driven by methods arising out of the Enlightenment era, scholars argued which events, or which aspects of their description, were authentic. Elaborate proposals, for example, were given about the way Israel came to possess the land of Palestine. The story of Joshua's conquest was not totally discounted as one scenario. Other explanations, however, were championed as more likely: migration, infiltration, internal revolution. To adopt the critical view of these and other events affects the way a theology will be formulated. To take another example: the development of the covenant idea will be portrayed differently if parts of Leviticus and Numbers are held to derive from a time considerably after Jeremiah. The theology outlined in this book does not adhere to the critical reconstruction of Israel's history, but following the example of G. von Rad adheres to the "confessed" rather than the reconstructed history.[9]

A Center for Biblical Theology?

Another vexing question for persons seeking a synthesis of the biblical material has been whether in "seeing the Old Testament whole" one should look for a theological center.[10] The reasons for organizing a theological summary around a single theme are several. The large amount of material and its disparate nature—genealogy, poetry, narrative, prophetic oracle—is vastly simplified if a theological center can be discerned. By means of a central concept one gets a handle on material that otherwise seems quite unmanageable. A second reason for organizing a theological statement around a center is that to do so is intellectually satisfying. To be able to classify material and, despite some artificiality, to do so around a governing theme, aids in the process of understanding. A third reason for reaching for a center is that a center offers some clarity as to how other Bible themes are to be related, and even how problematic texts are to be interpreted. If one of the goals of a biblical theology is to gain an appreciation and an understanding of the relative importance of the multiple themes, then the identification of a center greatly facilitates that goal. If the theme of covenant, as W. Eichrodt proposed, is front and center in Old Testament material, then the task of situating themes such as "sacrifice" and "kinship" is simplified. One goes a long way in explaining these by showing whether and to what extent they tie in to the theme of covenant. A fourth reason for readiness to identify a theological center is that by means of a center it becomes easier to connect the Old Testament to the New Testament. Although it has been debated whether the task of connecting the two testaments belongs to Old Testament theology, it is obvious that Christians cannot escape the challenge. That challenge is made easier, it is here claimed, if a center, in the form of an event or a concept, can be identified from the Old Testament.

Criticism about establishing a center for Old Testament theology has been vigorous. For one, ever since the renaissance and the impetus given to Old Testament theology in the 1930s, a variety of centers have been proposed. Among these proposals are the sovereignty of God, covenant, promise.[11] The range of proposals puts into some question the notion that the Old Testament has an identifiable center. Critics have charged that finding a center is a subjective preoccupation. Moreover, if the intent is to connect the Old Testament with the New Testament, then an extraneous agenda is introduced which may distort the research which should be aimed at laying bare the theology of the Old Testament "as is." Could it be, it is asked, that the desire to delineate a center is an urge peculiar to minds given to linear thinking, and that Hebrew thinking ill accords with such a mind-set?

Critics of a single center have made counterproposals. G. von Rad stressed the importance of a range of traditions (e.g., exodus, wilderness, royalty, Zion) which, like multicolored ribbons in the wind, alternately move into sight and then receded. Still others, like John McKenzie or William Dyrness, were content merely to list and elaborate biblical themes. Others, such as C. Westermann, S. Terrien, and W. Brueggemann, proceeded dialectically: there are opposites which, when placed adjacent to each other, function as a magnet, each pole with its sphere of influence setting up a dynamic or tension. So, for example, to follow S. Terrien, one can identify an aesthetic pole, as represented in the wisdom literature, but alongside it, somewhat in tension with it, is the ethical pole and its covenant sphere of influence.[12] Without question the penchant for finding a center needs to be tamed. What is advocated here as a way of organizing Old Testament theology is a modified notion of center, one which does not dismiss the notion, but conceptualizes "center" more in the nature of a nucleus of components. The center, so defined, it is here maintained, is captured in the expression, "God's design."

What Method(s) Should Be Employed?

To the list of issues—how to see the connection between history and faith; whether a center for the Old Testament can be justified—one can add another: by what method does one arrive at a biblical theology?[13] The options in the past six decades have included the following: description (G. E. Wright), confessional approach (G. von Rad), and the canonical approach (B. S. Childs). Without examining the options, a case can be made (though the procedure has been disputed) for identifying a biblical text unit as a clue to the organization of a biblical theology. Singling out a text which offers a grid for an Old Testament theology is the approach taken in this book. While such an approach is clearly not the only way of outlining a biblical theology, it is justified on several grounds.

Working from a biblical text block as a method of doing biblical theology is a legitimate procedure on the elemental ground that it is not unreasonable to expect that, as in a sermon or a book, the message, even though elaborated and complex, will be somewhere stated in a nutshell. G. von Rad isolated an early credo (Deut 26:5–10) as encapsulating Israel's faith.[14] Clearly a reason for a nutshell statement is clarity and reinforcement. With an array of books in the Old Testament canon, whose authors span centuries, one might well be wary of the bold move to find a biblical text which is programmatic. Still, the possibility should not be rejected out of hand. A second consideration is that scholars have in fact seized on less than a pericope, *viz.* a formula (e.g., Israel is Yahweh's people and Yahweh is Israel's God) as summarizing the foundational conviction of a book.[15] A legitimate objection to such a practice is that it is subjective. One finds what one is looking for. Or, an agenda in the theologian's life is imposed on a book. But control measures exist. The literary structure of an individual book, for example, serves as a control. For example, if William Holladay is correct that Jer 2:1–3 is a seed oracle for at least a portion of the book, then Jer 2:1–3 must be clearly factored into a theology of the book.[16]

Moreover, despite the hazards that attach to selecting a biblical text as theologically seminal, the hazard is not unlike procedures of others who—sometimes with fewer objective controls—parade "covenant" or "promise" as the organizing principle for an Old Testament theology. And even if less than ideal as a procedure, casting Old Testament material on a theological canvas with a biblical text block as a grid, as this book does, can be tested on its own merits. Does a particular text, if taken as a window into the entire Old Testament, assist in organizing the theology of the whole? This book answers that question in the affirmative. At the minimum, then, such a procedure may serve as a heuristic device. That is, the anchoring of a biblical theology in a particular text block may bring to light legitimate nuances that have otherwise been ignored or minimized.

The pages of this book unpack a biblical theology of the Old Testament which is governed by a textual block, namely Exod 5:22 – 6:8. Reasons for holding *this* particular text as pivotal are given in chapter one.[17] Would another text passage be as adequate? Perhaps only in testing other proposals could that answer be given. If Exod 5:22 – 6:8 is as key as argued here, then echoes of it could be expected elsewhere, which is indeed the case.

The proposals to employ various methods in "doing a biblical theology" lend adventure (and admittedly some confusion) to the task. As in any worthwhile endeavor, obstacles temporarily impede progress. But the rewards that emerge from a synthesis are so substantial that the efforts to surmount the obstacles can be joyfully embraced.

Notes

Chapter 1 A Pivotal Text about Yahweh and His Purpose

1. A brief discussion of methodological issues is found in the Appendix. An illustration of major proposals is found in Ben C. Ollenburger, Elmer A. Martens, and Gerhard Hasel, eds., *The Flowering of Old Testament Theology: A Reader in Twentieth Century Old Testament Theology, 1930–1990* (Winona Lake: Eisenbrauns, 1992). Cf. Gerhard F. Hasel, *Old Testament Theology: Basic Issues in the Current Debate*, 4th ed. (Grand Rapids: Eerdmans, 1991). Brief discussions of issues are given in Ralph Smith, *Old Testament Theology: Its History, Method, and Message* (Nashville: Broadman & Holman Publishers, 1993), pp. 72–93; Robert L. Hubbard Jr., Robert K. Johnston, and Robert P. Meye, *Studies in Old Testament Theology* (Dallas: Word Books, 1992), pp. 31–75; John Sailhamer, *Introduction to Old Testament Theology: A Canonical Approach* (Grand Rapids: Zondervan, 1995). Three recent books of collected essays relevant to methodological issues are: R. Knierim. *The Task of Old Testament Theology: Substance, Method, and Cases.* (Grand Rapids/Cambridge: Eerdmans, 1995); S. J. Kraftchick, C. D. Myers Jr., and B. C. Ollenburger eds., *Biblical Theology: Problems and Perspectives. In Honor of J. Christiaan Beker.* (Nashville: Abingdon, 1995); and H. T. C. Sun, Keith L. Eades, J. M. Robinson and G. I. Moller eds., *Problems in Biblical Theology: Essays in honor of Rolf Knierim.* (Grand Rapids: Eerdmans, 1997). An annotated bibliography on the various dimensions of Old Testament Theology is found in my *Old Testament Theology.* IBR Bibliographies #13 (Grand Rapids: Baker, 1997).

2. E.g., Walther Eichrodt, *Theology of the Old Testament*, 2 vols. (Philadelphia: Westminster Press; London: SCM Press, 1961, 1967). An author who eschews a single concept as the center is Gerhard von Rad, *Old Testament Theology*, 2 vols. (New York: Harper & Row; London: Oliver & Boyd, 1962, 1967).

3. E.g., On sovereignty, E. Jacob, *Theology of the Old Testament* (New York: Harper & Row; London: Hodder & Stoughton, 1958);

on communion, Th. C. Vriezen, *An Outline of Old Testament Theology*
(Newton, Mass.: Charles T. Branford; Oxford, Blackwell, 1956,
1970); on promise, Walter C. Kaiser Jr., *Toward an Old Testament
Theology* (Grand Rapids: Zondervan, 1978, 1991); on presence, S.
Terrien, *The Elusive Presence: toward a New Biblical Theology* (San
Francisco: Harper & Row, 1978); on election, H. D. Preuss, *Old
Testament Theology.* 2 vols., translated by L. G. Perdue (Louisville:
Westminster/John Knox, 1995). Cf. Brevard S. Childs, *Biblical
Theology of the Old and New Testaments: Theological Reflection on the
Christian Bible* (Minneapolis: Fortress Press, 1993); J. J. Niehaus, *God
at Sinai: Covenant and Theophany*, SOTBT (Grand Rapids:
Zondervan, 1995); and W. Brueggemann, *Theology of the Old
Testament: Testimony, Dispute, Advocacy* (Minneapolis: Fortress, 1997).

4. James Barr, "Trends and Prospect in Biblical Theology,"
Journal of Theological Studies 25:2 (1974), p. 272. Cf. *The Flowering of
Old Testament Theology*, pp. 43–57.

5. See E. A. Martens, "Tackling Old Testament Theology: Exod
5:22 – 6:8," *Journal of the Evangelical Theological Society* 20 (June
1977), pp. 123–132.

6. Critical scholarship assigns conjectured sources E and P to
the first chapters of Exodus, partly as a way of accounting for the
statement that the name Yahweh was not previously known when in
fact it is found frequently in Genesis. Problems with the
documentary theory are noted in R. W. L. Moberly, *The Old
Testament of the Old Testament* (Minneapolis: Fortress/Augsburg, 1992);
Gerhard Maier, *The End of the Historical Critical Method* (St. Louis:
Concordia, 1977); R. K. Harrison, *Introduction to the Old Testament*
(Grand Rapids: Eerdmans, 1969 / Tyndale Press, 1970). As for the
name Yahweh, said in Exod 6:2 not to be known before, the position
adopted here is that while the name was familiar to the patriarchs (it
occurs more than a hundred times in Genesis) its significance was
only now disclosed. For a different explanation built around
historical and theological considerations, cf. Moberly.

7. Tryggve N. D. Mettinger, *In Search of God: the Meaning and
Message of the Everlasting Names*, trans. F. H. Cryer (Philadelphia:
Fortress Press, 1987), pp. 14–49; R. W. L. Moberly, *Old Testament of
the Old Testament*, pp. 5–35; several essays in R. L. Hubbard et al.,
eds., *Studies in Old Testament Theology*, deal with images of Yahweh.

8. U. Cassuto, *A Commentary on the Book of Exodus* (Jerusalem: Magnes Press, ET 1967), p. 77.

9. See G. von Rad, *Old Testament Theology*, 1, p. 182.

10. W. Eichrodt, *Theology of the Old Testament*, 1, p. 191.

11. Brevard S. Childs, *The Book of Exodus* (Philadelphia: Westminster Press, 1974), p. 115 (=*Exodus*, SCM Press, 1974).

12. U. Cassuto, *Exodus*, p. 76.

13. B. S. Childs, *Exodus*, p. 119. Italics mine.

14. It is of interest, though hardly of theological consequence, that the reason given for the use of four cups of wine at the Jewish Passover is the fourfold promise of Exod 6:2–8. *Encyclopedia Judaica*, 13 (Jerusalem: MacMillan, 1971), p. 167.

15. James H. Cone: "The Exodus was the decisive event in Israel's history, because through it Yahweh revealed himself as the Savior of the oppressed people." "Biblical Revelation and Social Existence," *Interpretation* 28 (1974), p. 423; cf. David Daube, *The Exodus Pattern in the Bible* (London: Faber and Faber, 1963).

16. C. Westermann, *Blessing in the Bible and the Life of the Church* (Philadelphia: Fortress Press, 1978).

17. This schema obviously requires a judgment on the chronology of the sources, the books of the Old Testament. From a critical viewpoint the problems of dating are many. Still, attention to the general canonical shape of the Old Testament can represent a starting point, especially because it can be argued that the final shape of the canon and the historical claims of the books represent a valid theological position.

Chapter 2 Earlier Anticipation of God's Purpose

1. *Genesis: A Commentary* (Philadelphia: Westminster Press, 1961; London: SCM Press, 1979). C. Westermann comments: "But for what or for whom can creation be good? One cannot say for man, because man is a part of it. Nor can man say: for God, because God has created his work for everyone or for something. It can only mean that creation is good for that for which God intends it." *Creation* (Philadelphia: Fortress Press; London: SPCK, 1974), p. 61.

2. Walter C. Kaiser Jr., *Toward an Old Testament Theology* (Grand Rapids: Zondervan, 1978), p. 33.

3. The creation accounts are offered as history—a story of incidents connected in a cause and effect manner. The creation account is history in the sense that God at a given time created the world and man. Yet, whether we are to believe that creation was accomplished in a week of six 24-hour days is debatable; while certainly possible, the seven-day theory is not likely for several reasons. The first chapter is semi-poetic in form, and poetry allows for symbolism. The expression "and it was evening and it was morning" is like a refrain which is appropriate in poetry. This refrain is perhaps best regarded as a literary divider between the mosaics which give in turn the broad brush painting of the major elements of the world. There are, after all, other literary devices apart from historiography for telling a story; cf. Bernard Ramm, *The Christian View of Science and Scripture* (Grand Rapids, Michigan: Eerdmans, 1954; Exeter: Paternoster Press, 1964), p. 218ff. Cf. Henri Blocher, *In the Beginning* (Downers Grove, Ill./Leicester: Inter-Varsity Press, 1984), pp. 39–59; Gordon Wenham, *Genesis 1–15*, Word Biblical Commentary, vol. 1 (Waco, Tex.: Word Books, 1987), pp. 19, 39–40. Cf. John Sailhamer, *Genesis Unbound (Portland: Questar, 1996).*

4. See Walter Brueggemann, *Living Toward a Vision: Biblical Reflections on Shalom* (Pilgrim, NY: Shalom Resource Series, 1976); Perry B. Yoder and W. M. Swartley, eds., *The Meaning of Peace* (Louisville, KY: Westminster/John Knox, 1992).

5. The OT condemns all kinds of cross-breeding (Deut 7:3) as well as copulation with animals (Lev 20:16). The "sons of God" have been interpreted as angelic or royal personages, or, less likely, Sethites. See commentaries.

6. See C. Westermann, "Types of Narrative in Genesis," *Forschungen am Alten Testament*, 1964, p.53.

7. The general outline of this chart is from C. Westermann, "Types of Narrative in Genesis," p. 53.

8. The historicity of the patriarchs has been challenged, e.g., J. Van Seters, *Abraham in History and Tradition* (New Haven and London: Yale University Press, 1975), and defended, e.g., A. R. Millard and D. J. Wiseman, eds., *Essays on the Patriarchal Narratives* (Leicester: Inter-Varsity Press, 1980). Cf. William LaSor, D. A. Hubbard, and F. William Bush, *Old Testament Survey: The Message,*

Form, and Background of the Old Testament (Grand Rapids: Eerdmans, 1982), pp. 98–116.

9 Cf. Klaus Koch, *The Growth of the Biblical Tradition* (New York: Scribner; London: A & C. Black, 1969), pp. 111ff; and D. J. A. Clines, "What Does Eve Do to Help?" JSOTSup 94 (Sheffield: JSOT Press, 1990), pp. 67–84.

10. The four themes listed here should be compared with the three theme elements—posterity, relationship, land—noted in D. J. A. Clines, *The Themes of the Pentateuch,* JSOTSup 10 (Sheffield: JSOT, 1978).

Chapter 3 God's Design: Salvation

1. The complementary aspects of salvation, deliverance, and blessing are helpfully differentiated in C. Westermann, *Blessing in the Bible and in the Life of the Church* (Philadelphia: Fortress Press, 1979). My debt to him is obvious.

2. Brevard S. Childs, *The Book of Exodus* (Philadelphia: Westminster Press, 1979), pp. 240–253 (= *Exodus*, SCM Press, 1974). F. M. Cross, "Song of the Sea and Canaanite Myth (Exodus 15)," *Journal for Theology and the Church*, 5, 1968, pp. 1–25.

3. See Millard Lind, *Yahweh Is a Warrior* (Scottdale, Pa.: Herald Press, 1980); Peter C. Craigie, *The Problem of War in the Old Testament* (Grand Rapids: Eerdmans, 1978). Cf. also T. Longman III and D. G. Reid, *God Is a Warrior* (Grand Rapids: Zondervan, 1995).

4. C. B. Labuschagne, *The Incomparability of Yahweh in the Old Testament* (Leiden: E. J. Brill, 1966), p. 136. B. Albrektson has shown that pagan deities were also thought to act in history. *History and the Gods* (Lund: Gleerup, 1967).

5. Gerhard von Rad, *Holy War in Ancient Israel*, trans. M. J. Dawn (Grand Rapids: Eerdmans, 1991). See especially the Introduction by B. C. Ollenburger.

6. Cf. expositions on sacrifice in G. J. Wenham, *Leviticus*, NICOT (Grand Rapids: Eerdmans, 1979); John Hartley, *Leviticus*, Word Biblical Commentary (Dallas: Word Books, 1992).

7. Rolf Knierim, *Hauptbegriffe für Sünde im Alten Testament* (Gütersloh: Gütersloher Verlagshaus G. Mohn, 1965).

8. Now described as "purification" and "reparation" offerings; cf. Hartley *Leviticus*.

9. F. Brown, S. R. Driver, C. A. Briggs, *A Hebrew and English Lexicon of the Old Testament* (Oxford: Clarendon Press, 1907), p. 498.

10. The range of biblical images is described in John Driver, *Understanding the Atonement for the Mission of the Church* (Scottdale, Pa.: Herald Press, 1986).

11. Jose P. Miranda, *Marx and the Bible* (Maryknoll, NY: Orbis Books, 1974; London: SCM, 1977), pp. 78–81.

12. A helpful bibliography is found in M. Daniel Carrol R., "God and His People in the Nations' History: A Contextual Reading of Amos 1–2." *Tyndale Bulletin* 47.1 (1996) pp. 39-70.

13. J. H. Yoder, "Probing the Meaning of Liberation," *Sojourners* 5 (September 1976), p. 28.

14. For a discussion of war from a Christian pacifist approach see Waldemar Janzen, "War in the Old Testament," *Mennonite Quarterly Review* 46 (April 1972), pp. 155–166; John E. Toews and G. Nickel (eds.), The Power of the Lamb (Winnipeg: Kindred Press, 1986); and Millard Lind, *Yahweh Is a Warrior* (Scottdale, Pa.: Herald Press, 1980).

15. For a treatment of atonement in the image of conflict see Gustav Aulén, *Christus Victor* (New York: Macmillan, 1966; London: SPCK, 1970).

Chapter 4 God's Design: The Covenant Community

1. The most comprehensive and classical development of the covenant as the center of the Old Testament is Walther Eichrodt, *Theology of the Old Testament*, 2 vols. (Philadelphia: Westminster Press; London: SCM Press, 1961, 1967). See also J. Barton Payne, *The Theology of the Older Testament* (Grand Rapids: Zondervan, 1962); T. E. McComiskey, *The Covenants of Promise: A Theology of the Old Testament Covenants* (Grand Rapids: Baker, 1985); Paul Hanson, *The People Called: The Growth of Community in the Bible* (San Francisco: Harper & Row, 1986). Cf. J. J. Niehaus, *God at Sinai: Covenant and Theophany* (Grand Rapids: Zondervan, 1995) and H. D. Preuss, *Old Testament Theology*, 2 vols. (Louisville: Westminster/John Knox, 1995).

2. See H. W. Robinson, *Corporate Personality in Ancient Israel* (Philadelphia: Fortress Press, 1964). J. W. Rogerson criticizes Robinson for "a theory of Hebrew mentality" which is based on "untenable anthropological assumptions." Some of Robinson's

claims need modification; however Rogerson agrees that parts of the Old Testament appear to imply what might be called a "corporate personality." *Anthropology and the Old Testament* (Atlanta: John Knox; Oxford: Blackwell, 1978), pp. 55–58.

3. J. R. Porter, while not ruling out the concept of "corporate personality" elsewhere, concludes that in the legal aspects, as in Achan's sin, "corporate personality" was not the dominant functioning concept. "The legal aspects of the concept of 'Corporate Personality' in the Old Testament," *Vetus Testamentum* 15 (1965), pp. 361–380.

4. For a succinct discussion see Gordon J. McConville's article, "*bᵉrît*" *New International Dictionary of Theology and Exegesis*, I:747–55.

5. G. A. Mendenhall and G. A. Herion, "Covenant," in *Anchor Bible Dictionary*, ed. D. N. Freedman (New York: Doubleday, 1992), I:1170–1202. Cf. E. W. Nicholson, whose assessment on treaties is negative. *God and His People: Covenant Theology in the Old Testament* (Oxford: Clarendon Press, 1986), pp. 56–82.

6. The treaty from Ugarit is identified as RS 17,340.

7. J. A. Thompson, *The Ancient Near Eastern Treaties and the Old Testament* (London: Tyndale Press, 1964), p. 17.

8. Ibid.

9. There is not full agreement that Exodus 20 or Joshua 24 or Deuteronomy as here outlined are all formulated according to the treaty pattern. Even where this comparison is allowed, there are slight differences as to which statements are counterparts of the treaty elements. For good treatments see J. A. Thompson, *The Ancient Near Eastern Treaties and the Old Testament* (London: Tyndale Press, 1964); or J. Barton Payne, ed., *New Perspectives on the Old Testament* (Waco, Texas: Word, 1970); or Delbert R. Hillers, *Covenant: The History of a Biblical Idea*. Larry R. Helyer notes similarities and differences between the suzerainty treaties and the Sinai covenant in his *Yesterday, Today and Forever. The Continuing Relevance of the Old Testament* (Salem, Wisconsin: Sheffield Publishing Company, 1996), pp. 149–160.

10. See Jay G. Williams, *Ten Words of Freedom: An Introduction to the Faith of Israel* (Philadelphia: Fortress Press, 1971). Cf. D. L. Christensen. *Deuteronomy 1–11*, Word Biblical Commentary (Dallas: Word, 1991), pp. 105–129.

11. Thompson exemplifies the treaty pattern as applied in Joshua 24 as follows: preamble 2a; historical introduction 2b–13; general stipulations 14; specific stipulations 25; oath 16, 21, 24; witnesses 22, 27.

12. See M. G. Kline, *The Treaty of the Great King* (Grand Rapids: Eerdmans, 1963).

13. "Mekilta Exodus." C. G. Montefiore and H. Loewe, eds., *A Rabbinic Anthology* (New York: Schocken Books, 1974; London: Macmillan, 1938), p. 296.

14. The argument for this assertion, drawing on both Old Testament and New Testament, is made by E. A. Martens, "Embracing the Law: A Biblical Theological Perspective," *Bulletin for Biblical Research* 2 (1992), pp. 1–28.

Chapter 5 God's Design: Knowledge of God

1. Martin Buber, *I and Thou* (New York: Charles Scribner's Sons, 1970; London: T.&T. Clark, 1971). See commentaries, e.g., V. P. Hamilton, *The Book of Genesis: chapters 1–17*, NICOT (Grand Rapids: Eerdmans, 1990), pp. 131–141.

2. The historical nature of these reports and the material in Genesis generally, including the patriarchal stories, has been debated. Presuppositions enter, here as elsewhere, into both the investigation and the formulation of conclusions. There are problems both with the documentary source theory and with recent variations of it, as well as with the proposal that Moses is the author of Genesis. The existence of short histories written on clay tables as sources for Moses is a possibility. The expression "these are the generations" which occurs eleven times in the book of Genesis (2:4; 5:1; 6:9; 10:1; 11:10, 27; 25:12, 19; 37:2; 39:19) is a conventional way of concluding (some say beginning) an account on a tablet, and names indicate either the writer or the owner of the materials. If written tablets were not circulating widely, oral tradition may well have been. For a discussion of the problem see R. K. Harrison, *Introduction to the Old Testament* (Grand Rapids: Eerdmans, 1969; London: Tyndale, 1970), pp. 543–551. A fresh solution is in R. W. L. Moberly, *The Old Testament of the Old Testament* (Fortress, 1992).

3. For a comparison of the Babylonian story with the Genesis creation account see Alexander Heidel, *The Babylonian Genesis: the story of the creation* (Chicago: University of Chicago Press, 1951).

4. G. Ernest Wright, *God who Acts: Biblical Theology as Recital* (London: SCM Press, 1958).

5. Quoted in Brevard S. Childs, *The Book of Exodus* (Philadelphia: Westminster, 1974), p. 547 (= *Exodus*, London: SCM Press, 1974).

6. J. Barton Payne, *The Theology of the Older Testament* (Grand Rapids: Zondervan, 1962), p. 362.

7. I agree with Robert Traina on typology: "The best policy to follow . . . is to limit the exposition of Old Testament symbols to those which are explained within the Scriptures themselves." *Methodical Bible Study: A New Approach to Hermeneutics* (copyright 1952 by the author at Asbury Theological Seminary, Wilmore, Kentucky), p. 176.

8. John Gammie, *Holiness in Israel* (Minneapolis: Fortress, 1989).

Chapter 6 God's Design: Land

1. The writer acknowledges his debt to Professor W. H. Brownlee under whose direction he completed a dissertation on the subject of land: *Motivations for the Promise of Israel's Restoration to the Land in Jeremiah and Ezekiel* (unpublished dissertation, Claremont, California, Claremont Graduate School, 1972). Brownlee's unpublished essays, such as "the Theological Significance of the Land of Israel—A Key to Biblical Theology," have been stimulating and helpful. Excellent observations have been made by Christopher J. H. Wright. Cf. his article on "land" with bibliography in NIDOTTE 1:519–24

2. W. D. Davies, *The Gospel and the Land* (Berkeley: University of California Press, 1974), p. 6.

3. The passage, Deut 26:1–11, according to Gerhard von Rad, contains the "little credo," which for him is illustrative of the way in which a promise, and history in general, were conveyed from generation to generation. *Old Testament Theology*, 1 (New York: Harper & Row; London: Oliver & Boyd, 1962), pp. 122ff.

4. Quoted in W. Zimmerli, "Promise and Fulfillment," in C. Westermann, *Essays on Old Testament Interpretation* (London: SCM, 1963), p. 96.

5. There are eighteen explicit references in Deuteronomy to the Lord's promise of land to the patriarchs, and all but three speak

of God's giving it. Patrick D. Miller, *Deuteronomy* (Louisville: John Knox Press, 1990), p. 45. Cf. "Excursus: The Deuteronomic Theology of the Land," pp. 44–52.

6. A forceful presentation of the importance of the gift aspect of land is given by Walter Brueggemann, *The Land: Place as Gift, Promise, and Challenge in Biblical Faith* (Philadelphia: Fortress Press, 1977; London: SPCK, 1978).

7. David Daube, *Studies in Biblical Law* (New York: Ktav, 1969; London: Cambridge University Press, 1947), pp. 34f.

8. See Eberhard von Waldo, "Israel and Her Land: Some Theological Considerations" in Howard N. Bream, Ralph D. Heim, and Carey A. Moore, eds., *A Lamp unto My Path: Old Testament Studies in Honor of Jacob M. Meyers* (Temple University Press, 1974), p. 502.

9. J. G. Ploeger, quoted in *Theological Dictionary of the Old Testament* (Grand Rapids: Eerdmans, 1974), p. 403.

10. I am indebted for material in this chapter and for the diagram to C. J. H. Wright's careful analysis, *God's People in God's Land: Family, Land, and Property in the Old Testament* (Grand Rapids: Eerdmans/Exeter: Paternoster, 1990).

11. Ludwig Koehler, *Old Testament Theology* (Philadelphia: Westminster; London: Lutterworth, 1957), p. 151.

Chapter 7 Deliverance

1. R. H. Hiers, "Day of the Lord," *Anchor Bible Dictionary*, 2:82–83; cf. W. Van Gemeren, *Interpreting the Prophetic Word* (Grand Rapids: Zondervan, 1990), pp. 214–224.

2. Geerhardus Vos, *Biblical Theology* (Grand Rapids: Eerdmans, 1948; Edinburgh: Banner of Truth, 1975), p. 313.

3. The date of the book of Joel is uncertain. Some, because of its canonical position between Amos and Hosea, date it early. Others, because of Aramaisms, favor a post-exilic date. Joel is quite compatible with the pre-exile date, a dating here preferred, mostly because the nations mentioned in his book are enemies of pre-exilic Israel.

4. A. J. Everson, "The Days of Yahweh," *Journal of Biblical Literature* 93 (1974), pp. 329–337, cites several texts which describe and interpret past events: Lamentations 1–2; Ezek 13:1–9 (fall of

Jerusalem 587 BC); Jer 46:2–12 (Egyptian defeat at Carchemish, 605 BC); and Isa 22:1–4 (Sennacherib's campaign in Judah, 701 BC).

5. "To anoint" (*māšîaḥ*) is to spread a liquid. It is a word used in a non-religious sense, as to paint (*māšîaḥ*) a house (Jer 22:14) or to rub a shield with oil (Isa 21:5). In ceremonial religious ritual, oil was applied as well to persons, to such items as tabernacle, altar or laver (Exod 40:9–11). F. F. Bruce, *This is That: The New Testament Development of Some Old Testament Themes* (Paternoster, 1968), p. 89. S. D. Sachs, "Messiah," in *Baker Encyclopedia of the Bible*, ed. W. A. Elwell (Grand Rapids: Baker, 1988), 2:1446–1449. M. de Jong, "Messiah," *Anchor Bible Dictionary*, 4:777–788. W. C. Kaiser Jr., *The Messiah in the Old Testament* (Zondervan, 1995).

6. I owe this insight concerning Saul to Rolf Knierim, "The Messianic Concept in the First Book of Samuel," in F. T. Trotter, ed., *Jesus and the Historian* (Philadelphia: Westminster, 1968), pp. 20–51.

7. An additional rabbinic allusion is of interest for the rabbis treated the verb "increase" as a proper noun and so made Yinnon (increase) one of the names of the Messiah. Christians such as Isaac Watts, whose hymn "Jesus Shall Reign" is built on a Christological understanding of the psalm, have for generations seen Psalm 72 as describing someone in addition to the monarch in Israel, namely Jesus Christ. One could add other psalms to the discussion such as Psalm 110 for which see David M. Hay, *Glory at the Right Hand, Psalm 110 in Early Christianity* (Nashville: Abingdon, 1973).

8. For a summary of views see H. M. Wolf, "Solution to the Immanuel Prophecy in Isaiah 7:14 – 8:22," *Journal of Biblical Literature* 91 (1972), pp. 449–456. Cf. commentaries, e.g., J. N. Oswalt, *The Book of Isaiah 1–39* (Eerdmans, 1986), pp. 206–213.

Chapter 8 The Covenant Community and the New Functionaries: Kings, Prophets

1. See Walter C. Kaiser Jr., "The Blessing of David: a Charter for Humanity," in John Skelton, ed., *The Law and Prophets* (Philadelphia: Presbyterian & Reformed Publishing House, 1974), pp. 298–318.

2. E.g., J. Barton Payne, "Saul and the Changing Will of God," *Bibliotheca Sacra* 129 (1972), pp. 321–325.

3. R. E. Clements, "The Deuteronomistic Interpretation of the Founding of the Monarchy in 1 Sam. VIII," *Vetus Testamentum* 24

(1974), pp. 398–410. For a helpful discussion from the form-critical view see D. J. McCarthy, "The Inauguration of Monarchy in Israel—a Form Critical Study of 1 Sam. 8–12," *Interpretation* 27:4 (1973), pp. 401–412. See V. Philips Long, *The Reign and Rejection of King Saul: A Case for Literary and Theological Coherence*. SBL Diss. Series (Atlanta: Scholars Press, 1984).

4. Reliance on texts from Deuteronomy assumes an early, possibly Mosaic date for that book. In the critical view Deuteronomy originates in the seventh century, when the monarchy was a well-established institution, and was finally edited a century later.

5. Compare Ben C. Ollenburger, *Zion, the City of the Great King*, JSOTSup 41 (Sheffield: JSOT, 1987), pp. 23–80.

6. Other bases for belief in the security of Zion might presumably be the tradition of Jerusalem's invincibility (cf. 2 Sam 5:6) or the Melchizedek conquest tradition (cf. Ps 110:2–4 and II Q Melch. at Qumran). Cf. J. J. M. Roberts, "The Davidic Origin of the Zion Tradition," *Journal of Biblical Literature* 92 (September 1973), pp. 329–344; also a brief summary in Ollenburger, *Zion, the City of the Great King*, pp. 15–19.

7. J. Eaton, *Kingship and the Psalms* (Naperville: Allenson, 1975), p. 168.

8. John Bright's contrast between the Sinaitic and Davidic covenants is too sharply drawn. *Covenant and Promise* (Philadelphia: Westminster Press, 1976; London: SCM Press, 1977). Cf. McComiskey, *Covenants of Promise*.

9. W. VanGemeren argues for Moses as the fountainhead, *Interpreting the Prophetic Word*, pp. 28–34.

10. For a detailed essay see W. Eichrodt, "Prophet and Covenant: Observations on the Exegesis of Isaiah," in J. I. Durham and J. R. Porter, eds., *Proclamation and Presence* (London: SCM Press, 1970), pp. 167–188. Cf. R. E. Clements, *Prophecy and Covenant* (London: SCM Press, 1965).

Chapter 9 The Experience of God

1. For such a discussion see John Goldingay, "That You May Know that Yahweh Is God: a Study in the Relationship between Theology and Historical Truth in the Old Testament," *Tyndale Bulletin* 23 (1972), pp. 58–93.

2. Francis I. Andersen, *Job* (London: Inter-Varsity Press; Downers Grove: InterVarsity Press, 1976), pp. 61ff.

3. "Prayer of Lamentation to Ishtar," James B. Pritchard, ed., *Ancient Near Eastern Texts Relating to the Old Testament* (Princeton, NJ: Princeton University Press, 2–1955), p. 383.

4. Craig C. Broyles, *The Conflict of Faith and Experience in the Psalms: A Form-Critical and Theological Study*, JSOT 52 (Sheffield: JSOT Press, 1989). Cf. C. Westermann "The Role of the Lament in the Theology of the Old Testament," *Interpretation* 28 (1974), pp. 20–38, and other articles in that issue devoted to lament.

5. Quoted in Bernard W. Anderson, *Out of the Depths* (Philadelphia: Westminster, 1970), p. 86.

6. "The Hymn to Aton," *Ancient Near Eastern Texts*, p. 371.

7. Quoted in Kathryn Lindskoog, *C. S. Lewis: Mere Christian* (Glendale, California: Regal Books, 1973), p. 57.

8. D. J. A. Clines, *Job 1–20*, Word Biblical Commentary (Waco, Tex.: Word Books, 1989), pp. xxxvii–xlvii.

9. Claus Westermann, *Basic Forms of Prophetic Judgment Speech* (Philadelphia: Westminster; London: Lutterworth, 1967). Cf. P. D. Miller, *Sin and Judgment in the Prophets: A Stylistic and Theological Analysis* (Chico, CA: Scholars Press, 1982).

10. C. Westermann, *Prophetic Oracles of Salvation* (Louisville: Westminster/John Knox, 1991).

Chapter 10 Life and Land

1. R. Murphy, "The Kerygma of the Book of Proverbs," *Interpretation* 20 (1966), p. 9.

2. For a sustained argument on the affirmation of a this-worldly stance in the Old Testament see Walther Zimmerli, *The Old Testament and the World* (Atlanta: John Knox; London: SPCK, 1976).

3. See Henri Blocher, "The Fear of the Lord as the 'Principle' of Wisdom," *Tyndale Bulletin* 28 (1977), pp. 3–28.

4. See Roland Murphy, "Wisdom and Yahwism," *No Famine in the Land. Studies in Honor of John L. McKenzie* (Missoula, Montana: Scholars Press, 1975), pp. 117–126.

5. G. von Rad, *Old Testament Theology*, 1 (New York: Harper & Row; London: Oliver & Boyd, 1962), p. 443.

6. The link between wisdom and Torah, suggests Walter Kaiser Jr., is forged around the "fear of the Lord" concept: "The fear of the Lord more than any other phrase linked together the patriarchal promise with the law and wisdom." *Toward an Old Testament Theology* (Grand Rapids: Zondervan, 1979), p. 168. Although Kaiser acknowledges the motif of "life" as significant, he does not give to it the prominence that is suggested here. Bruce K. Waltke urges the covenant substratum for Proverbs. "The Book of Proverbs and Old Testament Theology," *Bibliotheca Sacra* 544 (October-December 1979), pp. 302–317.

7. Cf. Walther Zimmerli, "The Place and Limit of Wisdom in the Framework of the Old Testament Theology," *Scottish Journal of Theology* 17 (1964), pp. 146–158; Walter C. Kaiser Jr., "Wisdom Theology and the Center of Old Testament Theology," *Evangelical Quarterly* 50:3 (July-September 1978), pp. 132–146. R. E. Clements omits the wisdom writings in his *Old Testament Theology: A Fresh Approach* (Atlanta: John Knox; London: Marshall Morgan & Scott, 1978).

8. For a summary of the positions see John Ruffle, "The Teaching of Amenemope and Its Connection with the Book of Proverbs," *Tyndale Bulletin* 28 (1977), p. 29–68. Ruffle proposes indirect dependence on Egypt through an Egyptian scribe working at Solomon's court.

9. Much of the last half of the present chapter is indebted to W. Brueggemann's *The Land* (Philadelphia: Fortress Press, 1977; London: SPCK, 1978).

10. Cf. also E. A. Martens, "Yahweh's Compassion and Ecotheology," in Problems in Biblical Theology: Essays in Honor of Rolf Knierim. (Eds.) H. T. C. Sun, K. L. Eades, J. M. Robinson, G. I. Moller (Grand Rapids: Eerdmans, 1997), 234-248.

Part 4: Prologue
1. For a discussion of the issue of the unity and the authorship of Isaiah, see William LaSor, D. A. Hubbard, and F. W. Bush, *Old Testament Survey*, pp. 371–378, and commentaries.

Chapter 11 Deliverance
1. For a non-technical treatment of apocalyptic see D. S. Russell, *Divine Disclosure: An Introduction to Jewish Apocalyptic* (Minneapolis: Fortress, 1992); Leon Morris, *Apocalyptic* (Grand

Rapids: Eerdmans, 1972; London: Inter-Varsity Press, 1973). More technical are the books by Klaus Koch, *The Rediscovery of Apocalyptic* (Naperville: Allenson; London: SCM Press, 1972); J. J. Collins, *The Apocalyptic Imagination: An Introduction to the Jewish Matrix of Christianity* (New York: Crossroad, 1984); and J. J. Collins and J. H. Charlesworth, eds., *Mysteries and Revelations: Apocalyptic Studies since the Uppsala Colloquium* (Sheffield: JSOT, 1991).

2. H. H. Rowley, *The Relevance of Apocalyptic* (London: Lutterworth, 1963), p. 13.

3. R. J. Bauckham points to origins in both wisdom and prophecy, and stresses the positive contributions of apocalyptic writers. "The Rise of Apocalyptic," *Themelios* 3/2 (1978), pp. 10–23.

4. H. H. Rowley, *Darius the Mede and the Four World Empires of Daniel: A Historical Study of Contemporary Themes* (Cardiff: University of Wales Press, 1959). E. J. Young, *The Prophecy of Daniel* (Grand Rapids: Eerdmans, 1949) = *A Commentary on Daniel* (Banner of Truth, 1972). For other options, see John Goldingay, *Daniel*, Word Biblical Commentaries (Dallas: Word Books, 1989), pp. 50–52, 173–176.

5. Leon J. Wood, *A Commentary on Daniel* (Grand Rapids: Zondervan, 1973), p. 187.

6. Opinions vary as to the identity of the "saints of the Most High." A defender of these as Israel is Gerhard F. Hasel, "The Identity of the Saints of the Most High in Daniel 7," *Biblica* 56 (1976), pp. 173–192.

7. The literature is extensive. See John Goldingay, *Daniel,* pp. 169–172; and G. W. E. Nickelsburg, "Son of Man," *Anchor Bible Dictionary*, 6:137–150.

8. Paul Hanson, *The Dawn of the Apocalyptic* (Philadelphia: Fortress Press, 1975), pp. 315–316. Hanson focuses on the sociological context for the development of apocalyptic—an intra-community struggle between visionary and pragmatic-oriented groups.

9. F. F. Bruce, *This Is That: the New Testament Development of Some Old Testament Themes* (Exeter: Paternoster, 1968), p. 84.

10. Henri Blocher, *Songs of the Servant* (Downers Grove: InterVarsity Press; London: Inter-Varsity Press, 1975), p. 40. Cf.

Robert R. Ellis, "The Remarkable Suffering Servant of Isaiah 40–66"
Southwest Journal of Theology 34 (1991) 20–30.

11. Ibid., p. 75. Cf. Robert R. Ellis, "The Remarkable Suffering
Servant of Isaiah 40–66" *Southwest Journal of Theology* 34 (1991)
20–30.

Chapter 12 Covenant and Community in the Post-Exilic Period

1. Ronald Youngblood, *The Heart of the Old Testament* (Grand
Rapids: Baker, 1971), p. 42.

2. Isaiah, as has been stated earlier, addresses the situation of
the exile, whether or not the material in chapters 40–66 dates from
the prophet in the eighth century or from a successor in the time of
the exile.

3. An interesting treatment of the word "witness" as advocacy is
given from the book of Isaiah by Allison A. Trites, *The New Testament
Concept of Witness* (New York and London: Cambridge University
Press, 1977).

4. Salvation speech genres are designated by C. Westermann as
"assurance" and "proclamation," *Isaiah 40–66*, pp. 13, 67, 126, etc.
A helpful discussion is found in J. Hayes, *Introduction to Old Testament
Study* (Nashville: Abingdon, 1979). Cf. C. Westermann, *Prophetic
Oracles of Salvation* (1991).

5. E. A. Martens, "Motivation for the Promise of Israel's
Restoration to the Land in Jeremiah and Ezekiel" (unpublished
dissertation, Claremont Graduate School, Claremont, California,
1972), pp. 329ff.

6. Books and articles are numerous. For the classic treatment of
covenant see W. Eichrodt, *Theology of the Old Testament*, 2 vols.
(Philadelphia: Westminster; London: SCM Press, 1961, 1967); E. W.
Nicholson, *God and His People: Covenant Theology in the Old Testament*
(Oxford: Clarendon Press / New York: Oxford University Press,
1986); T. E. McComiskey, *The Covenants of Promise.* (Grand Rapids:
Baker, 1985). Cf. Gordon J. McConville's article on covenant in
NIDOTTE I:747–55.

Chapter 13 The Experience of God

1. "Cult means social worship through ritual performances;
anything less than this is not cult." J. L. McKenzie, *A Theology of the*

Old Testament (Garden City: Doubleday; London: Geoffrey Chapman, 1974), p. 37. Similarly W. Eichrodt defines cult as "the expression of religious experience in concrete external actions performed within the congregation or community." *Theology of the Old Testament*, 1 (Philadelphia: Westminster; London: SCM Press, 1961), p. 98.

2. Reading the word in question in Dan 9:21 as y^cp, "weary," rather than ^cwp, "fly."

3. R. A. Alexander, "Ezekiel," *The Expositor's Bible Commentary*, 6:943–952.

4. Paul Hanson has discerned a temple party and an anti-temple group active in the restoration period. *The Dawn of Apocalyptic* (Philadelphia: Fortress Press, 1975), pp. 161ff, 228ff. Whether or not his argument can be sustained, his work points to salient issues of temple theology.

5. Roddy Braun, *1 Chronicles*, Word Biblical Commentary (Waco, Tex.: Word Books, 1986), pp. xxv–xxix.

6. For Jesus' use of the temple as symbolic see Mark 15:48; John 2:19.

7. W. Zimmerli, "Knowledge of God according to the Book of Ezekiel," in *I Am Yahweh*, trans. D. W. Stott, ed. W. Brueggemann (Atlanta: John Knox Press, 1982), pp. 29–98.

8. A discussion of these mission models is given in G. W. Peters, *A Biblical Theology of Mission* (Chicago: Moody Press, 1972). Cf. John N. Oswalt, "The Mission of Israel to the Nations," pp. 85–95 in *Through No Fault of Their Own*, edited by W. V. Crockett and J. G. Sigountos (Grand Rapids: Baker, 1991).

9. W. Eichrodt, *Ezekiel* OTL (Philadelphia: Fortress, 1970), 586

Chapter 14 Land

1. In Jeremiah and Ezekiel announcements of a return to the land are found in Jer 3:11–20; 12:14–17; 16:10–18; 23:1–8; 24; 28:1–14; 30:1–3, 10–11; 31:2–14; 32:1–44; 42:1–22; 50:17–20; Ezek 20:39–44; 34:1–16; 35:1 – 36:15; 36:16–36; 37:1–14, 15–28; 39:21–19.

2. A discussion of the meaning and translation of *šûb š^ebût* may be found in E. A. Martens, "Motivations for the Promise of Israel's Restoration to the Land in Jeremiah and Ezekiel"

(unpublished dissertation, Claremont Graduate School, 1972), pp. 172ff.

3. Robert Bach, "Bauen und Pflanzen," in R. Rendtorff and Klaus Koch, eds., *Studien zur Theologie der Alttestamentlichen Überlieferungen* (Neukirchen: Neukirchener Verlag, 1961).

4. W. Eichrodt, *Ezekiel* (Philadelphia: Westminster Press, 1970), p. 497.

5. E. A. Martens, "Motivations," p. 205.

6. W. M. Clark, "Origin and Development of the Land Promise" (unpublished dissertation, Yale University, 1964), p. 16.

7. An essay by G. von Rad discusses the subject of land as rest, though with different presuppositions than those adopted in this book. "There Still Remains a Rest for the People of God," *The Problem of the Pentateuch and Other Essays* (New York: McGraw-Hill; London: Oliver & Boyd, 1966).

8. Cf. W. Brueggemann, *The Land* (Philadelphia: Fortress Press, 1977; London: SPCK, 1978), pp. 153ff. Brueggemann offers a vigorous treatment on the theological dimensions of "land" generally.

9. J. Klausner, *The Messianic Idea in Israel* (New York: Macmillan, 1955; London: George Allen & Unwin, 1956), pp. 117ff.

10. E. A. Martens, "Motivations," p. 353.

11. W. Brueggemann, *The Land*, p. 172.

12. Ibid., p. 179.

Chapter 15 Framing God's Design: Creation

1. E.g., H. J. Kraus, *Theology of the Psalms*, trans. Keith Crim (Minneapolis: Augsburg Publishing House, 1984), pp. 63ff; cf. G. von Rad, "The Theological Problem of the Old Testament Doctrine of Creation," in *The Problem of the Hexateuch and Other Essays* (London: SCM Press, 1966, 2–1984), pp. 131–143; reprinted in *Creation in the Old Testament*, ed. Bernard W. Anderson (Philadelphia: Fortress Press / London: SPCK, 1984), pp. 53–64. "It [the doctrine of creation] has always been related to something else, and subordinated to the interests and content of the doctrine of redemption" (p. 138).

2. R. Rendtorff claims that the last summary [Old Testament theology] to do so was G. E. Oehler's work in 1873: "'Where Were

You When I Laid the Foundation of the Earth?' Creation and Salvation History," chap. 9 in *Canon and Theology: Overtures to an Old Testament Theology* (Minneapolis: Fortress Press, 1993), pp. 92–113.

3. Ben Ollenburger, "Isaiah's Creation Theology," *Exod Auditu* 3 (1987), p. 69.

4. Ibid., p. 63.

5. "Mythopoeic and Theological Dimensions of Biblical Creation Faith," in *Creation in the Old Testament*, ed. B. W. Anderson (Philadelphia: Fortress Press / London: SPCK, 1984), p. 6.

6. See Terence E. Fretheim, "Nature's Praise of God in the Psalms," *Exod Auditu* 3 (1987), pp. 16–30, with a focus on Psalm 148.

7. "Theological Problem of the Old Testament Doctrine of Creation," p. 133.

8. R. J. Clifford, "Creation in the Psalms," in *Creation in the Biblical Traditions*, The Catholic Biblical Quarterly Monograph Series 24 (Washington, DC: The Catholic Biblical Association, 1992), 66.

9. "Creation in the Psalms," p. 64.

10. H. J. Kraus, *Theology of the Psalms*, p. 65.

11. The "dark side," namely the threat of evil in Psalm 104 over which God has mastery, is explored by Jon D. Levenson, *Creation and the Persistence of Evil: The Jewish Drama of Divine Omnipotence* (San Francisco: Harper & Row, 1988), 55–57.

12. For a provocative essay focusing on three metaphors in Proverbs 8—God as Procreator, God as Creator, and God as Co-creator—see Gale A. Yee, "The Theology of Creation in Proverbs 8:22–31," in *Creation in the Biblical Traditions*, ed. R. J. Clifford and J. J. Collins, The Catholic Biblical Quarterly Monograph Series 24 (Washington, DC: The Catholic Biblical Association of America, 1992), pp. 85–96.

13. These implications touch on human stewardship responsibility for the well-being of land, animals, and vegetation. For essays offering a biblical perspective: Wesley Granberg-Michaelson, ed., *Tending the Garden: Essays on the Gospel and the Earth* (Grand Rapids: Eerdmans, 1987); Calvin DeWitt, ed., *The Environment and the Christian* (Grand Rapids: Baker, 1991); L. Osborn, *Guardians of Creation: Nature in Theology and the Christian Life* (Leicester: Apollos [Inter-Varsity Press], 1993); L. Osborn, *Stewards of Creation: Environmentalism in the Light of Biblical Teaching* (Oxford:

Latimer House, 1990); cf. R. D. Land and L. A. Moore, *The Earth Is the Lord's: Christians and the Environment* (Nashville: Broadman Press, 1992).

14. C. Westermann, *Blessing: In the Bible and in the Life of the Church*, trans. Keith Crim, Overtures to Biblical Theology 3 (Philadelphia: Fortress Press, 1978).

15. Rendtorff, "Where Were You When I Laid the Foundation of the Earth?" p. 106.

16. In the Book of Wisdom (ca 100 BC) that connection is specifically made: it was wisdom present at creation by which Israel was saved (9:1–3, 18). Cf. Michael Kolarcik, "Creation and Salvation in the Book of Wisdom," in *Creation in the Biblical Traditions*, pp. 97–107.

17. R. Knierim, "Cosmos and History in Israel's Theology," *Horizons in Biblical Theology* 3 (1981), pp. 59–123; E. A. Martens, "The Oscillating Fortunes of 'History' in Old Testament Theology," in *Faith, Tradition and History: OT Historiography in Its Near Eastern Context*, edited by A. Millard, J. Hoffmeier, and D. Baker (Winona Lake: Eisenbrauns, 1994).

18. John Goldingay, "A Unifying Approach to 'Creation' and 'Salvation' in the Old Testament," in *Theological Diversity and the Authority of the Old Testament* (Grand Rapids: Eerdmans, 1987), 232.

Chapter 16 Framing God's Design: the World's Peoples

1. Cf. chap. 2 above.

2. The tripartite Hebrew canon is followed because (a) an Old Testament theology is a theology of the Hebrew Bible, and (b) the Bible of Jesus and the apostles was almost certainly the Hebrew ordering of books (Luke 24:44).

3. John Sailhamer, *The Pentateuch as Narrative* (Grand Rapids: Zondervan, 1992), p. 476.

4. Ridderbos, *Deuteronomy*, trans. Ed M. van der Maas (Grand Rapids: Zondervan, 1984), p. 296.

5. H. J. Kraus, *Theology of the Psalms* (Minneapolis: Augsburg Press, 1986), p. 32.

6. D. W. Van Winkle, "The Relationship of the Nations to Yahweh and to Israel in Isaiah xl–lv," *VT* 35 (1985), pp. 446–458.

7. Charles H. Scobie distinguishes two ways in which Israel relates to nations: incorporation (e.g., Ruth) and ingathering eschatalogically (e.g., Edom; cf. Isa 45:14–16). See "Israel and the Nations," *TB* 43:2 (1992), pp. 283–305.

8. A similar movement from the national to the international is evident in the Septuagint (and English) ordering of books. The books in the so-called Historical Division begin with Joshua and Judges, whose subject is Israel in Canaan, but end with Esther, the subject of which is a Hebrew in the Persian empire.

9. R. Rendtorff notes from Ps 98:3 how the particularist and the universalist are specifically linked. "Revelation and History: Particularism and Universalism in Israel's View of Revelation," chap. 9 in *Canon and Theology* (Minneapolis: Fortress Press, 1993), pp. 114–124.

10. Brevard S. Childs, *Biblical Theology of the Old and New Testaments* (Minneapolis: Fortress Press, 1992), p. 93.

Chapter 17 Divine Design and the New Testament

1. The nuances of the term "kingdom of God" are helpfully described both for the Old Testament and New Testament in G. R. Beasley-Murray, *Jesus and the Kingdom of God* (Grand Rapids: Eerdmans / Exeter: Paternoster, 1986).

2. Cf. George Eldon Ladd: "The Kingdom is God's kingly rule. It has two moments: a fulfillment of the Old Testament promises in the historical mission of Jesus and a consummation at the end of the age, inaugurating the Age to Come." *A Theology of the New Testament* (Grand Rapids: Eerdmans, 1974, rev. ed., by Donald Hagner, 1993), p. 58; cf. pp. 62–67.

3. "The one word that best characterizes Matthew's theological perspective is fulfillment" (R. T. France, "Matthew, Mark and Luke," chap. 16 in G. E. Ladd, *Theology of the New Testament*, p 219). Cf. G. N. Stanton: "The OT is woven into the warp and woof of this gospel [Matthew]; the evangelist uses Scripture to underline some of his most prominent and distinctive theological concerns." *A Gospel for a New People: Studies in Matthew* (Edinburgh: T & T Clark, 1992). Note Stanton's chap. 15: "Matthew's Use of the Old Testament," pp. 346–377.

4. *Israel's Scripture Traditions and the Synoptic Gospels: Stories Shaping Stories* (Peabody, MA: Hendrickson, 1994); for the hypothesis and pagination relative to Matthew's nuances, see p. 7.

5. C. Talbert, "The Gospel and the Gospels," *Interpretation* 33 (1979), pp. 354ff.

6. The passion event is in keeping with God's intention of deliverance exemplified at the exodus. The sayings, which call for a distinctive morality and lifestyle for Christ's followers, easily link with the Old Testament idea of the covenant community. The miracle stories represent one form of knowing or experiencing God. The revealer passages can be connected, though more distantly, with "land" which, as we noted, came to function as a revelation cipher.

7. *Jesus and the Kingdom of God*, p. 80.

8. G. E. Ladd, *Jesus and the Kingdom, The Eschatology of Biblical Realism*, 2nd ed. (Waco, TX: Word Books, 1969), p. 147.

9. Quoted in G. E. Ladd, *Jesus and the Kingdom*, p. 141.

10. W. D. Davies treats this text as one of four statements by Jesus in which "land" is mentioned. Davies considers it best to spiritualize land, giving it the meaning, "kingdom of God." *The Gospel and the Land* (Berkeley: University of California Press, 1974), pp. 359–362.

11. G. R. Beasley-Murray, *Jesus and the Kingdom of God* (Grand Rapids: Eerdmans / Exeter: Paternoster, 1986), 175.

12. Quoted in F. F. Bruce, *The Epistle of Paul to the Romans* (Grand Rapids: Eerdmans, 1971), p. 9. Italics mine.

13. Cf. Richard Hays, *Echoes of Scripture in the Letters of Paul* (New Haven: Yale University Press, 1989), pp. 34–83. In another vein, see N. T. Wright, *Romans and the Theology of Paul*, SBL 1992 Seminar Papers (Atlanta: Scholars Press, 1992).

14. Krister Stendahl, *Paul among Jews and Gentiles* (Philadelphia: Fortress Press, 1976), p. 27.

15. For the approach to the book of Romans I am indebted to my New Testament teaching colleague, Professor John E. Toews. "The Law in Paul's Letter to the Romans: A Study of Romans 5:30 – 10:13" (unpublished Ph.D. thesis, Northwestern University, 1977). Cf., J. D. G. Dunn, "the Justice of God," *Journal of Theological Studies* 43 (1992), pp. 1–22; and M. L. Soards, "Once Again the

'Righteousness of God' in the Writings of the Apostle Paul," *Bible Bhasham* 17 (1991), pp. 14–44.

16. Cf. Hays, *Echoes of Scripture*, chap. 3.

17. For example, "The question is the relationship between two communities and their co-existence in the mysterious plan of God." Krister Stendahl, *Paul among Jews and Gentiles* (Philadelphia: Fortress Press, 1976), p. 4; see also Johannes Munck, *Christ and Israel: An Interpretation of Romans 9–11* (Philadelphia: Fortress Press, 1968). J. D. G. Dunn, *Romans*, vol. 1 (Waco, TX: Word Books, 1988), liv–lviii.

18. W. Brueggemann, *The Land* (Philadelphia: Fortress Press, 1977; London: SPCK, 1978), p. 3, italics his.

19. W. D. Davies in discussing the topic of land in the Pauline epistles offers reasons for the sparse mention of land and concludes, "In the Christological logic of Paul, the land, like the law, particular and provisional, had become irrelevant." *The Gospel and the Land* (Berkeley: University of California Press, 1974), p. 179. Elsewhere however, in conjunction with Jerusalem and temple, Davies allows that Paul did not ignore the subject of land, but he "discovered" his inheritance "in Christ"—the land of Christians, "the new creation, if we may so express the matter" (p. 219).

Appendix

1. A recent attempt to incorporate both Old and New Testaments is Brevard S. Childs, *Biblical Theology of the Old and New Testaments* (Minneapolis: Fortress Press, 1993).

2. In recent years the term "Old Testament" has been critiqued on the basis that it is disparaging, and negatively affects dialogue between Christians and Jews. Proposals to remedy the situation include new designations such as The Hebrew Scriptures, the First Testament, *Tanak* (an acronym for *Torah, Nebi'im,* and *Kethubim* = Law, Prophets, and Writings, the three parts of the Hebrew Bible), and Prophets (with the New Testament designated, The Apostles). See Ralph L. Smith, *Old Testament Theology: Its History, Method and Message* (Nashville: Broadman & Holman Publishers, 1993), pp. 64–69; R. W. L. Moberly, *The Old Testament of the Old Testament: Overtures to Biblical Theology* (Minneapolis: Fortress Press, 1992), pp. 159–166; and John Miller, *The Origin of the Bible: Canon History.* (Paulist, 1995). In this book the traditional designation "Old Testament" will be employed.

3. For the history of the discipline, see Ben Ollenburger, "From Timeless Ideas to the Essence of Religion: Method in Old Testament Theology before 1930," in *The Flowering of Old Testament Theology. Sources for Biblical and Theological Study*, vol. 1, eds. B. C. Ollenburger, Elmer A. Martens, and Gerhard F. Hasel (Winona Lake: Eisenbrauns, 1992), pp. 3–19; on this and other issues discussed, see the Bibliography below; G. F. Hasel, *Old Testament Theology: Basic Issues in the Current Debate*, 4th ed. (Grand Rapids: Eerdmans, 1991), pp. 10–27; Jesper Høgenhaven, *Problems and Prospects of Old Testament Theology*, Biblical Seminar 6 (Sheffield: JSOT Press, 1988), pp. 13–27; Ralph Smith, *Old Testament Theology: Its History, Method, and Message* (Nashville: Broadman & Holman Publishers, 1993), pp. 21–64.

4. Ben C. Ollenburger, ed., *So Wide a Sea: Essays on Biblical and Systematic Theology*, IMS Text Reader 4 (Elkhart, Ind.: Institute of Mennonite Studies, 1991); G. F. Hasel, "The Relationship between Biblical Theology and Systematic Theology," *Trinity Journal*, n.s. 5 (1984), pp. 113–127.

5. Cf. the essays by E. A. Martens, "Biblical Theology and Normativity," and Ben C. Ollenburger, "Biblical and Systematic Theology: Constructing a Relation," in *So Wide a Sea*, pp. 19–35; pp. 111–145.

6. W. Eichrodt, *Theology of the Old Testament*, 2 vols., trans. J. A. Baker (Philadelphia: Westminster Press / London: SCM, 1961, 1967); W. C. Kaiser Jr., *Towards an Old Testament Theology* (Grand Rapids: Zondervan, 1978). See further G. F. Hasel, *Old Testament Theology: Basic Issues in the Current Debate*, pp. 172–193; J. Høgenhaven, *Problems of Biblical Theology in the Twentieth Century*, trans. John Bowden (Philadelphia: Fortress Press / London: SCM, 1986).

7. E.g., the sections on "Approaches" for each of fourteen theologians in *The Flowering of Old Testament Theology*, pp. 58–370; H. G. Reventlow, *Problems of Old Testament Theology*; W. Eichrodt, "Excursus," *Theology of the Old Testament*, vol. 1, pp. 512–520. See also R. Knierim, *The Task of Old Testament Theology. Substance, Method, and Cases*. (Grand Rapids/Cambridge: Wm. B. Eerdmans, 1995), and S. J. Kraftchick, C. D. Myers Jr., and B. C. Ollenburger, eds. *Biblical Theology. Problems and Perspectives. In Honor of J. Christiaan Beker.* (Nashville: Abingdon, 1995).

8. Elmer A. Martens, "The Oscillating Fortunes of 'History' in Old Testament Theology," in *Faith, Tradition and History: OT Historiography in Its Near Eastern Context*, eds. A. Millard, James Hoffmeier, and D. Baker (Winona Lake: Eisenbrauns, 1994), pp. 313–340.

9. Further discussion on the issue, especially G. von Rad's views, can be found in H. G. Reventlow, *Problems of Old Testament Theology*, pp. 59–124; and in J. J. Collins, "Is a Critical Biblical Theology Possible?" in *The Hebrew Bible and Its Interpreters*, eds. W. H. Propp, Baruch Halpern, and D. N. Freedman. Biblical and Judaic Studies from the University of California, San Diego, vol. 1 (Winona Lake: Eisenbrauns, 1990), pp. 1–17; G. F. Hasel, *Old Testament Theology: Basic Issues in the Current Debate*, pp. 115–138.

10. Discussion on the issue can be found in J. Høgenhaven, *Problems and Prospects of Old Testament Theology*, pp. 38–44; G. F. Hasel, *Old Testament Theology: Basic Issues in the Current Debate*, pp. 139–171; and H. G. Reventlow, *Problems of Old Testament Theology*, pp. 125–133.

11. Edmond Jacob, *Theology of the Old Testament*, trans. Arthur W. Heathcote and Philip J. Allcock (New York: Harper / London: Hodder & Stoughton, 1958); W. Eichrodt, *Theology of the Old Testament*; and Walter C. Kaiser Jr., *Toward an Old Testament Theology* (Grand Rapids: Zondervan, 1978).

12. S. L. Terrien, *The Elusive Presence: Toward a New Biblical Theology* (San Francisco: Harper & Row, 1978).

13. G. F. Hasel, *Old Testament Theology: Basic Issues in the Current Debate*, 4th ed., pp.28–114; Ralph Smith, *Old Testament Theology*, (Nashville: Broadman & Holman, 1993), pp. 72–93.

14. G. von Rad, *Old Testament Theology*, vol. 1, trans. David M. G. Stalker (New York: Harper & Row / Edinburgh: Oliver & Boyd, 1962), pp. 121–126.

15. John Goldingay, *Theological Diversity and the Authority of the Old Testament* (Grand Rapids: Eerdmans, 1987), pp. 141–152.

16. William L. Holladay, *The Architecture of Jeremiah 1–20* (Lewisburg: Bucknell University Press / London: Associated University Presses, 1976), pp. 30–34.

17. R. W. L. Moberly, who sees Exodus 3 and 6 as decisive in the inauguration of Mosaic Yahwism as distinct from patriarchal religion, adds strong support to our thesis. See *The Old Testament of the Old Testament* (Minneapolis: Fortress Press / Augsburg, 1992).

Bibliography

Note: For annotations on most of the books listed below, and for a more extensive bibliography (512 entries), see E. A. Martens, *Old Testament Theology*. IBR Bibliographies #13. Grand Rapids: Baker, 1997.

1. Basic Books on Old Testament Theology

Baker, D. L. *Two Testaments: One Bible*. Leicester: Inter-Varsity Press, 1976; Downers Grove: InterVarsity Press 1977, 1991.

Brueggemann, W. *Theology of the Old Testament: Testimony, Dispute, Advocacy*. Minneapolis: Fortress, 1997.

Childs, B. S. *Old Testament Theology in a Canonical Context* Philadelphia: Fortress, l986.

_____. *Biblical Theology of the Old and New Testaments*. Minneapolis: Fortress Press, 1992.

Clements, Ronald E. *Old Testament Theology: A Fresh Approach*. Atlanta: John Knox / London: Marshall, Morgan & Scott, 1978.

Dyrness, William. *Themes in Old Testament Theology*. Downers Grove: InterVarsity Press, 1979; Exeter: Paternoster, 1980.

Eichrodt, Walther. *Theology of the Old Testament*, 2 vols. Philadelphia: Westminster Press / London: SCM Press, 1961, 1967.

Hubbard, Robert L. Jr., Robert K. Johnson, and Robert P. Meye, eds. *Studies in Old Testament Theology*. Dallas: Word Books, 1992.

Jacob, Edmond. *Theology of the Old Testament*. New York: Harper & Row / London: Hodder & Stoughton, 1958.

Kaiser, Walter C. *Toward an Old Testament Theology*. Grand Rapids: Zondervan, 1978, 1991.

Knight, George A. F., *A Christian Theology of the Old Testament*. Richmond: John Knox, 1959.

Lehman, Chester. *Biblical Theology*, 1 Scottdale, PA: Herald Press, 1971.

McKenzie, John L. *A Theology of the Old Testament*. Garden City, NY: Doubleday / London: Geoffrey Chapman, 1974.

Niehaus, J. J. *God at Sinai: Covenant and Theophany*, SOTBT. Grand Rapids: Zondervan, 1995.

Ollenburger, B. C., E. A. Martens, and G. F. Hasel, eds. *The Flowering of Old Testament Theology: A Reader in Twentieth-Century Old Testament Theology, 1930–1990*, Sources for Biblical and Theological Study, vol. 1. Winona Lake: Eisenbrauns, 1992.

Payne, J. Barton. *The Theology of the Older Testament*. Grand Rapids: Zondervan, 1962.

Preuss, H. D. *Old Testament Theology*. 2 vols. Translated by L. G. Perdue. Westminster/John Knox, 1995.

Rad, Gerhard von. *Old Testament Theology*, 2 vols. New York: Harper & Row / London: Oliver & Boyd, 1962, 1967.

Smith, Ralph. *Old Testament Theology: Its History, Method and Message*. Nashville: Broadman & Holman Publishers, 1993.

Terrien, Samuel. *The Elusive Presence: Toward a New Biblical Theology*. New York: Harper & Row, 1978.

VanGemeren, W. *The Progress of Redemption: The Story of Salvation from Creation to the New Jerusalem*. Grand Rapids: Zondervan, 1988.

Vos, Geerhardus. *Biblical Theology*. Grand Rapids: Eerdmans, 1948; Edinburgh: Banner of Truth, 1975.

Vriezen, Th. C. *An Outline of Old Testament Theology*. Boston: Branford / Oxford: Blackwell, 1958, 2nd ed. 1970.

Westermann, Claus. *Elements of Old Testament Theology*, trans. Douglas W. Stott. Atlanta: John Knox Press, 1982.

Wright, George Ernest. *The Old Testament and Theology*. New York: Harper & Row, 1969.

Zimmerli, Walther. *Old Testament Theology in Outline*. Atlanta: John Knox / Edinburgh: T. & T. Clark, 1978.

2. Books on Key Old Testament Theology Motifs

A. Deliverance/Salvation

Beecher, Willis J. *The Prophets and the Promise*. 1905, reprinted Grand Rapids: Baker, 1975.

Blocher, Henri. *Songs of the Servant*. Downers Grove: InterVarsity Press / London: Inter-Varsity Press, 1975.

Craigie, Peter C. *The Problem of War in the Old Testament*. Grand Rapids: Eerdmans, 1978.

Daube, David. *The Exodus Pattern in the Bible*. London: Faber & Faber, 1963.

Farris, T. V. *Mighty to Save. A Study in Old Testament Soteriology*. Nashville: Broadman, 1993.

Hanson, Paul. *The Dawn of Apocalyptic*. Philadelphia: Fortress, 1975.

Hengstenberg, E. W. *Christology of the Old Testament and a Commentary on the Messianic Predictions*. Reprint: Grand Rapids: Kregel, 1956.

Kaiser, W. C. Jr. *The Messiah in the Old Testament*. SOTBT. Grand Rapids: Zondervan, 1995

Kidner, F. D. *Sacrifice in the Old Testament*. London: Tyndale Press, 1952.

Lind, Millard. *Yahweh Is a Warrior*. Scottdale, PA: Herald Press, 1980.

Longman, T. III and D. G. Reid. *God is a Warrior*. Studies in Old Testament Biblical Theology. Grand Rapids: Zondervan, 1995.

Morris, Leon. *Apocalyptic*. Grand Rapids: Eerdmans, 1972; London: Inter-Varsity Press, 1973.

Raitt, Thomas M. *A Theology of Exile. Judgment/Deliverance in Jeremiah and Ezekiel*. Philadelphia: Fortress Press, 1977.

Westermann, Claus. *Blessing in the Bible and the Life of the Church*. Philadelphia: Fortress Press, 1978.

Wright, G. Ernest. *God Who Acts: Biblical Theology as Recital*. London: SCM Press, 1952.

B. The Covenant Community

Bright, John. *Covenant and Promise*. Philadelphia: Westminster Press, 1976; London: SCM Press, 1977.

Dumbrell, W. J. *Covenant and Creation: An Old Testament Covenantal Theology*. Exeter: Patternoster, 1984; Grand Rapids: Baker, 1993.

Hanson, Paul D. *The People Called: The Growth of Community in the Bible*. San Francisco: Harper & Row, 1986.

Hillers, Delbert R. *Covenant: The History of a Biblical Idea*. Baltimore: Johns Hopkins Press, 1969.

Hubbard, Robert L., Robert K. Johnston, and Robert P. Meye, eds. *Studies in Old Testament Theology*. Dallas: Word Books, 1992.

McComiskey, Thomas. *The Covenants of Promise*. Grand Rapids: Baker, 1985.

Nicholson, E. W. *God and His People. Covenant Theology in the Old Testament*. Clarendon: Oxford, 1986, 1988.

Rogerson, J. W. *Anthropology and the Old Testament*. Atlanta: John Knox, 1979; Oxford: Basil Blackwell, 1978.

Sakenfeld, K. D. *Faithfulness in Action*. Philadelphia: Fortress Press, 1985.

Walton, J. H. *Covenant: God's Purpose, God's Plan*. Grand Rapids: Zondervan, 1994.

Williams, Jay G. *Ten Words of Freedom: An Introduction to the Faith of Israel*. Philadelphia: Fortress Press, 1971.

Wolff, H. W. *Anthropology of the Old Testament*. Philadelphia: Fortress Press / London: SCM Press, 1974.

Youngblood, Ronald. *The Heart of the Old Testament*. Grand Rapids: Baker, 1971.

C. Knowledge of God

Dentan, Robert C. *The Knowledge of God in Ancient Israel*. New York: Seabury, 1968.

Fretheim, Terence. *The Suffering of God*. Philadelphia: Fortress Press, 1984.

Gammie, John. *Holiness in Israel*. Minneapolis: Fortress Press, 1984.

Hedlund, R. E. *The Mission of the Church to the World: A Biblical Theology.* Grand Rapids: Baker, 1991.

Hildebrandt, W. *An Old Testament Theology of the Spirit of God.* Peabody, Mass: Hendrickson, 1995.

Labuschagne, C. B. *The Incomparability of Yahweh in the Old Testament.* Leiden: E. J. Brill, 1966.

Mettinger, T. N. D. *In Search of God: The Meaning and Message of the Everlasting Names.* Translated by F. H. Cryer. Philadelphia: Fortress, 1988.

Park-Taylor, G. H. *Yahweh: The Divine Name in the Bible.* Waterloo, Ont.: Wilfrid Laurier University Press, 1975.

Peters, George W. *A Biblical Theology of Missions.* Chicago: Moody Press, 1972.

Rowley, H. H. *Worship in Ancient Israel.* Philadelphia: Fortress Press / London: SPCK, 1967.

Senior, D., and C. Stuhlmueller. *The Biblical Foundations for Mission.* Maryknoll, NY: Orbis Books, 1984.

Snaith, N. H. *The Distinctive Ideas of the Old Testament.* London: Epworth Press, 1944.

Trible, Phyllis. *God and the Rhetoric of Sexuality.* Philadelphia: Fortress Press, 1978.

Westermann, Claus. *What Does the Old Testament Say about God?* Atlanta: John Knox / London: SPCK, 1979.

D. Land/Life

Birch, Bruce. *Let Justice Roll Down: The Old Testament, Ethics and Christian Life.* Louisville, KY: Westminster/John Knox, 1991.

Brueggemann, Walter. *The Land: Place as Gift, Promise, and Challenge in Biblical Faith.* Philadelphia: Fortress Press, 1977; London: SPCK, 1978.

Davies, William D. *The Gospel and the Land.* Berkeley: University of California Press, 1974.

Janzen, W. *Old Testament Ethics. A Paradigmatic Approach.* Louisville: Westminster/John Knox Press, 1994.

Kaiser, Walter C. *Toward Old Testament Ethics.* Grand Rapids: Zondervan, 1983.

Rad, Gerhard von. *Wisdom in Israel*. Nashville: Abingdon / London: SCM Press, 1972.

Wright, C. J. H. *God's People in God's Land: Family, Land and Property in the Old Testament*. Grand Rapids: Eerdmans / Exeter: Paternoster, 1990.

_____. *Living as the People of God*. Leicester: Inter-Varsity, 1983; = *An Eye for an Eye*. Downers Grove: InterVarsity Press, 1983.

Zimmerli, Walther. *The Old Testament and the World*. Atlanta: John Knox Press / London: SPCK, 1976.

E. Creation

Anderson, B. W., ed. *Creation in the Old Testament*. Philadelphia: Fortress Press / London: SPCK, 1984.

Clifford, R. J., and J. J. Collins, eds. *Creation in the Biblical Traditions*, the Catholic Biblical Quarterly Monograph Series 24. Washington, DC: The Catholic Biblical Association of America, 1992.

Dumbrell, W. J. *Covenant and Creation: An Old Testament Covenantal Theology*. Exeter: Paternoster, 1984.

Levenson, Jon D. *Creation and the Persistence of Evil: The Jewish Drama of Divine Omnipotence*. San Francisco: Harper & Row, 1988.

Westermann, C. *Creation*. Philadelphia: Fortress / London: SPCK, 1964.

F. Universalism/The World's Peoples

Scobie, C. H. H. "Israel and the Nations: An Essay in Biblical Theology," *Tyndale Bulletin* 43.2 (1992), pp. 283–305.

G. Old Testament/New Testament Relationship

Achtemeier, Elizabeth. *The Old Testament and the Proclamation of the Gospel*. Philadelphia: Westminster, 1973.

Baker, David. *Two Testaments, One Bible*, rev. ed. Leicester: Apollos [Inter-Varsity Press], 1991.

Bright, John. *The Authority of the Old Testament*. Nashville: Abingdon, 1967.

Bruce, F. F. *This Is That: The New Testament Development of Old Testament Themes.* Exeter: Paternoster, 1968.

Childs, Brevard S. *Biblical Theology of the Old and New Testaments: Theological Reflection on the Christian Bible.* Minneapolis: Fortress Press, 1993.

France, R. T. *Jesus and the Old Testament: His Application of Old Testament Passages to Himself and His Mission.* London: Inter-Varsity Press, 1971.

Helyer, Larry R. *Yesterday, Today and Forever. The Continuing Relevance of the Old Testament.* Salem, Wisconsin: Sheffield Publishing Company, 1996.

Ruler, Arnold A. van. *The Christian Church and the Old Testament.* Grand Rapids: Eerdmans, 1971.

Westermann, Claus. *The Old Testament and Jesus Christ.* Minneapolis: Augsburg, 1968.

H. A Place to Stand: Issues in Old Testament Theology

Hasel, Gerhard F. *Old Testament Theology: Basic Issues in the Current Debate,* 4th ed. Grand Rapids: Eerdmans, 1991.

Hayes, John H., and Frederick C. Prussner. *Old Testament Theology: Its History and Development.* Atlanta: John Knox / London: SCM Press, 1985.

Høgenhaven, Jepser. *Problems and Prospects of Old Testament Theology,* Biblical Seminary 6. Sheffield: JSOT Press, 1988.

Goldingay, John. *Theological Diversity and the Authority of the Old Testament.* Grand Rapids: Eerdmans, 1987.

Knierim, R. P. *The Task of Old Testament Theology: Substance, Method, and Cases.* Grand Rapids/Cambridge: Eerdmans, 1995.

Kraftchick, S. J., C. D. Myers Jr., and B. C. Ollenburger, eds. *Biblical Theology: Problems and Perspectives. In Honor of J. Christiaan Beker.* Nashville: Abingdon, 1995.

Martens, E. A. *Old Testament Theology.* IBR Bibliographies #13. Grand Rapids: Baker, 1997.

Moberly, R. W. L. *The Old Testament of the Old Testament.* Minneapolis: Fortress Press, 1992.

Ollenburger, B. C., E. A. Martens, and G. F. Hasel, eds. *The Flowering of Old Testament Theology: A Reader in*

Twentieth-Century Old Testament Theology, 1930–1990, Sources for Biblical and Theological Study, vol. 1. Winona Lake: Eisenbrauns, 1992.

Ollenburger, Ben C., ed. *So Wide a Sea: Essays on Biblical and Systematic Theology*, IMS Text Reader 4. Elkhart, IN: Institute of Mennonite Studies, 1991.

_____. "Biblical Theology: Situating the Discipline," in *Understanding the Word: Essays in Honor of Bernhard W. Anderson*. J. T. Butler, Edgar Conrad, and B. C. Ollenburger, eds. JSOTSup 37. Sheffield: JSOT Press, 1985, pp. 37–62.

Reventlow, Henning Graf. *Problems of Old Testament Theology in the Twentieth Century*, trans. John Bowden. Philadelphia: Fortress Press / London: SCM Press, 1985.

Sailhamer, John. *Introduction to Old Testament Theology: A Canonical Approach*. Grand Rapids: Zondervan, 1995.

Scobie, C. H. H. "The Challenge of Biblical Theology," *Tyndale Bulletin* 42 (1991), p. 31–61; "The Structure of Biblical Theology," *Tyndale Bulletin* 42 (1991), pp. 163–194.

Smith, Ralph. *Old Testament Theology: Its History, Method and Message*. Nashville: Broadman & Holman Publishers, 1993.

Sun, H. T. C., Keith L. Eades, J. M. Robinson and G. I. Moller eds. *Problems in Biblical Theology: Essays in Honor of Rolf Knierim*.Grand Rapids: Eerdmans, 1997.

Index of Subjects

Index of Authors

Index of Scripture Citations

411

Index of Hebrew, Greek, and Akkadian Words

3-33   2 ✓
37-70   4 ✓
91-111   5 ✓

71-90   6 ✓

113-137 7 ✓

141-168 8 ✓

22 169-191 9 ✓

23 193-216 10 ✓

19 217-236 11 ✓

~~24 239-313 12~~

339-313 12
75 PAGES